Fourth Edition

EFFICIENCY
OF
HUMAN
MOVEMENT

MARION R. BROER, Ph.D.

Professor Emeritus
University of Washington

RONALD F. ZERNICKE, Ph.D.

Assistant Professor of Kinesiology
University of California, Los Angeles

1979

W. B. SAUNDERS COMPANY

Philadelphia • London • Toronto

W. B. Saunders Company: West Washington Square
                           Philadelphia, PA   19105

                           1 St. Anne's Road
                           Eastbourne, East Sussex BN21 3UN, England

                           1 Goldthorne Avenue
                           Toronto, Ontario M8Z 5T9, Canada

Library of Congress Cataloging in Publication Data

Broer, Marion Ruth.

Efficiency of human movement.

Includes bibliographies and index.

1. Human mechanics.   2. Man — Attitude and movement.
 3. Kinesiology.   4. Sports — Physiological aspects.
 I. Zernicke, Ronald F., joint author.   II. Title.

QP301.B88 1979   612'.76   78–20742

ISBN 0–7216–2088–4

Efficiency of Human Movement   ISBN   0-7216-2088-4

Last digit is the print number: 9   8   7   6   5   4   3   2   1

To
RUTH B. GLASSOW
*whose early vision and constant enthusiasm
for gaining and promoting an understanding
of human movement has been a very
great inspiration*

PREFACE
to the Fourth Edition

Many additions and restatements required by the rapid expansion of understanding in the area of biomechanics have been included in this revision. Dr. Ronald Zernicke has collaborated in the preparation of the material and Dr. Richard Nelson has been a contributing author for Part Two, Basic Mechanical Principles Underlying Efficient Human Movement. Those familiar with the book in the past will find that, while Part Two has been enlarged to include many more formulas for the computation of forces, velocities, angles, etc., the **meanings** are still spelled out in language that those first encountering basic mechanics of human motion can understand. It is anticipated that those interested in mathematical solutions to certain basic movement problems will find additional material that will be helpful; those not concerned with mathematical calculations can concentrate on the explanations of concepts which, it is hoped, will be found to be stated with clarity.

The book addresses everyone interested in developing a basic understanding of efficient movement, whether the reader is a person playing recreational golf (or some other sport), a person working in the home or garden who is interested in avoiding undue fatigue and back strain, an individual with responsibility for the care of an invalid, or a teacher or student of human motion. Thus, in this edition stress has been placed more on learning and solving movement problems than on teaching. To this end the concepts formerly found in Part Six (Movement Education) have been restated and incorporated into Part One.

The special section dealing with nursing tasks (Part Five of the third edition) has been deleted but the universally important applications have been incorporated into Part Three, which applies basic mechanical principles to fundamental movements; these concepts are found particularly in

v

Chapters 10, which deals with problems associated with standing and which has been expanded to include lying; 16, which discusses pushing and pulling tasks; and 17, which involves lifting problems.

An Appendix, which enumerates all symbols and formulas found in the book and includes a brief summary of trigonometry as well as a conversion table for the metric system, has been added. Because of the controversy concerning conversion to metric usage at the present time, some of the problem examples in the book use metric measures, usually with English equivalents in parentheses, while others employ the more familiar British system of weights and measures.

All chapters of Part Four (Sample Applications of Basic Mechanical Principles to Various Activities) have been revised, some slightly but others extensively. The chapter on swimming has been expanded to include some fundamental mechanical concepts applicable to diving; the gymnastics chapter has been changed considerably and a new chapter applying mechanics to sample track and field activities has been added. Again I wish to emphasize that the discussion in these chapters includes **only samples** of **possible** applications. In no way is the purpose to present a complete mechanical analysis of any activity but rather to cite a **few examples** of applications to **selected segments** of each activity in the hope that they will spark interest so that the reader will be stimulated to think through every movement task with which he or she may be confronted whether it involves some mundane activity that must be performed in everyday living, an exercise read in some magazine, or a sport (recreational or competitive) and whether the task is inherent in playing the game or in handling the equipment for it.

MARION R. BROER

San Diego, California

PREFACE
to the First Edition

Movement problems have had to be met by each of us practically since we were born. Some of us have experienced greater success in the solution of these problems than have others. This book is written, not only as an aid to the teacher of movement, but also for any individual who desires to improve his efficiency. Since movement is involved in some way in every task, improvement in the efficiency of movement has far-reaching implications in the lives of all.

This book considers the questions: "What is efficient movement?" "Upon what is it based?" "What are the most basic laws which govern movement?" "What problems are involved in everyday, work and recreational activities and what are the factors that must be considered in their solution?"

The basic laws governing movement are discussed in simple language and explained so fully that a background in the science of physics is not needed in order to understand this discussion. The final section of the book is written to aid the teacher of students of all levels of ability in understanding the reason(s) for a student's inefficient performance, so that teaching can be geared to the correction of the **basic** cause(s) rather than to a description of a set series of movements established authoritatively. Since the value of a foundation course in the physical education activity program is being debated so widely, the final chapter is devoted to a discussion of the possibilities of this type of movement education.

It is my sincere belief that the generality of movement calls for a generality of understanding that cannot be gained through the limited experience of learning a specific method for performing a few specific activities, but rather through experiences which, even though they may be limited, lead to an understanding of the factors involved in movement and in the various methods for approaching the solving of motor problems.

This book does not give answers to those who seek definite descriptions **of the correct form** for various movement situations. It discusses problems involved in the execution of a variety of activities and the principles which must be considered in their solution. For example, the discussion of the golf drive does not in any way establish the "correct" length of backswing. It seeks to assist the reader in gaining an understanding of the **relationship** of the length of the backswing to the control of the clubhead and to the force which can be produced, so that the reader can choose intelligently that length of backswing which will be most efficient according to **his** strength and the **particular** purpose involved at any specific time.

The book is the result of over ten years of study and of experimentation with basic principles of movement. I am greatly indebted to many students as well as colleagues whose clear thinking has led to questions and discussions which have aided in the clarification of many of the ideas expressed. Since every discussion, whether with an individual or a class, brings greater understanding, the ideas that can be brought to bear on this subject will never be assembled completely and, in this sense, a book dealing with this subject will never be "finished."

It is my hope that the ideas which **are** expressed will stimulate the reader to question some of the traditional materials and methods and to search for **basic** causes so that through each movement experience, whether his own or that of one of his students, he will continue to increase his own understanding and thus will experience the thrill that comes with a new idea and the satisfaction that results from seeing the greater progress of his students, not only in the efficiency of their movement but also in their ability to think through problems and to make intelligent decisions.

It would not have been possible to write this book without the understanding, patience, encouragement, and concrete assistance of many individuals. For their constructive suggestions concerning various portions of the manuscript I am greatly indebted to Ruth Wilson, Katharine Fox, Elizabeth Culver, Ruth Abernathy and Laura Huelster; for the many hours willingly spent in the performance of the activities photographed, to Elizabeth Culver; for his excellent photography, to Mr. E. F. Marten; for assistance in lettering the photographs, to Helen Hamilton and Joan Armstrong; for encouragement to put these ideas into print, to many of my students of the past years as well as my colleagues; and finally, and most important, for stimulating me to question and to search I shall always be grateful to Ruth Glassow.

MARION R. BROER

Seattle, Washington

CONTENTS

PART FOUR   SAMPLE APPLICATIONS OF THE BASIC MECHANICAL PRINCIPLES TO VARIOUS ACTIVITIES

PART 1

CONCEPTS OF EFFICIENT MOVEMENT

EFFICIENT MOVEMENT

Movement is used in some way, to some degree, in every task accomplished by human beings. It is the first concern of the child; it has been said that life is movement, lack of movement is death. The person who moves efficiently usually feels more like being active and, as he adds years to his life, continues to be active more safely than his unskilled peers.[1] Thus, the learning of efficient mechanics early in life can enrich the later decades of life. In fact, "Faulty mechanics can hasten some of the aging process."[2]

Every individual needs to understand human movement so that any task — light or heavy, fine or gross, fast or slow, of long or short duration, whether it involves everyday living skills, work skills or recreation skills — can be approached effectively.

Although the variety of specific movement tasks that confront man is endless, those involving the large muscles of the body might be organized under four main headings. A task may be **supportive,** and the purpose may be only to support the body itself, or it may involve supporting some object or objects. It may demand **suspension** of the body in which case some segment of the body must be supported. Although the body itself is **suspended** from a bar, the **hands** are **on top of** the bar and are thus supported. Suspension tasks differ from supportive in that, in the former, gravity pulls the body's center of gravity downward into vertical alignment **below** the point of support while in supportive tasks, the body must maintain its center of gravity **above** the base or gravity will pull it downward away from the base. While an **object** may be suspended from the body, some part of the object is always supported and the body must adjust the center of gravity of the total, weight plus body, to keep this new center of gravity above the base; thus while the situation is suspension of the object, the task for the individual is one of support. A suitcase is suspended from the hand, **but** the fingers are under the handle and thus it is actually supported. A task may involve **motion** of the body as a whole or of one or more body segments, or of an object. And finally, the task may concern the problem of **receiving force,** either for the purpose of absorbing it, or resisting it so that the force will be returned to act on the object. For clarity various types of human movement tasks are outlined in Chart 1.

CHART 1.   ORGANIZATION OF LARGE MUSCLE HUMAN TASKS*

I. Supportive Tasks
  A. Supporting the body
      1. On more or less solid surface — standing, sitting, lying, kneeling
      2. On water — floating
  B. Supporting an object — holding

II. Suspension Tasks — Hanging
  A. From a solid object (e.g., bar)
  B. From an object free to move (e.g., rope, rings, etc.)

III. Tasks Involving Motion
  A. Moving the body
      1. Entire body
          a. On solid surface — walking, running, skipping, sliding, gallop-
             ing, taking off for jump, dive, vault, hurdle, climbing a ladder, etc.
          b. On an object free to move — climbing rope, performing on rings,
             paddling canoe, rowing, skiing, surfing, skateboarding, etc.
          c. Through the air
             1). With no support — diving, jumping, falling, etc.
             2). While suspended — pole vault, on rope, trapeze, etc.
          d. Through the water — swimming
      2. Body parts
          a. Neck and trunk — rotating, bending, stretching, etc.
          b. Extremities — bending, stretching, swinging, rotating, etc.
          c. Pelvis — tilting
  B. Moving objects
      1. Force supplied to object directly by body
          a. Giving initial velocity by keeping object in contact with body,
             or with object held by body, and then breaking contact and
             allowing object to move under the influence of gravity and
             other forces such as air resistance and friction, i.e., throwing,
             rolling
          b. Giving sudden impetus to object by momentary contact with a
             body part or an object held by body, i.e., striking
          c. Moving object by more or less constant application of force
             over distance and time, i.e., lifting, pushing, pulling, carrying,
             sweeping, etc.
      2. Force applied to object indirectly by the body. Force of the body acts
         on elastic or some other type structure which in turn supplies the force
         to move the object. Body action essentially a push or pull, e.g., shooting
         bow, sling shot, gun, etc.

IV. Tasks Involving Receiving Force
  A. Of moving body
      1. Landing   a. On solid surface
      2. Falling (weight out of control)   b. On non-resistive surface,
                                                       e.g., mats, pits, water, etc.
  B. Of moving object
      1. Body gains possession of object — dissipates force, "gives" to reduce
         jar of impact, i.e., catching
      2. Object rebounds from body or object held by body — body resists
         force of impact so force is returned to object, i.e., striking

*For a summary discussion of tasks organized in this manner, the reader is
referred to reference 3 and for exploratory experiences to the manual *Laboratory
Experiences; Exploring Efficiency of Human Movement.* W. B. Saunders Company,
1973.

With this variety of human movement tasks, the problem is to determine how, in a relatively short period of time, each individual can gain skill —not only in a few isolated sport activities but also efficiency in movement in general.

Movement can be, and has been analyzed from many points of view. Many questions have been asked and each has led to a somewhat different approach to the study of human movement. The first question which comes to mind is, "What does the movement look like?" This has been studied by observation and by analysis of still and motion pictures. Observation is the oldest, and for years has been the most widely used (and probably the most misused), method of analyzing movement.

To answer the question, "What muscles function to produce the movement?" students have referred to anatomy and kinesiology texts. Traditionally these have analyzed motion according to the positioning of the origins and insertions of the muscles crossing the joint or joints involved in the particular movement. More recently, this question is being answered by use of **electromyography** and current texts are reporting these findings.

The force platform has become one important tool in answering the question, "What forces are involved?" The computer is also proving to be invaluable in answering this and many other questions such as those dealing with the sequence and timing of body segments.

While rhythm is as important in swinging a golf club, shooting a basket or swimming the crawl stroke as it is in dancing the rhumba, the dancer has, in the past, given more attention to the question, "What is the rhythmic pattern of the movement?" and thus to the time-force-space relationship of various movements, than have others interested in movement analysis.

The area of movement analysis represented by the questions, "How does the movement feel?", "What kinesthetic sensations are involved?" has many interesting possibilities. As Steinhaus[4] indicated, it has very powerful implications since it is so vitally involved in the formation of many basic concepts such as those of the third dimension, roundness, etc.

Psychologists and physical educators are trying to answer the question, "What emotions are elicited by the movement?" The emergence of the importance of self-image and body concepts as they relate to response to movement has been one interesting result.

Regardless of the approach to analysis, the first question which must be considered is, "What is the purpose of the movement that is to be executed?" This can be answered in very specific terms according to the objective result desired, such as "to get the ball into the basket with a lay-up shot," or it can be answered in terms of the **force** requirements, such as, "to produce force to lift the body as high as possible and to move the ball upward with just enough force and spin to carry it over the rim of the basket." The method of movement analysis will vary according to the approach to purpose.

In approaching analysis from the standpoint of observation, too frequently every detail in the performance of the expert has been described, regardless of whether a particular position or movement is really basic to success or is simply some inconsequential matter of an expert's style. Many texts and other books concerning various sports analyze skill only by describing, in minute detail, how the performance of the expert looks or the way an expert thinks he moves. Unfortunately, many teachers (educators, coaches and professionals) have concentrated on skill patterns established authoritatively, and have presented them with the finesse of detail desired of the polished performer.[5] This implies that everyone attempting to learn the skill should attempt to reproduce all of this detail. Obviously, this is impossible for any beginner; in fact, it is doubly impossible since no two individuals have the same tool for movement. Body builds differ; psychological and emotional make-ups differ; no two persons can ever perform a skill in **exactly** the same way.

To be effective, observation of self and others must be concentrated on the methods employed for applying the basic principles of movement in order to produce the force(s) required to accomplish the purpose of the particular movement. Observation must be accompanied by the question "Why?" in the mind of the analyst. In other words, the analyst must ask, "What does each particular position or movement contribute to the performer's success in the production and application of the force required by the specific purpose and the variables of the situation?"

The basic tool for the performance of any movement task is the human body. Since the body cannot be "turned in on a new model" as can a car when its efficiency decreases, either it is used well or the individual fails to accomplish his purpose and/or suffers from fatigue or pain due to wasted energy or strain. It is not possible to anticipate every activity which each individual will sometime in his life be called upon to perform, and if this were possible there would not be time to learn them all specifically. Happily, this is not necessary.

The human body is essentially a system of weights (mass of body segments), levers (bones), and devices for producing force (muscular and nervous systems) operating within the physical universe and thus subject to the same universal forces as any other system of weights and levers. The human body and its movement possibilities are, therefore, governed by the physical laws and whenever an individual moves, he either applies the principles of body mechanics effectively or wastes energy and/or suffers strain or injury; thus it is important that each individual gain general concepts of body mechanics and that he understand the breadth of their effective application.

The laws of gravity, buoyancy, balance, motion, leverage, force, and impact must all be reckoned with. Only when lying down or sitting so that the body is completely supported can the force of gravity and the laws of equilibrium be discounted; buoyancy is important for all aquatic activities; the laws of motion and force must be considered when any movement is undertaken; and impact is involved whenever the moving body or a moving object contacts a surface as in landing from a fall, a jump, a leap, or in many gymnastic activities, as well as in the vast number of sports that use balls or other equipment that is caught or struck. Since the human body is a system of levers, almost all of which are third class, it is important to understand the law of leverage. The force limitations of a system of third-class levers must be understood if strain is to be avoided, and knowledge of the speed advantage of such a system makes possible the most effective use of the body, and various implements, in all activities.

"The importance of the application of the physical laws to human movement and the effect on the body of habitual failure to observe the principles dictated by these laws have long been understood and applied by those involved in rehabilitation (the corrective expert, physical therapist, and physical medicine specialist). The fact that mechanical stresses and pressures not only cause fatigue and strain with resultant pain but can cause adaptations in bones has been well known. The structural curves of the spine are familiar examples of such bony changes. The spine being an articulating column weighted at its ends not only bends, increasing its curvatures, but rotates laterally along its axis when the weight is off-center. A wealth of literature that deals with the mechanics of the feet, knees, hips, spine, and so on; the application of mechanics to the "postural" types of activities; the defects resulting from habitual use of poorly balanced positions and improper forces; as well as exercises and activities for the correction of these defects has been available through the years. Because of this, the term **body mechanics** came to be associated with the postural activities, and thus for many years was defined very narrowly."[6]

The term body mechanics has been used by many to mean various postures or corrective activities. To others, the term has stood for a group of activities that includes standing, walking, running, sitting, pushing, pulling and lifting, while still others have taken the view that all positions and movements involve body mechanics and therefore no such restrictive definitions are justified.

As long ago as 1914, Watts' knowledge of the importance of understanding mechanical principles was indicated by her statement, "When once these principles are understood, they may be applied, not only to definite exercises, but to all sports, as also to the unconscious everyday movement of life, with a certainty of finding a more complete order of activity, a stronger current of force, a new power of control."[7] However, it was not until 16 years later that the first book[8] dealing with the application of basic body mechanics to any except "corrective-type" activities was published, and another 25 years passed before any number of such publications began to appear.

"Coaches of performers in competitive athletics have realized that an understanding of the mechanics of the human body is essential to the development of the most highly skilled performers, and for years many have applied the principles to their respective sports. Many dancers have also made these applications to their area.

"Also, some physical educators who became interested in studying those students who had unusual difficulty with physical activities found that teaching basic mechanics seemed to increase the ability of these students to learn physical activities.

"More recently, those interested in increasing the 'normal' individual's performance in all types of physical activities have begun to realize that, regardless of skill level or activity, effective performance requires the application of the physical laws. Mechanics are as important to effective performance in a golf drive, a downhill ski run, or bowling as to a dance technique, competitive basketball, or an exercise for the correction of scoliosis."[9]

As individuals have come to understand that body mechanics is a broad term that implies the application of the physical laws to the human body at rest or in motion, the term has gradually given way to the broader term **biomechanics,** mechanics dealing with the living human being.

Every individual is constantly faced with the problems of moving and controlling the body masses so as to maintain stability at rest or in motion (or using instability to advantage) and of producing and controlling the force required by a particular purpose(s). In addition, many activities require moving and controlling objects that increase lever length and therefore may compound the mechanical problem. If the laws of mechanics are not applied effectively, either the purpose is not accomplished or the individual suffers strain or undue fatigue, or both.

If the basic principles are understood, knowledge important to all movement can be learned through any activity. McCloy stated that if these principles are taught, learners can readily apply them in the mastery of new activities. "For example, if a boy has learned to bat a baseball, he can readily learn to hit a golf ball as well as to kick a football accurately if he applies the common principles intelligently."[10]

Any teacher, coach or professional with several years' experience will have developed certain devices which have been successful in helping some individual(s) overcome faulty movement patterns. Thus the literature dealing with any sport is full of such devices which, although useful in correcting certain specific faults, are not necessary to the successful performance of the movement involved. Unfortunately, the difference between devices for correcting faults and the basic mechanical factors which **must** be applied if the particular purpose is to be accomplished is not always made clear to the individual who is attempting to execute effective movement. Some persons, confusing devices with necessary mechanics, have lumped several devices together to form a stereotyped pattern instead of using them only as specific problems arise. Golf is probably the best example of this; a more complete discussion can be found in Chapter 20. Another example is seen in the solution of the problems involved in learning to float on the back in water. The problem is to balance the body weight around the center of buoyancy. The placing of the arms in the water above the head and the drawing of the feet toward the body in the frog position are both **devices** for redistributing the weight. Some individuals may need to apply one, others may need to apply both, while still others, because of their body builds, may need neither. It is useless for all, regardless of personal buoyancy, to assume the same position. The mechanical factors involved in floating must be understood by all and then each can make the adjustments in position required by his or her own body build.

As various skills are analyzed from the standpoint of the mechanics involved, it becomes obvious that there are some basic patterns of movement that require only slight adjustments according to the various purposes. Although many have thought that dance has little in common with football, basketball or baseball, comparison of pictures indicates that many of the same movements are found in dance and in these sports (Figs. 1–1 to 1–6). While the object in the dance picture of Figure 1–2 is a bouquet and that in the basketball picture a ball, the objective of the dancers and basketball players is the same, namely to project the body upward to gain possession of an object. The similarity in resulting motion is obvious. The pictures of

Text continued on page 12

Figure 1–1. Movements in Dance and Football. Seattle Times, November 4, 1959.

Figure 1–2. Movements in Dance and Basketball. Seattle Sunday Times, March 10, 1957.

Figure 1–3. Movements in Dance and Basketball. Seattle Sunday Times, March 10, 1957.

Figure 1–4. Movements in Dance and Baseball. Speaking of Pictures; Ball players and ballerinas have a lot in common, Life, 26:22–24, April 11, 1949.

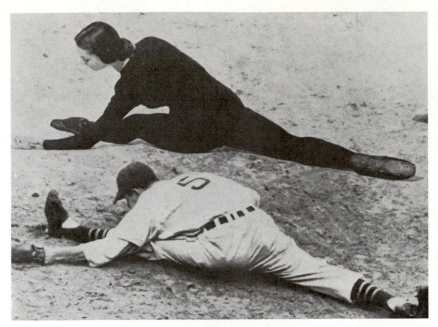

Figure 1–5. Movements in Dance and Baseball. (See Fig. 1–4.)

Figure 1–6. Movements in Dance and Baseball. (See Fig. 1–4.)

Figure 1–7. Movements in Ice Skating and Football. Seattle Post Intelligencer, November 3, 1955.

dancers superimposed on those of baseball players (Figs. 1–4, 1–5 and 1–6) indicate considerable similarity in movements and positions.

Changing direction is accomplished the same way on the ice and on the football field (Fig. 1–7) and the movement used to drive a stake looks much like that used to hit a golf ball (Fig. 1–8).

Figure 1–8. Movements in Driving a Stake and Hitting a Golf Ball. (Source not known.)

When the objects involved in the activities pictured in Figure 1–9 are removed it is almost impossible to determine exactly which of many activities is being performed in each picture sequence. It might be interesting for the reader to try to identify each sequence. Is the first a striking or throwing skill? Which specific skill is being performed?

These pictures are not offered as examples of perfect "form" but rather as examples of the way one particular individual moved when applying approximately the same force in the performance of three different skills. Figure 1–10 shows clearly which activities are being performed. Many other activities use this general pattern, e.g., bowling, horseshoe pitching, and hockey. The last is somewhat modified owing to the fact that two hands are used to control the long implement more readily.

There are also many activities that use a similar overhand pattern (Fig. 1–11). Whether throwing, serving a tennis ball, hitting an overhead badminton clear, or smashing a tennis ball or a badminton shuttle, the individual is executing essentially the same movement pattern. The purpose of each causes some adjustments, but the basic mechanics remain the same.

Actually there may be more difference in movements which are effective in applying various degrees of force in a given activity than in those applying similar degrees of force when executing seemingly different activities. There is not one basic pattern of movement for any activity; there is a pattern for maximum force production and this is adjusted as less force is required to accomplish the specific purpose. Adjustments to less force will be accomplished differently by different individuals. Of course, the purpose may be to deceive an opponent, in which case the obvious factors involved in maximum force may be included in the movement and much more energy expended than needed for the resultant flight of the ball or shuttle. In fact, additional energy is expended to reduce force at impact. However, the movement satisfies the purpose which is to deceive the opponent.

There is also a sidearm pattern (Fig. 1–12); in the basketball throw for distance, a tennis drive, badminton drive, or batting, the body movement is essentially the same.

While there are some differences in the several movement patterns involved in the various throwing and striking activities, all follow the same basic mechanical principles. This was recognized by Tittle, former professional football quarterback, when he stated, "The motion in passing is a lot like the motion in any throw, or even in hitting a golf ball or baseball."[11] The factors he discussed are the body position, weight transference, length of backswing and follow-through.

The subject pictured here performed these same activities while electromyographic records of the function of 68 muscles were made.* Analysis of these records indicated that there was considerable similarity in the functioning of the leg muscles while performing the underhand throw and the volleyball serve. The pattern of muscle function was the same for the badminton serve, except that the activity was considerably less since the weight transference was less for this activity which required less force. As might be anticipated, the greatest difference in muscle function during the

---

*These electromyograms can be found in reference 12.

Text continued on page 24

UNDERHAND PATTERN

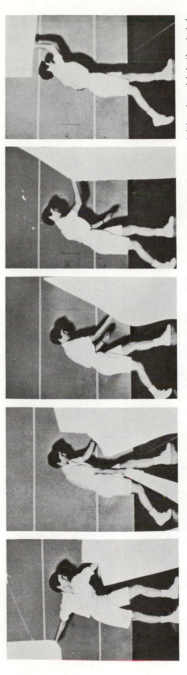

Figure 1–9. Sequence of photographs shows the subject performing skills associated with three activities in which the total body movement patterns are similar. Areas have been eliminated from the illustration which give clues to the activity. Can you identify the activity in each sequence? What skill is demonstrated? (See Fig. 1–10.)

UNDERHAND PATTERN

THROW

VOLLEYBALL SERVE

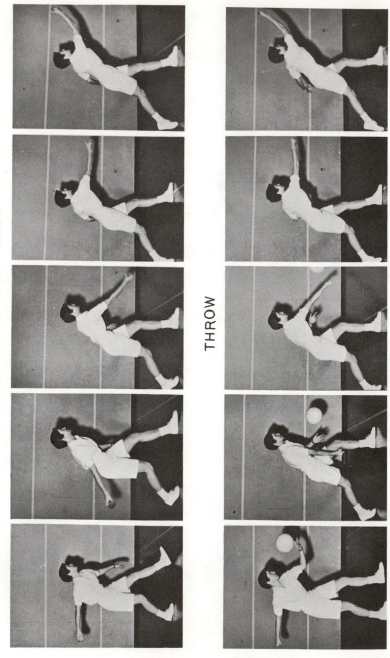

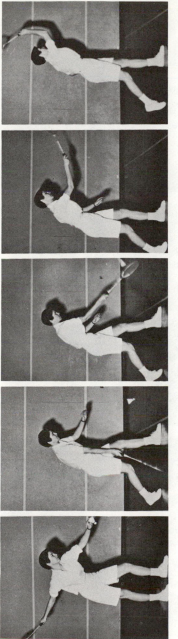

BADMINTON SERVE

Figure 1–10. Photographs from Figure 1–9 are unmasked to show the actual skills involved. Note the almost identical positions at each stage of the skill performance. Note: Since these are still pictures taken during different service attempts, the foot positions may appear to indicate a step. Actually no step was taken; only weight transference was used.

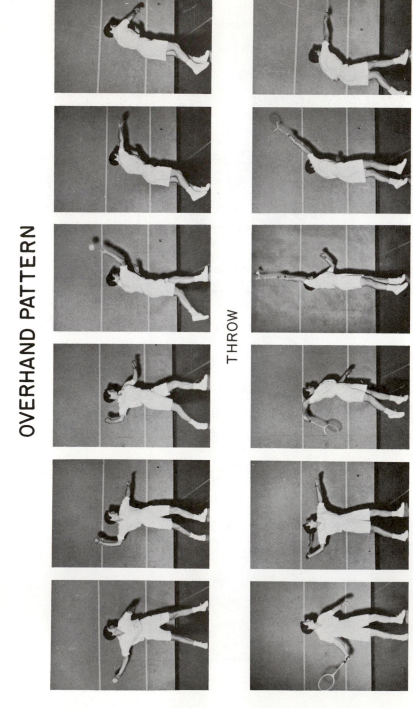

OVERHAND PATTERN

THROW

BADMINTON CLEAR

TENNIS SERVE

Figure 1–11. Similar patterns are seen in the execution of skills employing an overhand movement. Note the body positions immediately prior to the beginning of the forward swing and at each stage of the movement.

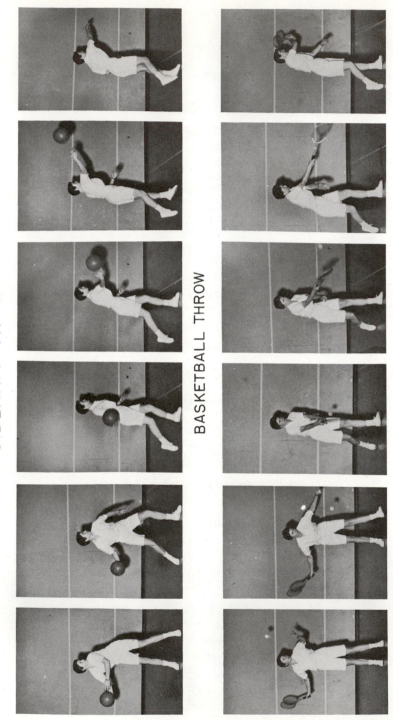

SIDEARM PATTERN

BASKETBALL THROW

TENNIS DRIVE

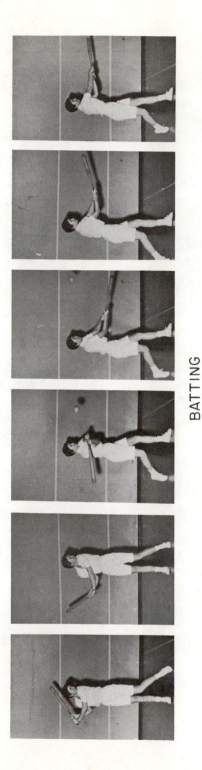

BATTING

Figure 1-12. Some differences caused by the toss of the ball for tennis and two hands on the bat can be noted but the similarity in basic body movement is still obvious:

ONE FOOT JUMP—HEIGHT
RUNNING APPROACH

BASKETBALL LAY-UP

VOLLEYBALL SPIKE

DIVING HURDLE

Figure 1–13. The movement patterns used in three skills which require conversion of forward momentum to upward momentum are very similar.

performance of these three activities was found in the left arm since this hand was used to support and toss the volleyball and to drop the shuttle. The muscle action indicating the toss of the ball was different from that indicating the drop of the shuttle and these were absent from the records of the throw. The right arm function was almost identical for the three activities, the one real difference was in the greater activity in wrist and finger flexors during the badminton serve and throw than in the volleyball serve reflecting differences in specific purposes. Since in the throw the ball is held in the hand, no force of impact is involved and the light badminton equipment causes relatively little reaction force to be resisted at impact while necessitating the development of great racket speed just before impact, but the force of the heavier volleyball against the hand requires considerable wrist stabilization.

Both leg and arm action were found to be similar in the overhand throw, badminton clear and tennis serve (Fig. 1–11). There were slight differences in the functioning of the right arm muscles during the overhand throw, but the two striking activities were almost identical.

The sidearm pattern activities pictured here (Fig. 1–12) again appeared to be very similar. The left arm was less active during the tennis drive than the basketball throw. The arm pattern for batting was found to be more similar to the other activities than anticipated. An outstanding difference was seen in the left triceps' action which was considerably greater in batting. This, of course, was expected since the left arm was actively used in applying force.

When the leg action for the throws — underhand, overhand, sidearm — was compared, it was found that muscle function for all three patterns was very similar. It was apparent that there was a general pattern of leg action which, with minor adjustments, this subject used when executing various throwing and striking activities **requiring considerable force.** There also appeared to be some general patterns of arm and trunk muscle function that were used for different skills with slight adjustments according to specific purpose.

Another interesting pattern is seen in those activities that require a one foot jump for height, i.e., basketball lay-up, volleyball spike and diving (Fig. 1–13). Diving was not included in the electromyographic study, but the leg action for the volleyball spike and basketball lay-up was found to be almost identical. More activity in the abdominal muscles was required by the striking activity, and there was a clear difference in arm action in the two activities. Since one is a striking action which brings the arm forward-downward and the other a pushing action which moves the hand upward, this was to be anticipated. Although the action of the upper body when in the air was different, the movement pattern used to convert forward momentum to upward momentum to lift the body into the air was clearly the same.

In taking the pictures of the one foot jump it was found that this individual jumped from the left foot and raised the right knee when performing a lay-up shot in basketball or a volleyball spike. However, on the diving board she raised the left knee and took off from the right foot. When questioned about this change in body movement, she replied that when learning to dive, an instructor had insisted that she start her steps on the right foot and lift the left knee in executing a diving hurdle. She reported that it had been extremely difficult for her to learn the running front dive. In approximately 45 minutes of practice this student was able to perform a better dive using a lift of the right knee (her normal movement pattern) than she had been able to achieve after some eight years of raising the left knee on the diving hurdle. How frequently is movement development hindered by a performer attempting to repeat exactly, or a teacher requiring that a student use, a stereotyped form which has perhaps been successful with someone else but may not be his normal movement?

The locomotor patterns are applicable in many different activities. Walking is fundamental to almost all. There are slight changes due to purpose. If the objective is a smooth, gliding movement of the body, the walk is executed differently than if the purpose is to economize on energy over a long period of time. However, basically it is still the same pattern. The similarity between the crawl kick and the walking pattern is frequently overlooked. Running is used in a wide variety of activities. Whether the slide, gallop, skip, and pivot are used in the various dance activities, or in covering the tennis, badminton or basketball courts, the mechanics are the same. The need to adjust the center of gravity to change direction is the same in all activities. Twists and turns while the body is in the air are executed in the same manner in diving, gymnastics, dance and some basketball shots. The movement involved in changing from the front to the back float is essentially the same as that of the dance roll using the shoulder lead. If injury is to be avoided the principles involved in falling must be followed whether the individual is sliding into base, executing a dance fall, or losing his equilibrium in skiing or any other activity. The mechanical laws are applicable in many seemingly very different situations.

The mechanical principles that determine effective performance of the so-called basic skills (e.g., standing, walking, running, sitting, pushing, pulling, lifting) are applicable to all movements, and the skills which are incorporated in various sports use basically the same patterns. There may be modifications required by differing purposes. This broadness of application is shown in Chart 2; the sports which use the various basic skills, either the identical movement patterns or patterns that are basically the same although somewhat modified, are listed under each basic skill.

Since the individual is on his feet in all sport activities, with the exception of sports such as canoeing, crew, riding, sailing and swimming, knowledge of the principles of, and skill involved in, maintaining a well-balanced standing position have broad application. Actually, although the individual is in a horizontal position in swimming, the principles of alignment of the various body segments are the same as in the vertical position and thus knowledge of standing principles is applicable even to swimming. Canoeing, crew and riding involve sitting rather than standing and the principles of a well-balanced sitting position, which are the same as those of a well balanced standing position, are applicable to these activities.

In many sports which include running — and the list is long — only short runs with rapid changes in direction may be involved (basketball, racket games). Other sports demand that longer distances be covered quickly (softball and baseball, football, field hockey, soccer, speedball, lacrosse).

CHART 2. INTERRELATIONSHIP OF "BASIC SKILLS" AND VARIOUS ACTIVITIES

Standing	Walking	Running and Stopping	Jumping, Leaping, Hopping, etc.	Landing and Falling	Sitting	Pushing and Pulling	Holding, Lifting, Carrying	Throwing° and Catching	Striking°
All activities except: Canoeing Crew Riding Swimming Sailing	All activities except: Archery Canoeing Riding Shuffle-board Weight Lifting Note: use of walking coordination in crawl kick, in swimming	Badminton Baseball-Softball Basketball Dance Football Handball Hockey Lacrosse Racketball Speedball Speed-away Squash Rackets Tennis Track and Field	Basketball Dance Diving Gymnas-tics Skiing Track and Field Volleyball	Baseball-Softball Basketball Dance Football Gymnastics Skiing Tumbling Track and Field Volleyball Wrestling	Canoeing Crew Contem-porary Dance Riding Sailing	Archery Canoeing Crew Dance Fencing Riding Sailing Shot Put Shuffle-board Swimming Wrestling	Canoeing Dance Tumbling Weight Lift-ing Wrestling Note: Carry-ing equip-ment for many activi-ties such as: Golf, Skiing, etc.	Baseball-Softball Basketball Bowling (throwing) Deck Tennis Football Gymnastics (spotting-catching) Lacrosse Track and Field Speedaway Speedball Some applica-tion of throw-ing to: Hockey (Roll-in) Soccer (Goalie)	Badminton Baseball-Softball Basketball Bowling Boxing Football Golf Handball Hockey Pool and Billiards Racketball Squash Rackets Soccer Speedaway Speedball Table Tennis Tennis Volleyball

°Use the same basic movement patterns.

However, in all of these the ability to stop and change direction suddenly is also important. Only in some of the track events, in running to first base in baseball or softball, or in dance, can the individual gradually slow his run to a stop. Skill in running and stopping is the same whether in basketball or tennis, hockey or a dance technique.

To be successful in basketball, volleyball, or diving one must be able to project the body weight into the air. Many gymnastic events also demand height of body projection. In dance and track, the individual must be able to apply projecting force upward or outward depending upon the particular purpose.

Any projection of the body into the air is, of course, inevitably followed by a forceful contact of the body with the floor or ground. Also, at any time the body is moving rapidly a fall may result. Therefore, it is important that individuals taking part in any motor activity understand the principles of **force absorption** and become skilled in their application. In some activities, such as dance and gymnastics, force absorption is involved in the performance of the actual skill. In others it is the natural aftermath of the skill, as in landing from a jump in basketball, volleyball, track. While falling or landing is not involved in the actual skill of skiing (except in jumping), the importance of understanding principles of force absorption and skill in their application cannot be overlooked if injury is to be avoided. Hilleboe and Larimore[13] reported that falls at work account for 20 per cent of all work injuries and that falls are the largest single cause of accidental death in the home; this is a particular problem for the elderly. Tasks involving lifting, carrying, and moving or placing various materials, machine parts and other objects account for a high per cent of all work injuries.

Many agree that it is important to understand the principles of holding, carrying, lifting, pushing and pulling because of their application to work and daily living but still fail to appreciate the importance of this knowledge in sport activities. What is the skill involved in archery except pulling? The body, the canoe, the shell, the rowboat move through the water as a result of a push or pull exerted against the water. The horse slows as a result of pressure against his mouth caused by a pull on the reins, and the action that moves the fencing foil toward the opponent is essentially a push, as is the action that projects the shot.

A canoe must be lifted and carried to and from the water and launched without damage to the craft or strain of the back of the carrier. Partners must be supported in figure skating and most forms of dance. Many activities involve the carrying of heavy equipment and if carried or lifted incorrectly strain can result. The golf cart has relieved the golfer of the task of carrying his heavy bag of clubs; however, unless an electric cart is used the golf bag and cart must still be pulled and the bag must be lifted in and out of the car trunk. Knowledge of the mechanical principles involved in the tasks of pushing, pulling, lifting and carrying can be skillfully employed in a wide variety of sports as well as in daily living and work tasks.

If skill in the basic throw and strike patterns (pp. 13–24 and Figs. 1–10, 1–11, and 1–12, pp. 16–21) and an understanding of the principles involved are gained, much time can be saved in learning specific sport skills at a later date.

It is interesting to note that striking is used in more sports than is throwing. A common concept is that throwing is the most used of the basic skills with the possible exceptions of standing, walking and running. Probably this idea can be attributed to the wide use of throwing in various games of low organization. It is reasonable that the basic throw-strike patterns should be learned first with the object held in the hand and these patterns can then be applied to the more difficult tasks involving contact with an object (striking).

Some may question the inclusion of basketball in the list of sports that apply striking. In dribbling, the player does strike rather than throw the ball, and in turn the ball strikes the floor and the principles of rebound operate. The principles of striking are also important to success in basket shooting whenever the backboard is contacted.

Actually, movement pattern and mechanical similarities among different activities are not surprising if the purpose of the movement is considered in terms of the required amount of force and its direction, rather than simply in terms of getting the ball over the net, into the basket, or over the plate.

In discussing the execution of a motor skill the terms "good form" and "poor form" are frequently used. One may encounter disagreement on what is good form for a particular skill. The discussion usually arises because of a confusion of "mannerisms" with form, or the definition of form. Historically, good form has been determined by analyzing the performance of an individual who has been unusually successful in a particular activity. The concept of good form has changed from time to time because an individual who looked different from the accepted model demonstrated even greater success. There has been failure to consider the possibility that an individual may be having success, despite certain incorrect mechanics, by compensation and extra expenditure of energy, or that an individual who uses his body well mechanically may have certain mannerisms which, while they do not necessarily detract from his success, **are not the reasons** for it.

In general, the causes for disagreement on form are little mannerisms which, because they have been noted in some highly skilled player's movement, have become a part of the accepted picture of the form of the particular activity. Many of the points which are so often questioned, points of form on which there is disagreement, are simply these little mannerisms that are independent of the basic mechanics involved in efficient execution of the skill. In fact, differences in styles with which individuals execute a skill may be due to structural differences. An unusual style in one individual may be a necessary compensation that in another individual would be detrimental to efficiency. Performers and teachers "need to recognize that many somewhat different movements may be efficient and correct for a given purpose, depending upon the individual doing the performing."[14] In discussing skiing technique Hutter stated that "style is the highly personal application of technique. And technique . . . is the natural, logical and most economic application of mechanics and use of physical laws in any given skiing situation."[15] Ariel compared one who coaches according to "what looks best" to an engineer who would remove a beam from a bridge because a survey of a hundred drivers indicated that 75 per cent thought that the bridge looked better without the beam; he pointed out that people are subject to the same physical laws as are bridges.[16]

In summarizing literature dealing with motor learning Hellebrandt stated, "There are many ways in which the same goal can be reached, and man unconsciously picks and chooses among the gamut of those available, easing the burden of fatigue . . ., and thus extending the range and sensitivity of his movement vocabulary. The physical therapist, shop foreman, physical educator or coach may wish to impose upon the human subject some precise and specific technique of movement, but an infinitely wise living machine . . . makes its own autonomous adjustments. Instead of suppressing these, we would do well to study them."[17]

One person looking at the picture of the underhand pattern (page 16) criticized the "form" of the underhand volleyball serve because it was his belief that the ball should not be tossed on the service. Actually, the only thing that is important to the success of the service is that the ball be contacted with the required amount of force on the correct spot so that the force is through the center of gravity in the direction and at the angle required by the purpose. If the individual tosses the ball and is successful in contacting the ball properly, why should anyone insist that the ball be held? Obviously, when the ball is held the problem of timing of toss and contact is not involved. Therefore, it may be expedient to suggest to the beginner that the ball be held. However, this does not mean that it is incorrect to toss the ball. Mechanically it is the point of contact that is important. It is necessary to understand the difference between those principles that are basic and must be followed if efficient movement is to result, and the little extras that are determined by individual differences or preferences.

Individuals should not confuse themselves by trying to give attention to many small details that do not actually affect the efficiency of the movement. Instead they should concentrate on those movements or controls required in applying the basic mechanics. The individual's mannerisms will eventually develop and little individual differences — so long as they do not interfere with the mechanics — will not be important. **Good form is not a set pattern but rather the movement, or movements, which accomplish the purpose with the least expenditure of energy.** Metheny stated that form in all activities is based on an understanding of two fundamental principles, "(1) how to conserve energy by proper use of the body and its parts, and (2) how to expend energy intelligently and efficiently to accomplish a given purpose."[18] It is only through such understanding that relationships between various movements of the body and between various activities can be seen. Just as two sentences which express different ideas use many of the same words, so also do movement tasks which accomplish different specific purposes use many of the same basic neuromuscular patterns in applying the same basic mechanics.

In 1956, Huelster stated that, owing to the structure of the human body and its muscular function, there are elements of movement common to all specialized techniques.[19] Examination of the various pictures presented previously certainly indicates that there are many common elements upon which the learning of future skills can be based. The principles of balance, force production, motion and leverage are identical regardless of the activity. Common elements would be much more apparent if learning were approached from the standpoint of several questions. What is the purpose of this movement (or activity)? Purpose should be considered, not only in the very specific terms of hitting the tennis ball over the net, but in the broader terms of force production — whether a maximum production of force or controlled force is needed. What are the elements of the particular situation which could affect force requirements? What basic mechanical laws are applicable? How can the purpose be accomplished with the least strain and least expenditure of energy? Why is this method more effective (in terms of basic physical laws)?

Such an approach should aid in the realization that each activity is not a completely new pattern of movement but is largely familiar, although some specific adjustments may be necessitated by the purpose of the specific activity. It should clearly indicate that no activity demands a stereotyped pattern of movement but rather that its effectiveness is determined by its mechanics, degree of energy expenditure, and rhythmic quality. H'Doubler has stated that ". . . all purposeful activities such as the activities of play and work expressed in pushing, pulling, striking, hauling, throwing or their associated expressions in the technique of sports, or their abstractions in the creative movements of dance, have their forms set by the laws of body mechanics and the symmetries of physical movement."[20]

Movement is essential in everyone's life and is influenced not only by body build but also by personality traits. An individual's movements have certain characteristics by which he can be recognized by those who know him well even when his face is not distinguishable. Some persons' movements are large and expansive, while those of others are small and restricted. The movements of some are always very direct and those of others indirect. Some individuals are habitually quick in moving while others move more slowly. Within the framework set up by the neuromuscular equipment, body build and personality of the individual, the physical laws operate.

There are mechanical principles that govern all movement and determine what the body can and cannot do. These principles are the same regardless of the type of activity, whether dance, sports, everyday tasks, or work tasks. The **specific** purposes and motivations may be different but all use the same tool (the body) and the same medium (movement), and body movement is governed by physical laws. If these basic principles are understood, knowledge important to all skills can be learned through any specific movement experience. There may be slight variations because of a difference in equipment to be manipulated, but the bulk of a movement pattern may be identical with that used in a **seemingly** very different specific skill.

The individual approaching the learning of golf should realize that the **principles** he learned in tennis can guide him in determining the most effective method for hitting a golf ball. If the knowledge and skills gained through one activity are to form a base on which to build in other movement situations, one must carefully consider possible applications to other sport techniques and to activities of everyday living in light of similar force purposes, although the actual tasks may seem quite different. In learning, concern should center around, not what the individual looks like as he moves, but around an understanding of the efficiency of the movement — its mechanics, degree of energy expenditure and rhythmic quality.

Degree of energy expenditure is dependent upon purpose. If the purpose of the particular activity demands an all-out effort, such as a throw for distance, all of the factors which can contribute to greater velocity at the end of the throwing lever should be employed and maximum expenditure of energy is called for. On the other hand, if the purpose is to serve the badminton bird from the front of one service court to the front of the diagonally opposite service court (short service), few of the factors involved in force production are required. Since the movement of the arm alone can produce sufficient force for the purpose, the longer backswing and additional muscular strength which are added to the movement by body rotation simply waste energy. The foot position is unimportant since body rotation is not needed and the force produced is not sufficient to upset body equilibrium even if the base is relatively small.

In analyzing any movement task, the problem involved must be determined in terms of force purposes and all aspects of the situation that could affect the desired result; the basic mechanics that are applicable are then ascertained; and in light of past experience with similar movement patterns, methods for applying the mechanical principles in the solution of the problem(s) are explored. Through this type of meaningful exploration an individual not only can determine the best solution for accomplishing the present task with the least strain and energy expenditure but also can gain insights which can be useful in solving future movement problems.

Problem solving is an active process; learning takes place as insight dawns. Just as in any other learning situation, for effective **motor** learning the learner must be involved beyond simply trying to produce a movement described or demonstrated by someone else. He needs to be involved in analyzing the task, considering possible solutions in light of the situational variables and his own physical equipment, and deciding which movements have the greater chance for success according to the particular force purpose(s). He must remember that his unique physical and emotional make-up make it impossible for him to perform any activity in exactly the same manner that someone else does; that in trying to do so he may actually interfere with his own skill development.

The case of the diver (p. 24) required by a teacher to lift her left knee on the hurdle although her normal movement pattern for a one foot vertical jump called for a right knee lift is an excellent example. It is not possible to go out on the golf course on Monday and reproduce the same movement pattern used by one of the pros regardless of the accuracy of the observation of his performance seen on television the previous day. Careful observation can lead to an understanding of the basic mechanics which must be applied, even though various professionals may move somewhat differently when applying them. Seldom is there just one way to execute any skill; there may be several possible methods, each with its advantages and disadvantages. Individuals must learn to weigh these and make a final choice on the basis of **all** the factors involved.

Learning by problem solving is more likely to lead to the development of generalizations which make future application of the material possible. Through this process similarities in movements and in principles are likely to become obvious. Knapp[21] stated that positive transfer is easier and more likely to occur when the learner is on the look-out for similarities and differences and when attention is centered on underlying principles of wide application; that if an individual practices an activity without perceiving relationships, learning is likely to be highly specific to that particular situation.

Each motor learning experience should develop or strengthen concepts that will last a lifetime. Individuals need to understand the ways in which the body mechanism changes through the years and to learn the adjustments in movement that may be required to continue to move efficiently. Insight into the interrelationships of the body mechanism and movement is important to an understanding of effective body mechanics in relation to the aging process.[22]

For a specific movement learning experience to be valuable beyond the immediate purpose, the individual must learn to analyze the variables of each situation, the purposes of the movement in terms of the amount of force required and the direction in which the force must be applied to accomplish the particular purpose. Then, after considering basic mechanics, he must determine the various ways that his body segments could be moved to produce the required force. He must understand the physical principles by which the body operates, the many basic movement patterns and also the method for attacking a movement task so that he can determine for himself those movements that will be most effective for accomplishing the purpose regardless of the movement task that he wishes to perform.

Thus determination of the movements required for efficient performance of any movement task involves three major steps. First, the task must be analyzed from the standpoint of the type of motion desired, the forces necessary to cause the desired motion and the variables that affect the specific situation. Next the mechanical principles that are applicable to such a situation must be considered. The **final** step involves determination of the movements which could result in application of the mechanical laws to produce the required amount of force in the desired direction.

In analyzing force requirements both the magnitude and direction of the required force as well as the point of application must be considered. Force requirements are determined by the **variables of the specific situations** as well as by the purpose of the task. Some situations involve objects, others do not, and the problems to be solved will be different if only movement of the body itself is required than if objects must be moved. If an object is to be moved, its size, weight and shape greatly affect the force requirements and the movements that can be successful in accomplishment of purpose. It is impossible to use the same motions to project the relatively small, round but heavy shot as to project the softball; nor will the identical movement pattern used to throw a softball overhand be successful with the large basketball. The solution will be different if force must be applied over a considerable or a short distance and/or time; if success is dependent upon speed of motion rather than strength; if the object can be held or must be contacted while moving and, if contact is involved, whether the object is stationary or moving; if it involves contact between the moving body and a resistive surface or one that moves on contact; if the task requires linear or angular motion.

The types of surfaces involved, both from the standpoint of their hardness and restitution and the coefficient of friction, must be considered, whether the individual wishes to move the body across a surface, project it from a surface, drop it onto a surface, or project an object with a surface which is a part of the body or of an object attached to the body. The medium through which the movement must take place is another consideration. If the body is to be moved through the air the problem is quite different from that involved in moving it through water. The size of the area in which movement of the body or of an object is permitted is also a factor. Movements can be very different if space is restricted rather than unrestricted. Many situations include obstacles to movement either of the body or an object. In this case height of the obstacle or perhaps its width or depth will affect the solution of the task. The task of projecting a ball over a net is quite different when the net is seven and one-half feet high as opposed to three feet high; it is also different when the force for projection must be applied three feet from the net as opposed to thirty feet.

The task may require more force than the body's muscular and leverage systems can produce and thus may require employment of an object which can increase force potential through the advantageous use of leverage; or the speed required may dictate that an object be used to increase speed potential through lengthened leverage.

Thus any movement task, common or unusual, can be solved efficiently if the movements to be made are determined as a result of a thorough understanding of all variables of the specific situation and the resultant force requirements rather than from reading a description of some one else's movements. Since not all tasks which may be encountered, in fact only a relatively small percentage of them, have been described and since individuals differ, it is important to understand how to go about analyzing and solving movement tasks.

An understanding of the mechanics of a given situation makes it possible for an individual to determine **why** he failed to accomplish his purpose; why the ball went too low, or to the right, or beyond the end line. He can then decide on the changes in movement required for success. The important thing is for each individual to learn how to produce and control force, how to use his body levers effectively, how to absorb force without injury and how to maintain balance or use instability to advantage in achieving his purpose.

It must be recognized that an understanding of human movement must be approached from an anatomical, physiological, neurological and psychological as well as a mechanical basis. Since human movement takes place only as a result of neuromuscular activity, the importance of the neurophysiological aspects of movement and motor learning is obvious.

Also it must be recognized that various individuals have different body rhythms; some can adjust easily to superimposed speeds and rhythms, others cannot. Those who can are successful in various dance activities and synchronized swimming. Those who cannot may move easily in activities which they can perform in their own timing, but may experience great difficulty in activities that demand a set rhythm. In situations in which movement in a superimposed rhythm or at a specific speed is not necessary to the purpose of the activity, it is well for each individual to develop skill in his own tempo. Using music in the development of various swings, such as the golf swing, may be useful in helping to induce a relaxed swinging motion as opposed to a more percussive hitting motion; for some it could also be an aid in the establishment of a feeling for the rhythmic pattern involved. However, it would seem unwise to continue musical accompaniment for a long period or for several persons to attempt to maintain the same rhythm. Music may be a useful **device** in helping some to relax but it must be understood that it may hinder the learning of those whose normal body rhythms do not coincide with the superimposed rhythmic stimulus.

Studies have indicated that the learning of a motor skill which involves both speed and accuracy proceeds most effectively when both are emphasized from the beginning. Accuracy developed at a slow tempo may be lost when the movement is speeded up, but there is little loss of speed when emphasis is placed on accuracy. Therefore, while it may be expedient to go through a pattern of movement in slow motion in order to develop an understanding of sequence, continued practice at this tempo is a waste of time.

The human mechanism is endowed with certain reflexes upon which effective patterns of movement can be built. The mechanical principles are applied in light of their effect upon this biological mechanism; while the mechanical approach to the study of movement is vital to total understanding, the other aspects cannot be overlooked. However, one book cannot cover this vast area. The main thrust of this book, therefore, is limited to the understanding and application of the mechanical basis of movement.

It is the purpose of this book to help each individual understand the way to proceed in the solution of a movement task; to understand the most fundamental mechanical principles as they relate to human movement (Part Two); to point up the mechanics involved in the skills fundamental to all activities — those used in the accomplishment of daily tasks as well as sport and dance techniques (Part Three); and to suggest **a few** applications to **some** common activities (Part Four). In short its purpose is to help each individual develop his ability to use his body effectively in the performance of **all** movement tasks demanded of him, whether these tasks involve skills of everyday living, work or recreation.

REFERENCES

1. Scott, M. Gladys: Retardation of Aging, *Encyclopedia of Sport Sciences and Medicine*. New York, The Macmillan Company, 1971, p. 1186.
2. *Ibid.*, p. 1185.
3. Broer, Marion R.: *Introduction to Kinesiology*. Englewood Cliffs, New Jersey, Prentice-Hall, Inc., 1968, pp. 35–87.
4. Steinhaus, Arthur H.: *Toward an Understanding of Health and Physical Education*. Wm. C. Brown, Publishers, 1963, p. 33.
5. Movement Group Report, *Workshop Report: Purposeful Action*. Washington, D.C., The National Association for Physical Education of College Women, 1956, p. 93.
6. Broer, Marion R.: Body Mechanics, *Encyclopedia of Sport, Sciences and Medicine*. New York, The Macmillan Company, 1971, pp. 184–186.
7. Watts, Diana: *The Renaissance of the Greek Ideal*. New York, Frederick A. Stokes Company, 1914, p. 36.
8. Glassow, Ruth B.: *Fundamentals in Physical Education*. Philadelphia, Lea and Febiger, 1932.
9. Broer, 1971, *loc. cit.*
10. Johnson, Warren, ed.: *Science and Medicine of Exercise and Sports*. New York, Harper and Brothers, 1960, pp. 62–63.
11. Tittle, Y. A.: Secrets of a Pro Quarterback. *Sports Illustrated*. 9:14–52. October 6, 1958.
12. Broer, Marion R., and Houtz, Sara Jane: *Patterns of Muscular Activity in Selected Sport Skills: An Electromyographic Study*. Springfield, Charles C Thomas, 1967.
13. Hilleboe, Herman E., and Larimore, Granville W.: *Preventive Medicine*. Philadelphia, W. B. Saunders Company, 1965, p. 21.
14. Movement Group Report, *loc. cit.*
15. Hutter, M. K.: Technique Today: An Evaluation. *Skiing*, 17:2:100, November, 1964.
16. Moore, Kenny: Gideon Ariel and His Magic Machine, *Sports Illustrated*, 47:8:54–55, August 22, 1977.
17. Hellebrandt, F. A.: The Physiology of Motor Learning. *Cerebral Palsy Review*, 10:4:13, July–August, 1958.
18. Metheny, Eleanor: *Body Dynamics*. New York, McGraw-Hill Book Company, Inc., 1951, p. 5.
19. Huelster, Laura J.: Comments on the Calling We Profess. *Workshop Report: Purposeful Action*. Washington, D.C., The National Association for Physical Education of College Women, 1956, p. 14.
20. H'Doubler, Margaret N.: *Movement and Its Rhythmic Structure*. Madison, Wisconsin, Kramer Business Service, 1946, p. 8.
21. Knapp, B.: *Skill in Sport*. London, Routledge and Kegan Paul, 1963.
22. Scott, *op. cit.*, p. 1185.

PREREQUISITES TO EFFICIENT MOVEMENT

2

While the bulk of this book deals with the application of the basic physical laws to movement, the base to which the physical laws are applied must be considered. There are certain physical, mental, and emotional prerequisites that must be recognized and dealt with as need arises.

PHYSICAL PREREQUISITES

The degree to which movement can be effective may be influenced by body build, reaction time, strength, power, flexibility, endurance, and acuity of the senses. The importance of each of these is dependent upon the demands of the movement task to be performed. For example, while reaction time is not an important factor in most tasks of the lifting, pushing and pulling, or carrying type, it is extremely important in many sports such as tennis, basketball and badminton. There are, however, sports in which reaction time does not play an important role, for example, golf and bowling. It is significant in any survival activity involving dodging or falling. This is obvious when one is crossing a street and a car suddenly bears down. Effective automobile driving depends upon a quick reaction time. Acuity of the senses, ability to make quick decisions and movement time are all involved in reaction time.

Strength, on the other hand, is extremely important to many tasks of the lifting-carrying type, while it assumes a less prominent role in some sport activities. However, strength of the muscles that control pelvic position is important in most activities. The trunk must be stabilized as a base for effective action of the extremities. Arm and shoulder girdle strength may be of concern in archery, bowling, canoeing, swimming, skiing, gymnastics, and field activities; strength of the legs is involved to some extent in almost all activities, but is particularly important in basketball, fencing, riding, gymnastics, skiing and track; wrist strength is essential in tennis; finger and wrist strength in archery. An understanding of the compensations students

35

are likely to make for lack of strength is extremely important in teaching. For example, if a student persists in swinging the bowling ball in an arc around the body even though he understands the contribution of a straight swing to accuracy, in all probability he lacks the strength to control the ball when it is farther from his center of gravity. He swings it in an arc because in this way the ball can be kept close to his body (shorter resistance arm, p. 80) and is, therefore, easier to control.

Or, if a bowler turns his right foot (if right-handed) diagonally outward, thus making the approach irregular because of the outward as well as forward push from the right foot, he may lack the strength necessary to keep the trunk erect when adjusting to the added weight of the ball on the right side of the body. Therefore, he turns the right foot somewhat to enlarge the base on the side of the weight. In both cases, the answer is not to reiterate the proper swing or the proper approach, but rather to give him an understanding of his problem, to provide a lighter ball, and to suggest exercises which will strengthen the weak muscles.

If a right handed beginner in tennis continually hits to the right, it should be determined whether he lacks the wrist strength to withstand the force of the ball against the racket and gives with the wrist, thus turning the racket face to the right. This fault can be corrected by helping the player understand the reason the ball went to the right and that "squeezing" the racket at impact will help to stabilize the wrist. Also exercises should be suggested to strengthen wrist muscles. It will do no good to continue to tell the player to keep the racket face straight ahead on contact, since the strength to do this is lacking. It is important to understand that since the ball hits the racket far from the fulcrum of the lever involved, the force of the ball against the racket is magnified.

Also the individual who, in hitting a tennis drive, continually draws the arm in so that the elbow is close to the side, may be compensating for lack of strength. Since, with the elbow well bent, the impact is taken at the end of a shorter lever, it can be withstood with less strength than when the player reaches for the ball with an extended arm (a longer lever). It is also easier to swing the shortened arm-racket, since the resistance to angular movement is reduced (moment of inertia is less). Here again, the player needs to be helped to understand his problem and be given suggestions for ways to increase strength. This last fault, that of hitting with the elbow close to the body, may also be due to a spatial judgment problem.

MENTAL PREREQUISITES

Through the years an individual develops a spatial concept of the distance that he can reach. The length of his arm is familiar to him and he can quickly judge how closely to approach an object that he wishes to strike with his hand. When he is given a tennis racket that lengthens his reach by approximately 24 inches and is expected to make rapid judgments as to how closely to approach the ball in order to hit with an extended arm plus racket, the habit of a lifetime may be so ingrained that he approaches the ball at his normal striking distance (arm length). While swinging he finds that he is too close to the ball and draws the elbow toward the body to shorten the reach. In the long run, learning time may be reduced if, when a new implement is introduced, some time were taken to help the individual gain the new spatial concept. Perhaps some of these problems arise because it has been taken for granted that these new spatial concepts are developed immediately and automatically.

Time also needs to be spent in developing the timing concept peculiar to badminton. Over the years an individual develops a concept of the timing of the flight of a ball. Since the shuttle is affected more than a ball by air resistance, its flight is different and, therefore, this concept of the speed with which objects fall must be adjusted if an individual is to be successful in the game of badminton.

Whenever a moving object is involved, not only must one judge the speed of its movement, but also its distance and height, as well as the force which will result from contact with it, must be assessed.

Rhythmic judgment — the ability to "feel" the beat, judge time duration, stress and intensity — is involved in all movement. The ability to perceive quickly and make quick decisions adapted to the situation, to remember past movement experiences (not only the results of moving in a certain way but the **feeling** of the movements) so that they can be applied in the solution of new motor problems, and to understand the mechanics of effective movement, are all important.

EMOTIONAL PREREQUISITES

Despite the physical and mental capabilities of the student, teaching will not be effective unless there is a feeling of need for, or desire to learn, the particular skill involved. For example, a student being taught to serve in tennis found that when she lifted her racket forward and up with a bent arm and contacted the ball just slightly above her head, she could get the ball over the net and into the service court. When she attempted the circular backswing and a high contact she was successful less frequently. Since she had a greater feeling of success with the short swing and arched slow service, she was resistant to instruction which described the "correct form." This student was then approached from the standpoint that the purpose of the service is to put the ball into play **in such a way that it would be difficult for an opponent to return it,** the ease with which her service could be returned and the reasons for this. A demonstration of balls being dropped from the height at which she was hitting and a height that she could reach, indicated to her the difference in the distance that the two balls had to fall, and thus the time available to get a ball hit with horizontal force over the net. The difference in the speed with which the racket could be moving at contact when her short backswing was used as compared with a longer circular backswing was made clear to her through her own experimentation. Her response to this approach was, "This makes sense. I'll try it." Discussion of purpose followed by teaching through problem solving is an excellent method for making the student aware of the necessity for following the principles basic to a particular task, and creating a realization of need and thus a **desire to learn.**

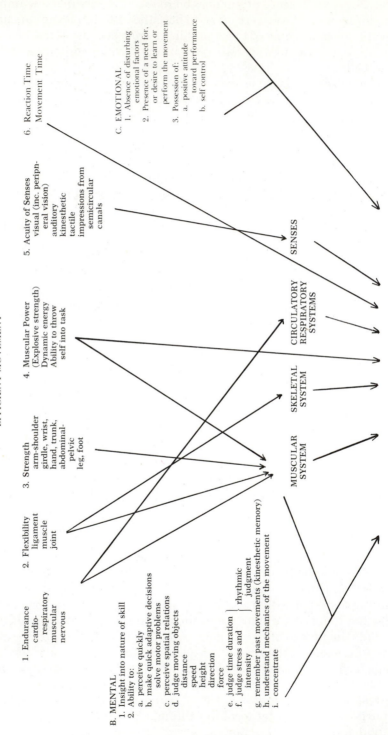

CHART 3

PREREQUISITES TO
EFFICIENT MOVEMENT

1. Endurance
   cardio-
   respiratory
   muscular
   nervous

2. Flexibility
   ligament
   muscle
   joint

3. Strength
   arm-shoulder
   girdle, wrist,
   hand, trunk,
   abdominal-
   pelvic
   leg, foot

4. Muscular Power
   (Explosive strength)
   Dynamic energy
   Ability to throw
   self into task

5. Acuity of Senses
   visual (inc. periph-
   eral vision)
   auditory
   kinesthetic
   tactile
   impressions from
   semicircular
   canals

6. Reaction Time
   Movement Time

B. MENTAL
1. Insight into nature of skill
2. Ability to:
   a. perceive quickly
   b. make quick adaptive decisions
      solve motor problems
   c. perceive spatial relations
   d. judge moving objects
      distance
      speed
      height
      direction
      force
   e. judge time duration ⎱ rhythmic
   f. judge stress and   ⎰ judgment
      intensity
   g. remember past movements (kinesthetic memory)
   h. understand mechanics of the movement
   i. concentrate

C. EMOTIONAL
   1. Absence of disturbing
      emotional factors
   2. Presence of a need for,
      or desire to learn or
      perform the movement
   3. Possession of:
      a. positive attitude
         toward performance
      b. self control

MUSCULAR
SYSTEM

SKELETAL
SYSTEM

CIRCULATORY
RESPIRATORY
SYSTEMS

SENSES

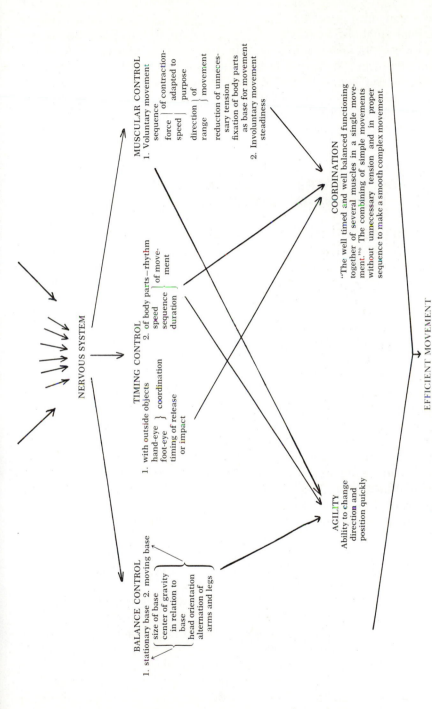

NERVOUS SYSTEM

MUSCULAR CONTROL
1. Voluntary movement
   sequence
   force ⎫ of contraction-
   speed ⎬ adapted to
   direction ⎫ purpose
   range ⎬ of
   movement
   reduction of unneces-
   sary tension
   fixation of body parts
   as base for movement
2. Involuntary movement
   steadiness

TIMING CONTROL
1. with outside objects
   hand-eye ⎫ coordination
   foot-eye ⎬
   timing of release
   or impact
2. of body parts — rhythm
   speed ⎫ of move-
   sequence ⎬ ment
   duration ⎭

BALANCE CONTROL
1. stationary base 2. moving base
   size of base
   center of gravity
   in relation to
   base
   head orientation
   alternation of
   arms and legs

AGILITY
Ability to change
direction and
position quickly

COORDINATION
"The well timed and well balanced functioning
together of several muscles in a single movement."* The combining of simple movements
without unnecessary tension and in proper
sequence to make a smooth complex movement.

EFFICIENT MOVEMENT

The combining of coordinated movements to produce the force required by the
particular purpose and to apply it through the most advantageous point, in the
most advantageous direction with the least expenditure of energy.

*Kraus, Hans: Therapeutic Exercises in Pediatrics. *Medical Clinics of North
America,* 31:629, May, 1947.

The teacher must also recognize the fact that disturbing emotional factors may block efficient movement. This is tremendously important in teaching swimming where fear of loss of support when the feet are taken off the bottom can, unless realistically dealt with, cause great retardation of learning. Fear must also be recognized in sports involving oncoming objects and body contact. In fact, fear of something new can be involved in most any movement situation. The pointing up of similarities to other activities and application to the new activity of known patterns and basic principles encountered previously can go far in doing away with this fear of the unknown by showing that the "new" activity is, after all, made up of elements that are largely familiar.

ORGANIZATION OF PREREQUISITES AND CONTROLS LEADING TO EFFICIENT MOVEMENT

An attempt to chart the organization of the various prerequisites and controls that lead to efficient movement can be found in Chart 3. This chart shows clearly the importance of the nervous system to human movement. Obviously, efficient movement is impossible without its smooth functioning. In any movement all systems of the body are brought into play and work through the nervous system to produce **balance, timing,** and **muscular** control. These three types of control depend to varying degrees on the items listed in the chart under **physical, mental,** and **emotional** prerequisites. One of these prerequisites may be more important to one of the three controls and another, to another.

Balance control involves the ability to adjust the center of gravity effectively in relation to any base, stationary or moving. Because of the importance of the eyes and semicircular canals to balance, head orientation is fundamental to this ability. In addition, when the body is in motion; the use of the arms and legs in alternation to assist balance is involved.

The individual must be able to time the contractions of various muscle groups so that he can produce motion at the speed, in the sequence, and for the duration of time which will result in the force required by the given purpose. This **timing control** sets the rhythm of his movement. He must be able to time his movements with those of objects, whether he is using his upper or lower extremities (or other body segments), to impart force to, or absorb force from, an object. This ability has been labeled "hand-eye" and "foot-eye" coordination.

The speed, range and resultant force of a movement must be adapted to the purpose. The degree to which direction is controlled determines accuracy. The fixation of certain body segments is essential if other segments are to have a base for action. All of these are involved in **muscular control.** In addition, muscular control involves the ability to relax — the ability to keep muscles which can in no way contribute to the maintenance of the position or execution of the movement, from contracting. The fact that the ability to relax is as much a motor skill as any movement, is too frequently overlooked.

Balance control, timing control, and muscular control are all mutually interrelated. For example, muscular control provides the means for control of balance; timing control is certainly involved in sequence of voluntary movement which is an important part of muscular control. The three types of control together lead to what has been termed **agility** — the ability to change direction and/or position quickly — and to **coordination.** Kraus has defined coordination as "the well-timed and well-balanced functioning together of several muscles in a single movement."[1] It might be defined further as the combining of simple movements without unnecessary tension, in proper sequence to make a smooth complex movement. When coordinated movements are combined to produce the force required by the particular purpose and to apply it at the most advantageous point, in the most advantageous direction and with the least expenditure of energy, the result is **efficient** movement.

The importance of teacher and student understanding of the basic mechanical principles — principles of balance, force production, and control — is obvious. While body size, shape, strength, and so forth, are factors in the determination of the success attainable in physical performance, the degree to which an individual can approach his potential depends upon the way in which he uses his physical, mental, and emotional attributes. "The degree of success in most physical activities is determined by the manner in which forces are applied. Through more effective use of available forces, a small man can outwrestle a larger man, a short-statured golfer can outdrive a taller golfer, a person with a short arm can throw farther than another with a long arm, and a weak-muscled person can move a heavier load than a strong-muscled person."[2]

REFERENCES

1. Kraus, Hans: Therapeutic Exercises in Pediatrics. *Med. Clin. North America*, 31:629, May, 1947.
2. Morehouse, Laurence E., and Cooper, John M.: *Kinesiology*. St. Louis, C. V. Mosby Company, 1950, p. 117.

ADDITIONAL READING

Fitts, P. M. and Posner, M. L.: *Human Performance*. Brooks/Cole Publishing Co., Belmont, California, 1967.
Keele, S. W.: *Attention and Human Performance*. Pacific Palisades, California, Goodyear Publishers, 1973.
Marteniuk, R. G.: *Information Processing in Motor Skills*. New York, Holt, Rinehart and Winston, 1976.
Sage, G. H.: *Introduction to Motor Behavior: A Neuropsychological Approach*. Reading, Massachusetts, Addison-Wesley Publishing Co., 1977.
Schmidt, R. A.: *Motor Skills*. New York, Harper and Row, 1975.
Wickstrom, R. L.: *Fundamental Motor Patterns*. 2nd Edition. Philadelphia, Lea & Febiger, 1977.

PART 2

BASIC MECHANICAL PRINCIPLES UNDERLYING EFFICIENT MOVEMENT

Consulting Author
RICHARD C. NELSON, Ph.D.
Professor
The Pennsylvania State University

INTRODUCTION
TO PART TWO

This section of the book has been greatly expanded by the inclusion of mathematical solutions for many movement problems. However, this need not cause a problem for the reader who is just beginning to study the mechanics of human movement; he can concentrate on the explanations of basic concepts which are still spelled out **simply** and clearly, and skip, to whatever degree desired, the mathematical solutions and more advanced material which have been added in this edition. Those readers with more background will find considerably more material covering all the steps in various mathematical calculations of forces, velocities, angles and so forth. Thus it is hoped that this edition will be more useful to those with some background or those who wish to gain a greater depth of understanding, without lessening its usefulness for those who are encountering the basic mechanics of human motion for the first time and who may not be interested in, or ready for, the more difficult mathematical calculations.

CENTER OF GRAVITY AND EQUILIBRIUM

3

GRAVITY

The discussion of gravity might be considered to be more properly presented in the chapter dealing with **force.** Technically, gravitational force constitutes the attraction of each mass-particle in the universe for every other mass-particle. Because this particular force is different from any other in that it is **constantly** acting on every object, whether stationary or moving, it is important to gain a basic understanding of its effects before considering any other mechanical principles. The concept of **center of gravity** and the principles of balance are based on an understanding of the fundamental effects of gravity.

The force that keeps individuals and objects on the earth's surface is the result of the gravitational attraction of two bodies; technically it is directly related to the product of the two masses (object and earth) and inversely related to the square of the distance between them $(m_1 \times m_2 \div d^2)$. The slight differences in the mass of people or objects as compared to the mass of the earth results in a constant value for the effect of gravity near the earth. However, as the distance between the earth's center and the object increases, the gravitational attraction decreases. In fact objects can move so far from earth as to be outside earth's gravitational field (the influence of its mass) as seen in space flights.

Because the earth is somewhat flattened at the poles, the distance from its surface to its center is thirteen miles greater at the equator than at the poles. While this difference appears to be minor when one considers the size of the earth, it does affect events which involve flight of an object or the body through the air, for example the long jump, shot put, golf, and so on. Olympic records indicate important differences attributed to location. Distances for javelin, hammer throw, shot put and long jump have been found to be less in Helsinki, Finland (60° N. latitude) than in Columbus, Ohio (40° N. latitude). Mexico City, located near the equator (20° N. latitude) and at an altitude of approximately a mile, provided an ideal environment for throwing and jumping events. Increase in altitude not only places the performer farther from the earth's center and thus decreases gravitational pull, but also, it reduces the resistance to the performer's (or object's) movement through the air since the air is less dense (p. 78).

Because gravity is caused by the attraction between the earth and each person and each object and since **each particle** of each object is involved, many parallel forces result; when these are added together the **resultant** is a single force from the center of the earth's mass to the center of the mass of each object (person). Thus the force of gravity is always exerted in a vertical direction downward toward the center of the earth and can be considered to act on the center of the mass of each object, person or body segment. For this reason the center of mass of a body or object is known as the **center of gravity.** Since the force of gravity pulls vertically toward the center of the earth, the line passing from the center of gravity downward (toward the center of the earth) is known as the "line of gravity." When a person stands on a scale, gravitational force pulls him downward but any motion is resisted by springs in the scale; this resistance is registered on the scale and is known as the person's weight.

CENTER OF GRAVITY

The **center of gravity** has been described as the point about which a body balances, or as the point at which the weight of the body can be considered to be concentrated. No matter how irregular the shape of an object or body, it has a point about which it will balance. If a single force equal to the weight of the body (or in other words equal to gravity's pull) could be applied vertically upward at the body's center of gravity, the body would be supported in equilibrium, no matter how it were turned about its center of gravity.[1]

In the case of any rigid symmetrical body with uniform density, such as a ball or block, the center of gravity is located at the geometric center. It is not as easy to predict the location of the center of gravity in an irregularly shaped object. Not only is the human body irregular in shape, but also it has moving parts and therefore, its shape is constantly changing and its center of gravity is dependent upon the position of its various segments at that time. The height of the center of gravity above its base when the human body is in its erect standing position (feet together, arms at sides) can be found by application of the law of leverage (p. 81). One end of a long board is placed on the platform of a scale. Across each end

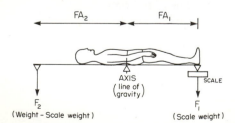

Figure 3–1. Forces and force arms involved in determining center of gravity in supine position.

of this board is a leg which is tapered to a fine edge; one leg is shorter than the other so that when the long leg rests on the floor and the short one is on the scale, the board is level. After the short leg is placed on the scale platform, the scale is set to zero to take the board's weight out of the calculation (Fig. 3–1).

The individual lies on the board with the soles of his feet even with the end of the board and with his arms along his sides. The scale is read. The distance from the soles of his feet to his center of gravity can be calculated by Equation 3.1:

DLG = distance scale end board to line of gravity (distance line of gravity)

$$DLG = \frac{D(W - SW)}{W}$$

W = **subject's total weight**

SW = weight registered on scale (scale weight)

D = total length of board

$$F_1 \times FA_1 = F_2 \times FA_2 \text{ (see Fig. 3–1)}$$

$$SW \times DLG = (W - SW) \times (D - DLG)$$

$$SW \times DLG = D(W - SW) - DLG(W - SW)$$

$$(SW \times DLG) + [DLG(W - SW)] = D(W - SW)$$

$$DLG [SW + (W - SW)] = D(W - SW)$$

total weight

$$DLG = \frac{D(W - SW)}{W} \tag{3.1}$$

If the individual stands on the board facing away from the scale with his heels a known distance from the scale end of the board, the anteroposterior position of the center of gravity in his body can be calculated; if he stands with his side to the scale, the lateral position of the center of gravity in his body can be calculated.

Recently Kelley and Zentz[2] have suggested a simplified process which dispenses with the need for mathematical calculation. A line is inscribed across the upper surface of the board halfway between its two pivot points. This method requires that, after the short leg of the board is placed on the scale, the scale be read rather than set to zero. After the scale reading for the board alone has been determined, one half of the individual's weight is added to the scale. The individual then lies supine on the board, feet toward the scale end, and shifts position until the scale balances. The distance from the center line of the board to the soles of the individual's feet is measured to find the height of his center of gravity above his base.

In the normal standing position with the arms hanging at the sides, the center of gravity in the adult male is 54 to 57 per cent of the total height from the floor and that of women, 53 to 56 per cent of the height; it is approximately centered in the anteroposterior and lateral planes. The position will vary somewhat with body build. Emphasizing these results of the height of the center of gravity to support a hypothesis that a difference in height of center of gravity contributes to variations in the physical performance of males and females has doubtful validity, since the ob-

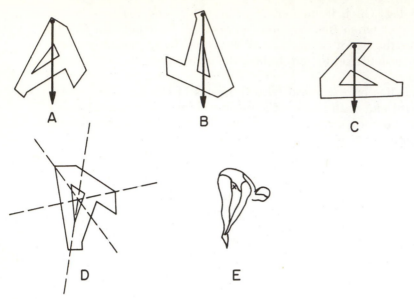

Figure 3–2. A, B, C, D; Finding center of gravity of uneven shape. E; Comparison with pike position.

served difference in center of gravity height is small and considerable overlap of the two distributions is evident. In general, the center of gravity in the human body can be thought of as being located in the region of the hips. However, any movement of a body part will shift the center of gravity in the direction of the movement (p. 52).

The shape of an object may be such that the center of gravity is actually outside the object itself. When considering the location of the center of gravity of a doughnut, for example, it is seen that it lies, not within the doughnut itself, but in the **center of the hole.** This situation can occur in many irregularly shaped as well as round objects. When a string with a weight and a V-shaped piece of cardboard are **freely** suspended from a pin which is inserted in three different points of the cardboard (Fig. 3–2 A,B,C), and the lines where the string crosses the cardboard in each position are drawn across the piece of cardboard, it is found that the three lines intersect in space, **not** on the cardboard (the actual object) (Fig. 3–2D). The point of intersection indicates the center of gravity. The similarity of this piece of cardboard to the pike position of the body is obvious (Fig. 3–2E).

The body assumes many positions in which its center of gravity is outside the body itself. In general, when two parts of the body are at an angle, the center of gravity is on a line which joins the centers of gravity of the two segments[3]; it is closer to the segment with the greater weight. When in a pike position the center of gravity of the total body lies on a line connecting the center of gravity of the trunk and arms segment with the center of gravity of the lower extremities and pelvis. When the arm is flexed at the elbow, the center of gravity of the total arm lies on a line connecting the center of gravity of the forearm with the center of gravity of the upper arm.

Law of Falling Bodies

The magnitude of the force of gravity is stated in terms of its **acceleration effect** (increase in velocity, see p. 63) which at sea level is 32.17 feet per second per second. For purposes of calculation this can be considered to be 32 feet per second per second (32 ft/sec²) without undue error resulting. The law of falling bodies states that **in the absence of air friction,** all bodies, regardless of size and weight, will fall with the same acceleration. If the distance an object has fallen is known, the time taken to fall to earth can be easily calculated by using Equation 3.2:

$$D_v = \tfrac{1}{2} g t^2$$

D_v = vertical distance

g = acceleration of gravity

t = time

(3.2)

A ball will fall 8 feet in 0.71 second.

$$8 = \tfrac{1}{2}(32)t^2$$

$D_v = 8$

$g = 32$

$t = ?$

$8 = 16\ t^2$

$8/16 = t^2$

$t = \sqrt{0.5}$

$t = 0.71$

If the time in which a ball fell is known, the vertical distance which it fell can be determined. For example, if a ball hit the floor one half second after release and was given no upward force to counteract the pull of gravity or downward force to add to the pull of gravity, one would know that it fell four feet.

$D_v = ?$

$g = 32$

$t = 0.5$

$D_v = \tfrac{1}{2}(32)(0.5)^2$

$D_v = 16 \times 0.25$

$D_v = 4$

While a freely falling object falls 4 feet in one half second, it falls 16 feet in one second and 64 feet in two seconds; the acceleration (increase in velocity) is obvious.

This downward acceleration of 32 feet per second per second takes place **independently of any horizontal motion.** If one body falls freely from rest at the same time that another is projected horizontally **from the same height,** both will strike the ground at the same time. However, they will strike in different places. This is explained in Chapter 9, Projection.

BALANCE

Since balance is of considerable importance in the execution of most human positions and motions, an understanding of its various aspects is essential. Sometimes the purpose of a particular activity demands stability, at other times instability. If the mechanical principles involved are understood maximum advantage can be taken of the forces present.

A body is balanced when its center of gravity is positioned over its supporting base. If the line of gravity passes outside the base, the body moves downward until a new base which is directly below the center of gravity is established. The action of slowly sliding a book over the edge of a table demonstrates this principle. As soon as the book's center of gravity has passed the edge of the table the book falls to the floor where it rests on its side and a base is again established which is under its center of gravity. A gymnast swinging on a bar will come to rest with his center of gravity directly below his point of support, while in a handstand above the bar the center of gravity must be directly above the bar. The point of balance in a suspension task is with the center of gravity vertically below the base (point of support) while in a support task it must be directly above the base.

The nearer to the center of the base the line of gravity falls, the more stable the body. Conversely, the nearer the line of gravity falls to the edge of the base, the more precarious is the equilibrium. One can experiment with this principle by standing with the feet slightly apart, weight centered, and asking a partner to push toward the right against the left shoulder and then, standing with the weight on the right foot, again asking the partner to push against the left shoulder. It will be noted readily that balance is more easily maintained when the weight is in the center of the stance because greater movement of the center of gravity is required before the line of gravity passes outside the base, in this case falls beyond the outside edge of the right foot.

Another factor which determines how far the center of gravity can move without falling outside the base is the **size of the base.** Obviously, **the larger the base, the more stable the body.** The center of gravity can move a greater distance without falling outside the base. In any activity in which stability is important the base of the body should be large enough so that the shifting of the center of gravity due to movement of the body, or body parts, will not cause the line of gravity to fall beyond the base.

This principle accounts for the greater stability of the four-point as compared with the three-point stance used by football linemen. By placing both hands on the ground, the base is made rectangular in shape and the area is greater than that of the triangular base of a three-point stance. However, the triangular base formed by the head and hands results in the largest base possible when performing a head stand, the alternative being to place the hands in line with the head which narrows considerably the base from front to back. Difficulty attributable to a small base of support is involved in performing on a balance beam, ice skating and ballet when dancing on the toes; one reason for the great difficulty in maintaining a handstand is the small anteroposterior base of support.

In making the base larger, however, several factors must be considered. The first of these is **the direction from which the opposing or expected force is coming or body segments are moving.** If a person anticipates being pushed from the **front** he should place one foot forward and lean forward (shift weight forward). This widens his base forward-backward and shifts his center of gravity and thus his line of gravity toward the front foot, increasing the distance the center of gravity can be moved in the direction of the anticipated force (backward) before the line of gravity passes beyond the back edge of the base (the rear foot). If a push from the **left side** is anticipated the feet should be **spread apart sideways** and the weight shifted to the left to maximize stability by increasing the distance the line of gravity can move before falling beyond the right foot. Thus it is seen that **to increase stability the base should be enlarged in the direction of the force to be opposed or produced.**

Additional stability is gained by shifting the body weight so as to move the line of gravity in the direction from which the force is anticipated. When standing on a moving bus, the sway of the bus from side to side can best be offset by placing the feet apart laterally; when the bus is slowing down or speeding up, stability is increased by placing the feet apart forward-backward. Stability in a given direction is in proportion to the horizontal distance of the center of gravity from the edge of the base toward which a given force is effective.

This same principle applies when the body segments are moving forcefully. When attempting to throw a ball as far or as fast as possible, first with the feet together, then with the feet in a lateral stride and finally in an anteroposterior stride, it is obvious that balance is more easily maintained with the anteroposterior position because this widens the base in the direction of forceful body motion.

If the forward-backward stride position is taken first with the right foot forward and then with the left forward, this last experiment can point up another factor in base enlargement — **the restriction of joint action.** As a right-handed person throws a ball with the right foot forward, it can be noted that backswing is definitely restricted due to the position of the hip joint. When the left foot is forward, the right hip is freed and a longer backward rotation is possible. When trunk rotation is required the feet should be spread in such a way that the pelvic rotation (which always results from a forward-backward stride) is in the direction of the required trunk rotation. Then maximum rotation is possible and, if less than maximum rotation is needed, the rotation of the spine is minimized. Therefore, **any widening of the base to give greater stability should be accomplished in such a way that movement in the joints is not restricted, or strain put on any joint.** There must always be a margin for movement in all directions if injury to a joint is to be avoided in case a sudden force is contacted.

In making the base wider another factor which must be considered is **the direction of the force which is exerted by the individual against the ground.** When a person increases the area of the base of support either by moving the feet apart laterally or by placing one foot forward of the other the **angle of the leg-foot segment with the surface** becomes an important factor and the importance of **friction** is magnified. As this angle decreases (as the feet are spread farther apart) the **horizontal component** of the force produced by the body (feet) against the surface increases. The reaction to this horizontal force is dependent upon the friction between the feet and the surface. Whether or not a widening of the base is effective depends on the forces involved (horizontal component of the force produced by the body against the surface and friction). If friction is adequate (that is, the coefficient of friction is relatively high), a wide base increases the ability to resist a force from or to exert a force in the direction of the base widening. However, when friction is insufficient to oppose the horizontal component of the force of the feet against the surface, increasing the base size is **not** desirable. When standing on ice or other slippery surfaces, a wide base contributes to instability; the feet are literally pushed out from under the body. All principles which apply to a given situation must be observed. If only some of them are observed results will not be as expected.

Whenever one body part moves away from the line of gravity in one direction, the center of gravity shifts within the body in the same direction. Another body segment must move in the opposite direction to keep the center of gravity above the same point of the base. If the movement shifts the center of gravity **beyond** the edge of the base, there must be considerable adjustment of segments in the opposite direction to keep it over the base **or** a new base must be established which is under the shifting center of gravity. One can experiment with this principle simply by standing with the back to the wall, heels against the wall, and attempting to lean forward. It is immediately obvious that the bending of the upper body forward shifts the center of gravity beyond the forward edge of the base (the toes), and either the body falls forward or one foot is shifted forward to establish a new base which is under the forward moving center of gravity. However, if one moves a foot or so from the wall the bend can be performed with no loss of balance because the hips are free to move backward to balance the forward moving trunk and thus keep the forward moving center of gravity of the body over the base (the feet).

Since various body segments are constantly moving, the center of gravity of the body is constantly shifting. If one stands in a well-balanced position with arms at sides and the weight centered on the feet, and raises both arms forward-upward to shoulder height, the front half **and** the upper half of the body are weighted more and thus the **center** of body weight is now farther forward and upward **within** the body than in the

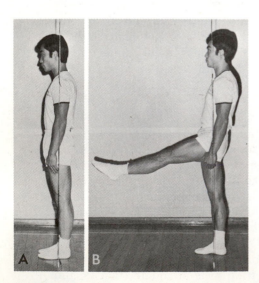

Figure 3–3. Body shift backward to keep the forward shifting center of gravity over the base.

normal (arms at sides) position; the center of gravity has shifted forward-upward **within the body.** Just how much the center of gravity moves is dependent upon the weight of the arms (segment being moved) relative to the weight of the total body and the distance the arms are moved. Movement of a leg a specific distance, for example, has a greater effect on the center of gravity's location than moving an arm the same distance. Whenever segments move there is an unconscious adjustment of the body to keep the center of gravity centered over the feet. For example, when the arms move forward-upward the adjustment of the body is backward.

Raising both arms to the right shifts the center of gravity to the right and upward within the body; the reflex adjustment to keep the center of gravity over the base (the feet) moves the total body left. A further example of this principle is seen in Figure 3–3. When one leg is lifted forward-upward, it is easy to see the shift of the body backward to keep the forward moving center of gravity over the support foot.

External weights added to the body become part of the total body weight and affect the location of the center of gravity, displacing it in the direction of the added weight. The center of gravity that must be kept over the base, if the individual holding an object is to remain standing, is the center of the weight of the body **plus** the weight of the added object. This new center of gravity is on a line that connects the center of gravity of the body and that of the weight (Fig. 3–4). The effect of the weight increases as its distance from the body becomes greater. This involves leverage and is discussed in detail in Chapter 5. However, it should be noted that the closer to the body the weight is held, the less it changes the location of the center of gravity and the less the effort necessary to hold it. This can be demonstrated easily by holding a heavy book close to

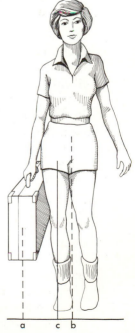

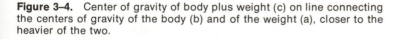

Figure 3–4. Center of gravity of body plus weight (c) on line connecting the centers of gravity of the body (b) and of the weight (a), closer to the heavier of the two.

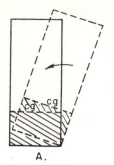
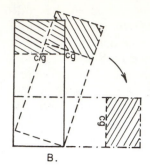

Figure 3–5. Comparison of the stability of two objects with centers of gravity (cg) at different heights.

the body and then at arm's length. The more the position of the total body-plus-weight is adjusted as a unit to keep the center of gravity over the base, the less energy required to hold the weight. The balance of each body segment over the segment below is not disturbed and the body is used as a whole to counterbalance the weight.

The lower the center of gravity the more stable the body. The potential rotating force of a weight that is high increases as the weight is lifted (Chapter 5, Leverage). The higher the center of gravity, the less the object must tip before the line of gravity falls outside the base. Object "A" (Fig. 3–5) is weighted so that its center of gravity is low. It can, therefore, be tipped 15 degrees and the line of gravity still falls within the base. When the force which is tipping it is released, the object settles back on its original base. Object "B," however, has been weighted so that its center of gravity is high. When it is tipped to the same angle, the line of gravity falls outside the base and the object falls until it lies on its side, having established a new base which is under the center of gravity.

Some activities are more difficult because of a relatively high center of gravity. Walking on stilts is one example; another is canoeing. Better balance is obtained by kneeling in the bottom of the canoe than by sitting on the seat because of the difference in height of the center of gravity. Stability in skiing is improved when the hips, knees and ankles are flexed, thereby lowering the center of gravity. In any activity when equilibrium is precarious in the standing position, a crouching, kneeling, or sitting position should be assumed. This lowers the center of gravity and increases stability. The same principle is followed when, in contemporary dance, ballet or conditioning exercises, the beginner is given exercises while sitting or lying on the floor. With the problem of maintaining balance eliminated or minimized, the student is free to concentrate on the movements which strengthen specific muscles or increase flexibility. The more advanced student with better control of his balance will be able to perform the techniques in a standing position.

Forward (or backward) rotating motion increases stability. While the object is rotating about one axis it has great inertia to rotation about another axis. This is why, although it is extremely difficult to balance a bicycle which is still, it is easy to balance a bicycle which is in motion.

Sensory Function in Balance. The integration of stimuli from several receptors is important in the maintenance of balance; information may arise from the vestibular apparatus of the inner ear, the visual system, the organs of touch and the end organs of the kinesthetic sense (receptors in tendons, ligaments and joints). Whenever the head is rotated for any period of time, either by rolling or twirling, the fluid in the inner ear is put into motion. Because of inertia (pp. 65–66), this motion of fluid continues after the movement of the head has stopped and gives the individual a sense of continued motion although the body is actually still. When the individual attempts to make adjustments to this false sense of motion a reeling movement may result. The degree to which this can be conditioned in different individuals by training is questionable. However, it is obvious from watching a beginner the first day he attempts a forward roll, and the same individual after several weeks of gymnastic instruction that the training has been effective. While a beginner, after executing **one** forward roll, may feel considerable dizziness and have difficulty controlling his movements, the more seasoned gymnast can execute several rolls or flips in succession and maintain control of his subsequent movements. In dance techniques involving whirling, this effect of the semicircular canals can be minimized by holding the head still momentarily between sudden turnings rather than moving it constantly in the circular motion.

During dynamic movements, those with relatively high accelerations, the vestibular apparatus contributes substantially to the control of balance. During quiet standing, however, the accelerations of the body are so slight that the vestibular apparatus has relatively little influence on maintenance of the upright stance. A person with a loss of vestibular function may be able to stand normally, but cannot be expected to walk on a balance beam successfully.[4]

The visual system is a significant factor in the control of balance. In normal standing there is a definite increase in the amount of body sway when a person is blindfolded.[5] The importance of vision to balance can be demonstrated by standing on one foot with the eyes open and then closing the eyes. The difficulty of maintaining the balance with the eyes closed is immediately apparent. The eyes give a point of reference and therefore, are important in the maintenance of body balance. Obviously, as the body sways during standing, the head moves also and certain properties of the optic flow pattern specify that movement.[6] Recent experiments[7] have re-emphasized the potent influence of visual proprioception in the control of balance. Even during dynamic motion the importance of vision should not be underestimated. For example, in the dance technique previously mentioned the dancer focuses the eyes on some object during a part of every rotation.

In general, the focus should be in the direction of intended movement, since the body tends to follow the direction of the head. In walking a balance beam and running, the focus should be ahead. One of the problems of the beginner in diving is his tendency to focus downward toward the board instead of upward and outward in the direction he wishes to move. Morehouse and Cooper[8] suggest that balance during movement is best maintained if focus is taken on an object that is at least 20 feet ahead, since the ocular muscles must make continual adjustments to keep the object in view when focus is taken on an object less than 20 feet from the individual.

Musculoskeletal proprioception, arising from joints, muscles, tendons and ligaments, also has a major role in the control of position and balance.[9] Complex and abundant information is available constantly; specifically, information concerning (1) the static position of joints, (2) the onset, duration and range of joint movements, (3) the velocity and acceleration of joint movements, and even (4) the pressure and tension on joint structures not related to the movements, should be available to a person's higher neural centers to assist in the control of balance.[10]

In addition to the musculoskeletal information, the organs of touch are important in helping to control body sway. Sensations from the soles of the feet are particularly important. During forward swaying of the body, the organs of touch are stimulated by increased pressure on the balls of the feet at the same time that joint receptors are sensing the change in lower extremity joint positions and motions. Therefore, information from both senses, touch and kinesthetic, may be used to determine the need for strengthening the contraction of calf muscles to stop forward sway and begin to move the body backward, thereby maintaining balance.

As a person stands normally, precise interplay occurs between the changing distribution of forces exerted by muscles crossing the joints of the lower extremities, especially the ankle joints, and the changes in the centers of gravity for various body segments. There is an important distinction between the point where the line of gravity cuts the base of support and the location of the **center of pressure** in the base of support (Fig. 3–6). Because of the leverage system (Chapter 5) at the ankle joint, the center of pressure in the feet normally is located slightly forward of the line of gravity during standing. It is the application of pressure at a location toward the balls of the feet that provides a counterbalancing force to the forward rotation of the body around the ankle joint. Fluctuations of the center of pressure provide a sensitive evaluation of postural stability

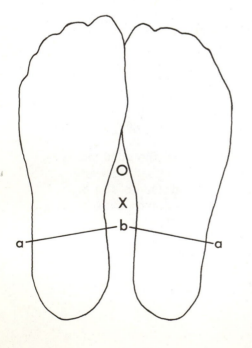

Figure 3–6. Location of the center of pressure in the standing position. The X indicates a location of the center of gravity projection on the base of support. The lines connecting a and b represent the axes of rotation at the ankle joints. The O shows a position of the center of pressure of the supportive forces to be slightly anterior to the position of the center of gravity.

1 cm

and steadiness.[11] A clear distinction between the location of the line of gravity and the position of the center of pressure in the base of support can be seen as an individual slowly moves from a standing to a squatting position. During descent, the line of gravity falls relatively close to the center of the base of support, thereby insuring a stable movement.

In contrast, movements of the center of pressure within the base of support may appear very erratic. The center of pressure applied to the bottom of the feet may shift rapidly from the lateral portion of the feet to the medial and from the front to a more posterior position. Movements of the center of pressure are directly related to changes in contraction forces of muscles controlling the ankles and feet. The rapid changes in the center of pressure that relate to movements of the feet and ankles permit smooth and controlled motion of the total body's center of gravity.

A similar situation can be seen in a hand stand; the center of pressure, now located within the base of the supporting hands, is constantly changing because of variations in the forces exerted by muscles in the hands, forearms and shoulders of the skilled gymnast. The total body center of gravity, however, is smoothly and carefully maintained above the base of support. The center of pressure and center of gravity are intimately interrelated as an individual controls body balance.

SUMMARY

The center of gravity of any body is that point at which all of the object's weight can be considered to be concentrated, or the point about which the object balances. For the human body (erect, arms at sides position) the center of gravity falls approximately in the center (front-to-back and side-to-side) of the hip region. However, as body segments move, the center of gravity of the total body shifts in the direction of the movement of the segment(s). A body remains in a state of equilibrium as long as its center of gravity is situated over the base of support, and the more nearly it is centered above the base, the greater the stability.

In general, stability is increased when the base is enlarged and/or the center of gravity is lowered. To be effective widening of the base must be in the direction of the force to be opposed or produced by the body; if the widening is accompanied by a shift of weight in the direction of the force, stability is enhanced further. In widening the base consideration must be given to possible joint restriction as well as to the friction between the feet and the surface. If an external weight is added to the body, stability becomes dependent upon the combined center of gravity (body plus weight) in relation to the base. Since these principles have many practical applications in daily activities as well as in sports their understanding is basic to the achievement of efficient positions and movements.

Opposing forces are constantly at work in the body so that the task of holding these in equilibrium is always present. When opposing forces acting on the body are equal, stability is maintained. When opposing forces are not equal, stability is disturbed until additional force is available. If the requirements for additional force are too great, strain results.

REFERENCES

1. Weber, Robert L., White, Marsh W., and Manning, Kenneth V.: *College Physics*. New York, McGraw-Hill Book Company, Inc., 1952, p. 110.
2. Kelley, David L., and Zentz, Gerry A.: Direct Read-off Center of Gravity Board. Paper presented, National Conference on Teaching Kinesiology, University of Illinois, Urbana-Champaign, June 9, 1977.
3. Williams, Marian, and Lissner, Herbert R.: *Biomechanics of Human Motion*. Philadelphia, W. B. Saunders Company, 1962, p. 17.
4. Birren, J. E.: Static Equilibrium and Vestibular Function, *Journal of Experimental Psychology*, 35:127–133, 1945.
5. Edwards, A. S.: Body Sway and Vision, *Journal of Experimental Psychology, 36*:526–535, 1946.
6. Gibson, J. J.: *The Senses Considered as Perceptual Systems*. Boston, Houghton-Mifflin Company, 1966.
7. Lee, D. N., and Lishman, J. R.: Visual Proprioceptive Control of Stance, *Journal of Human Movement Studies*, 1:87–95, 1975.
8. Morehouse, Laurence E., and Cooper, John M.: *Kinesiology*. St. Louis, C. V. Mosby Company, 1950, p. 137.
9. Granit, R.: *The Basis of Motor Control*. New York, Academic Press, 1970.
10. Smith, J.: *Mechanisms of Neuromuscular Control*. Los Angeles, University of California–Los Angeles Printing and Production, 1974.
11. Murray, M. P., Seireg, A., and Sepic, S. B.: Normal Postural Stability and Steadiness; Quantitative Assessment, *Journal of Bone and Joint Surgery, 57A*:510–516, 1975.

ADDITIONAL READING

Dyson, Geoffrey: *The Mechanics of Athletics*. London, University of London Press, Ltd., 1970.
Hay, James: *The Biomechanics of Sports Techniques*. Englewood Cliffs, Prentice-Hall, Inc., 1973.
Krause, Jo, and Barham, J.: *The Mechanical Foundations of Human Motion*, C. V. Mosby Company, 1975.

MOTION

4

Motion implies a change of place or position. It involves direction and speed. Motion of a body or object, or any part thereof, is brought about when a force of sufficient magnitude to overcome the object's inertia is applied to it.

TYPES OF MOTION

Observation of people and objects in motion indicates that there is an almost endless variety of ways in which they move. They may move along the ground, through the water, freely through the air, or through the air while attached to another object. The body itself may move through the air while some body part is attached to an object which in turn may be still or moving,* and objects may move through the air while attached to some body part, implement or machine, or freely under the influence of a previously applied force, gravity and air resistance. They may move in a straight, curved, or angled path; they may slide, roll, swing, bounce, rotate, or sail through the air. However, when the basic characteristics of all these movements are studied, it is found that there are actually two types of motion — linear and angular — and all movements can be classified as being **essentially** one or the other, or a combination of the two.

Linear motion, also called **translatory,** is characterized by the progression of the body as a whole with all parts moving the same distance, in the same direction, at the same rate of speed. A block pushed straight across the floor moves linearly. The human body experiences linear motion when it is carried forward in a train, bus, plane or car.

The second type of motion, **angular (rotary),** is characterized by motion in an arc about a fixed point (axis or fulcrum). Examples of this type of motion are found in the spinning of a record on a turntable, the turning of a wheel, a spinning ball, the use of a paper cutter or any lever, giant swings on the high bar, rapid turns of an ice skater, motion of a discus thrower and movement of most segments of the human body. This motion may involve a

---

*Examples of such movement are movements performed on the horizontal bar (a body segment attached to a still object) and on a trapeze (a moving object).

small arc or a full circle; the record, wheel and spinning ball move in a full circle, while the paper cutter and most levers move in a smaller arc.

Many objects, including the human body, may experience linear movement of the whole by means of angular motion of some of their parts. In walking the human body experiences linear motion as a result of the angular motion of its legs. The movement of the legs that carries the body as a whole linearly is actually a series of two angular motions. The upper end of the thigh and the body attached to it rotate forward around the foot as an axis. The axis then shifts to the hip joint and the leg rotates forward around this joint (Chapter 11, Walking). In skiing downhill the skier experiences pure linear motion, but in skiing cross-country his linear motion results from the angular motion of his extremities. The same is true of the child on roller skates, although the skates themselves always move linearly as a result of the angular (rotary) motion of their wheels.

Frequently objects have a form of motion that is not **strictly** linear but rather curvilinear. The flight of a ball, an arrow, in fact any projectile (Chapter 9), carries out this curvilinear motion. The motion is linear at the start but gravity, air resistance, and friction act upon the object to make the motion curvilinear. It is possible for this motion to be an actual arc, or even a complete circle. Frequently circular motion is indicated as a third type of motion; actually it is a form of angular motion if all parts move in an arc about an axis, or curvilinear if the object moves as a whole in a circular path. An excellent example of this type of motion — a person riding on a merry-go-round — was noted by Wells.[1] The person is moving as a whole in a circular path. The merry-go-round itself is, of course, experiencing angular motion since it is turning about its axis. An ice skater in performing a figure eight experiences curvilinear motion. He moves in a curved path and is not rotating about an axis with which he is in contact. A discus moves in a circular path during the thrower's turn. Since it is held in the hand it becomes a part of the arm-hand lever that is rotating around the moving axis of the feet and therefore, during this time, it could be said to be in angular motion. However, it is in a situation similar to the person on the merry-go-round and thus could be considered to be moving curvilinearly. Once released it moves linearly but the path is made curvilinear by gravity.

Linear Motion

Displacement describes the location of an object which has moved from a specified point. It may or may not be the same as the distance it has traveled. Consider the motion of a baseball player running the bases. When he arrives at first base he has traveled a distance of 90 feet, and his displacement from home plate is 90 feet at an angle of 45 degrees. When the batter reaches second base (assuming he runs in a straight line from base to base) he has covered a distance of 180 feet; however, his displacement from home plate is only 127 feet at a 90 degree angle. Upon reaching home plate he has run a total distance of 360 feet, and yet his **displacement** is zero. Thus the difference between distance and displacement is that **distance** is a **scalar quantity** and **displacement** is **a vector quantity** (involving distance and direction).

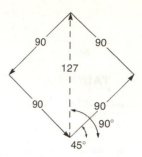

Displacement of baseball runner compared to actual distance traveled.

The units used to describe linear displacement are those of length: inches, feet, centimeters, meters, and so on.

Speed and Velocity. The **velocity** of an object is the **rate of change of its position.** In order to determine the velocity of an object at a given time, the distance moved, the direction of motion and the time elapsed must be known. **Speed** involves only the distance moved in a **certain time without regard to direction. Speed** is a **scalar quantity** while **velocity** is a **vector quantity** since it involves direction as well as distance moved in a given time.

Velocity is an important factor in many sport events but is often implied rather than explicitly calculated. If the distance and direction are the same for all runners, the one who runs the course in the least amount of time is said to be the fastest. Thus football players may be timed on a 40 yard dash to determine their speed. Examples of typical times are shown in Table 4–1.

This measure of speed is, however, only a measure of **average speed.** The average speed or velocity of an object can be calculated as follows:

$$\bar{V} = \frac{D}{t}$$

$\bar{V}$ = average velocity
D = distance   (4.1)
t = time

Calculation of the average velocities obtained by the football players in the previous example shows that **when distance is the same** for all contestants, time places the runners in the same relationship as does average speed (Table 4–2). The relationship between time and velocity is inverse; the lower the time, the higher the speed.

This concept is important for physical educators and coaches since in sports in which speed is the objective, it is measured by time. Most runners don't know their average speeds since they deal in time almost exclusively. Milers may speak of 58 second laps, or of a 4 minute mile pace. Swimmers

TABLE 4–1. RELATIVE POSITION OF TYPICAL TIMES OF COLLEGIATE FOOTBALL PLAYERS

POSITION	DISTANCE (YD)	TIME (SEC)	PLACE°
Linebacker	40	5.21	2
Back	40	5.02	1
Lineman	40	5.46	3

°Lower speed is better.

TABLE 4–2.   RELATIVE POSITION OF TYPICAL VELOCITIES
OF COLLEGIATE FOOTBALL PLAYERS

POSITION	DISTANCE (YD)	VELOCITY (YD/SEC)	PLACE°
Linebacker	40	7.68	2
Back	40	7.97	1
Lineman	40	7.33	3

°Higher velocity is better.

also deal in time. Men freestylers speak of 11 second laps (25 yards). When a swimmer or runner prepares for a race he will note his own lap times as well as those of the other participants. This helps to plan strategy since lap time gives more information than does total race time.

In the preceding example (Table 4–2), the runners all started at zero velocity and yet they averaged 7.68, 7.97 and 7.33 yd/sec; thus they must have run faster than their average velocities during part of the run. In fact, although average football players will take 2 seconds to complete a 10 yard dash, they can complete a 40 yard dash in 5 seconds. The average velocity during the 10 yard dash would be 5 yards per second (10 yd/2 sec) while that for the 40 yard dash would be 8 yards per second (40 yd/5 sec). This is because a great deal of the time measured for the 10 yard dash is actually spent getting into motion (overcoming inertia and accelerating from zero velocity at the start).

If an individual drives from one city to another (300 miles) in six hours, the **average** speed is 50 miles per hour. However, some time is spent going 0 mph (at red lights), a small amount of time at 20 mph (in traffic) and a large amount of time driving faster than 50 mph. Actually, speed is often changing; it is necessary to accelerate after each light, slow down for the traffic and then speed up again. Speed during such a drive is variable. If this driver had a cruise control which was set at 55 mph and this speed was maintained for 1 hour, during that hour speed would be constant.

In the previous examples **average velocities** or **speeds** were involved. By **average velocity is meant a speed which represents the distance an object has travelled in a certain amount of time.** If these velocities were calculated over shorter and shorter time periods, eventually a velocity which represents the distance traveled in an instant would be obtained: this is called **instantaneous velocity.** Instantaneous velocities are important in projection problems. For example, the distance a ball will travel depends on its velocity at the instant of release. A volleyball may be spiked at a speed of 65 mph; this would be the instantaneous velocity of the ball.

The units for velocity are an expression of distance and time: 10 ft/sec (3.05 m/sec) is read 10 feet per second; 60 mph (96.5 km/hr), 60 miles per hour; and 25 cm/sec, 25 centimeters per second.

A velocity of 10 ft/sec means that an object is traveling at a speed that would move it 10 ft if it continued to move at that speed for 1 second. It does not mean that the object will necessarily travel 10 feet; other forces may interfere with its continued motion at that speed so that its velocity may be changed before it has moved that far. A velocity of 60 mph means that an object is traveling at a speed which would cause it to move 60 miles if it continued to move at that speed for 1 hour, but gives no indication of how far it does travel. Although a volleyball may be spiked at a velocity of 65 mph, it does not travel 65 miles; within a second it contacts the floor or some other object which causes it to change speed and direction. What does 25 cm/sec mean?

In many instances times of less than 1 second are involved but it is more convenient to represent velocity in a base of one time unit. For example, while 50 mph = 25 miles/30 min = 12.5 miles/15 mins, the first term is the easiest to comprehend.

Acceleration. The **rate of change in velocity** is called **acceleration.** In physical education when people are timed over short distances such as 10 yard dashes or shuttle runs, the purpose is not to measure how fast they can move but how fast they can **change** their motion.

If at the start of a swimming race two swimmers leave the blocks with the same velocity (12.5 ft/sec), the swimmer who comes off the blocks first has the greatest average acceleration; he develops take-off velocity in less time. Initially both swimmers have a velocity of 0 feet per second; if one leaves the blocks in 1.0 sec and the other in 0.9 sec, the second swimmer will have the greatest average acceleration.

$$\bar{a} = \frac{V_f - V_i}{t}$$

$\bar{a}$ = average acceleration
V_f = final velocity
V_i = initial velocity (4.2)
t = time

swimmer 1

$$\bar{a} = \frac{12.5 \text{ ft/sec} - 0}{1 \text{ sec}}$$

$$\bar{a} = 12.5 \text{ ft/sec}^2$$

swimmer 2

$$\bar{a} = \frac{12.5 \text{ ft/sec} - 0}{0.9 \text{ sec}}$$

$$\bar{a} = 13.9 \text{ ft/sec}^2$$

These examples of acceleration are **average** accelerations and do not indicate instantaneous acceleration at any specific point in time.

Acceleration is independent of the magnitudes of the velocities involved. Velocities of different magnitudes can **change** at the same rate. Note the following examples.

1. $V_i = 10$ ft/sec $\qquad V_f = 30$ ft/sec $\qquad t = 0.5$ sec

$$\bar{a} = \frac{30 \text{ ft/sec} - 10 \text{ ft/sec}}{0.5 \text{ sec}} = 40 \text{ ft/sec}^2$$

2. $V_i = 1000$ ft/sec $\qquad V_f = 1020$ ft/sec $\qquad t = 0.5$ sec

$$\bar{a} = \frac{1020 \text{ ft/sec} - 1000 \text{ ft/sec}}{0.5 \text{ sec}} = 40 \text{ ft/sec}^2$$

In both examples the average acceleration is 40 ft/sec², although the actual velocities are markedly different. This means that the velocity of each object **will increase** by 40 ft/sec for every second of its motion; obviously this does **not** mean that the objects have the same velocity.

From the examples given it is seen that when calculating acceleration, the units of the numerator are velocity units and those in the denominator are time units. Typical units are meters/sec², feet/sec² and inches/sec².

When speaking of velocity or displacement, sign convention denotes direction. Movement to the right or upward is specified as positive while motion to the left or downward is negative. When used to describe acceleration the meaning of the sign may be confusing because it depends on both the direction of the motion and the increase or decrease in velocity. This is exemplified in the following:

1. As a gymnast rebounds off the trampoline he accelerates his body from 0 ft/sec at the low point of the bed to some positive take-off velocity (V is upward).

$$\bar{a} = \frac{V_f - V_i}{t} \qquad \begin{array}{l} V_i = V \text{ at low point} \\ V_f = V \text{ at take-off} \end{array}$$

$$\bar{a} = \frac{V_f - 0}{t}$$

Since t is always positive and the final velocity (upward) is positive, the **acceleration is positive;** in this case the acceleration is a **speeding up in a positive** (+) direction.

2. As the gymnast continues to move upward his motion slows due to gravity until his vertical velocity (V_f) becomes zero.

$$\bar{a} = \frac{0 - V_i}{t} \qquad \begin{array}{l} V_i \text{ now V at take-off} \\ V_f \text{ now V at high point} \end{array}$$

t is positive, V_i is positive (upward), thus $\bar{a}$ is negative

For this portion of the flight the **acceleration is negative** (−) **indicating slowing down in a positive direction** (up).

3. The gymnast then falls to the trampoline with some negative (−) velocity (downward direction).

$$\bar{a} = \frac{-V_f - 0}{t} \qquad \begin{array}{l} V_i \text{ now V at high point (0)} \\ V_f \text{ now V at contact with trampoline} \\ \quad \text{(negative because motion is downward)} \end{array}$$

V_f is (−), t (+)

∴ $\bar{a}$ is negative

Thus a negative (−) **acceleration can also indicate speeding up in a negative direction** (downward).

4. Finally the gymnast depresses the trampoline and is slowed down to zero velocity.

$$\bar{a} = \frac{0 - (-V_i)}{t} \qquad \begin{array}{l} V_i \text{ now V as first contact bed} \\ V_f \text{ now V at low point of bed (0)} \end{array}$$

V_i is (−), t (+)

∴$\bar{a}$ is positive

TABLE 4–3.   RELATION OF ACCELERATION SIGN TO DIRECTION OF MOTION AND CHANGE IN SPEED

MOTION	DIRECTION°	ACCELERATION
increasing speed	+	+
decreasing speed	+	−
increasing speed	−	−
decreasing speed	−	+

°Note: + means to the right or upward
    − means to the left or downward

Thus **a positive acceleration may mean speeding up in a positive direction or slowing down in a negative direction,** while **negative acceleration may mean slowing down in a positive direction or speeding up in a negative direction.** Therefore in interpreting acceleration it is important to know the direction of motion. (See Table 4–3.)

Newton's Laws of Motion.   Newton formulated three basic laws of motion. His **First Law** states that **an object which is at rest or in motion will remain at rest or in motion at the same speed, in a straight line, unless acted upon by a force.** Force must be applied to set any object in motion or to change its motion, either its speed or its direction. This tendency of a body or object to remain in its present state of motion, to resist change, is known

© 1972, Archie Comic Publications, Inc.

Figure 4–1.   Examples of the effect of inertia. "Gasoline Alley" cartoon reprinted through the courtesy of the Chicago Tribune-New York News Syndicate, Inc.

as **inertia.** The resistance of a body to a change in its state of motion depends upon its mass and the speed at which it is moving.

Mass can be thought of as a quantity of resistance to change possessed by an object. Whereas an object's weight may fluctuate due to gravitational effects, its mass is constant. **Weight** is obtained by multiplying body mass by its gravitational acceleration. Since gravitational acceleration is the same for all objects at a given location, inertia can be considered to be dependent upon weight and velocity. Generally speaking, the heavier the object and the faster it is moving, the more force necessary to overcome its inertia (change its state of motion). Once movement is started it takes less force to maintain a given speed than to change speed. It follows then, that the greater the use of inertia the less energy required to maintain motion. While the glide in certain swimming strokes saves considerable energy, it is important that the swimmer execute a second stroke before forward momentum from the first has been lost (due to water resistance). If the glide is maintained until momentum is lost, the energy saved by the glide will have to be used in overcoming inertia on each stroke.

The operation of this law is seen constantly. For example, an understanding of the law of inertia makes it possible to anticipate the inability to maintain contact with the greased golf club (Fig. 4–1) as the direction of motion of the hands is changed or to predict the result of stopping motion of the swing. It explains why Rufus (Fig. 4–1) falls as he steps off the moving merry-go-round (friction stops his feet but his body motion continues); why a ball continues to move after it is released; why people standing in a bus tend to fall forward when the bus comes to an abrupt stop. It points up the danger of allowing a small child to stand on a car seat as well as the reason for using seat belts.

The **Second Law of Motion** states that **when a body is acted upon by a force, its resulting acceleration is proportional to the force and inversely proportional to the mass.** It is expressed by Equation 4.3:

$$a = \frac{F}{m} \qquad \text{acceleration} = \frac{\text{Force}}{\text{mass}} \tag{4.3}$$

$$F = m \times a \qquad \text{Force} = \text{mass} \times \text{acceleration}$$

In other words, given an object of a certain **mass,** the greater the force applied to it, the greater the acceleration of the object (the faster it will change velocity). Anyone who has attempted to throw a medicine ball knows that it takes more force to change the velocity of a medicine ball than to accelerate a softball.

On the other hand, given a **certain force** applied, the greater the mass of the object, the less the acceleration (the longer the time it will take to change its velocity). If force applied to a given mass is doubled, acceleration will be doubled; but if force is maintained and the mass is doubled, acceleration will be halved.

It is possible to substitute Equation 4.2 into Equation 4.3:

$$F = ma$$

$$F = \frac{m(V_f - V_i)}{t}$$

$$F = \frac{mV_f - mV_i}{t} \qquad (4.4)$$

The quantity mass times velocity (mV) is referred to as **momentum.** When trying to catch an object such as a softball or football the purpose is to stop it ($V_f = 0$). When V_f is replaced by zero the above formula becomes:

$$F = \frac{-mV_i}{t}$$ (The (−) sign means that the respective directions of force and velocity are opposite.)

The greater the momentum of an object (its mass and/or its velocity) or the less the time during which the force is applied to stop it, the greater the force required. Since an object's mass remains the same, the two factors that determine how much force must be applied to a given object to stop it are the speed of the object just as it is contacted and how long the force is applied to slow it down. The faster the object is moving and the less time involved in stopping it, the greater the force which must be applied. Thus the force required to catch a given ball is less when the force is applied over a longer period of time.

Newton's second law can also explain how to increase the speed of an object. In this case the final velocity (V_f) would have a value and the initial velocity (V_i) would be equal to zero. Thus

$$F = \frac{mV_f}{t} \quad \text{or} \quad mV_f = F \times t$$ (positive since force and velocity in same direction)   (4.5)

Thus to speed up a given object the quantity ($F \times t$) must be increased. This quantity ($F \times t$) is called **impulse.** The same final momentum can be reached by an infinite number of combinations of forces and times. For example:

$$F \quad \times \quad t \quad = \quad mV$$

$$10 \text{ lb} \times \ 5 \text{ sec} = 50 \text{ lb-sec}$$
$$5 \text{ lb} \times 10 \text{ sec} = 50 \text{ lb-sec}$$
$$25 \text{ lb} \times \ 2 \text{ sec} = 50 \text{ lb-sec}$$

Newton's Third Law of Motion states that **to every action force there is an equal and opposite reaction force;** or for every force exerted by one body on another an equal and opposite force is exerted on the first by the second. The human body moves because of this reaction force — some body segment(s) exert(s) force against some surface and the reaction from the surface moves the body.

The effect of the equal and opposite reaction force is readily seen when the swimmer or canoe paddle pushes backward exerting a backward force against the water. The water moves backward with a certain velocity depending on the forcefulness of the stroke, and at the same time, the equal and opposite force produced by the water pushing forward against the arm or canoe paddle moves the swimmer or canoe forward. The effect of the two forces is not obvious when a runner pushes backward against the earth and the equal and opposite force produced by the earth causes him to move forward, because of the tremendous mass of the earth in relation to the mass of the runner.

A runner is propelled forward with a force equal and opposite to that with which he pushes backward against the ground, provided that there is sufficient friction and resistance to prevent slipping. The result of the equal and opposite force is obvious when one attempts to run in sand. Since the sand is not solid and the mass of each grain in contact with the foot is so small, the grains of sand move readily (considerable velocity) in response to the runner's backward push. The forward force exerted by them against the runner is slight. Only when the grains of sand have become packed so that they become, in effect, a part of a large solid mass is enough force exerted to move the runner forward with any speed. Thus it is easier to run in the hard packed sand close to the edge of the water than in the drier and softer sand farther from the water's edge.

When the body is unsupported in the air, as it is in diving and many gymnastic stunts, and a body part moves, the equal and opposite reaction of other parts of the body can be seen. This principle is, therefore, important in fancy diving, in performance on the trampoline and in any stunts executed in the air.

Angular Motion

Angular motion occurs when all particles of an object move in an arc around a fixed point. The concepts and relationships presented for linear motion also apply to angular motion, the principal difference being that the movement is circular rather than linear and the symbols used to depict various components are necessarily different.

Displacement.   The most commonly used symbol to identify angular displacement is the Greek letter **theta** (θ) which is analogous to distance (**D**) in linear motion. Three units of measurement are common for θ: degrees, revolutions and radians. Since one revolution (a complete circle) contains 360°, revolutions can be converted to degrees by multiplying by 360° and degrees are changed to revolutions by dividing by 360°. If a wheel makes 3½ revolutions, it turns through 1260° (3.5 × 360°). Conversely if it were turned through 580°, it would make 1.61 revolutions (580° ÷ 360°).

The **radian,** though less commonly used, is a very important unit of angular displacement. It **is the ratio of the arc of a circle to its radius.** In Figure 4–2, **r** represents the radius (not to be confused with radian) of the circle and **S** represents the arc (distance along the circumference of the circle) through which the distal end of the object (X) would be moved, if

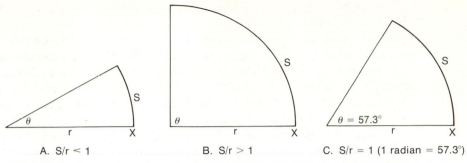

A. S/r < 1   B. S/r > 1   C. S/r = 1 (1 radian = 57.3°)

Figure 4–2. Comparison of angles for various relationships of cricle arc (S) to radius (r).

moved through an angle θ. In the first diagram (A), the distance **S** is clearly less than the length of the radius **r**, therefore the ratio of the arc (**S**) to the radius (**r**) is less than one (**S/r** < 1). In diagram B, the arc (**S**) is greater than the radius (**r**); the ratio of **S** to **r** is greater than one (**S/r** > 1). The third diagram (C) has an arc distance that is equal to the radius length and thus the ratio **S/r** = 1. This situation occurs when the angle (θ) is 57.3°; thus when an object has moved through 57.3° it has moved one radian. A full circle (360°) is equal to 6.28 radians (360° ÷ 57.3°). It should be noted that 6.28 is equal to 2π (π = 3.1416); thus since angular displacement (θ in radians) (Equation 4.6) is the ratio of the arc of the circle (displacement) to its radius, the formula for the circumference of a circle (Equation 4.7) is 2 π times its radius (2 π r).

$$\theta \text{ (in radians)} = \frac{S}{r} \quad \text{or} \quad S \text{ (displacement)} = \theta \times r \quad \quad (4.6)$$

$$\text{For circumference of circle} : S = 360° \times r$$
$$\text{circumference} : S = 2\pi r \quad \quad (4.7)$$

It is often necessary to convert degrees to revolutions and/or radians, revolutions to degrees or radians, and radians to degrees or revolutions; the processes are outlined in Table 4–4. These units describe only the displacement of an object undergoing angular motion.

TABLE 4–4. CONVERSION OF DEGREES, REVOLUTIONS AND RADIANS

CONVERSION DESIRED	PROCESS	EXAMPLES
revolutions to degrees	revolutions × 360°	3 rev × 360° = 1080°
degrees to revolutions	degrees ÷ 360°	1440°/360° = 4 rev
degrees to radians	degrees ÷ 57.3°	700°/57.3° = 12.2 rad
radians to degrees	radians × 57.3°	4.3 rad × 57.3° = 246.4°
revolutions to radians	revolutions × 6.28	3.7 rev × 6.28 = 23.2 rad
radians to revolutions	radians ÷ 6.28	34.3 rad/6.28 = 5.5 rev

Velocity.   As in linear motion the speed of an object is a function of the distance it moves and the time it takes to complete the movement. Thus the units used for angular velocity are a combination of angular displacement and time: revolutions/minute, radians/second and degrees/second. Records are commonly referred to as 45's or 33's, meaning that their rates of spin are 45 rev/min and 33 rev/min respectively. The symbol used to represent angular velocity is the Greek letter **omega** (ω); this is analogous to the letter **V** used to represent linear velocity.

Angular velocity is determined by calculating the change in displacement for a given change in time. Thus velocity means the same thing (rate of change of position) whether it refers to angular or linear motion; only the symbols are different. For angular motion the definition of velocity depicted in symbols would be:

$$\omega = \frac{\theta_f - \theta_i}{t} \qquad \begin{array}{l} \theta_f = \text{final angle} \\ \theta_i = \text{initial angle} \end{array} \qquad (4.8)$$

Thus a diver who wishes to complete a one and a half dive while in the air 1.19 seconds must spin 454°/sec. One and a half revolutions is 540° (1.5 × 360°) that must be completed.

$$\omega = \frac{\theta_f - \theta_i}{t} \qquad (\theta_i = 0)$$

$$\omega = \frac{540° - 0}{1.19 \text{ sec}} = 454°/\text{sec}$$

Acceleration.   Many sports involve projecting an object such as a ball with a high velocity. In order to accomplish this one must accelerate the arm from zero angular velocity to some large value by the instant of release.

As in linear motion, **acceleration** is the **rate of change of velocity.** Once again the concept is the same, only the units and symbols are different. The units for angular acceleration represent a change in angular velocity per unit of time. Common units are radians/sec² and degrees/sec². The symbol for angular acceleration is α (alpha).

To calculate the angular acceleration of an object when the velocities and time are known, Equation 4.9 is used:

$$\alpha = \frac{\omega_f - \omega_i}{t} \qquad (4.9)$$

If a gymnast on the high bar starts with an angular velocity of 3°/sec and changes to 140°/sec in 0.5 sec, what is his angular acceleration?

$$\alpha = \frac{140°/\text{sec} - 3°/\text{sec}}{0.5 \text{ sec}} = 274°/\text{sec}^2$$

Momentum.   The **angular momentum** possessed by a body undergoing angular motion is equal to its moment of inertia times its angular velocity ($I\omega$). When the sum of the external torques exerted on an object is equal to zero, the angular momentum is conserved. This is very important for any skill an athlete performs in the air. Consider the following: if angular momentum is conserved, then the quantity $I\omega$ must remain constant throughout the performance. When a diver leaves the board he has a certain quantity of angular momentum. For example, if in a layout position his moment of inertia (I) is 11 slug-ft^2 and his angular velocity (ω) is 2.21 rad/sec, his angular momentum would be:

$$I\omega_1 = 24.3 \text{ slug-ft}^2/\text{sec}$$

If the diver goes into a tuck position his moment of inertia (I_2) decreases because of the shorter distance from the axis to the center of the mass of his body. Since his angular momentum must remain constant, his angular velocity must increase. If his tuck position moment of inertia (I_2) is 2.58 slug-ft^2:

$$I_1\omega_1 = I_2\omega_2$$
$$24.3 = I_2\omega_2$$
$$24.3 = 2.58 \; \omega_2$$
$$9.42 \text{ rad/sec} = \omega_2$$

His angular velocity has increased from 2.21 rad/sec in the layout position to 9.42 rad/sec in a tuck. If the diver went into a pike position and his moment of inertia (I_3) was then 4.89 slug-ft^2, his angular velocity would be greater than for the layout but less than for the tuck. Once again the total angular momentum must be equal throughout the time in the air.

$$I_1\omega_1 = I_3\omega_3$$
$$24.3 = 4.89 \; \omega_3$$
$$4.97 \text{ rad/sec} = \omega_3$$

Since it is possible to obtain a larger angular velocity for a given torque value with a small moment of inertia rather than with a large moment of inertia, the tuck dive is easier than the pike, which is easier than a layout. Diving judges are aware of these differences and so differing point values are assigned to the difficulty factor for a rotating dive in each of these positions. A gymnast is also aware of the comparative ease of rotating in tuck as opposed to layout. A gymnast who does not have enough time to complete a front somersault in layout position tucks to increase his spin rate. Although ice is not completely frictionless skaters are able to increase their spin rate by pulling the arms in close to the body; they then extend the arms to slow down.

LaDue and Norman[2] point out that the true length of the radius of rotation is the distance from the center of rotation to the center of gravity of the mass away from the center of rotation. In other words, in twisting and twirling the true radius of rotation is not the distance from the center of rotation to the fingertips, but rather the distance to a point somewhere in the general location of the elbow which would be the **center of gravity** of the part of the body to that side of the center of rotation. In the case of a somersault the radius would extend to a point closer to the knees than the toes. However, the radius of rotation, and thus the moment of inertia, decreases as the extremities are brought in close to the body.

Technically the moment of inertia (I) is the product of mass and the square of the radius of gyration (**k**). The radius of gyration differs slightly from the radius of rotation (**r**), but the concept of increased moment of inertia with greater concentration of weight toward the periphery is the same, regardless of which is used. Since calculation of the true radius of gyration is complicated and the difference is slight, for purposes of this book, the formula for moment of inertia which uses the radius of rotation is suggested $(I = mr^2)$. The greater the moment of inertia, the more difficult it is to change angular velocity; the longer the radius of rotation or the radius of gyration, the greater the moment of inertia.

The increase in angular velocity with a shortened radius of rotation can be demonstrated effectively by attaching a string to a small weight and putting the other end of the string through a hole bored in a piece of wood. Moving the wood in a small horizontal circle gives force which moves the weight in a circle, since it is held by the string. If, while the same amount of force is being applied to move the wood at the same speed, the string is suddenly pulled up so that the distance from the point where it crosses the wood to the weight (radius of the weight's circle) is shortened, the increase in speed of the weight can be seen clearly.

Relationship Between Linear and Angular Motion

A great deal of movement is not strictly linear or rotary (angular) but rather a combination of the two. For example, the act of walking takes place because of the angular motion of the legs but the body as a whole is moved linearly. A car, train, bicycle, bus or wheelbarrow, in fact anything on wheels moves linearly as a result of angular motion of its wheels. Although the human body is restricted to angular motion at each joint, the angular motions of segments may be combined to obtain overall linear motion. This happens in the thrust in fencing and boxing, the push shot in basketball, in the shot put, and in any push or pull executed by the hands and arms. In executing a jump for height the various segments (levers) of the legs experience angular motion which gives upward linear motion to the body as a whole.

When the body, or an object, is carried forward as a whole owing to the movement of another object — such as when an individual rides in a car, a boat or on a horse — it acquires the motion of the object to which it is attached and due to inertia it tends to keep moving in that same direction and at that speed. When the vehicle or horse stops suddenly, the individual is likely to move forward off the seat (saddle) due to the resulting inertia he has developed because of the movement of the car, boat or horse. (See Fig. 4–1.) A ball or discus held in the hand acquires the same angular motion as the hand and if the contact is released it continues to move with the speed and **in the direction the hand was moving at release** until acted upon by another force; thus after release it moves linearly tangent to the arc of hand motion.

Even though an object is made to move in a circle it has a tendency to move in a straight line. Two forces are acting on it: the force causing motion and the force holding the object to the center of the arc. A stone whirled on the end of a piece of string is itself experiencing linear motion but is attached to an axis by means of the string. Therefore, the motion, while the string is in contact with the axis, is really angular. However, if the string is released, contact with the axis is broken, and the force bringing about motion causes the stone to move in a linear path (made curvilinear by gravity). The force pulling toward the center of motion (toward the axis) has been commonly known as **centripetal force.** The outward pull is an equal and opposite action force known as **centrifugal force.** This outward force is caused by the object's inertia, since the object, although forced to move in an arc by inward force, has a tendency to move in a straight line.

If the force holding the object to its circular or curved path is suddenly released, the object's inertia keeps it moving **in the same direction** and at the same speed that it was moving at that instant; thus the object **will fly off in a straight line (linear motion), tangent to the arc through which it was moving at the moment of release.** This force depends on weight of the object, its speed, and the radius of curvature of the arc (see Formula 4.10[7]).

$$F_c = \frac{m\omega^2}{r} \quad \text{or} \quad \text{Centripetal force} = \frac{\text{mass} \times \text{angular velocity}^2}{\text{radius}} \qquad (4.10)$$

This force must increase as the mass (for practical purposes, the weight) increases, but since it must increase as the **square** of the velocity, speed is a greater factor than is weight. Increasing the length of the radius, however, **decreases** the centrifugal force and the shorter the radius, the greater the centrifugal force.

The linear velocity of an object is equal to its radius of rotation times its angular velocity. This relationship is found by dividing both sides of Equation 4.6 for angular displacement by time:

$$S = r \times \theta$$

$$\frac{S}{t} = \frac{r\theta}{t} \quad \text{or} \quad \frac{S}{t} = r \times \frac{\theta}{t} \qquad (4.11)$$

The quantity θ/t equals angular velocity and, since S (displacement along the arc) is analogous to distance in linear motion, S/t equals linear velocity. Thus the symbols for linear and angular velocity can be substituted in the above formula:

$$V = r\omega^* \quad \text{(linear velocity} = \text{angular velocity} \times \text{radius)}$$

$$\text{or} \quad \omega = \frac{V}{r} \quad \text{(angular velocity} = \text{linear velocity} \div \text{radius)} \qquad (4.12)$$

Given a **certain angular velocity,** the longer the radius, the greater the linear velocity, and the shorter the radius, the less the linear velocity. However, if **linear velocity is constant,** the longer the radius, the less the angular velocity, while a shorter radius increases the angular velocity.

The variation in linear velocity with a change in length of radius is demonstrated in Figure 4–3. If three performers in a marching band stand on spots 0, 1 and 2 on the bottom line and the whole line pivots from the

*ω must be expressed in radians/unit time for this conversion.

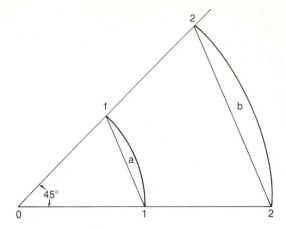

Figure 4–3. Comparison of distance traveled when radius varies. If covered in same time, linear velocity varies with length of radius.

horizontal through a 45° angle, they will finish on the upper line. The performer starting on spot 1 walks a distance **a**, the performer on spot 2, a distance **b** while the one at 0 simply pivots in place. If the line is to remain straight, performers 1 and 2 must reach their new positions in the same amount of time; since 2 must move farther than 1, he must walk faster (his linear velocity must be greater). Both 1 and 2 move through the 45° angle in the same amount of time so their angular velocities are the same although their linear velocities are different.

This concept is important in sports performance. If the angular velocity can be maintained, a longer lever gives a greater linear velocity. Thus when performing skills in which a large linear velocity is desirable, the longest lever that can be controlled should be used. For example, in golf the longest club is chosen for the drive, a volleyball or tennis ball is struck with a straight arm and a kicker attempts to have a straight leg at contact with the football.

While a body's resistance to any change in **linear** motion (inertia) depends entirely on its mass, its resistance to change in **angular** motion (moment of inertia) depends not only on its mass but also on the distribution of its mass around the axis. Thus the greater the **inertia** of an object (its mass), the more difficult it is to change its **linear** motion (start it moving, speed it up or slow it down); the greater its **moment of inertia** (its mass and the distribution around the axis) the more difficult it is to change its **angular** motion.

Just as linear acceleration varies directly with the force and inversely with the mass (Newton's Second Law: a = F/m), angular acceleration (α) varies directly with the force producing rotation (torque) and indirectly with the moment of inertia (I).

$$\alpha = \frac{Torque}{I} \quad \text{or} \quad Torque = I\alpha \qquad (4.13)$$

For a given moment of inertia, the greater the torque applied the greater the angular acceleration; for a given torque, the greater the moment of inertia (either the mass or the distance of its center of gravity from its axis) the smaller the angular acceleration.

The runner who flexes his knees during the swinging phase, the volleyball spiker who flexes the arm for the wind up and the batter who chokes up on the bat are all decreasing the moment of inertia by bringing the center of gravity of the mass being moved closer to the axis of rotation in order to increase the angular acceleration. Just before contact the spiker straightens the arm to maximize the linear velocity for contact.

The **factors which determine the type of motion** that will result when force is applied are the point at which the force is applied and the pathway of movement available to the object or body. If force is applied through the center of gravity of the object, and the object is free to move in the direction in which the force is applied, linear motion will result. Force applied uniformly against an entire side of an object, or equal forces applied equidistant from the center of gravity, can be considered to be the same as a single force applied through the center of gravity, since the forces on all sides of the center of gravity are balanced. If force is applied away from the center of gravity of the object, the object will rotate. This, of course, is the way spin is put on a ball. If an object is not free to move linearly — one end is held in place or meets interference — the object will rotate whether or not the force is applied through the center of gravity. For example, if one were pushing a large carton on wheels across a clear surface and the force were applied through the center of gravity, it would move linearly in the direction of the force. However, if the left wheel contacted a stick, rock or other obstacle that interfered with its forward movement, the carton would begin to turn to the left even with a centered force. Friction commonly causes angular motion even though force is applied through the center of gravity. If friction is such that the base of an object does not move readily, force applied through the center of gravity will cause the object to tip. Since the top is freely movable but friction interferes with the movement of the bottom, the force is more effective in moving the top than the bottom and the object tips. Since, by definition, a lever has a fixed point, angular motion always results when a force sufficient to overcome its moment of inertia is applied at **any point** on a lever.

FACTORS MODIFYING MOTION

There are several factors which modify motion. Any of these may be a help or a hindrance depending upon the situation. The first of these is **friction.** Friction, the force which opposes the motion of one object across the surface of another object, depends upon the characteristics of the two surfaces and on the force(s) pushing the two surfaces together. It is expressed as a coefficient of friction. A given degree of friction force will prevent movement until the moving force exceeds a certain level after which sliding occurs. Once movement has started, the sliding friction force decreases below that reached just prior to movement. This **in part** explains why it is easier to keep an object sliding than it is to start it moving.

The coefficient of friction between two objects can be found by placing

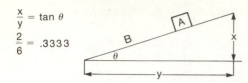

$$\frac{x}{y} = \tan \theta$$

$$\frac{2}{6} = .3333$$

Figure 4–4.   Calculation of coefficient of friction.

one object on the second and slowly tilting the second until the first begins to slide downward. The tangent of the angle of the surface of the second object with the horizontal at the instant the first object **begins to slide** gives the coefficient of friction between the two objects. This can be calculated by dividing the height to which one end of the second object had been lifted when the first began to slide, by the distance from the angle to the point directly below the end of the lifted object.[4] If one end of the surface (B, Fig. 4–4) had been raised 2 inches (x), when A began to slide down B and the distance from the angle to the point below the end of object B was 6 inches (y), the tangent of the angle formed (θ) would be 0.3333, which would be the coefficient of friction between surfaces A and B.

The coefficient of friction is **independent of area** of surfaces in contact[5] and is dependent **only** on the total force pushing the two surfaces together and on the types of surfaces involved. When an object is moved across a surface, the total force pushing the surfaces together depends on the weight of the object plus any additional force pushing downward. In other words, whether the base of a 50 pound object is four feet or eight feet square, the friction between it and any given surface is the same. When the **force pushing the two surfaces together** is changed or the **material of either** surface is changed, the coefficient of friction is different. Since when an object rests on a horizontal surface the force of gravity acts perpendicular to the surface, friction resisting motion across a horizontal surface increases

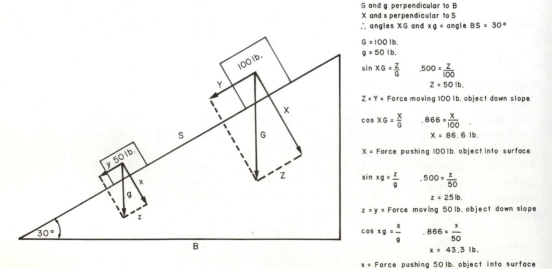

G and g perpendicular to B
X and x perpendicular to S
∴ angles XG and xg = angle BS = 30°

G = 100 lb.
g = 50 lb.

$\sin XG = \frac{Z}{G}$ $.500 = \frac{Z}{100}$

Z = 50 lb.

Z = Y = Force moving 100 lb. object down slope

$\cos XG = \frac{X}{G}$ $.866 = \frac{X}{100}$

X = 86.6 lb.

X = Force pushing 100 lb. object into surface

$\sin xg = \frac{z}{g}$ $.500 = \frac{z}{50}$

z = 25 lb.

z = y = Force moving 50 lb. object down slope

$\cos xg = \frac{x}{g}$ $.866 = \frac{x}{50}$

x = 43.3 lb.

x = Force pushing 50 lb. object into surface

Figure 4–5.   Forces effective against 50 and 100 pound weights on slope of 30 degrees.

proportionally with weight, i.e., the greater the weight of the object to be moved, the greater the friction to be overcome. While greater weight does increase the force pushing an object against a sloping surface (force perpendicular to the surface) and thus increases the force resisting motion (friction), it does not retard the **downhill motion** because the greater weight also increases the force parallel to the slope which tends to move the object downhill (Fig. 4–5). These two forces, perpendicular (Fig. 4–5, X) and parallel (Fig. 4–5, Y) to the slope, increase proportionately. The greater weight would make the movement of the heavier object **uphill** more difficult because of the greater force pushing the surfaces together (X compared to x).

If some downward force is added to the weight of the object, friction is increased proportionally. If one pushes a heavy piece of furniture with the hands toward its top edge, the force applied is downward as well as forward. The downward component is not only wasted as far as forward motion is concerned, but it also adds to the difficulty of the task by increasing the friction to be overcome.

The friction between the shoes of athletes and the playing surfaces on which they move is of critical importance to successful performance. The advent of a variety of artificial surfaces and new sport shoes has made it increasingly difficult to determine the best combinations. If the friction is inadequate slipping and sliding occur; if it is too great, the stops are too abrupt and in some cases this leads to painful toe, ankle or knee injuries. Friction is altered when the surface becomes wet. The speed and mobility of football, field hockey and soccer players are greatly reduced when they must play on wet, muddy surfaces; baseball games cannot be played if the playing surface becomes too wet. Shoes with various types of cleats and spikes are used to increase friction in sports such as football, field hockey, baseball, soccer, and track and field.

In some sport activities it is desirable to minimize friction. Downhill skiers apply wax to their skis as a means of reducing friction and thereby increasing speed. Because the surface of the snow (and thus the friction) changes drastically with different weather conditions, the type of wax must be varied according to the condition of the snow at a given time. Bobsled runs are iced to permit maximum speed of the sled to be reached. Smooth ice is required in speed skating competition to enhance the gliding phase of the stroke. Bowlers dry their hands and chalk their fingers to reduce friction between their fingers and the inner surface of the holes in the ball and thereby assure a more consistent release of the ball. Furthermore, the lanes are treated regularly with a special oil as a means of providing standard conditions.

In addition to static and sliding friction, many sport and daily activities are influenced by rolling friction. The force to be overcome from rolling friction is considerably less than that of static or sliding friction. Therefore, whenever possible a heavy load is put on wheels when it must be moved. Rolling friction is exemplified in the contact between a bicycle wheel and road surface and a ball rolling over the ground as in golf, soccer or field hockey. The harder the surface over which the object rolls, the less the force of rolling friction. The effect of the surface can be seen in contrasting putting on a dry, closely mowed golf green as opposed to a rain soaked green. In extreme cases, some players have even used a number five or six iron to avoid having to roll the ball through wet areas.

Friction is a help to man in the performance of tasks necessitating the application of a diagonally forward and upward force to (or through) the human body — tasks in which he must push downward and backward against the supporting surface. Without it the runner, broad jumper, thrower, or pusher could not exert maximum force without danger of slipping, because the backward component of his diagonal force would have no force to resist it and push back against him. On the other hand, friction hinders the movement of any object being pushed or pulled as well as that of a rolling ball.

The **drag** of the medium through which an object moves, commonly known as **air** and **water resistance,** is also a factor that modifies motion, as is **lift.** Without air resistance a sailboat could not move, an airplane could not fly. On the other hand air resistance can be a great hindrance to movement. Unless it is a tailwind, the golfer, the football punter or the runner finds that air resistance hinders movement considerably. Badminton, because the light weight and lack of compactness of the shuttle make it so responsive to air pressure, is extremely difficult to play outdoors unless the air is unusually still.

Water resistance is somewhat different from the other factors mentioned in that it both assists and hinders movement **at the same time.** It is essential to the propulsion of the body, or boat, through the water and at the same time it hinders its progress. (This is discussed more fully in Chapters 7 and 25.)

The final factor that modifies motion is **gravity.** While this force must be considered in all movement, it has been discussed in Chapter 3 and, therefore, is not included here.

The magnitude of the applied force relative to the magnitude of the resistance is the all-important factor causing motion.[6] In all movement tasks one needs to understand the methods for taking advantage of these forces when they contribute to the movement, and for minimizing them when they hamper the movement.

REFERENCES

1. Wells, Katharine F.: *Kinesiology.* 5th ed. Philadelphia, W. B. Saunders Company, 1971, p. 79.
2. LaDue, Frank, and Norman, Jim: *This is Trampolining.* Cedar Rapids, Iowa, Torch Press, 1956, pp. 73–74.
3. Tricker, R. A. R., and Tricker, B. J. K.: *The Science of Movement.* New York, American Elsevier Publishing Company, Inc., 1967, p. 263.
4. Weber, Robert L., White, Marsh W., and Manning, Kenneth V.: *College Physics.* New York, McGraw-Hill Book Company, Inc., 1952, p. 74.
5. *Ibid.,* p. 71.
6. Wells, Katharine F.: *op. cit.,* p. 77.

ADDITIONAL READING

Dyson, Goeffrey: The Mechanics of Athletics. London, University of London Press, Ltd., 1970, pp. 70–98. (angular motion)

Faria, I., and Cavanagh, P. R.: The Physiology and Biomechanics of Cycling. New York, John Wiley, 1977. (angular motion)

Hays, James: The Biomechanics of Sports Techniques. Englewood Cliffs, New Jersey, Prentice-Hall, Inc., 1973. (linear motion)

Kuhlow, A.: "Analysis of Competitors in World Speed-Skating Championship," Nelson and Morehouse, eds. Biomechanics IV. Baltimore, University Park Press, 1974. (linear motion)

Northrip, J., Logan, G., and McKinney, W.: Introduction to Biomechanic Analysis of Sport. Dubuque, Wm. C. Brown Company, 1974. (angular and linear motion)

Ramey, M.: "The Use of Angular Momentum in the Study of Long Jump Take-offs," in Nelson and Morehouse, eds., Biomechanics IV. Baltimore, University Park Press, 1974, pp. 144–148. (angular motion)

5

LEVERAGE

Levers are used many times a day, in the kitchen, the garden, the workshop, and on the sportsfield. When a knife is used to lift a lid, a bottle opener to pry off the top of a bottle, a nutcracker to crack the shell of a nut, scissors to cut cloth, the head of a hammer to pull out a nail, a wheelbarrow to transport a load, a crowbar to lift a heavy rock, or when any segment of the body is moved, leverage is involved.

In the discussion of motion it was pointed out that a force applied through the center of gravity of an object that is **free to move** produces linear motion but applied to an object which is **fixed** at some point, this force produces angular motion. Since a **lever** is defined as a **rigid object with a fixed point** (axis or fulcrum), a force applied at any point produces angular motion. Obviously to cause motion the force must be sufficient to overcome the lever's moment of inertia (p. 74).

PRINCIPLE OF LEVERS

The product of the force applied (its magnitude) and the perpendicular distance from the line of force application to the axis is called the **moment** or **torque.** The perpendicular distance from the point of force application to the axis is known as the **force arm** (FA). Thus the 10 pound force in Figure 5–1A causes a torque of 50 in-lbs.

$$M(T) = F \times FA \qquad \text{Moment (or torque)} = \text{Force} \times \text{Force Arm} \qquad (5.1)$$
$$M(T) = 10 \text{ lbs} \times 5 \text{ in} = 50 \text{ in-lbs.}$$

Because this force tends to produce **counterclockwise** rotation it is considered to be positive (+); one that tends to cause **clockwise** rotation is negative (−). If two forces act on a lever in opposite directions as exemplified in Figure 5–1B, one would tend to produce positive rotation and the other, negative. In this example the 20 pound resistance force acting 5 inches from the axis is offset by the 10 pound force acting at a point 10 inches from the axis. The moment (torque) of the 20 pound force is −100 in-lbs and that of the 10 pound force is +100 in-lbs. Since the sum of the moments equals zero, no rotation occurs. Thus a lever is in equilibrium (balanced) when the moment of the clockwise force (force times the length of force arm) is equal to the

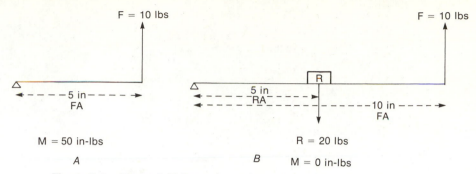

Figure 5–1. Moment, M (torque), produced by the force acting on a lever.
A, A single clockwise moment.
B, A clockwise force and counterclockwise resistance.

moment of the counterclockwise force (resistance times the length of the resistance arm).

$$F \times FA = R \times RA \qquad (5.2)$$

Any additional force will produce motion.

It should be noted that in the example given (Fig. 5–1B), only 10 pounds of force are required to support the 20 pound weight. This is said to provide a "mechanical advantage" since the magnitude of the force required is less than that of the weight supported. A mechanical advantage occurs when the force arm is greater than the resistance arm (FA > RA). In other words, the ratio of force arm to resistance arm is greater than 1 (FA/RA > 1).

It must be emphasized that frequently a force is **not** exerted at a 90 degree angle to the lever to be balanced or moved and thus the force arm is **not** the distance along the lever to the point of force application as it is in Figure 5–1, where the forces are effective at right angles to the lever. As indicated earlier the force arm is the **perpendicular** distance from the axis to the line of the force. If the lever shown in Figure 5–1B were at a 30 degree angle with the horizontal and the force acted at a 55 degree angle to the lever while the resistance acted at a 60 degree angle, the force and resistance arms would no longer be 10 and 5 inches respectively (Fig. 5–2). The perpendicular distance from axis to line of force would be 8.2 inches (not 10) while the resistance arm would be 4.3 inches (not 5). The force moment would then be +82 in-lbs and the resistance moment would be −86 in-lbs; thus the resistance would cause rotation of the lever in a clockwise direction. The 10 pound force would still have a mechanical advantage but this advantage would be only 1.9 (8.2 in/4.3 in) as compared to the value of 2.0 in the previous example. Since the magnitude of the weight is twice that of the force, the force cannot balance the weight.

When the axis lies between two forces (or force and resistance), the lever (or object) is in equilibrium only when the forces have a common line of action. The forces acting on a teeter-totter will be balanced when the weight

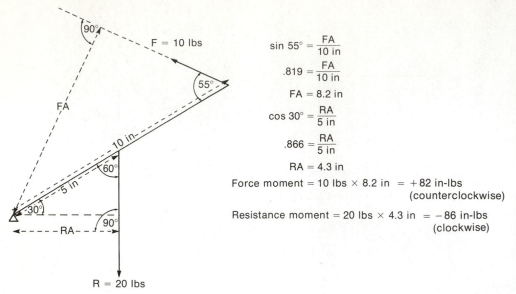

$$\sin 55° = \frac{FA}{10 \text{ in}}$$

$$.819 = \frac{FA}{10 \text{ in}}$$

$$FA = 8.2 \text{ in}$$

$$\cos 30° = \frac{RA}{5 \text{ in}}$$

$$.866 = \frac{RA}{5 \text{ in}}$$

$$RA = 4.3 \text{ in}$$

Force moment = 10 lbs × 8.2 in = +82 in-lbs
(counterclockwise)

Resistance moment = 20 lbs × 4.3 in = −86 in-lbs
(clockwise)

Figure 5–2. FA and RA are perpendicular distances from axis to lines of forces, thus are shorter than the distance from axis along lever to point of force application.

of one child multiplied by his distance from the fulcrum of the board is equal to the weight of the child on the other end of the board times his distance from the fulcrum (Fig. 5–3A). The forces applied at either end have a common line of action; both are vertically downward. However, if two equal forces are applied to a top as indicated in Figure 5–3B, motion will result. The forces acting on the top will not be in equilibrium, even though the forces are equal and are applied equidistant from the point of rotation, because both torques are positive and therefore their sum is not zero.[1]

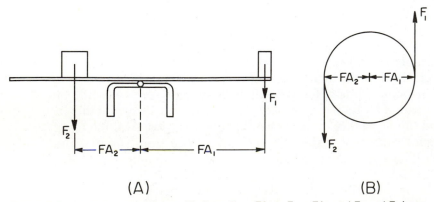

(A)   (B)

Figure 5–3. *A*, teeter-totter in equilibrium; $F_1 × FA_1 = F_2 × FA_2$ and F_1 and F_2 have common line of action; F_1 tends to produce clockwise rotation (negative torque) while F_2 tends to produce counter-clockwise rotation (positive torque). *B*, looking down on a top; $F_1 = F_2$ and $FA_1 = FA_2$ thus $F_1 × FA_1 = F_2 × FA_2$ but motion will result because both produce positive torque.

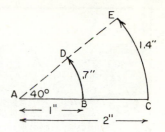

Figure 5–4. Relationship of length of lever to speed and range of movement. C moves twice as far (to E) as B (to D) in the same time and thus has twice the linear velocity.

As indicated earlier (page 46), the **center of gravity** of any body is that point about which the weight is balanced. Since each of the particles of the object is pulled downward by gravity, each exerts a **torque** (moment) about any given point. There is only one point about which all of these torques are equal to zero; this is the center of gravity.[1]

The longer the force arm, the less force it takes to balance a lever, and the longer the weight or resistance arm, the more force required to balance it. Thus one use of a lever is to gain a mechanical (force) advantage so that a small force exerted far from the axis is, in effect, converted to a larger force which is exerted closer to the axis.*

Another function of a lever is to gain speed and/or range of motion, and these are linked together. If two levers move through an angle of 40 degrees at the same velocity (Fig. 5–4) the tip of the longer lever (AC) travels much farther than the tip of the shorter lever (AB), and because it covers a longer distance (CE) in the same time that the shorter lever covers the shorter distance (BD), it must travel faster. When a lever moves about its axis, the distance that all points on the lever move is proportional to their distance from the axis. If a point is twice as far from the axis, it will move twice as far and, therefore, its linear velocity will be twice as great.

The example of the marching band line cited in the discussion of the relationship between angular and linear motion (p. 73) is another illustration of this function of a lever. Thus, as stated earlier, **if angular velocity can be maintained,** lengthening a lever increases linear velocity at the distal end. Therefore, in golf, as more distance and greater linear velocity are desired, longer clubs are chosen. Obviously then, for strength tasks a lever with a long force arm in relation to the weight arm should be used, and when range or speed of motion of relatively light weights are desired, the resistance arm should be lengthened.

TYPES OF LEVERS

Levers are of three types; they are classified according to the relationship of the axis (point about which each rotates) and the points of application of the force and of the resistance to be overcome.

When the axis (or fulcrum) is located between the points of application of the force and of the resistance, the lever is of the first class. The **first class**

---

*Efficiency can be accurately calculated by the length of the lever arm only when friction is not involved.

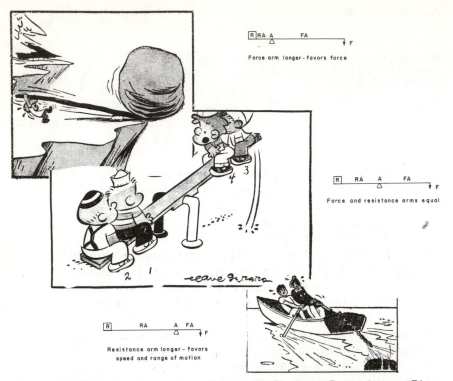

R RA A   FA

Force arm longer - favors force

R   RA   A   FA

Force and resistance arms equal

R   RA   A FA

Resistance arm longer - favors
speed and range of motion

Figure 5–5. First class levers. A = axis (fulcrum); F = force; R = resistance; FA = force arm (distance from force to axis); RA = resistance arm (distance from resistance to axis). Cartoon at top reprinted through the courtesy of the Chicago Tribune-New York News Syndicate, Inc. ''Archie'' cartoon: ©1972, Archie Comic Publications, Inc.

lever may have force and resistance arms that are equal (i.e., the force and resistance are applied equidistant from the axis), the force arm may be longer than the resistance arm (force applied farther than is the resistance from the axis) in which case the lever favors **force,** or the resistance arm may be longer (the force is applied closer to the axis than is the resistance) in which case the lever favors **speed** (Fig. 5–5). The first class lever may favor speed and range of motion **or** force, depending upon the relative lengths of the force and resistance arms. Some examples of this type of lever are the teeter-totter, crowbar, oar, scissors, extension of the ankle when the foot is not weight bearing and extension of the elbow when the upper arm is flexed and rotated so that the forearm is horizontal to the shoulders. Because the olecranon process of the ulna on which one of the extensors inserts crosses the axis of the elbow, the force is applied to the forearm on the side of the axis opposite to the resistance (applied at the center of gravity of the arm). When the upper arm, with flexed elbow, hangs down at the **side of the body,** lowering of the forearm is caused by gravity unless the elbow is forcibly extended; the flexors are active in controlling the lowering of the forearm. The action of the flexors involves third class leverage.

The **second class lever** always has a force arm which is longer than the resistance arm, since the resistance is applied between the axis and the point

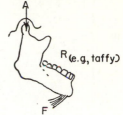

Figure 5–6. Second class levers
—favor force.

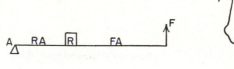

of application of the force. Therefore it favors force; a force mechanical advantage is always present at the expense of speed and range of motion. Examples of this class of lever are found in the wheelbarrow, the nutcracker and a door opened by use of the knob. It is difficult to find a specific example within the human body of a second class lever system; opening the jaw when chewing sticky taffy is one possibility (Fig. 5–6).

In the **third class lever** the force acts at a point between the axis and the resistance and, therefore, the resistance arm is always longer than the force arm (Fig. 5–7). This type of lever favors range of motion and speed at the expense of force; a mechanical (force) **dis**advantage is always present. Flexion of the lower arm and extension of the lower leg are examples of this class of lever. In fact, the human body is essentially a system of third class levers. The force required to hold a weight in the hand is much greater than the weight itself; this is exemplified in Figure 5–8. Since muscles of the human body insert near the joints (axes for rotation) and the segments that must be supported or moved are relatively long, the muscles function at a severe mechanical (force) disadvantage. As a result, muscles must produce large forces to cause motion of body segments. This emphasizes the importance of muscular strength and of understanding the most advantageous methods for using the available strength as well as the need to use tools to perform heavy tasks. On the other hand it points up the effectiveness of the body for tasks requiring speed of motion.

There are many levers which fall into different classes depending upon the way in which they are used. A door is a second class lever when opened or closed by applying force to the knob, an act which takes little force. The resistance (the center of gravity of the door) is between the point of application of force (the knob) and the axis (the hinges). However, when the door is closed by a mechanical device it becomes a third class lever since the force is applied between the hinges and the center of the door (Fig. 5–9). Experimentation with pushing open a door by pressure at the knob, the middle of the door, and close to the hinges shows clearly how much the force necessary to produce the same movement of the door increases as the force arm becomes shorter.

Figure 5–7. Third class levers favor speed and range of motion.

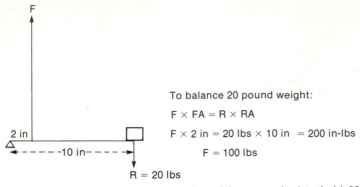

To balance 20 pound weight:

$F \times FA = R \times RA$

$F \times 2 \text{ in} = 20 \text{ lbs} \times 10 \text{ in} = 200 \text{ in-lbs}$

$F = 100 \text{ lbs}$

R = 20 lbs

Figure 5–8. Schematic representation of force required to hold 20 pound weight in hand.
 Note: All of force is effective in supporting the weight since force is applied at right angle (90°) to the lever.

The actions involved in shoveling dirt and paddling a canoe are similar in that both involve a combination of two leverage actions (first and third class). When the force is applied by the top hand, the shovel or paddle functions as a first class lever with the fulcrum at the lower hand and the resistance acting against the far end. However, some force is at the same time applied by the lower hand; this results in third class leverage, since the fulcrum for this lower hand force is the upper hand and the lower hand force is applied between the fulcrum and the resistance.

LEVERS OF THE HUMAN BODY

In the human body the lever is the bone, the fulcrum is the joint at which the movement takes place, and the force is supplied either by the contraction of the innervated muscles or by gravity acting on the various body masses. Muscular force is applied at the point where the muscles insert on the bone. Since muscles pull at an angle and the effective force arm is the **perpendicular** distance from the line of force application to the axis, the length of the force arm for a muscle **cannot** be determined by measuring the

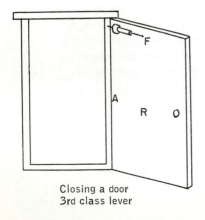

Closing a door
3rd class lever

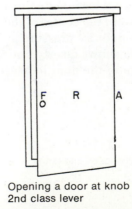

Opening a door at knob
2nd class lever

Figure 5–9. Leverage of a door.

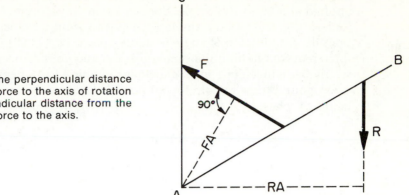

Figure 5–10. FA is the perpendicular distance from the line of the force to the axis of rotation and RA is the perpendicular distance from the line of the resisting force to the axis.

distance along the bone from the axis to the point of insertion. The perpendicular distance from the **line of muscle pull** to the joint must be determined (Fig. 5–10). This is complicated further by the fact that the angle of pull is not constant as it is when pulling an object such as a sled, because the pull of the muscle(s) results in rotation of the body segment and thus constantly changes the angle of pull (Fig. 5–11). If this angle is at right angles (90°) to the segment (lever), the total force exerted combines with the force arm to create the muscle moment. However, if the angle is less than or greater than 90 degrees a portion of the force is "wasted" as far as producing rotation is concerned although it may be useful in joint stabilization.

Using the example in Figure 5–8, this effect can be illustrated; the force required to hold, without movement, the 20 pound weight when the force

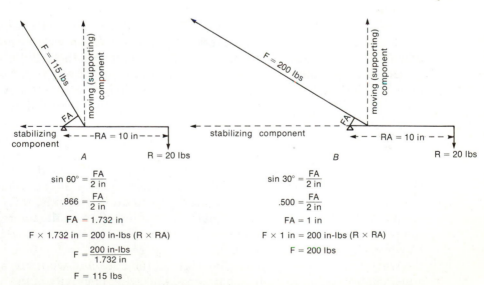

$$\sin 60° = \frac{FA}{2 \text{ in}}$$

$$.866 = \frac{FA}{2 \text{ in}}$$

$$FA = 1.732 \text{ in}$$

$$F \times 1.732 \text{ in} = 200 \text{ in-lbs } (R \times RA)$$

$$F = \frac{200 \text{ in-lbs}}{1.732 \text{ in}}$$

$$F = 115 \text{ lbs}$$

$$\sin 30° = \frac{FA}{2 \text{ in}}$$

$$.500 = \frac{FA}{2 \text{ in}}$$

$$FA = 1 \text{ in}$$

$$F \times 1 \text{ in} = 200 \text{ in-lbs } (R \times RA)$$

$$F = 200 \text{ lbs}$$

Figure 5–11. Comparison of length of FA and F required to hold a given weight as the angle of force with the lever changes. Note change in relationship of moving (supporting) component of the force to the stabilizing component.

acts at 90 degrees (shown in Fig. 5–8, p. 86) is 100 pounds. If the force were applied at a 60 degree angle, the force arm would be reduced from 2 to 1.7 inches (Fig. 5–11A) and the force required would increase from 100 to 115 pounds. A reduction of angle to 30 degrees (Fig. 5–11B) would increase the force required to hold the same object to 200 pounds because the force arm would be reduced to 1 inch; a further reduction to 15 degrees would require a 385 pound force to hold the 20 pounds because the force arm would then be 0.52 inches.

$$\sin 15° = \frac{FA}{2 \text{ in}}$$

$$.259 = \frac{FA}{2 \text{ in}}$$

$$FA = .52 \text{ in}$$

$$F \times .52 \text{ in} = 20 \text{ lbs} \times 10 \text{ in}$$

$$F = \frac{200 \text{ lbs}}{.52 \text{ in}} = 385 \text{ lbs}$$

As the component of force that is effective in holding the weight is decreased, the component which stabilizes (pulls back toward) the joint increases. This stabilizing, clearly seen in Figure 5–11, has been termed by Cates[2] as the "internal work" of the muscle as opposed to its "external work," that which accomplishes the movement of the bone. He states, "As the angle of pull departs from a right angle, internal work . . . begins to be performed and, to that extent the power to do external work . . . is lost."[3] This angle of force application (of pull) in the human body depends upon the angle of attachment of the muscle involved and **not** on the angle between the two bones or body segments; for example, when the elbow is flexed at 90°, the biceps does not pull at 90° but at an angle less than 90°.

When the angle of pull is greater than 90° a small dislocating force (pulling away from the joint) is present but this occurs only rarely and only when the muscle has shortened to such an extent that there is little force remaining. Also, other muscles assisting the movement help to stabilize the joint.[4] "When several muscles act together to produce a single movement, they act at different points and at different angles. In this way they help to steady and guide the segment throughout the movement."[5]

In Figure 5–11 the weight of the forearm (body segment supporting the weight) was disregarded in order to simplify the problem. In reality, the resistance includes the weight of the body part plus any added weight, and is applied at the center of gravity of the body part plus the added weight. For example, if the forearm is being raised the elbow is the axis, the force is supplied by the flexor muscles at their point of insertion on the forearm, and the resistance is the weight of the forearm applied at its center of gravity. However, if a book were held in the hand, the resistance would then become the weight of the forearm **plus** the weight of the book and would be applied considerably farther from the elbow since the center of gravity of the forearm **plus** the book would be closer to the hand with the book; how much nearer to the hand would depend on the weight of the book.

While the force of gravity always acts in a downward direction, the actual **effect of gravity on human motion** varies with the direction of the motion. Any motion in a downward direction is assisted by gravity, while motion directed upward is opposed by gravity. It is considerably easier to touch one's toes while standing (aided by gravity) than to do the same when supported by the feet in an upside-down position (opposed by gravity). Performing a sit-up on an inclined plane with the feet higher than the head is more difficult than with the head above the feet. A sit-up done on a horizontal surface is easier than one on an inclined plane with the feet higher. Also, the first part of the sit-up is most difficult and it becomes progressively easier as the trunk becomes more upright. Not only is this because the first motion requires the overcoming of inertia but also because the distance from the center of gravity of the trunk-head segment (segment being lifted) to the axis of rotation or the hip joint (RA) becomes progressively shorter; as a result the resisting moment becomes less.

In the same way that the force arm is reduced with a change in the angle of the force, the resistance arm is decreased as the angle of pull of the resistance changes. Thus the resistance moment is decreased and the force required to hold the weight decreases. Using the previous example, in which a 100 pound force exerted 2 inches from the axis was required to hold a 20 pound weight 10 inches from the axis, rotating the lever 30 degrees from the horizontal, it is seen that the resistance arm is reduced to 8.7 in and the resistance moment to 174 in-lbs (Fig. 5–12). **Assuming that the force to hold this weight is still exerted at 90 degrees to the lever,** it would take 87 pounds of force instead of 100.

$$F \times 2 \text{ in} = 174 \text{ in-lbs (see Fig. 5–12)}$$
$$F = 87 \text{ lbs}$$

If the lever were rotated 60 degrees, the RA would be 5 in and the resisting moment 100 in-lbs (Fig. 5–12). The force (at 90°) required to hold the weight at this angle would be:

$$F \times 2 \text{ in} = 100 \text{ in-lbs}$$
$$F = 50 \text{ lbs}$$

This example shows clearly that while it required 100 pounds of force to hold the 20 pound weight when the lever was horizontal, a force of only 50 pounds was required when the lever was rotated to an angle of 60 degrees (if force still applied at 90°).

Holding a heavy book with the forearm horizontal and then flexing the elbow to raise the book closer to the shoulder demonstrates this reduction in required force. It points up clearly the fact that gravity, although being of constant value, does not necessarily have a constant effect. The lifting of a weight through 180 degrees illustrates the overall variation in the effect due to gravity. Excluding the additional force needed to overcome inertia, the moment of the resistance is zero at the beginning, reaches maximum at 90 degrees and returns to zero at 180 degrees (the top). Figure 5–13 illustrates this phenomenon. In positions A and C the line of the resistance force is

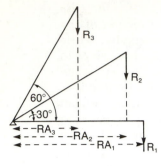

Given: R = 20 lbs; RA_1 = 10 in

$$\cos 30° = \frac{RA_2}{10 \text{ in}}$$

$$.866 = \frac{RA_2}{10 \text{ in}}$$

$$RA_2 = 8.7 \text{ in}$$

Moment for RA_2 = 20 lbs × 8.7 in = 174 in-lbs

$$\cos 60° = \frac{RA_3}{10 \text{ in}}$$

$$.500 = \frac{RA_3}{10 \text{ in}}$$

$$RA_3 = 5 \text{ in}$$

Moment for RA_3 = 20 lbs × 5 in = 100 in-lbs

Figure 5–12. Comparison of length of resistance arm (RA) and resistance moment as lever angle changes.

through the axis and thus the resistance arm is zero and no resistance moment is created. As the weight is moved up to point B the resistance arm and the component of the weight acting at right angles to the forearm both increase steadily until the weight reaches maximum at point B, beyond which both decrease.

With few exceptions, the levers of the body are of the third class. They have a shorter force than resistance arm since the muscles insert close to the joint and the weight is concentrated farther from the joint. The human body, therefore, favors speed and range of motion at the expense of force.

On the whole, the levers of the human body are long and therefore, the distal ends can move rapidly. Therefore "wide movements of the body can be made with speed, but at the expense of large muscle forces."[6] The human body performs easily those tasks which involve fast movement with light objects, throwing a ball, for example. When heavy work is demanded the human body must use some type of machine such as a crowbar to gain a force advantage. Sport instruments lengthen the levers of the body still further and greatly increase the speed of the object imparting force, but their

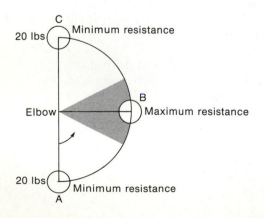

Figure 5–13. Area of greatest resistance (shaded) for a weight lifted through 180 degrees.

use also adds greatly to the muscular effort required. A relatively small difference in the weight of a piece of sports equipment (since this weight is so far from the axis) makes a considerable difference in the demand made on the muscles that are involved in moving it. Therefore, it is important that each individual use equipment suited to **his** or **her** strength.

Leverage of the human body rarely, if ever, involves a single body part (a simple lever). Instead movement results from a system of levers functioning together. Even when movement of a single lever does take place, many other parts of the body must be immobilized. When the force produced by the human system of levers is dependent upon speed at the extremity, the levers function in sequence, each coming into action at the time that the one before approaches its maximum speed. However, when many levers are brought into a heavier task, such as pushing, they need to function simultaneously (Chapter 6, Force).

REFERENCES

1. Beiser, Arthur: *The Mainstream of Physics.* Reading, Massachusetts, Addison-Wesley Publishing Company, Inc., 1962, p. 58.
2. Cates, H. A., and Basmajian, J. V.: *Primary Anatomy.* 3rd ed. Baltimore, Williams and Wilkins Company, 1955, p. 107.
3. Ibid.
4. Wells, Katharine F.: *Kinesiology.* 5th ed. Philadelphia, W. B. Saunders Company, 1971, p. 93.
5. Ibid., p. 99.
6. Williams, Marian, and Lissner, Herbert R.: *Biomechanics of Human Motion.* Philadelphia, W. B. Saunders Company, 1962, p. 61.

6 FORCE

Motion results only when sufficient force is applied to overcome the object's inertia. **Force** can be defined as **any influence that can change the state of motion of a body;** to start or stop motion, to accelerate or decelerate, to change direction. Essentially this force is either a push or a pull which may or may not result in motion.

Motion of the human body may be caused by internal or external forces. The principal source of internal force must be supplied by innervated muscles, whether the body is producing force to move itself or some object, or to react to an externally applied force. Since for the most part muscles exert force by shortening (**concentric contraction**), the force exerted by them results in a pull. However, if the muscular contraction is resisted by an equal and opposite force so that no motion results, it is said to be an **isometric contraction.**

Some movements are actually **caused** by gravity (or some other outside force) while the force applied by the muscle contraction **controls** the motion through offering resistance to the external force. This is termed **eccentric contraction** (lengthening contraction) as opposed to concentric contraction (shortening contraction). If the upper arm is held along the side with the elbow flexed so that the lower arm is at right angles to the upper arm and then the elbow is extended slowly, it is gravity that causes the extension. By placing the other hand on the biceps the eccentric contraction of these flexor muscles can be felt as they control the lowering of the arm. However, if the elbow is extended **very rapidly,** gravity assists the motion but the extensors must also contribute to the extension (concentric contraction). It is possible for full extension to result from relaxation of all the muscles that cross the elbow joint. In this case the weight of the forearm accelerates it downward; in other words the effect of gravity causes the motion **with no interference** from muscular contraction.

When an individual who is standing "flexes" his hips, knees and ankles slowly, gravity is the force which actually causes the motion; the individual **allows** gravity to flex the joints at the desired speed through a lengthening (eccentric) contraction of the extensor muscles of these joints. The primary external forces result from contact with other persons, moving sports equipment (balls, hockey pucks, etc.) or machines, and from friction between contact surfaces, air resistance, water resistance and the downward force of gravity.

GRAPHIC REPRESENTATION AND CALCULATION OF FORCES

All forces have certain common characteristics which make possible the evaluation of their effects. The first of these is **magnitude** or quantity of the force; this is measured in pounds (lbs) in the British system and newtons (N) in the metric system. A second important factor is the **direction** of the force since the effect of a force can be quite different if its direction of application is changed. Related concerns are the actual **point** on an object **where the force is applied** and the **time** of force application.

Since force has both magnitude and direction it is defined as a vector quantity. In contrast, a scalar quantity has magnitude only. A force (vector) can be represented by a line with an arrowhead at one end; the length of the line indicates its magnitude and the arrowhead its direction.

Summation of Forces.   A simplified example can be seen in a tug-of-war in which two groups of children pull on a rope in opposite directions. Within each group all youngsters are assumed to be pulling in the same direction. Thus, it is necessary to merely add the magnitudes of their forces together to obtain a total or resultant force. If the two groups were each composed of four children and their maximum possible forces known, the tug-of-war could be described graphically. Table 6–1 contains assumed force values.

These forces can be summed vectorially using the graphic method. Each of the forces (vectors) is drawn to a scale that represents the appropriate magnitude. For each group the second child's force is diagrammed at the end of the first child's vector; the third child's at the end of the second's, and so on (Fig. 6–1A). The total force for each group is indicated by the length of the line from the point where the first vector begins to the end of the fourth vector (Fig. 6–1B). Since the forces within each group are applied in the same direction, they can be added together to find the total force for each group. The two total forces which are in opposite directions can be added algebraically (that is, taking into account the sign of the force according to direction). If the direction to the left is defined as negative (Group A) and that to the right as positive (Group B), the resultant (R) of the two forces is −10 pounds (44.5 N) (Fig. 6–1C). This means that all of the forces applied by all of the children reduce to a single 10 pound (44.5 N) force in favor of Group A (to the left on the diagram).

This example describes a greatly simplified situation in which all forces are either directed along the same path (parallel) or are in direct opposition. It is the only case in which forces can be added and subtracted algebraically.

TABLE 6–1.   FORCES EXERTED BY CHILDREN IN TUG-OF-WAR

CHILD	GROUP A Force	GROUP B Force
1	20 lbs (89.00 N)	20 lbs (89.00 N)
2	40 lbs (178.00 N)	25 lbs (111.25 N)
3	30 lbs (133.50 N)	30 lbs (133.50 N)
4	20 lbs (89.00 N)	25 lbs (111.25 N)

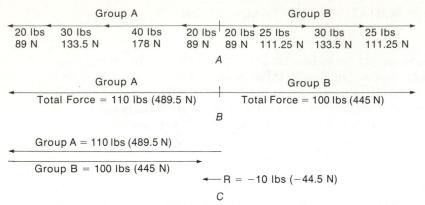

Group A				Group B			
20 lbs	30 lbs	40 lbs	20 lbs	20 lbs	25 lbs	30 lbs	25 lbs
89 N	133.5 N	178 N	89 N	89 N	111.25 N	133.5 N	111.25 N

A

Group A	Group B
Total Force = 110 lbs (489.5 N)	Total Force = 100 lbs (445 N)

B

Group A = 110 lbs (489.5 N)

Group B = 100 lbs (445 N)

R = −10 lbs (−44.5 N)

C

Figure 6–1. Forces exerted by two groups of children in tug-of-war and resultant (R) (sum of these forces).

A more common occurrence involves forces which intersect at some angle as shown in Figure 6–2.

When an object is acted upon by two forces, the movement is in the direction of the **resultant** of the two forces. Also, it is obvious that the resultant (vector sum) of a vertically upward force of 20 newtons and a horizontal force of 40 newtons is not 60 newtons (20 N + 40 N) nor is it 20 newtons (40 N − 20 N). How can these forces be added? One solution is to

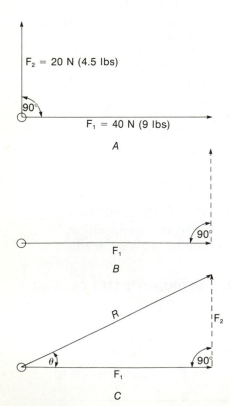

F_2 = 20 N (4.5 lbs)

90°

F_1 = 40 N (9 lbs)

A

90°

F_1

B

R

F_2

θ

90°

F_1

C

Figure 6–2. Summation of forces acting at right angles to each other.
    A, Two forces plotted to scale at right angles.
    B, F_2 drawn from head of F_1 at same angle to F_1.
    C, Resultant drawn from origin of F_1 to head of F_2.

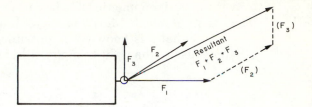

Figure 6–3. Addition of three forces. Note (F₂) drawn from end of force 1 and (F₃) drawn from end of (F₂); sum represented by line from point of application of the three forces to the end of (F₃). Note: (F₂) equal in both magnitude and direction to force 2 and (F₃) equal to force 3.

use the graphic method, which first requires that both vectors be drawn to scale (Fig. 6–2A; 1 cm = 8 N). Then the vectors are repositioned with the tail of one (in this case F_2) intersecting with the head of the other (F_1) making certain that the angle between the two vectors (90°) is maintained (Fig. 6–2B). A line is drawn from the origin (O) (tail of F_1) to the head of the last vector (in this case, F_2), and an arrowhead is placed at the **end** of this line (not at its origin). This line represents the vectorial sum of forces F_1 and F_2 and is called the **resultant** (R) (Fig. 6–2C). To complete the problem, the length of this line is measured to determine the magnitude of the resultant, and the angle between R and F_1 must be measured with a protractor to describe its direction of application. The length of the resultant (R) is found to be approximately 5.5 centimeters (equivalent to 44 newtons) and the angle is approximately 26 degrees. The resultant force is stated to be approximately 44 N at 26°.

The graphic method can be used to add any number of forces provided each succeeding force vector is plotted at the same angle as its original and is drawn to scale. The **tail of the vector being plotted must be located at the head of the preceding vector and must be parallel to the force it represents.** When all vectors are plotted in this manner, the resultant is then drawn from the origin (tail of all **original forces**) to the head of the last vector (Fig. 6–3).

This method is unlikely to produce a precise answer since it depends upon how accurately the vectors can be drawn and measured. This limitation can be overcome by using trigonometry to determine the resultant of all forces acting on a given object. Again the acting forces are drawn with the second force drawn from the head of the first parallel to its original direction so that it will be at the same angle. The resultant is then drawn from the tail of the first force to the head of the second.

To determine the resultant of the two forces given in the previous problem using trigonometry, the same triangle is drawn (Fig. 6–2C) and the angle between the resultant and F_1 is labelled θ. For this angle the line representing F_2 is the side opposite and that representing F_1 is the adjacent side. The formula for the tangent of an angle can be used to determine the value of θ.

$$\tan \theta = \frac{\text{side opposite}}{\text{side adjacent}} \qquad (6.1)$$

$$\tan \theta = \frac{20 \text{ N}}{40 \text{ N}}$$

$$\tan \theta = .5000$$

By use of a trigonometric table (see p. 415) an angle of 26°34′ is found to have a tangent of .50004; thus θ is approximately 27°.

Now that θ is known it is possible to determine the resultant (R), the hypotenuse of the right triangle; either sine or cosine could be used.

$$\sin \theta = \frac{\text{side opposite}}{\text{hypotenuse}} \quad (6.2) \qquad \cos \theta = \frac{\text{side adjacent}}{\text{hypotenuse}} \quad (6.3)$$

$$.44724 = \frac{20 \text{ N}}{R} \qquad\qquad\qquad .89441 = \frac{40 \text{ N}}{R}$$

$$R = \frac{20 \text{ N}}{.44724} \qquad\qquad\qquad R = \frac{40 \text{ N}}{.89441}$$

$$R = 44.7 \text{ N} \qquad\qquad\qquad R = 44.7 \text{ N}$$

It is possible to calculate R by the geometric formula: the square of the hypotenuse is equal to the sum of the squares of the other two sides of a right triangle.

$$R^2 = F_1^2 + F_2^2 \qquad\qquad\qquad (6.4)$$

$$R^2 = 20 \text{ N}^2 + 40 \text{ N}^2 = 400 + 1600 = 2000 \text{ N}$$

$$R^2 = 2000 \text{ N}$$

$$R = 44.7 \text{ N}$$

Thus the resultant of forces F_1 and F_2 is a force of 44.7 newtons acting at an angle of 26°34′, a more precise answer that differs very little from the one found by the graphic method. Trigonometry is applicable **only** when the problem contains a right angle. Summing forces that are not acting at right angles becomes more complicated unless tthe graphic method is used.

An example of two forces is seen when a spinning ball bounces on the floor; the ball reacts according to the **resultant** of the rebound force which would be normal for its angle of approach and the spin force (see Chapter

Figure 6–4. Two components of a diagonal force. Note the greater horizontal force in relation to vertical force when a longer rope is used.

8). When a racket strikes a spinning ball, three forces are involved: the effective force from the racket, the rebound force caused by the ball's motion and the spin force.

Determination of Components of a Single Force Acting at an Angle. The previous discussion has dealt with the problem of adding two or more forces together to obtain a single resultant. It is also important in many situations to determine the two components, normally one vertical and the other horizontal, of a single force. For example, in pulling a heavy load, the force may be applied at various angles to the direction of motion of the load and thus will have a horizontal component in the direction of motion and a vertically upward component (Fig. 6–4).

If a force of 45 newtons (approximately 10 lbs) is applied at an angle of 40° to the horizontal, how much force is effective for forward motion and how much is effective upward? To determine the horizontal and vertical components trigonometry can again be used since the vectors are at right angles to each other. The first step is to sketch a diagram of the original force (Fig. 6–5A). Then, by dropping a vertical line from the head of the force (F) to the horizontal, the head end of the horizontal component (F_h) can be determined; a horizontal line drawn from the head of the force (F) to a point vertically above the point of origin of the force locates the head of the vertical force (F_v) (Fig. 6–5B). To solve for F_h and F_v it is necessary to reposition F_v at the head of F_h, that is, to draw a line representing F_v from the head of F_h vertically upward to the head of the force (F). (See Figure 6–5C.) Since the magnitude of the hypotenuse (F) is known to be 45 newtons, the vertical component (F_v) can be calculated by using the sine of the 40° angle, while the cosine can be used to find the horizontal component (F_h).

$$\sin \theta = \frac{F_v}{F} \qquad\qquad \cos \theta = \frac{F_h}{F}$$

$$\sin 40° = \frac{F_v}{45 \text{ N}} \qquad\qquad \cos 40° = \frac{F_h}{45 \text{ N}}$$

$$.643 = \frac{F_v}{45 \text{ N}} \qquad\qquad .766 = \frac{F_h}{45 \text{ N}}$$

$$F_v = 28.9 \text{ N (6.5 lbs)} \qquad\qquad F_h = 34.5 \text{ N (7.8 lbs)}$$

Thus the original force of 45 newtons has an upward effect of approximately 29 newtons and a horizontal effect of approximately 35 newtons. If a force of the same magnitude were applied at an angle nearer the horizontal (for example, 30°) the value of the horizontal force would increase, while that of the vertical force would decrease because they would have the same vector sum (the original force). If the angle were increased (for example, 60°), the vertical force would increase while the horizontal component would decrease for the same reason.

Figure 6–4 illustrates a practical application of this concept. A longer rope results in a given force being more effective in the forward direction. Because the hand is at the same height regardless of the rope length the

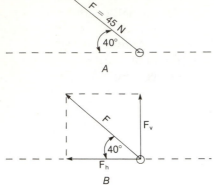

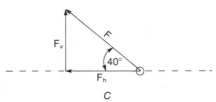

Figure 6–5. Dividing diagonal force (F) into its vertical (F$_v$) and horizontal (F$_h$) components.

longer rope results in a reduced angle with the horizontal and, as a result, the horizontal component is greater and the vertical component is less. A shorter rope, because of its higher angle of application, shorter forward component and greater upward component of force, could be more effective when friction is a great problem, since the upward component would tend to lift and thus reduce friction. In general, the more nearly the force is applied in the direction of the desired motion the more effective the force since less force is wasted. However, in many situations the second component of a diagonal force may be useful either in counteracting some other force acting on the object or in accomplishing the specific purpose. Whether or not an upward force is desirable in a pulling task depends upon the amount of friction to be overcome. The greater the friction the more upward component of force is desirable.

If a diagonally downward force is applied to an object resting on the floor, the force exerted is divided into a vertical downward component and a horizontal forward component. The floor, exerting upward force against the object, prevents its moving in the exact direction of the applied force and it moves in the only direction in which it is free to move, forward. The downward component is effective only in increasing friction (p. 76) and thus hinders the forward movement. When force is applied in a diagonally upward-forward direction, as when pulling an object with a rope, the force exerted again has two components, one in the direction of desired movement (forward) and the other upward (against gravity and therefore reducing friction) (Fig. 6–4). A longer rope results in a given force being more effective forward while a shorter rope results in more upward force and so could be more effective if friction is a great problem.

An understanding of the horizontal and vertical components of a diagonal force and the relationship of these to various purposes is important

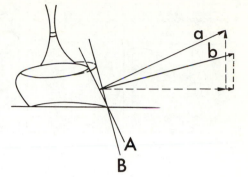

Figure 6–6. Horizontal and vertical components of diagonal forces applied to ball by moving clubheads with different angles.

whether one is determining the length of a rope for pulling; the angle of the body for walking, running, jumping, the angle of any throw or strike. Just as a longer rope is used to pull an object on wheels when friction is inconsequential (greater horizontal component of force) and a shorter rope is used to increase the upward component when friction is a great problem, a golf club with a more vertical face is chosen to gain greater horizontal force when playing into the wind but, when the wind is from the rear, a more open-faced club is used to give a greater upward component. As a result, the ball will stay in the air longer (more force combating gravity) and give the wind time to carry it forward. Compare Figures 6–4 and 6–6. These are two very different activities but the identical mechanical principle is involved, that of the horizontal and vertical components of a diagonal force.

CONSIDERATIONS IN FORCE APPLICATION

In applying force, whether to move the body or some object, the objective of the movement must be considered. It is necessary to consider whether the desired outcome calls for a maximum production of force available in the body or a controlled application of force. An all-out effort, and therefore maximum force, is required if the purpose is to throw as far or as fast as possible, or to jump as far or as high as possible. On the other hand, many a putt has been missed in golf because too much force was used, and many a catch has been fumbled because the ball came to the receiver from a short distance too forcefully. In applying force one must consider the amount of force to be applied (its magnitude), the direction of its application, the point of application, and the distance over which it is applied.

Magnitude of Force. The first point concerning magnitude has already been stated, that is, that the force must be sufficient to overcome the inertia of the object plus any other resisting forces, if movement is to result. The greater an object's mass, and any resistive forces such as friction and the surrounding medium of air or water, the greater its inertia and the more force necessary to move it. Because of every object's tendency to maintain its state of motion (inertia) it takes more force to start an object moving than to keep it moving. When additional forces such as friction are added to inertia, starting motion may require a magnitude of force so great that it is difficult

Figure 6–7. Examples of force required (to overcome inertia and resisting forces) which is greater than can be controlled once object starts to move. "Archie" cartoons: ©1972, Archie Comic Publications, Inc. "Gasoline Alley" cartoons reprinted through the courtesy of the Chicago Tribune-New York News Syndicate, Inc.

or impossible to control the object's motion once its initial inertia plus other force(s) are overcome and the object is underway. This is the force problem faced by Skeezix and Mr. Lodge (Fig. 6–7); more force was required by the suction of the cup and the friction of the stuck drawer than could be effectively controlled once the objects started to move.

The amount of force produced depends upon the magnitude of the propelling force and its duration. The magnitude of the force in turn depends on the mass and speed of the object imparting the force. The greater the mass of the object, and the faster that it is moving, the greater the force imparted, all other things being equal. A slowly moving object can have great momentum if it is very heavy (train, truck, etc.). A small light object can have great momentum because of the speed with which it is moving (bullet, arrow, golf ball, etc.). As indicated earlier, velocity is the product of average acceleration and the time over which the acceleration takes place. Thus, the greater the distance, and thus the time over which an object is accelerated, the greater the velocity; the longer the force is applied to the object, the greater the force imparted, all other things being equal.

The greatest total force is attainable when all of the forces that can contribute to the desired outcome are employed at their maximum and in sequence. All body segments that can contribute to the desired movement should be used if maximum force is the objective. The fewer **noncontributing** muscles that are contracted, the less energy is wasted. Muscles **can** contribute to a movement while not being **directly** involved in its production by carrying out the extremely important task of a restraining or holding action which involves considerable tension within the muscle.[1] A movement is considered to be efficient when opposing muscle groups work in harmony. If both groups contract with the same amount of force at the same time no movement results, only tension and fixation. If they do not work in harmony, jerky or uncontrolled movement results. Frequently, difficulty in learning a skill arises because of a generalized contraction caused by an emotional disturbance such as fear of the water, fear of any unknown, or feelings of frustration. The tension of the beginning swimmer is well known. In such cases contraction of muscles which **in no way contribute** to the desired movement wastes energy and may interfere with the production of the movement.

Difficulty in producing effective movement may also result from an individual's failure to stabilize certain body segments so that they can become a base for the segment which must move. A crawl stroke is not effective unless the trunk and shoulder girdle are fixed as a base upon which the arms can act. Nor can the breast stroke be effective if the pelvis is not fixed so that it is a solid base for leg action. In throwing a baseball, the feet against the floor must provide a base for leg action, the pelvis, for trunk action and the trunk, for shoulder and arm action.

The body may produce a great deal of force but unless there is a firm base for the action, force is not effective. Thus, **the effectiveness of a force produced by the body is dependent upon the fixation of the origins of the muscles involved, by other muscles, to give a firm base on which to act, and upon the interaction between the body and the supporting surface.** For example, in pushing, the scapulae must be held against the ribs. An individual whose rhomboid muscles have been affected by poliomyelitis cannot push effectively because his applied force moves the scapulae out away from the ribs. Also, there must be sufficient friction between the feet and the ground so that the feet do not slide backward, or the force will push the body backward rather than the object forward.

Strong tasks require the body to resist considerable equal and opposite force. To resist such force there must be effective fixation through many body segments. If one were to attempt to push an automobile, it would be useless to approach the car on the run and attempt to push it when contact was made. Rather the whole body is set in the position for maximum forward pushing force (Chapter 16) and then the force is applied. Less energy is required to carry out a heavy task when the muscles that are to perform the given work get set before contacting the load.[2] For an individual with weak wrists, even contacting the fast moving tennis ball at the end of the long lever becomes a heavy task and therefore, it is wise for this individual to set the wrist muscles before starting the swing.

The body, being a system of third class levers (Chapter 5), can be an effective instrument for the production of speed of relatively light objects. Obviously, the faster the muscular contraction the faster the end of the lever will move and therefore, speed of muscular contraction is an important factor in the velocity imparted in all relatively light tasks (for example, throwing, striking).

On the other hand, the slower the muscular contraction, the less the energy required.[3] For relatively light speed tasks such as throwing a ball, fast muscular contraction is needed since force is dependent on speed; while for strong tasks a slow, steady maximum contraction is needed. When the body wishes to produce the considerable amount of force required to move a very heavy object, it is wise to make use of tools that give a force advantage. (See Chapter 5.)

When several muscle groups are cooperating in the production of force for a given purpose, the total effective force is the sum of the forces produced by all groups if all are applied in the same direction and in the proper sequence. When forces are added successively, each should be applied when the one before has reached its peak (**is moving with its greatest velocity and least acceleration**).[4]

Plagenhoef reported studies indicating that deceleration of the first segment as the next begins its motion aids in the increase of velocity of the second segment. This same sequence continues from segment to segment. "The timed sequence of one segment helping the next will produce the maximum velocity of the last segment with the minimum muscle force at each joint."[5] This deceleration of the preceding segment acts to "stabilize" the axis for the motion of the second segment. In sequential action the first segment rotates around its axis, the second rotates around the moving end of the first segment, and the third around the moving end of the second.[6] Thus, to gain maximum rotation of the second around **its** axis (the end of the first), the first segment must decelerate. If maximum force is to be produced in relatively light tasks in which the force is largely dependent upon speed (for example, throwing and striking skills), the contractions should be sequential, starting at a fixed point and moving through the body, reaching the extremity last. Each part should be brought into the movement when the part below has reached its maximum speed and begins deceleration. However, in heavy tasks such as pushing, the forces are applied simultaneously. The total effective force is limited by the weakest force of the group.

Obviously, more force is available from strong than from weak muscles. When a task demanding a good deal of force is involved, the stronger the muscles called into play, the more efficient the action and the less the muscular strain. To avoid strain the strongest muscles that are available to the particular task to be performed should be used. All muscles are not equal in potential maximum force and, therefore, are not equally adapted to the task of supplying force. The magnitude of muscular force is directly proportional to the number and size of the muscle fibers contracting.[7] This is referred to as the cross section of the muscle. Strength of a muscle group can be increased by use, but to increase strength a muscle must be overloaded; either the intensity of contraction or its duration (or both) must be greater than is normal for the muscle. As was pointed out in Chapter 2, many of the difficulties which are encountered in the performance of sport skills are due to lack of strength. The individual may understand the mechanics of the skill but if he lacks the strength to carry them out no amount of discussion of his incorrect movement will be of help to him. Exercises to condition the weak muscles are essential to increase their capacity to produce force.

Within limits, the more a muscle is lengthened the greater its potential force. As it shortens, its force diminishes. Zoethout and Tuttle[8] state that in an active muscle the amount of energy liberated during contraction increases as the initial length of the muscle increases.

When the internal resistance of a muscle is decreased before the maximum task is undertaken, less energy is required to carry out the task, indicating the importance of the use of some method for warming up the muscles to be involved. Internal resistance can be reduced by submaximal contractions and by warming the muscles with hot water, methods which gradually increase circulation through the muscle. There has been some argument in the literature concerning the importance of warm-ups. While it may be possible to produce maximum force without previous warm-up, the muscular soreness which may result is familiar to all. Until more evidence to the contrary is available, it seems reasonable that increasing circulation gradually before making an all-out muscular effort is advisable.

Direction of Application of Force. Unless hindered by some other force such as gravity, off-center friction, or an obstacle in the pathway, an object will move in the direction of the force applied to it. In walking, running or jumping the direction of the force applied by the push-off of the foot is determined by the relationship of the center of gravity to the foot at the moment of take-off. Since in order to move itself, the body is dependent upon the reaction force from an outside medium (ground, water, another object), the force produced by the body must be applied in the direction opposite to that of the desired movement.

Point of Application of Force. If linear motion is desired, the more nearly through the center of gravity the force is applied the less the force required to move a given object. When force is applied through the center of gravity **and** the object is free to move, linear motion results. If, however, the object is not free to move, if there is a great deal of friction or an obstacle in its path, angular motion results. If one point is fixed, it rotates around the fixed point no matter where the force is applied. The farther from the center of gravity the force is applied the more the object tends to rotate (turn or tip). When forward force is applied toward one end of an object the total object will move forward **but at the same time** it will rotate. In other words, unless there is considerable friction or some other obstacle to motion, both ends will move but the end nearest the point of force application will move forward faster. An object tends to rotate if force is applied above or below or on either side of the center of gravity instead of through the center of gravity. The farther from the center of gravity the force is applied, the less force necessary to rotate the object.

Distance Over Which Force Is Applied. Inasmuch as force depends upon mass and acceleration

$$F = m \times a \text{ (Newton's Second Law, p. 66)}$$

and acceleration is the velocity divided by time

$$V = at \text{ (pp. 63–64)} \qquad \text{or} \qquad a = \frac{V}{t}$$

it follows that the velocity of an object of a given mass (m) depends upon both the amount of force and the length of time that it is applied.

$$F = m \times \frac{V}{t} \qquad \text{or} \qquad F \times t = m \times V$$

Since the amount of force depends upon its duration as well as its magnitude, more force can be applied to an object when it is applied over a longer distance. If a ball is kept in contact with the racket for a short time, more force is applied than if the ball hits and immediately leaves the racket. The greater the distance over which the force is applied, the greater the amount of work done. Work is determined by multiplying the force by the distance over which it is applied

$$W = F \times D \qquad\qquad \begin{aligned} W &= \text{work} \\ F &= \text{force} \\ D &= \text{distance} \end{aligned} \qquad (6.5)$$

This formula applies only when the force is constant over the total distance. If a sled is dragged 10 feet (3.048 m) by a constant application of a 15 pound (66.75 N) force, 150 ft-lbs (203 joules) of work is done. If the sled were given an initial push and then allowed to slide (no further force applied) 10 feet, no work is done while it slides, only while the original push is being given.

If an individual weighing 120 pounds (54.4 kg) walks up a flight of stairs that has a **vertical height** of 30 feet (9.1 m) the distance over which the force is applied is the height of the stairs; thus the vertical work is the weight lifted multiplied by the stair height, or 3600 ft-lbs (4881 joules).

$$\begin{aligned} \text{vertical work} &= \text{ht} \times \text{wt} \\ &= 120 \text{ lb} \times 30 \text{ ft} \\ &= 3600 \text{ ft-lbs} \end{aligned} \qquad (6.6)$$

If the individual were to **run** up the same stairs, the vertical work would remain the same; the difference in the two methods of climbing the stairs lies in the time taken to complete the work, not the amount of work done.

The **time rate of doing work** is called **power**. If walking up the stairs took 4.5 seconds and running, 2 seconds:

$$\text{Power} = \frac{F \times D}{t} = \begin{array}{cc} \text{walk} & \text{run} \\ \dfrac{3600}{4.5} & \dfrac{3600}{2} \end{array} \qquad (6.7)$$

$$= 800 \text{ ft-lbs/sec} \qquad 1800 \text{ ft-lbs/sec}$$

Running up the stairs requires more power than walking up.

In applying force the type of task must be considered. If the purpose is to apply as much force as possible in a relatively light task such as hitting a tennis ball, the force would be applied as long as possible. If, however, the purpose is to lift a heavy load with as little strain as possible one would lower the body only as far as necessary to contact the load, thus keeping to a minimum the distance the body weight must be lifted.

ENERGY

The human body may apply force directly to objects through a continual application of force (Chapters 16 and 17), contact over a period of time during which motion is developed followed by release (Chapter 18) or by instantaneous contact (Chapter 19). In addition the body frequently applies force to objects indirectly. Both direct and indirect application require the expenditure of **energy.** Energy, a scalar quantity, may be thought of as **the capacity to do work;** it may be mechanical, chemical, electrical, thermal, light or nuclear. When analyzing the mechanics of human motion, mechanical energy assumes the important role.

Mechanical energy can be divided into two types: potential and kinetic. A body (or object) possesses **potential energy** by virtue of **its position,** which may be related to its absolute location in space or its change in shape (deformation). In lifting, work done on an object is stored as potential energy; the object has gained a certain amount of stored energy which potentially may be converted into energy of **motion (kinetic energy).** An object that is any distance above the ground has potential energy because gravity is constantly acting upon it; the higher the object above the ground, the greater the amount of energy that is stored.

$$P.E. = wt \times ht$$

P.E. = potential energy
wt = weight of object (mass × g)   (6.8)
ht = height of object above ground

As a jumper goes over a high jump or pole vault bar, his potential energy may be determined by multiplying his weight by the distance of his center of gravity above the pit. A spring board diver has potential energy just by standing on the end of the diving board, but at the maximum height of his flight during the dive, his potential energy is greater because the height above the water is greater.

Potential energy is also stored in an object when that object is deformed (strain energy). The molecules in an object resist a change in the shape of the object; the potential energy that is stored may be used to restore the object to its original shape. The use of potential energy from deformation is seen in the catapult, a sapling tree tied to a stake and an archer's bow (Fig. 6–8). Potential energy can be seen even in a buoyant barrel held down by an anchor line (Fig. 6–8); the volume of the barrel has displaced the water and buoyant force pushes against the barrel.

The energy of deformation is important in many sport activities. A bow is bent (deformed) and the string is released to impart energy to the arrow. The strings of a tennis racket "deform" thus storing energy which is released against the ball. A gymnast deforms the bed of a trampoline, storing potential energy in the bed. When a diver hurtles onto a board he imparts energy to the board by deforming it; this energy of deformation is given back to the diver as the board regains its original shape. Balls struck by rackets, bats and clubs are given potential energy due to their flattening. The use of the fiberglass pole, which bends to a greater degree and thus stores more energy than previous poles, allowed pole vaulters to raise the vaulting record by

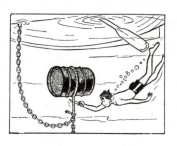

Figure 6–8. Examples of potential energy. "Archie" cartoons: ©1972, Archie Comic Publications, Inc.

one foot in just one year; prior to the advent of the fiberglass pole the record had stood for sixteen years.

Much of the importance of potential energy is related to its conversion to **kinetic energy,** energy inherent in an object (or body) by virtue of its **motion.**

$$K.E. = \frac{1}{2}\,mV^2$$

$$\begin{aligned} K.E. &= \text{kinetic energy} \\ m &= \text{mass of object} \\ V &= \text{velocity of object} \end{aligned} \qquad (6.9)$$

The interplay between potential and kinetic energies reveals their importance in efficient human motion. A vivid example is seen in the act of bouncing on a trampoline. As the gymnast lands on the bed, it begins to deform (stretch downward) and develop stored energy. The cause of the stretching of the bed is the gymnast's kinetic energy that starts to be converted to potential energy as he contacts the surface. Some of his kinetic energy is converted to sound and heat, but a major portion is converted to stored energy in the trampoline bed. As the deformation (potential energy) of the bed increases, the descent of the gymnast is slowed; as his downward velocity decreases his kinetic energy decreases very rapidly ($\frac{1}{2}mV^2$); thus the kinetic energy of the gymnast's motion is converted into stored energy of the trampoline bed. When potential energy is maximum (when the bed will stretch no more) the gymnast's motion has been stopped by the bed and his **kinetic energy is zero.** The stored energy of the bed, however, instantly begins to move the gymnast upward. As the bed returns to a normal position, the gymnast gains velocity and with it, kinetic energy.

From the time that the gymnast leaves the surface of the trampoline until he reaches the maximum height of his flight, he loses kinetic energy (energy of motion) and gains potential energy (energy of position). At the very top of his flight, all of the kinetic energy which he had as he left the trampoline bed has been converted to potential energy; his velocity is **zero** at the point where his **height,** or position, above the trampoline is **maximum.** As he begins his descent, he loses potential energy (height) and gains kinetic energy (increased downward velocity) because of the acceleration of gravity. During the entire flight, the total mechanical energy (P.E. + K.E.) is conserved; the potential and kinetic energies are **inversely** related in this case. When he hits the surface of the trampoline to begin the next bounce, kinetic energy is maximum and potential energy, zero. The same conversion between kinetic and potential energy occurs on every bounce.

A quantitative verification of this energy relationship can be seen by assigning values to the variables in a jump for height example.

If an individual weighing 135 pounds were to jump upward with a velocity of 8.91 feet per second, his kinetic energy would be 166 ft-lbs.

$$K.E. = \frac{1}{2} mV^2 \qquad m = \text{mass and } V = \text{velocity}$$

$$= \frac{1}{2} \frac{135 \text{ lb}}{32.2 \text{ ft/sec}^2} \times (8.91 \text{ ft/sec})^2$$

$$= 2.096 \times 79.388 = 166.4 \text{ ft-lbs}$$

This energy would enable him to rise against gravity's pull for 0.277 seconds.

$$a = \frac{V_f - V_i}{t} \qquad \begin{array}{l} a = \text{acceleration of gravity (since rising, } -) \\ V_f = \text{final velocity (high point } = 0) \\ V_i = \text{initial velocity} \end{array}$$

$$-32.2 \text{ ft/sec}^2 = \frac{0 - 8.91 \text{ ft/sec}}{t}$$

$$t \times -32.2 \text{ ft/sec}^2 = -8.91 \text{ ft/sec}$$

$$t = \frac{-8.91 \text{ ft/sec}}{-32.2 \text{ ft/sec}^2} = .277 \text{ sec}$$

At the high point of the jump he would be at zero velocity and thus his kinetic energy would be zero but his potential energy would then be 166 ft-lbs. He would have reached a high point of 15 inches.

$$D_v = \tfrac{1}{2} \, gt^2$$

$$= 16 \text{ ft/sec}^2 \times .277 \text{ sec}^2$$

$$= 1.23 \text{ ft.} = 14.8 \text{ in}$$

To crosscheck that the high point was actually approximately 15 inches, the potential energy at high point can be determined:

$$P.E. = wt \times ht$$

$$P.E. = 135 \text{ lbs} \times 1.23 \text{ ft}$$

$$P.E. = 166.1 \text{ ft-lbs}$$

As the jumper drops this 15 inches, he gains the kinetic energy that he lost while he rose through the air so that when he again makes contact with the surface his kinetic energy is 166 ft-lbs. If he lands on a trampoline, this energy is expended to deform the bed but what if he lands on ground? The ground is resistive; its contour is not easily altered and thus it has little ability to store energy. Thus when landing on a resistive surface, the jumper himself must dissipate the energy involved safely. Some of the energy is given up as heat and sound but most is returned to (used to do work on) the jumper; if he remains rigid, all will be returned at once and this can cause injury to the jumper. How can this energy be dissipated safely?

FORCE ABSORPTION

In a great many movement tasks the individual is concerned not only with the efficient production and application of force, but also with the stopping of motion or receiving of force. The problem of force absorption involves the maintenance of equilibrium while receiving the kinetic energy of a moving object without injury or rebound resulting. Injury and rebound can only be avoided by the reduction of the shock of impact. The force of impact depends upon the weight of the moving object (objects) and the speed with which it (they) is (are) moving.

The human body must be able to absorb effectively the force created by its own momentum as well as the force of many other moving objects. This force may be in a horizontal direction as when an individual is running, skating, skiing, or performing a series of forward rolls, and wants to stop; or when he wants to stop an object that is rolling or sliding. It may be in a vertical direction as when an individual drops from a jump or a pole vault, falls from a wall and lands on the ground; or when he attempts to catch some object dropping straight down through the air. In this case, because of the acceleration of gravity, the momentum of the individual or object, and therefore the force to be received, increases rapidly with the distance that he, or the object, falls.

The force that must be received is frequently a combination, i.e., the object or individual is moving through space at an angle and two forces are, in effect, operating (a horizontal and a vertical component). This is the situation when catching a thrown or batted ball, or when landing from a long jump, a dive over obstacles, a fall or jump from a moving object. If an individual steps from a moving bus the friction between the ground and feet stops the motion of the feet, but the forward motion acquired from the motion of the bus throws the body forward and he falls forward and downward. If a cantering horse suddenly shies and turns to the left, the forward momentum of the rider, unless he has a firm seat, throws him straight ahead out of the saddle. If the velocity of skis is suddenly decreased due to a spot of deep soft snow, the skier must have excellent control of his weight to avoid falling forward.

In all these cases as soon as the individual's center of gravity falls beyond the edge of his base, gravity and momentum due to inertia take over and both vertical and horizontal components of forces are involved. Whenever gravity is involved, that is in any movement which is not purely horizontal, kinetic energy — energy due to motion — increases rapidly as the height from which the individual or object falls increases. This is due to the acceleration of gravity.

Regardless of whether the problem involves absorption of force created by the motion of the human body itself or by the motion of some object, of whether the force is horizontal, vertical or a combination of the two, the same principles must be applied if injury or rebound is to be avoided.

The more sudden the loss of kinetic energy, the more likely is injury or rebound to occur. Conversely, the more gradual the reduction of this force, the less likely is injury or rebound to occur. This means that force must be absorbed, or spent, gradually, **by increasing the distance and the time over which the force is absorbed.** One method for accomplishing this is to provide a partially nonresistive surface for the impact. If when he lands on the floor, the kinetic energy of the jumper discussed earlier can be returned to him over a time and distance, it can be "absorbed" through the jumper's body doing work by "giving" as he lands, that is, moving through a distance (W = F × D).

The same principle applies to catching any object. When a ball is thrown it approaches the individual with a certain kinetic energy dependent on its mass and velocity. If a ball capable of performing 100 ft-lbs of work (K.E. = 100 ft-lbs) is contacted well in front of the body and the catcher "gives with the ball" moving the hands through 2.5 feet, he must resist the ball with 40 pounds of force in order to stop it and he will feel a reaction force of 40 pounds.

$$W = F \times D$$

$$100 \text{ ft-lbs} = F \times 2.5 \text{ ft}$$

$$F = 40 \text{ lbs}$$

If the ball were caught by moving the hands only 6 inches (0.5 ft) the force would be magnified greatly.

$$W = F \times D$$

$$100 \text{ ft-lbs} = F \times 0.5 \text{ ft}$$

$$F = 200 \text{ lbs}$$

If the area of impact is small more force must be absorbed per unit area than if it is large. For example, if 100 foot-pounds of force is received by one square inch of surface all of the force (100 ft-lbs) acts against this small area. If however, this same force is received by 20 square inches of surface, each square inch receives only 5 foot-pounds of force since the force is then distributed over the larger area. **The greater the area over which the force is taken, the less force per unit area.**

Since a force applied at any point other than through the center of gravity tends to rotate the body, equilibrium is a problem that must be considered in any force absorption task. The nearer to the center of gravity the force is received and the more nearly the center of gravity is kept over the center of the base, the easier stability can be maintained.

The above applications of the principles of force absorption apply whenever the surface is resistive to any degree, i.e., the surface does not part and allow the body or moving object to move through it. However, absorption of the force involved when the body meets a **non**resistive surface (the particles of the surface do part, e.g., water) presents a different problem. If a partially nonresistive surface is penetrated the movement of the body (or object) contacting it is not stopped and there is little reaction force to be absorbed. A small surface penetrates more readily than a large surface area and thus there is less force of impact against the body from a penetrable surface when a **small** surface makes contact than when the surface is large. Application of the principles in this situation is discussed on page 202.

The force absorption tasks most frequently faced by the human body involve landing from a fall, landing from a jump, and catching. The application of the above principles to these tasks is discussed in Chapters 13, 14 and 18.

SUMMARY OF PRINCIPLES

Production and Application of Force

1. Force is defined as any influence that can change the state of motion of an object.

2. A force can be represented by a line with an arrowhead; length of line indicates magnitude, the arrowhead, direction.

3. Forces can be summed graphically or algebraically.

4. Diagonal forces can be broken down into their vertical and horizontal components.

5. Force must be of sufficient magnitude to overcome inertia for movement to result.

6. The greater the mass of the object imparting force and the faster it is moving, the greater the force imparted.

7. The greater the time and the distance over which acceleration can be developed, the greater the velocity possible.

8. The longer the force is applied to an object, the greater the total force imparted.

9. The more contributing muscles used, the more force obtainable.

10. The fewer noncontributing muscles used, the less energy wasted.

11. The stronger the muscles called into play for a task demanding a good deal of force, the more efficient the action and the less the muscular strain.

12. The faster the muscular contraction the greater the speed at the end of the moving lever and the greater force produced against an object contacted; the slower the speed of contraction, the less the energy required.

13. In relatively light tasks the more sequential the movement, the more velocity obtainable.

14. The more the muscles that are to perform a given task get set before contacting the load, the more they can resist the equal and opposite force and the less the energy required to carry out a heavy task.

15. The effectiveness of a force produced by the body is dependent upon the fixation of the origins of the muscles involved (by other body muscles) to give a firm base on which to act, and upon the interaction between the body and the supporting surface.

16. Within limits, the more fully a muscle is lengthened the greater the force that it can exert.

17. An object acted upon by two forces moves in the direction of the resultant of the two forces.

18. If linear motion is desired, the more nearly through the center of gravity the force is applied, the less force required to move a given object.

19. The farther from the center of gravity the force is applied, the less force necessary to rotate the object.

20. If force is applied to an object that has one fixed point, rotation always results unless the force is applied through the point of fixation.

21. The greater the distance over which a constant force is applied, the greater the amount of work done.

Energy

1. Energy, a scalar quantity, may be thought of as the capacity to do work.

2. Mechanical energy can be divided into two types: potential and kinetic.

3. Potential energy is energy possessed by an object by virtue of its position, either its absolute location in space or its change in shape (deformation or strain energy).

4. Kinetic energy is energy possessed by an object by virtue of its motion.

Force Absorption

1. When a moving body (or object) strikes a resistive surface, the larger the surface area making contact with the surface the less the force of impact per unit area; when the surface is non-resistive (will part) the smaller the surface area making contact the more likely the penetration and thus the less the force of impact.

2. When a moving body (or object) strikes any surface, the greater the time and distance over which the motion is stopped, the more gradual the absorption of the force of impact and the less the reaction force against the body (or object).

3. When the moving body strikes a resistive surface, the more the center of gravity is vertically aligned above the base the more easily equilibrium is regained.

4. When a moving object strikes the body, the nearer to the body the object is contacted the less the angular force against the body; the nearer to the center of gravity of the object contact is made the less the angular force against the object; the larger the body's base in the direction of the object's motion the greater the stability of the body.

REFERENCES

1. Crouch, James E.: *Functional Human Anatomy.* Philadelphia, Lea and Febiger, 1965, p. 205.
2. Lee, Mabel, and Wagner, Miriam M.: *Fundamentals of Body Mechanics and Conditioning.* Philadelphia, W. B. Saunders Company, 1949, p. 148.
3. *Ibid.,* p. 146.
4. Bunn, John W.: *Scientific Principles of Coaching.* Englewood Cliffs, New Jersey, Prentice-Hall, Inc., 1955, p. 67.
5. Plagenhoef, Stanley: *Patterns of Human Motion.* Englewood Cliffs, New Jersey, Prentice-Hall, Inc., 1971, p. 55.
6. *Ibid.,* p. 48.
7. Wells, Katharine F., and Luttgens, Kathryn: *Kinesiology.* 6th ed. Philadelphia, W. B. Saunders Company, 1976, p. 292.
8. Zoethout, William D., and Tuttle, W. W.: *Textbook of Physiology.* St. Louis, C. V. Mosby Company, 1952, p. 103.

ADDITIONAL READING

Hay, James: *The Biomechanics of Sport Techniques.* Englewood Cliffs, N.J., Prentice-Hall, Inc., 1973.
Kuhlow, A.: "Analysis of Competitors in World Speed-Skating Championship," eds. Nelson and Morehouse. *Biomechanics IV.* Baltimore, University Park Press, 1974.
Northrip, J., Logan, G., and McKinney, W.: *Introduction to Biomechanic Analysis of Sport.* Dubuque, Iowa, Wm. C. Brown Company, 1974.

FLUID DYNAMICS 7

Although few are aware of it, all sports are performed in a fluid environment; that is, all sports involve moving through air, water or both. In some cases the effects of fluid resistance can be neglected while in others they become very important. Fluid resistance varies with the physical characteristics of the object, its size, shape and weight per unit volume, and with its speed of movement. The larger the surface of resistance, the lighter the object per unit volume and the faster it is moving through the fluid, the more it is affected by fluid resistance. This means that a light object with a large surface area is slowed more by fluid resistance than a compact small object. This is the cause of the difficulty which is experienced by many beginners when attempting to hit a shuttlecock. In shot-putting, on the other hand, the effects are negligible since the shot is heavy for its volume and has a relatively small velocity. In events such as golf, skiing, swimming, baseball, discus, javelin and sailing, the effects of the resistance of the air or water on movement are very important.

BUOYANCY

While buoyancy does not affect all movement as does gravity, it is extremely important in all aquatic activities.

Archimedes' principle states that a body wholly or partially submerged in a fluid is buoyed up by a force equal to the weight of the displaced fluid.

This force of buoyancy is actually the resistance of the fluid to downward motion of an object caused by gravity. Acting in an upward direction, it counteracts the force of gravity to various degrees, depending upon the weight and volume of the object or body which is immersed in the fluid. If an object placed in water displaces an amount of water equal in weight to the weight of the object, the object floats. If the water displaced weighs more than the object weighs, the object floats partly out of the water. It will be pushed up by the water until the part under the water displaces an amount of water weighing as much as the total object. If the water displaced weighs less than the object, the object sinks (Fig. 7–1).

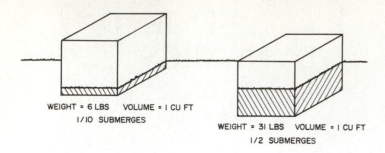

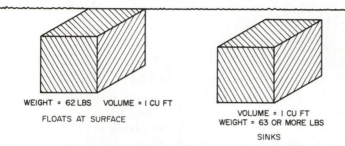

Figure 7–1. Buoyancy of blocks of various weights but of constant volume placed in water. (Water weight approximately 62 pounds per cubic foot.)

Just as there is a point about which the forces of gravity acting on an object in the atmosphere are balanced (center of gravity), there is also a point about which the buoyant forces acting on an object in water are balanced; this point is called the **center of buoyancy**. It is located at the center of volume of an object (body). In any symmetrical object with uniform density these two points (centers of gravity and buoyancy) are in the same spot and this object will remain balanced when placed in water; whether or not it will float depends on whether its weight is greater or less than that of an equal volume of water. However, an irregularly shaped object or one with segments of varying density may have a center of buoyancy in a different spot from its center of gravity. In this case, gravity, acting downward on the center of gravity, rotates the object around the spot where the force of buoyancy is acting upward (center of buoyancy); the object will rotate until the two forces, gravity and buoyancy, are in vertical alignment, and then will sink or float depending upon the relationship of the two forces (whether the object weighs more or less than the weight of an equal volume of water).

Ghesquire and Kavonen[1] stated that buoyancy in swimmers is determined by three principal factors: the lean body mass (heavier than water), body fat (lighter than water), and the air in the lungs (lighter). The functional residual capacity may have a greater effect on buoyancy than adipose tissue. Thus, it is often helpful to inhale while trying to float.

For most people the problem is not whether or not they can float but in what position. Since buoyancy depends upon the relationship between weight and volume, the heavier the individual for his size (volume) the less

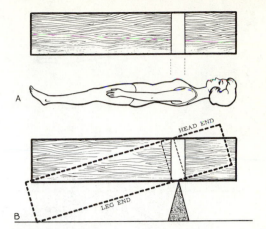

Figure 7–2. Tendency of body to rotate around the chest area.

buoyant he is. Normally the human body floats because its specific gravity (weight per unit volume) is less than that of water. The degree of buoyancy is dependent upon body build. Bone and muscle have a higher specific gravity than does adipose tissue. Bodies which are made up largely of bone and muscle are less buoyant than those containing a high percentage of fat. For this reason females, on the whole, are more buoyant than males.

The chest area containing the lungs filled with air is very light for its size, and is the most buoyant segment of the body. Thus, normally this is the center of buoyancy. However, if the legs are large because of adipose tissue which is relatively light and contain relatively underdeveloped muscles, they also may be lighter than the weight of the volume of water they displace and thus they may float. In this case, with both the legs and chest area pushed to the surface of the water (both buoyant), the center of buoyancy would be between the two and may coincide with the center of gravity; this individual would float in a horizontal position. This situation might be likened to a long box which is held with the two hands under its two ends.

Although in the air the body rotates around its center of gravity, in the water the fulcrum becomes the center of buoyancy. For most people, the center of gravity, approximately in the region of the hips, is toward the feet from this fulcrum (center of buoyancy). The legs are likely to have a high percentage of bone and muscle and therefore their specific gravity is high. Also the leg end of the body lever is longer (distance from the chest to the center of gravity of hips, legs, feet) than the head end (distance from the chest to the center of gravity of shoulder, neck, head). The farther the weight from the fulcrum (in this case center of buoyancy), the greater its effect (Chapter 5, Leverage). All these factors cause the body to be overbalanced at the leg end and it tends to rotate around the chest as the fulcrum and the legs sink (Fig. 7–2). The only time that the legs do not exert an angular force on the body is when they displace a volume of water that weighs as much as, or more than, they weigh.

However, this condition does not exist in the majority of persons and thus most people's feet sink until the center of gravity is below the center of buoyancy (Fig. 7–3). The buoyancy and balance of the human body in the water can be increased by enlarging the volume of the body without increas-

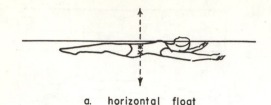

a. horizontal float

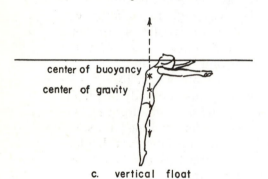

b. angle float

Figure 7–3. Floating positions resulting from various locations of the center of buoyancy.

center of buoyancy

center of gravity

c. vertical float

ing its weight and by raising the center of gravity so that it is brought closer to the center of buoyancy, thus decreasing the length of the weight arm.

The jellyfish float position, in which all segments of the body are as close as it is possible to get them to the center of buoyancy, and the lungs are filled with air adding to the volume of the chest area, is the most buoyant position which can be assumed by the human body. The centers of gravity and buoyancy are at approximately the same point. It is the position used to determine whether an individual who is having trouble floating on the back possesses sufficient buoyancy to make a back float possible, if certain adjustments in position are made. If, even though the lungs are filled, the individual sinks in the jellyfish float it is useless for him to attempt a **motionless** float on his back.

Since in most individuals the center of gravity is considerably lower in the body than is the center of buoyancy, when a motionless horizontal position is taken the legs sink. As they sink they gather momentum because of the acceleration caused by the force of gravity. This momentum may pull an individual down under the surface of the water even though his body buoyancy would normally cause him to float at an angle well above the vertical. While the buoyancy force can support the weight of the body, it is not great enough to overcome the momentum built up by the dropping of the legs. Therefore, it is important to place the body vertically in the water before assuming the motionless floating position. The legs, having no downward momentum to overcome, will be lifted to the point of balance according to the buoyancy of the particular individual. The practice of kicking the feet to the surface in assuming the floating position causes many relatively buoyant individuals to draw the conclusion that they are unable to float.

In floating on the back most persons need to redistribute the body weight around the center of buoyancy. Moving the arms to a position in the water above the head both lengthens and adds weight to that part of the body lever which is above the fulcrum (center of buoyancy) and is effective in helping to balance the heavier legs. It raises the center of gravity within the body, bringing it closer to the center of buoyancy. The center of gravity can be raised further by flexing the knees and drawing the feet toward the body in the frog position. This shortens the leg end of the body lever while maintaining the full resistive surface area of the legs. Arching the back and laying the head back into the water moves the center of gravity back within the body and thus the legs need to drop less before it reaches vertical alignment with the center of buoyancy. This position tends to expand the chest, aiding full breathing which adds volume and places more of the head in the water, displacing an additional volume of water. Buoyancy varies considerably with the amount of air in the lungs. A less buoyant individual may be able to float only when his lungs are filled completely. If this person wishes to float motionless it is necessary for him to take quick deep breaths, holding each until he is lifted far enough in the water that the drop accompanying the next exhalation will not put his mouth and nose under water.

Raising the head always tends to lower the feet in the water. The body lying in the water is a first class lever revolving around its center of buoyancy and might be likened to a teeter-totter. When one end of a teeter-totter is lifted the other end drops.

Many beginners are afraid in the water because they assume that they will sink. Actually the sinker is very rare. The problem is to learn to balance the body so that the mouth and nose can be out of the water at regular intervals to allow breathing. Buoyancy rather than its lack can, however, be a considerable problem for many individuals first learning to manipulate their bodies in the water. A person with very buoyant legs finds it difficult to replace the feet on the bottom. Frequently this inability to get the feet down under the body into a more accustomed position causes as much, or more, panic than the idea that the body will sink. It is, therefore, extremely important that such a person understand the problem, the reasons for it, and the mechanics for dealing with it.

Since in this case the legs displace a volume of water that weighs as much or more than they, the lever must be shortened to remove the mechanical advantage gained by the force of buoyancy when the lever is long. When the knees are brought in to the chest, the body lever is shortened, making it easier to rotate the hips downward by the force applied by the arms. When the body is on its back with the arms extending outward from the shoulders (approximately), a downward and forward force exerted by the arms lifts the upper body and pulls the hips down and backward. The equal and opposite reaction force rotates the body around its center of buoyancy. Tucking in the chin as the arms pull helps to drop the hips. When in a prone position with the arms on the water overhead, the downward and backward force of the arms lifts the upper body and, if the leg lever has been shortened by flexion of hips and knees, pulls the hips forward. The forceful lifting of the head also aids in dropping the hips. Once the hips are beneath the chest, extension of the legs sends the feet down to the bottom. Extension before this time simply puts them diagonally out in the water above the bottom and the force of buoyancy lifts them again to the surface.

DYNAMICS

Once an object starts to move through a fluid it is affected by dynamic forces. The magnitude of these forces depends on the object's speed, position and the material of which it is composed.

Drag.   Drag is defined as the **force of resistance to an object's motion through a fluid.** In air, this is commonly known as **air resistance.** Drag may be due to **friction** or to **pressure. Friction drag** varies with the surface of the object. Raine[2] studied the drag on a downhill ski racer and found that friction drag could add 0.03 seconds to each minute of a downhill race. This discovery resulted in the design of smooth covers for ski boots, and clothing with smoother lines. While friction drag is of little concern to the recreational swimmer, it must be considered by the competitive swimmer. When swimmers shave down for a race they are attempting to reduce friction drag.

Pressure drag depends mainly on the cross-sectional area of the object in the direction of its motion (Fig. 7–4). To decrease pressure drag a position which minimizes the cross-sectional area of the body must be adopted — for example, a planed body in swimming. The fact that resistance varies with the sine of the angle of the surface facing the direction of motion was reported as far back as 1888 by Saint-Venant[3] (Fig. 7–5).

In the crawl stroke the head position is important not only in maintaining the basic alignment of body segments but also in maintaining a planed position of the body. Breathing during the stroke must be accomplished without lifting the head to avoid sinking of the feet and thus an increased angle of the body and greatly increased pressure drag. In skiing, a downhill racer tries to remain in a tuck or egg position as much as possible to reduce the drag.[4] This also applies to the ski jumper who attempts to gain a large velocity by minimizing drag.

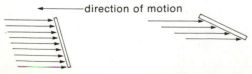

direction of motion

Large Pressure Drag   Smaller Pressure Drag

Figure 7–4. Comparison of cross-sectional areas facing direction of motion with different angles of object and of resultant drag.

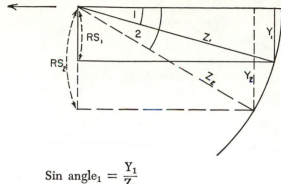

$$\text{Sin angle}_1 = \frac{Y_1}{Z_1}$$

$$\text{Sin angle}_2 = \frac{Y_2}{Z_2}$$

$$Z_1 = Z_2$$

$$\frac{\text{Sin angle}_1}{\text{Sin angle}_2} = \frac{\dfrac{Y_1}{Z}}{\dfrac{Y_2}{Z}} = \frac{Y_1}{Y_2}$$

$Y_1 = $ Resistive Surface (RS$_1$) caused by angle$_1$

$Y_2 = $ Resistive Surface (RS$_2$) caused by angle$_2$

$$\frac{\text{Sin angle}_1}{\text{Sin angle}_2} = \frac{RS_1}{RS_2}$$

Resistance varies with the sine of the angle of inclination.

Figure 7–5. Relationship of resistive surface to sine of angle.

In other activities an individual may wish to increase drag. In sailing, the sails are set to increase drag to speed the motion of the boat. In skydiving, the performer adopts a layout position in order to slow his fall. In extremely high speed car races, a parachute is released at the end of the race to increase the resistance to motion and help slow the car.

In many activities the pressure drag of the fluid both assists and resists the same motion. While without it a swimmer could not move through the water, it also serves as a resistance to forward motion. Thus the swimmer, oarsman or canoeist presents the smallest possible cross-sectional area in the forward direction to minimize the pressure drag resisting progress of the body or boat, while he presents the broadest area in the opposite direction (backward) to increase the force resisting the backward motion of the hand or oar and thus propelling him or the boat forward. A freestyle swimmer attempts to maintain a horizontal position to decrease pressure drag; at the same time he uses an open-hand position to increase the resistance to the hands' motion backward so that he can obtain a greater thrust.

Swimmers also experience **wave drag.** Swimming pools built with deck and water levels which are even help to decrease wave resistance.

Lift. As an object travels through a fluid the force perpendicular to its path of motion is termed **lift.** For an object travelling horizontally, **lift forces** cause the object to move to the right or left or to move up or down. When objects in the air are affected by lift forces they tend not to follow a parabolic

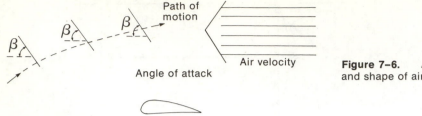

Path of
motion

Angle of attack

Air velocity

Figure 7-6. Angle of attack (β) and shape of airfoil.

Airfoil shape

path (p. 148). However, their exact path is not easily described. Some sport objects that attain lift are javelins, baseballs, golf balls, volleyballs and discuses. These objects are said to "fly."

The upward lift of an object can be changed by varying the **angle of attack** or the shape of the object. The angle of attack is defined as the angle that the surface of the projected object facing the direction of motion makes with the horizontal (Fig. 7-6). An initial javelin angle of 35 degrees is optimal when combined with a 42 degree projection angle.[5] Optimal angles of attack vary for objects of different shapes and for different angles of projection. If an object were projected with a 90 degree angle of attack (Fig. 7-7), it would move forward with its greatest surface area leading. This effect would create a very large pressure drag causing the object to stall (lose all horizontal velocity). Stalling is characteristic of shuttlecocks (Fig. 7-8). When the horizontal velocity has been overcome by air resistance, gravity is the only force acting on the shuttle and so it falls straight downward. Thus when distance is the objective, the angle of attack must give a large lift/drag ratio; that is, a large amount of lift compared to the amount of drag. Since drag on an object increases greatly with increased velocity, sports involving smaller velocities may allow greater angles of attack. In ski jumping off medium hills (velocity of 20 to 25 m/sec), the optimum angle of attack is 30 degrees, whereas for jumps from long hills (velocity of 25 to 30 m/sec) the best angle ranges from 15 to 23 degrees.

The best examples of the airfoil shape, the wings of an airplane, are designed to cause a low pressure area on top of the wings with higher pressure under the wings; thus there is a lift force and the plane flies. Some

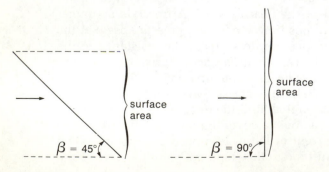

surface area

surface area

$\beta = 45°$

$\beta = 90°$

Figure 7-7. Comparison of surface areas for same object moving forward at 45 degree and at 90 degree angles of attack.

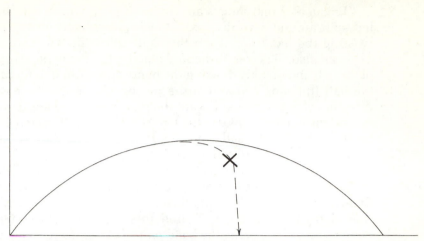

Figure 7–8. Horizontal velocity overcome by air resistance at point X; object stalls.

race cars are built with reverse airfoils (spoilers) so that the lift forces are directed downward, helping to create more friction (greater force pushing the two surfaces, tires and road, together). Ski jumpers try to hold their bodies in an airfoil shape to gain lift in order to stay in the air a little longer.

Magnus Effect. This results when an object spins as it moves through the air. The effect is seen in the flight of tennis balls, volleyballs, and baseballs and is particularly obvious in the golf slice and hook.

A ball may spin (turn) around an axis which passes through the center of the ball horizontal to the ground (horizontal axis) or an axis vertical to the ground (vertical axis) (Fig. 7–9).

When a ball is spinning around a **horizontal** axis in such a way that the **top** of the ball is **moving forward** (in the same direction the ball is moving), the ball is said to have **top spin** or **forward spin.** If the top of the ball is **moving backward** (away from the direction of flight), it is said to have **back spin.**

Top spin can be demonstrated by placing a ball on the desk or floor and moving the top forward and downward (away from the individual causing the movement and in the direction of flight if the ball were moving). If the top of the ball is moved backward and downward, back spin is demonstrated.

When a ball is spinning around a **vertical** axis so that the **front** of the ball (the side facing the direction of flight) is moving to the right the ball is said to have **right spin** and when the front is moving left, **left spin.**

Figure 7–9. Balls spinning around horizontal and vertical axes.

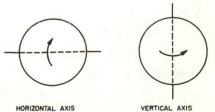

HORIZONTAL AXIS   VERTICAL AXIS

Frequently individuals are confused as to which is right and which is left spin around a vertical axis. Placing one hand on top of the ball and twisting the hand rapidly to the right starts the ball spinning clockwise. This can also be accomplished by placing the flat hand along the right side of the ball and quickly drawing the hand backward. In both cases the **front of the ball** (the side away from the person giving the force and toward the direction of flight) moves toward the right while the back of the ball (the side toward the person) moves to the left (right spin). If the hand on top of the ball twists to the left, the ball is given left spin (counter-clockwise). The **front** of the ball moves toward the left (left spin).

Spin is further complicated by the fact that it is possible to turn the ball to the right and left around a horizontal axis parallel to the direction of flight. (The horizontal axis for forward and back spin is at right angles to the line of flight.) Movement around this "parallel" horizontal axis can be demonstrated by placing the hand on top of a ball and moving the top to the right and downward (right spin) and then to the left and downward (left spin). Actually this type of spin is seldom used.

When a ball moving at a high velocity is spinning about its axis, pressure is built up on one side and reduced on the other, since the surface of the ball tends to drag a little air along with it. On the side where the air resistance to forward motion is in opposition to that of the air moving around the ball, a high pressure area is built up. On the opposite side of the ball the two forces are in the same direction and the velocity of the moving air is increased causing a low pressure area. The ball tends to move toward the side where the pressure is least. Since with forward (top) spin the pressure is built up on the top of the ball and reduced under the ball, the ball tends to drop more rapidly than normal. Thus tennis drives and serves can be given a high velocity and still be kept inside the court. With back spin the pressure is built up under the ball and reduced above the ball causing it to tend to remain in the air longer since this pressure overcomes some of gravity's pull (Fig. 7–10). The back spin ball may even seem to rise or curve upward in the air.

When a ball spins to the right around a **vertical** axis, the pressure is built up on the left curving the flight to the right. When spinning to the left the

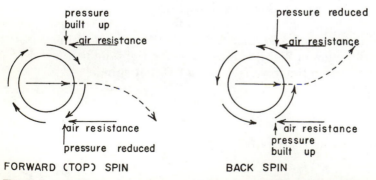

FORWARD (TOP) SPIN   BACK SPIN

Figure 7–10. Effect of forward and back spin on path of ball (looking at side of ball).

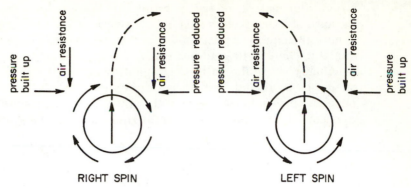

Figure 7–11. Effect of left and right spin around a vertical axis on path of ball (looking down on ball).

pressure is built up on the right curving the flight to the left (Fig. 7–11). Right and left spin around a **horizontal** axis are rarely encountered. However, a diagonally right (and top) spin is imparted by the American twist serve in tennis (see p. 320). Since this type of spin builds air resistance toward the top of the ball on the side toward which the top is spinning (right if spinning right) the ball curves toward the opposite direction (right spin curves ball to left) when spinning **around a horizontal axis.**

All of the effects of spin are greatly magnified by a head wind because of increased air resistance (drag) to the flight of the ball. Spin has more effect in curving the flight of a light than of a heavy ball because the greater momentum of the heavy ball makes it less responsive to air pressure.

Hicks reported that a ball with no spin at all may curve if its seams are in unequal positions on the two sides. "As air moves around an object, eddies begin to form. At the point where these eddies form, a surface irregularity can, surprisingly 'smooth out' the air flow and minimize the drag effect of this turbulence. This is known as tripping the boundary layer."[6] This means that if a ball can be thrown with no spin at all but so oriented to the air stream "that its seams trip the boundary layer on one side and not on the other," there is more drag on one side and the ball curves. Hicks reported a study which indicated that a ball with no spin but with its seams oriented to trip the boundary layer of air on one side and not on the other curved more than a ball with spin.

Terrell[7] became interested in the strange action of a ball with little or no spin and questioned Dr. Corrsin of Johns Hopkins University who offered the following "educated guess." He theorized that, because a ball is a blunt rather than a streamlined object, the flow of air around it is always irregular. Generally the flow is relatively smooth on the top and sides of the ball, but once the air stream reaches the back of the sphere it becomes confused. Instead of adhering smoothly to the surface of the ball it breaks away, some of it whirling back into space, some of it being sucked in close behind the ball to form a turbulent wake. "This is much like the wake behind a boat, whirling vortex of eddies and current and agitated air."[8]

He stated further that the point at which the smooth stream of air breaks away from the ball is called the separation point and that the separation line around the back of the ball is formed by these countless separation points. Because of many factors such as the seams of the ball, imperfections of the spherical shape, and gusts of wind, this separation line is erratic rather than straight. The swirling eddies cause unbalanced sideways pressures which eventually cause the ball to change direction and this change in direction cannot be predicted. In fact, the direction of a ball may change more than once. Because spin smooths out the air flow and causes the separation points to occur farther back it has a stabilizing effect on the flight of a ball.

REFERENCES

1. Ghesquire, J. L., and Kavonen, M. J.: Anthropometric Factors Affecting Buoyancy in the Africans, *First International Symposium on Biomechanics in Swimming*, eds. Lewille, L. and Clarys, J. P., 1971, pp. 175–182.
2. Raine, A. E.: "Aerodynamics of Skiing." *Science Journal*, 6:3:26–30, March, 1970.
3. de Saint-Venant, M.: Resistance des Fluides. *Memoirs de L'Academie des Sciences de L'Institute de France*, Tome Quarante-Quatrieme (Deuxieme Serie), 1888, p. 27.
4. Raine, op. cit.
5. Soong, T. C.: The Dynamics of Javelin Throw. *Journal of Applied Mechanics*, 42:2:257–262, June 1975.
6. Hicks, Clifford B.: The Strange Forces of the Air. *Popular Mechanics*, 111:6:127, June, 1959.
7. Terrell, Roy: Nobody Hits It. *Sports Illustrated*, 10:26:14–19, June 29, 1959.
8. *Ibid*, p. 18.

ADDITIONAL READING

Briggs, Lyman J.: Effect of Spin and Speed on the Lateral Deflection of a Baseball and the Magnus Effect for Smooth Spheres. *American Journal of Physics*, 27:589–596, November, 1959.

Cochran, Alstair, and Stobbs, John: *The Search for the Perfect Swing*. Philadelphia, J. B. Lippincott Company, 1968.

Hay, James: *The Biomechanics of Sports Techniques*. Englewood Cliffs N. J., Prentice-Hall, Inc., 1973.

Northrip, John W., et al.: *Introduction to Biomechanic Analysis of Sport*. Dubuque, Wm. C. Brown Company, 1974.

Soong, T. C.: The Dynamics of Discus Throw. *Journal of Applied Mechanics*, 98:4:531–536, December, 1976.

Streeter, V., and Wylie, E.: *Fluid Mechanics* (6th ed.). New York, McGraw-Hill Book Company, 1975.

IMPACT

8

When a moving object meets a resistance greater than its own momentum it will rebound from that resistance. The force of the rebound depends on the magnitude of the resistance (firmness of the surface), the velocity and mass of the object itself, its coefficient of restitution (elasticity, i.e., its ability to retake its shape after being flattened by the force of impact), the friction involved in the impact and the loss of energy to the impact. Skills involving impacts are involved in a majority of sports (Chapter 19).

Law of Conservation of Momentum

The law of conservation of momentum states that when two or more objects collide with each other, momentum is conserved; the total momentum after impact is equal to the total momentum before impact. In other words, when a bat meets an oncoming ball the total resulting momentum is the sum of the momentum of the bat (the mass of the bat times its speed) and the momentum of the ball (the mass of the ball times its speed). The difference between the two momentums determines the direction of the resulting motion; it is in the direction of the greater momentum. If the momentum of the bat is greater than that of the ball, the momentum of the bat is decreased, and the ball is given reverse momentum equal to the sum of the two original momentums minus the momentum which the bat still has. Dissipating forces such as energy lost in friction, sound and heat will, of course, reduce this.

Coefficient of Restitution

The coefficient of restitution of an object is a measure of its elasticity upon striking a given surface. When an official drops a ball and checks to see how high it bounces on a playing surface he is measuring the coefficient of restitution (e).[1]

$$e = \sqrt{\frac{\text{height bounced}}{\text{height dropped}}} \tag{8.1}$$

An object which, when dropped from a height of 16 inches rebounds to 16 inches, has a coefficient of restitution equal to 1.

$$e = \sqrt{\frac{16}{16}} = \sqrt{1} = 1$$

If the object only rebounds to a height of 12 inches it has a coefficient of restitution of .87.

$$e = \sqrt{\frac{12}{16}} = \sqrt{\frac{3}{4}} = .87$$

The factors which influence the coefficient of restitution are temperature, the object's composition, the composition of the surface it contacts and the speed of the impact. For most sport skills the composition of the object is specified in the rules and is therefore, standardized. Usually the height of bounce on a given surface is also standardized so this does not become a factor in competition; however, it may be a consideration for the recreational player since balls do lose elasticity with age and use. Also a tennis player who moves from a concrete to a clay or grass court finds that the bounce of the ball is altered.

Since a coefficient of restitution of less than 1 means that the ball bounces to a height less than that from which it was dropped, it indicates that mechanical energy has been lost in the impact. Thus the vertical velocity of an object when it leaves the surface is less than when it contacts that surface. Table 8–1 shows that balls have a coefficient of restitution on wood of less than 1 and further, that a ball moving at game speed actually has a lower rebound than under drop conditions and this change is greater for soft than for hard balls.

TABLE 8–1.   COEFFICIENT OF RESTITUTION OF VARIOUS BALLS WHEN DROPPED AND PROJECTED TO WOOD SURFACE*

TYPE OF BALL	DROPPED	PROJECTED 50–60 MPH
Baseball	.50	.44
Basketball	.75	.64
Golf Ball	.60	.58
Handball	.80	.50
Lacrosse Ball	.70	.60
Paddleball	.70	.45
Squash Ball	.52	.40
Softball	.55	.40
Super Ball	.90	.85
Tennis Ball	.74	.52
Volleyball	.75	.68

*Adapted·from Plagenhoef.[2]

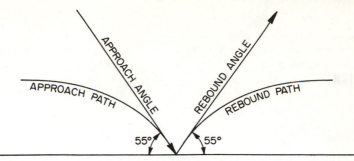

Figure 8–1. Angle of approach is tangent to arc of ball's path; discounting restitution, deformation of surface or ball, friction and spin, rebound angle is equal and opposite.

ANGLE OF REBOUND

When a ball approaches the floor from directly above, the entire bottom of the ball is depressed symmetrically making the force of rebound the same from all parts of the bottom of the ball and it bounces straight upward. However, when a ball approaches at an angle to the floor, the back of the bottom of the ball is depressed more than the front* and the rebound force throws the ball forward and upward. Because of gravity a ball moving forward through the air approaches a surface in a curved path. Its angle of approach is determined by the tangent to the arc of flight at the point of contact (Fig. 8–1). The angle at which it strikes determines how far back on the bottom of the ball the greatest depression comes and therefore, how much the rebound will be forward. The smaller the angle of approach the farther back will be the area of greatest depression and the more forward will be the rebound.

If there were no "give" (deformation) of the surface which an object struck (surface perfectly resistive), no friction involved in the impact, no spin on the ball and the ball had perfect restitution, a ball would rebound at an angle equal to its angle of approach (Fig. 8–1). While there are many situations in which the surface is resistive and some do not involve spin, friction is always involved to some degree and as Table 8–1 indicates, balls do not have perfect restitution; thus, in reality, the angle of rebound is very seldom the same as the angle of approach. For many situations the degree to which the rebound angle is modified is slight enough that, for all practical purposes, the recreational player can assume a rebound angle that approximates the angle of approach if spin is not involved. However, when the ball is spinning or when the impact involves considerable loss of vertical velocity due to a low coefficient of restitution, a large amount of friction or a surface that "gives," the angle will be modified markedly.

Vertical Velocity Loss. The reduction of vertical velocity on rebound due to a coefficient of restitution less than 1 causes a reduction in angle of rebound for all approach angles **except** when the ball approaches the surface at 90 degrees. When a ball is dropped or projected straight downward no horizontal velocity is involved in the approach to the surface, and therefore,

*Front of the ball is considered to be that part toward the direction of ball's movement.

BEFORE IMPACT

Given:
  approach velocity
  V_a = 50 ft/sec
  approach angle
  θ_a = 45°

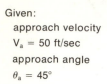
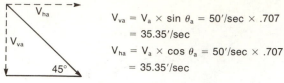

$V_{va} = V_a \times \sin \theta_a = 50'/sec \times .707$
        $= 35.35'/sec$
$V_{ha} = V_a \times \cos \theta_a = 50'/sec \times .707$
        $= 35.35'/sec$

Note: For 45° angle, sin = cos thus
        $V_v = V_h$

AFTER IMPACT (Rebound)

Given:
  coef. restitution = .5

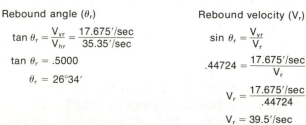

V_{vr} = coef. rest. $\times V_{va}$ = .5 $\times$ 35.35'/sec = 17.675'/sec

Rebound angle (θ_r)

$\tan \theta_r = \dfrac{V_{vr}}{V_{hr}} = \dfrac{17.675'/sec}{35.35'/sec}$

$\tan \theta_r = .5000$

$\theta_r = 26°34'$

Rebound velocity (V_r)

$\sin \theta_r = \dfrac{V_{vr}}{V_r}$

$.44724 = \dfrac{17.675'/sec}{V_r}$

$V_r = \dfrac{17.675'/sec}{.44724}$

$V_r = 39.5'/sec$

Figure 8–2. Trigonometric solution indicating reduction of rebound angle caused by loss of vertical velocity at impact because coefficient of restitution is less than 1 (assuming same horizontal velocity). Note: The *relationship* between vertical and horizontal velocity has changed and thus the rebound angle is not equal to the angle of approach.

the ball will bounce straight upward regardless of a loss in vertical velocity. However, when a ball approaching a surface **at an angle** loses vertical velocity the rebound angle is reduced. This can be verified by trigonometry. If a ball with a coefficient of restitution of 0.5 approaches a resistive surface at an angle of 45 degrees with a velocity of 50 feet per second, it will rebound at an angle of approximately 27 degrees with a velocity of approximately 40 feet per second (Fig. 8–2).

Obviously, the angle of rebound depends on the **relationship** between vertical and horizontal velocities; if the vertical velocity changes at impact, the relationship changes. When only the **coefficient of restitution** is considered, the angle of **rebound is less** than the angle of approach; how much less depends on how much the coefficient is below 1. If there is a loss of horizontal velocity as well as vertical velocity, this reduction is less.

Horizontal Velocity Loss. As the ball strikes the surface the **coefficient of friction** becomes a factor because the surface of the ball slides across the impact surface. The force due to friction works against the horizontal component of the impact velocity, and thus the horizontal velocity of the re-

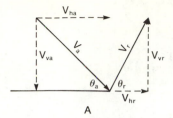

A

Horizontal velocity reduced (¹/₂) by friction and vertical velocity as before impact; rebound angle higher.

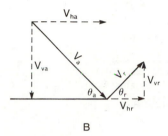

B

Horizontal velocity reduced (½) by friction and vertical velocity reduced (½) by coefficient of restitution; rebound angle = angle of approach.

Figure 8–3.   Effect of reduced horizontal velocity on angle of rebound; importance of *relationship* between horizontal and vertical velocities. A illustrates angle of rebound affected **only** by friction which reduces horizontal velocity. B illustrates angle of rebound affected by both friction and a coefficient of restitution less than 1 so that both horizontal and vertical velocities are reduced in proportion.

bound is less than that of approach; this **raises** the rebound angle (Fig. 8–3A). Plagenhoef[3] reported that the coefficient of friction alone causes a 14 degree increase in angle when the angle of approach is 45 degrees. This increase tends to offset the change in angle caused by a loss of vertical velocity in that it brings the **relationship** of the two velocities closer to that before impact; how much the two offset each other depends on the friction and the coefficient of restitution. The faster the ball is moving at impact with the surface, the greater the force pushing the two surfaces together and thus the greater the friction involved in the impact.

If, in the problem in Figure 8–2, in which the vertical velocity was cut in half, the coefficient of friction were such that the horizontal velocity were also halved, the rebound angle would remain the same as approach (disregarding other factors such as spin, etc.) since both the vertical and horizontal velocities would be reduced in proportion (Fig. 8–3B).

Spin.   Spin causes a sliding of the bottom of the ball across the surface creating a friction force which is effective in the direction opposite to that of the motion of the bottom of the ball; therefore, the rebound is the **resultant** of the **rebound force without spin** and this **friction force**. The friction force against a ball with top spin (bottom of ball moving backward) is forward while that against a back spinning ball (bottom moving forward) is backward. A ball with top spin approaching from directly above (90°) bounces up and forward rather than straight upward while a ball with back spin bounces

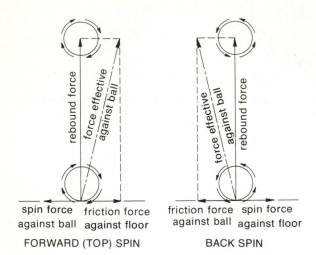

spin force against ball   friction force against ball

friction force against ball   spin force against floor

FORWARD (TOP) SPIN

BACK SPIN

Figure 8–4. Effect of top spin and back spin on bounce of ball approaching floor at ninety-degree angle (looking at side of ball).

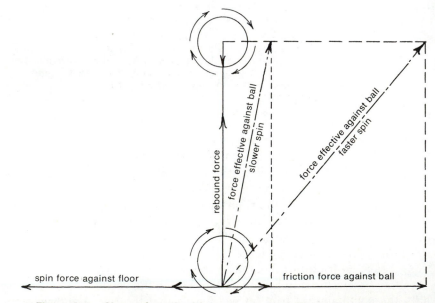

spin force against floor   friction force against ball

Figure 8–5. Change in path of forward spinning ball with increase in spin.

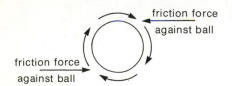

friction force against ball

friction force against ball

Figure 8–6. Looking down on ball with right spin approaching floor at ninety-degree angle.

up and backward (Fig. 8–4). If the ball is spinning very fast, the magnitude of the force caused by the spin is greater and the resultant is, therefore, more forward (Fig. 8–5). If the ball has back spin it will bounce backward rather than straight up (Fig. 8–4).

Right or left spin about its **vertical axis** as the ball aproaches the floor from directly above (90° angle) does not affect the direction of the rebound. Since the entire bottom of the ball is depressed, the friction against the forward part of the ball is same as that against the back part of the ball (Fig. 8–6). These two forces, being in direct opposition, neutralize each other and the ball bounces straight upward. The spin will be either stopped or reversed depending upon the force of impact and speed of spin. If the forces are not great the spin will be stopped, but if the ball is spinning with considerable speed the friction force will reverse the spin. If the ball is spinning left or right around its **horizontal axis,** the rebound is in the direction of the spin. The entire **bottom** of a right spinning ball is moving to the left and therefore the friction force is to the right and the ball bounces to the right.

When a ball with back spin **approaches the surface at an angle less than 90 degrees,** the friction force is increased; the friction force is effective in a backward direction because the bottom of the ball is moving forward and thus is in opposition to the direction of the ball's motion. It reduces the horizontal velocity more than if there were no spin and causes the bounce to be shorter and at a higher angle (Fig. 8–7).*

Top spin reduces the friction involved in the impact of a ball approach-

---

*To simplify the presentation, the effects of coefficient of restitution, friction, and so on, have been disregarded in the diagrams.

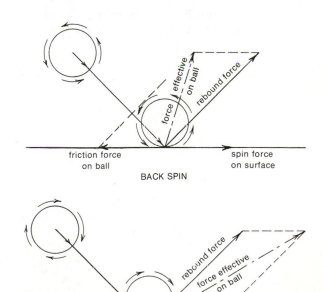

Figure 8–7. Effect of top spin and back spin on bounce of ball approaching floor at an angle. Note: back of ball is depressed more than front.

friction force on ball   spin force on surface

BACK SPIN

spin force on surtace   friction force on ball

FORWARD (TOP) SPIN

ing at an angle since the bottom of the ball pushes forward horizontally with less force than if the ball were not spinning. In fact, the spinning bottom actually pushes backward helping to overcome friction and adding to the ball's forward velocity. Thus the horizontal component of the velocity does not decrease as much as when there is no spin involved; with fast top spin, the ball's horizontal velocity after impact can be greater than that before impact. The effect of this forward force from spin is a lower angle of rebound and a lengthened bounce (Fig. 8–7).

Confusion arises because a ball with very fast top spin may actually bounce **higher** than one with no spin. This may appear to be in contradiction to the above discussion. However, it must be remembered that a fast moving ball with fast top spin meets considerable air resistance, and the spin will make it drop faster as it moves through the air, causing the ball to **approach** the surface at a greater angle than would be anticipated for its angle of projection. Thus, even though the top spin **reduces** this angle, the resulting angle of rebound may be higher than that of a ball projected at the same angle with no spin which would approach the surface at a lower angle (Fig. 8–8). Top spin reduces the angle of rebound from what would be normal for the angle of approach; it does not necessarily cause a ball to rebound lower than another ball with no spin and thus a different angle of approach.

Because of the friction when a ball with no spin strikes a horizontal surface the bottom of the ball is retarded but the top of the ball continues at the same speed (inertia). Thus the friction of impact and the forward momentum of the ball act together to cause a force that tends to rotate the ball forward causing the ball striking the floor with no spin to leave the floor spinning forward. Since the friction force is in the same direction as the spin of a top spinning ball, its spin velocity is increased. However, this force is in opposition to the direction of the spin of a back spinning ball and thus the back spin is stopped, or if the forward velocity is great in relation to the speed of the back spin, the spin is reversed.

Right and left spin do not alter the height of the bounce, but a ball with

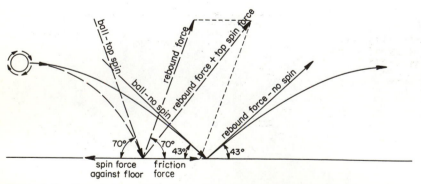

Figure 8–8. Comparison of bounces of ball with considerable top spin and ball with no spin. Note: Even though the final force effective against the top-spinning ball is lower than its *angle of approach*, it may be higher than that of a ball with no spin because it approaches the surface at a greater angle.

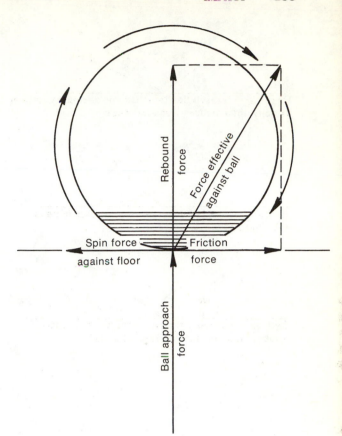

Figure 8–9. Direction of bounce of right-spinning ball approaching floor at an angle (looking down on top of ball spinning right around a vertical axis). Note: Left-spinning ball would bounce in the opposite direction (left).

right spin approaching the floor **at an angle other than 90 degrees**, regardless of which axis it is spinning around, bounces to the right and one with left spin bounces to the left. Since friction force is greater on the **back** of the ball approaching a surface at an angle (back depressed more), the **direction of spin of the back of the ball determines the direction of the rebound**. The back of a ball spinning to the right around its vertical axis is turning left and therefore, the friction force against the ball is to the right (Fig. 8–9). Since the **back of a ball** spinning to the left around its vertical axis is turning right, the force is to the left and the ball rebounds left. A ball spinning to the left or right about its **horizontal axis** also bounces in the direction of its spin since the entire bottom of the ball is moving in the direction opposite to the spin. (The bottom of a right spinning ball moves to the left.) Again, friction stops the right or left spin, and the forward momentum of the ball together with friction causes most balls to rebound with some top spin.

Figure 8–10 summarized the effects of coefficient of restitution, friction, back and top spin on the angle of rebound and the resultant velocity. These drawings assume that the ball is experiencing only one effect at a time. In reality an object experiences a **net effect** due to the angle of approach, coefficient of restitution, coefficient of friction and any spin on the ball. Under certain conditions various factors may tend to offset others and in another situation their effects may be summed to cause an even greater

Coefficient of restitution less than one decreases vertical velocity, thus reduces   rebound angle.

Friction decreases horizontal velocity, thus increases rebound angle.

Back spin increases friction, decreases horizontal velocity, thus increases   rebound angle.

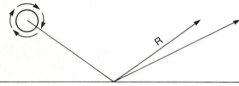

Top spin reduces friction, increases horizontal velocity, thus reduces rebound angle.

Figure 8–10. Summary of effects of *isolated* factors on rebound angle. R = Theoretical angle of rebound if none of these factors was acting.

deviation from the so-called "normal" angle of rebound. Actually, the chances of an object having equal angles of impact and rebound are very small.

REFERENCES

1. Plagenhoef, Stanley: *Patterns of Human Motion.* Englewood Cliffs, Prentice-Hall, Inc., 1971, p. 82.
2. *Ibid,* p. 83.
3. *Ibid,* p. 85.

PROJECTION

9

Actually the physical laws governing projectiles have already been discussed. However, since so many sport activities involve a performer and/or an object that is projected, it seems expedient to relate these physical laws to this topic.

In free fall the performer or object has an initial velocity of zero and gravity is the force causing motion; in projection, the body (or object) is given an initial velocity and then allowed to move under the influence of outside forces (i.e., gravity, air resistance and, when released along a surface, friction). This means that the body itself is a projectile in any jump or dive and, **therefore,** its path through the air is determined by these laws in the same way as that of a thrown or struck object.

The initial velocity of a projected object can be supplied by the body in many ways. It can be supplied by a person **directly** to an object, as when the object is held by a body part or in an implement held by the body (such as the crosse for lacrosse), and is moved through the air rapidly and then released (throwing). A direct application of force is also made when the object is momentarily contacted by a moving body part or by an implement held or attached to the body (striking); and when the body projects itself. Force is applied **indirectly** to a projectile when a person moves some part of an object which in turn applies the force to the object to be projected. By using an elastic type of device such as a slingshot, an individual indirectly applies force to a projectile. An archer's bow acts in the same way. The individual applies force to bend the bow, storing **potential energy** (energy resulting from its deformation) in the bow which, when released, is transformed into **kinetic energy** (energy due to motion). A gun is a mechanical device by which an individual applies force indirectly to the bullet by pulling the trigger. The firing pin applies the force which results in the movement of the bullet.

A projectile undergoes linear motion; when released above the ground its motion is made curvilinear by the force of gravity acting on it throughout its flight. It may, at the same time, be experiencing angular motion if it spins while moving through the air.

Examples in which an individual becomes a projectile include: falling, diving, vaulting in gymnastics, jumping on trampoline, hurdling, high jumping, long jumping, jumping to spike or block in volleyball, skydiving, jump shooting in basketball and leaping in dance. The flight of sport objects such as a baseball, tennis ball, golf ball, basketball, shuttlecock, shotput, discus, javelin, soccer ball, and football also represent projection. Although the objective in each case may be different (maximum height, speed, or length of throw or hit), all of these projectiles are subject to the same underlying mechanical principles; the main factors of interest are the time of flight (speed), vertical displacement (height) and horizontal displacement (distance).

Once the performer or object is in the air only two naturally occurring external forces act upon it: gravity and air resistance. The latter force is very important in such sports as ski jumping and skydiving because velocity is quite high and flight time relatively long, and in javelin and discus events because of the aerodynamic characteristics of these implements. Certainly air resistance (especially under windy conditions) affects such outdoor sports as golf, tennis, baseball, soccer, and football. However, in many sports involving projectiles air resistance plays an insignificant role. For this reason and in the interest of simplifying the following presentation, the force due to air resistance is considered negligible, that is, equal to zero.

AIR RESISTANCE NEGLECTED

Vertical Projection.   The simplest projection consists of an object being projected vertically upward (90° takeoff angle) as when a cheerleader jumps, a juggler tosses a ball straight up in the air or an individual performs a vertical jump test. When an object (body) is projected **straight upward,** directly in opposition to the force of gravity, its speed gradually diminishes until the force with which it was projected is neutralized by the pull of gravity. At this point it comes to rest ($V = 0$) and immediately begins to fall back toward the earth. When it reaches the point at which it was projected, its speed is equal to the speed at which it was originally projected, i.e., the deceleration of the upward flight is equal to the acceleration of the downward flight, or the upward motion is the same as the downward motion in reverse. The height to which an object will climb depends upon the speed with which it is projected. This relationship is expressed in Equation 9.1:

$$V^2 = 2gD_v \quad \text{or} \quad D_v = \frac{V^2}{2g} \tag{9.1}$$

$$\frac{\text{height of projection}}{\text{(vertical distance)}} = \frac{\text{projecting velocity squared}}{2 \times \text{acceleration of gravity}}$$

If a ball were projected straight upward with a velocity of 20 feet per second, it would climb to a height of 6.25 feet.

$$D_v = \frac{V^2}{2g}$$

$$D_v = \frac{(20'/\text{sec})^2}{2 \times 32'/\text{sec/sec}}$$

$$D_v = \frac{400'/\text{sec}}{64'/\text{sec/sec}}$$

$$D_v = 6.25'$$

The vertical distance from release to highest point can also be calculated by another fundamental formula:

$$D_v = V_i t + \frac{1}{2} gt^2 \qquad (9.2)$$

If **downward** flight were to be calculated, the initial velocity (V_i) would be zero; the ($V_i t$) quantity in this formula would also be zero and could be eliminated, making the formula the same as that for a free falling object:

$$D_v = \frac{1}{2} gt^2 \qquad (3.2)$$

Since downward distance, time and velocity are all equal to upward distance, time and velocity, Equation 3.2 can be applied to problems involving either a falling object or an object projected **straight upward.**

However, to find height of projection (vertical distance) by use of Equation 3.2, time must be known and to determine time, vertical distance must be known. If only projecting velocity is known the height of projection must be calculated by Equations 9.1 or 9.2 or time may be found by applying the basic acceleration formula:

$$a = \frac{V_f - V_i}{t} \qquad (4.2)$$

When an object is projected straight upward all vertical acceleration is caused by gravity and the **a** in Equation 4.2 can be replaced by **g** (acceleration of gravity). Because the ball slows down as it climbs in a positive direction (up), and speeds up as it drops downward, this acceleration is negative ($-32'/sec^2$). Substituting the projecting velocity ($20'/sec$), the final velocity (0) and the acceleration of gravity into Equation 4.2, the time needed to reach the high point is found to be .625 seconds.

$$-32'/sec/sec = \frac{0 - 20'/sec}{t}$$

$$-32'/sec/sec \times t = -20'/sec$$

$$t = \frac{20'/sec}{32'/sec/sec}$$

$$t = .625 \text{ sec (time to reach high point)}$$

It can be seen that the basic formula (9.2) and the simplified version (3.2) give the same projection height as does Equation 9.1:

Basic Formula

$$D_v = V_i t + \frac{1}{2} at^2$$

$$D_v = V_i t + \frac{1}{2} gt^2$$

$$D_v = 20'/sec \times .625 \text{ sec} - 16'/sec^2 (.625)^2$$
$$D_v = 12.5 - 6.25 = 6.25'$$

Simplified Formula

$$D_v = \frac{1}{2} gt^2$$

$$-D_v = -16'/sec^2 (.625)^2$$
$$-D_v = -6.25'$$
$$D_v = 6.25'$$

It must be noted that when the ball is decelerating in a positive direction (up), D_v is positive but the quantity $\frac{1}{2}gt^2$ is negative (negative acceleration). When the simplified formula (3.2) which finds the time for the ball to drop is used, D_v is negative (down) and the acceleration is also negative since the ball is now accelerating downward (negative direction).

Thus there are two formulas applicable to finding the distance (height) of a vertical projection:

$$D_v = \frac{V^2}{2g} \quad \text{or} \quad D_v = V_i t + \frac{1}{2}at^2 \text{ (simplified to } D_v = \frac{1}{2}gt^2)$$

Also one of two formulas can be used to find time to high point:

$$D_v = \frac{1}{2}gt^2 \quad \text{or} \quad a = \frac{V_f - V_i}{t} \quad (a = g)$$

Which formula is chosen depends upon whether height of projection, time or only velocity of projection is known.

Since in the given problem, it was found that it would take .625 seconds for the ball to reach its highest point, the **total time** of flight (T) would be twice that, or 1.25 seconds.

This example serves to emphasize the important fact that the **vertical velocity** at release (takeoff) is the sole determinant of the **vertical height** and **time of flight.** Also, the time required to reach the high point is exactly equal to the time needed for the ball to fall from that point to the initial takeoff level, and the initial vertical velocity is the same as the velocity of the ball at the instant it reaches the **takeoff point** during its descent.

Non-vertical Projection. With the exception of a straight upward or straight downward projection, a horizontal component is involved in the projecting force. An object may be projected with purely horizontal velocity and then all vertical velocity is caused by gravity; it may be projected at an angle (other than 90°) to the horizontal in which case the projecting velocity has both a horizontal and a vertical component (Fig. 9–1). **The downward force produced by gravity acts only on the vertical component of the projecting force and is independent of any horizontal force.** The relationship between the horizontal and vertical components of a projecting force depends on the angle of release.

In sports involving projectiles, a wide range of projecting angles are used because of diverse purposes. High angles of projection (near 90°) are necessary in volleyball blocking, basketball jump shooting, and diving. Medium angles (near 45°) are noted in throwing events such as the javelin, discus, shotput and hammer throw. Low angles of projection occur in the long jump, throws in baseball and softball, kicking in soccer, and archery.

Figure 9–1. Ball projected with force V at angle θ has horizontal component V_h and vertical component V_v.

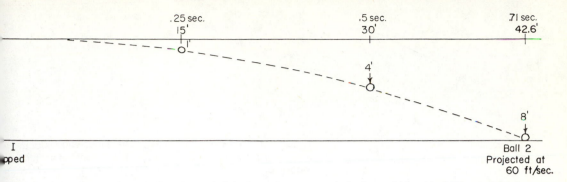

Figure 9–2. Paths of two balls released eight feet above ground. Both would land in 0.71 second (air resistance neglected).

Projectile angles even below the horizontal are present during ski jumping and starts in swimming. It is clear from these examples that no single projection angle is optimal for all situations.

If an object is given an initial force that is **strictly horizontal,** a vertical force caused by the pull of gravity brings about acceleration in a vertical direction (downward) throughout the flight. If one object falls freely from rest at the same time another is projected **horizontally from the same height,** both will strike the ground at the same time, but in different places. The freely falling object will strike directly under its point of release while the one projected horizontally will go as far out as the forward force can carry it in the time gravity takes to pull it to earth from the height at which it was released. In other words, if these two balls were released at a height of eight feet, both would hit the ground 0.71 second later ($D_v = \frac{1}{2}gt^2$, Equation 3.2). If one was given a forward (horizontal) velocity of 60 feet per second, it would hit 42.6 feet ahead of the point of release or forward of the dropped ball that had no horizontal velocity (Fig. 9–2).

$$D_h = V_i \times t + \frac{1}{2}at^2 \quad (D_h = \text{horizontal distance}) \qquad (9.3)$$

$$D_h = 60'/\text{sec} \times .71 \text{ sec} + 0 \text{ (air resistance discounted)}$$
$$D_h = 42.6 \text{ ft}$$

If air resistance is discounted, horizontal acceleration is zero and thus the quantity ($\frac{1}{2}at^2$) is zero. If there is no vertical component, as in horizontal projection, gravity acts on the projectile as on any freely falling object. The time taken to hit the ground depends only on the height of release and so can be altered only when the projecting force is applied either straight upward (all force opposing gravity), diagonally upward (vertical component opposing gravity), or diagonally or straight downward (vertical component or all force added to gravity).

Just as in a vertical projection the vertical component of the projecting force is decelerated by the pull of gravity as the object climbs to the high point in its path, the point where the vertical component of the projecting force is neutralized by gravity, and is accelerated as it drops from the high point. The time required to reach the highest point equals the time taken to fall back downward **to the height at which the object was originally project-**

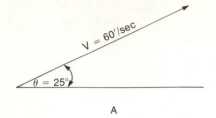

A

Figure 9–3. *A* Soccer ball kicked at 25° angle with velocity of 60'/sec. *B* Vertical and horizontal components of projecting force.

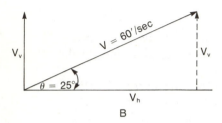

B

ed. Also, when it returns to the height from which it was projected, its velocity is the same as the projection velocity.

This important concept, that **once the ball is in flight gravity acts only on the vertical component of the projecting velocity,** is often difficult to understand unless the vertical and horizontal components are treated separately. The following represents a typical projectile problem in which three aspects are of interest: (1) time of flight, (2) vertical height at high point, and (3) horizontal distance covered. The activity consists of a soccer kick from the ground at an angle (θ) of 25° with the horizontal and an initial velocity of 60 feet per second along the path of projection (Fig. 9–3A).

1. **Time.** The time can be calculated directly from the projecting velocity and angle (Equation 9.5); however, in order to clarify the above concept, it will be calculated first from the vertical velocity. To do this it is necessary to first calculate the **vertical** and **horizontal** components of the projecting force (Fig. 9–3B). Moving the vertical velocity vector (V_v) as indicated in the figure completes a right triangle and the projecting velocity represents its hypotenuse. Since the sine of the angle is equal to the vertical velocity (side opposite) divided by the hypotenuse (projecting velocity), the vertical velocity equals the projecting velocity times the sine of the angle (Equation 6.2); and the horizontal velocity equals the projecting velocity times the cosine of the angle (Equation 6.3).[1]

$$\sin \theta = \frac{V_v}{V} \quad \text{or} \quad V_v = V \sin \theta \tag{6.2}$$

$$\cos \theta = \frac{V_h}{V} \quad \text{or} \quad V_h = V \cos \theta \tag{6.3}$$

$$V_v = 60'/\text{sec} \times .42262 = 25.3572'/\text{sec} \ (25.4)$$
$$V_h = 60'/\text{sec} \times .90631 = 54.3786'/\text{sec} \ (54.4)$$

The **time** from takeoff to the highest point in the arc can be calculated from the vertical velocity by the same procedure used in the example of the ball projected straight upward (90°). Since it is only the **vertical** velocity that is affected by gravity, this component controls time of flight; thus vertical velocity is used in the formula as original velocity. Obviously the final velocity is zero (at high point) and all acceleration is due to gravity; thus

$$a = \frac{V_f - V_i}{t} \quad \text{or} \quad t = \frac{V_f - V_i}{a} \tag{4.2}$$

becomes
$$g = \frac{0 - V_v}{t} \quad \text{or} \quad t = \frac{-V_v}{-32'/\text{sec}^2} \quad \left(t = \frac{V_v}{g}\right) \tag{9.4}$$

$$t = \frac{-25.4'/\text{sec}}{-32'/\text{sec}^2}$$

$$t = .79375 \text{ sec. } (.79)$$

Since vertical velocity is equal to the projecting velocity times the sine of the angle, this same result can be found directly from the projecting velocity by Equation 9.5:

$$t = \frac{V \sin \theta}{g} \tag{9.5}$$

$$t = \frac{60'/\text{sec} \times .42}{32'/\text{sec}^2} = .79 \text{ sec}$$

Since this time represents only the first half of the flight it must be doubled to obtain the total flight time (T).

$$T = 2 \times .79 \text{ sec} = 1.58 \text{ sec}$$

$$\text{or}$$

$$T = \frac{2V \sin \theta}{g} \tag{9.6}$$

$$T = \frac{120'/\text{sec} \times .42}{32'/\text{sec}^2} = 1.58 \text{ sec}$$

2. **Vertical Distance (height).** Knowing the time from the kick to the high point makes it possible to calculate the vertical distance (D_v) the soccer ball will climb. Again the original velocity involved is the **vertical veloci-ty** and the acceleration is due to gravity (g).

$$D_v = V_i t + \frac{1}{2} a t^2 \text{ becomes } D_v = V_v t + \frac{1}{2} g t^2 \tag{9.2}$$
$$D_v = [25.4'/\text{sec} \times .7937 \text{ sec}] + [-16'/\text{sec}^2 \times (.79375 \text{ sec})^2]$$
$$D_v = 20.16' - 10.08'$$
$$D_v = 10.08' \ (10.1)$$

Equation 3.2 gives the same result:
$$D_v = \frac{1}{2} g t^2 = 16 \times (.79375 \text{ sec})^2 = 10.08'$$

3. **Horizontal Distance.** The horizontal distance a projectile travels depends on the horizontal component of the projecting velocity and its **total time** of flight and can be calculated by using the same basic distance formula (9.2). However, the distance is now horizontal distance (D_h), initial veloc-

ity is horizontal velocity (V_h) and the acceleration is the change in velocity caused by air resistance. Since in this discussion air resistance is considered to be negligible (0), the basic formula (9.2):

$$D = V_i t + \tfrac{1}{2} at^2 \quad \text{becomes} \quad D_h = V_h T.$$

The time used must be the total time of flight (t = T). Thus the soccer ball would travel approximately 85 feet from the point of kick to landing.

$$D_h = 54.4'/\text{sec} \times 1.58 \text{ sec} = 86'$$

Since the soccer ball **lands at the same height from which it is projected** (ground), when both the original and projection angles are known, the horizontal distance, in this case called **range** (R), can be found by use of Equation 9.7:

$$R = \frac{V^2}{g} \sin 2\theta \qquad (9.7)$$

$$= \frac{(60'/\text{sec})^2}{32'/\text{sec}^2} \times \sin(2 \times 25°)$$

$$R = \frac{3600'/\text{sec}^2}{32'/\text{sec}^2} \times \sin 50°$$

$$R = 112.5 \times .766 = 86'$$

It must be emphasized that Equation 9.7 is applicable **only** when release and landing heights are the same.

The steps in solving this type of projectile problem are summarized as follows:
1. Calculate vertical and horizontal components of projecting (actual) velocity.
2. Determine time to high point using vertical velocity. Double this time for total time of flight.
3. Find vertical distance using vertical velocity and time to high point.
4. Calculate horizontal distance using horizontal velocity and total time of flight.

This method of calculating the time and distance variables is applicable to situations in which the **takeoff and landing points are at the same level.** Under these conditions it can be shown that for a given velocity the greatest horizontal distance can be achieved when the takeoff angle is 45° degrees. When the takeoff velocity in the previous example (60 ft/sec) is used to calculate the time and distance components for takeoff angles from 15 degrees to 90 degrees at 15 degree increments the values contained in Table 9–1 are found.

It can be seen from Table 9–1 that the lower the angle of projection the greater the horizontal component in relation to the vertical component of the projecting velocity (Fig. 9–4). Therefore, when an object is projected at a low angle the horizontal velocity resulting from a given projecting force is

**TABLE 9–1.   SUMMARY OF TIME AND DISTANCE VALUES FOR
A TAKEOFF VELOCITY OF 60 FT/SEC AT SPECIFIED ANGLES
(air resistance negligible)**

ANGLE OF TAKEOFF (degrees)	VERTICAL VELOCITY (ft/sec)	HORIZONTAL VELOCITY (ft/sec)	TOTAL TIME OF FLIGHT (sec)	VERTICAL DISTANCE (feet)	HORIZONTAL DISTANCE (feet)
15	15.5	58.0	0.97	3.8	56.3
30	30.0	52.0	1.88	14.0	97.4
45	42.4	42.4	2.65	28.1	112.5
60	52.0	30.0	3.25	42.2	97.4
75	58.0	15.5	3.62	52.4	56.3
90	60.0	0	3.73	56.0	0

relatively high but the vertical velocity is low and therefore does little to resist gravity's pull. As a result, the object does not stay in the air long enough to cover much distance. If the angle of projection is large, the vertical component of the projecting velocity is larger and thus keeps the object in the air longer, but since the horizontal component is relatively small, the distance covered is small.

With air resistance negligible, any variation from the 45 degree angle of projection, whether above or below, will result in the same loss of distance **at the point straight out from the point of release** (take off). The example used for Table 9–1 shows that for angles of 30 and 60 degrees (45° ± 15°) the vertical distances vary ± 14.1 feet and the horizontal distance ± 15.1 feet; for 15 and 75 degree angles (45° ± 30°) the variations are ± 24.3 feet (D_v) and ± 56.2 feet (D_h).

Very often the takeoff and landing points are at different levels as in all throwing events in track and field, volleyball serves, pitching and other throws in baseball, diving, high jump, tennis serves and many others. The

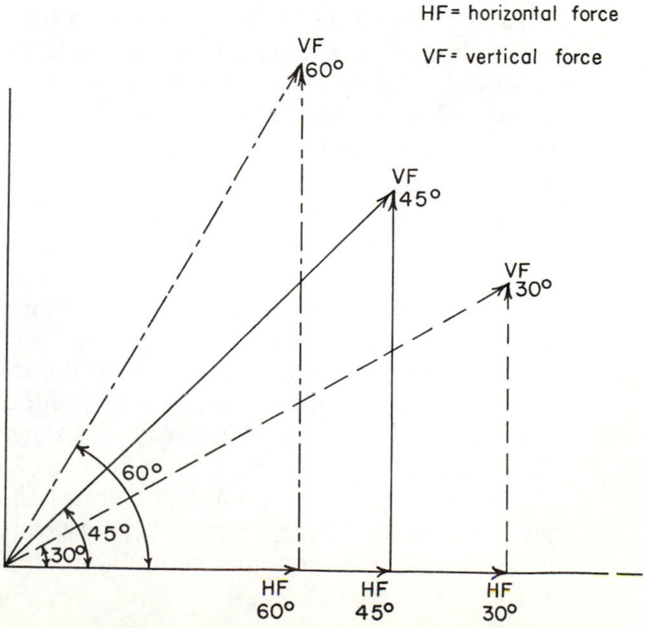

Figure 9–4. Relative magnitude of horizontal and vertical components of a given force applied at various angles.

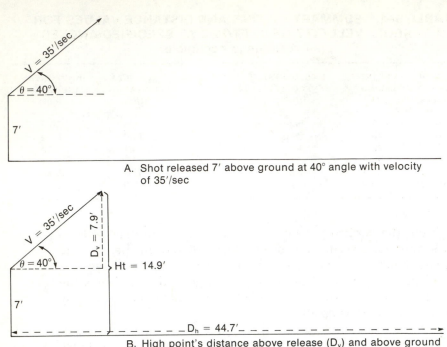

A. Shot released 7′ above ground at 40° angle with velocity of 35′/sec

B. High point's distance above release (D_v) and above ground (Ht) and horizontal distance (D_h)

Figure 9–5. Example of *non*-vertical projection; shot released at angle *above* horizontal.

height of release is a very important consideration in most of these activities.

In a typical example, the shotput, the point of release ranges from approximately 6 to 8 feet depending upon the size and technique of the shotputter. The following problem includes the calculation steps necessary **when the takeoff and landing heights differ.**

A shotputter releases the shot at a height of 7 feet above the ground with an initial velocity of 35 ft/sec at an angle of 40° with the horizontal (Fig. 9–5A). What would be the horizontal distance traveled by the shot from a point directly below the release to the landing point? Since the release is above the ground (landing point), the range formula for finding horizontal distance (Equation 9.7), is not applicable. At first glance it might appear that the problem should be divided into two parts; from release to the point where the shot returns to release level and from that point to the ground. Such an approach is possible but is complicated by the fact that at the division point the vertical velocity is not zero as it is at the high points.

A simpler approach is to first consider the problem from release to high point and then from that point to the ground. In addition to involving less complicated calculations, it also can be used when the landing point is above takeoff (release) level, as in hitting to an elevated green in golf.

As in the previous example, the time to high point, vertical and horizontal components of the projecting velocity, vertical distance to high point and total time must all be found before horizontal distance can be calculated.

1. **Time to High Point.** Before time to high point can be calculated the vertical velocity must be known, and since horizontal velocity is required later in the problem, it too is calculated.

$$V_v = Vsin\ \theta \qquad\qquad V_h = Vcos\ \theta$$
$$V_v = 35'/sec \times .64279 \qquad V_h = 35'/sec \times .76604$$
$$V_v = 22.5'/sec \qquad\qquad V_h = 26.8'/sec$$

The time to the high point can now be calculated.

$$t = \frac{V_v}{g}$$

$$= \frac{22.5'/sec}{32'/sec^2}$$

$$= .703\ sec$$

2. **Vertical Distance to High Point.** Knowing vertical velocity and time, it is now possible to calculate the vertical distance (above release) to the high point.

$$D_v = V_v \times t + \frac{1}{2}\ gt^2$$
$$D_v = [22.5'/sec \times .703\ sec] + [-16'/sec^2\ (.703\ sec)^2]$$
$$D_v = 15.8' - 7.9' = 7.9'$$

Since the shot was released 7 feet above the ground and the high point is 7.9 feet above the point of release, the total vertical distance of the high point above the ground is 14.9 feet (Fig. 9–5B).

3. **Total Time of Flight.** The total time of flight is the time to the high point plus the time from the high point to the ground. Since gravity acts only on the vertical velocity and the shot is at zero velocity when it begins its descent from the high point, the formula for a freely falling object (Equation 3.2) can be used.

$$D_v = \frac{1}{2}gt^2 \quad (D_v = distance\ high\ point\ to\ ground)$$

$$14.9\ ft = 16\ ft/sec^2 \times t^2$$

$$t^2 = \frac{14.9'}{16'/sec^2}$$

$$t^2 = .931\ sec$$

$$t = .965\ sec$$

The total time (T) can now be found:

$$T = (t\ to\ high\ point) + (t\ high\ point\ to\ ground)$$

$$T = .703\ sec + .965\ sec = 1.668\ sec$$

4. **Horizontal Distance.** The horizontal distance can now be calculated by using the horizontal component of the projecting velocity and the total time of flight, **assuming that air resistance is negligible** so that the velocity remains constant throughout the flight.

$$D_h = V_h t + \tfrac{1}{2} at^2 \qquad (\tfrac{1}{2} at^2 = 0; t = T) \qquad\qquad (9.2)$$

$$D_h = V_h T$$

$$D_h = 26.8'/\text{sec} \times 1.668 \text{ sec} = 44.7'$$

Since the distance that a projectile travels is dependent upon **height of release, projecting velocity** and **angle of projection,** it is possible to determine the horizontal distances that will result from various combinations of these three factors. The results of such an approach are reported by Miller and Nelson (Table 9–2).

Careful scrutiny of the tabulated data indicates that the optimum angle increases as the velocity increases for all three release heights. However, as the release height increases the optimal angle decreases for all velocities. Miller and Nelson point out that of the three factors, velocity is the most important and this aspect of the performance should be emphasized even if the optimum height of release and angle of projection are not obtained.

Since in most throwing activities the ball is released some feet above the ground, when distance is the objective, it is better to err by throwing at an angle less than optimum than at an equal angle higher than optimum (for example, ±15°). While equal angles above and below optimum result in the same loss of horizontal distance **at the point horizontally out from the point of release,** the ball projected at the higher angle drops more vertically and thus by the time the ground is reached it has travelled less distance horizontally (Fig. 9–6). If the ball is caught at approximately the same height that it

TABLE 9–2. SHOTPUT DISTANCE AS A FUNCTION OF THE CONDITIONS AT TAKEOFF*

RESULTANT RELEASE VELOCITY (ft/sec)	HEIGHT OF RELEASE					
	Six ft		Seven ft		Eight ft	
	Optimum Angle (°)	Distance (ft)	Optimum Angle (°)	Distance (ft)	Optimum Angle (°)	Distance (ft)
26	38–39	26.32	37–38	27.10	37	27.87
28	39	29.75	38–39	30.55	38	31.34
30	40	33.42	39	34.24	39	35.05
32	40–41	37.32	40	38.16	39	38.99
34	41	41.47	40–41	42.32	39–40	43.16
36	41	45.86	41	46.73	40	47.58
38	42	50.49	41	51.37	40–41	52.23
40	42	55.36	41–42	56.25	41	57.13
42	42	60.48	42	61.38	41	62.27
44	42	65.85	42	66.76	42	67.65
46	43	71.46	42	72.37	42	73.28

*Table from Miller and Nelson.[2]

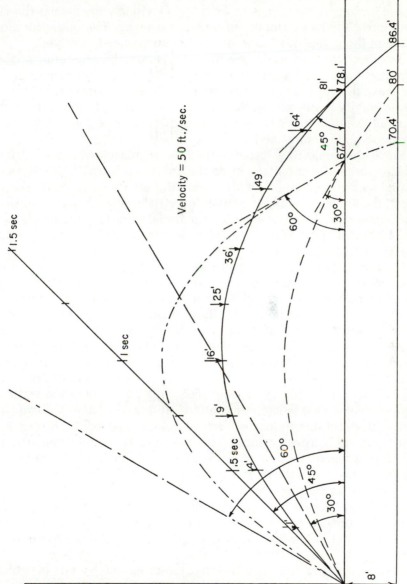

Figure 9–6. Paths of objects projected at various angles (air resistance not considered).

was projected, there is no distance advantage for a ball projected at an angle 15 degrees below optimal as opposed to one 15 degrees above; however, time is gained. A low angle means that the ball will not travel as high and thus the time in the air will be less.

To gain maximum distance is not always the purpose of projection. Frequently speed is the essential factor and if an object is to reach its destination as fast as possible, the angle of projection should be as small as possible to carry it the necessary distance. Obviously the greater the velocity, the lower the angle can be for a given distance. **The optimum angle of projection then, depends upon the particular purpose involved.**

An object approaches the ground at approximately the same angle as it was projected. If projected from the ground the angles are equal. If projected from **above** the ground they are equal **at the line of projection extended,** but because gravity is still acting, the path from this point to the ground is not a completely straight line but curved somewhat downward and the angle with the ground is, therefore, slightly larger.

Since the projecting force applied to an object which is thrown or struck, is in the direction tangent to the arc through which the throwing or striking segment (or implement) is moving at the moment of release or impact, the arc and the point on that arc at which the object is released or struck, determine the angle at which the initial force is applied. Methods for controlling this angle are discussed in the chapters dealing with throwing and striking (Chapters 18 and 19).

On the basis of the previous discussion and examples, a number of characteristics of projectile motion can be identified. When air resistance is negligible the horizontal velocity remains constant while the vertical velocity begins with an initial positive value and decreases to zero during flight to the high point. From that point, the vertical velocity increases until it reaches the same vertical velocity it possessed at release; this occurs at the same height as the release point. However, the vertical velocity during descent is considered to be negative because of the downward direction of motion. The actual velocity of the projectile (vector sum of the vertical and horizontal velocities) is maximum at release and diminishes during ascent to the high point due to loss in vertical velocity. At the highest point, the instant that the vertical velocity reaches zero, the actual velocity is at a minimum; it equals the horizontal velocity only. The actual velocity then increases so that when the release height is reached (air resistance negligible) it is the same as the projecting velocity.

As a consequence of the changing vertical component of the velocity, the object follows a curved flight path denoted as a **parabola.** Under the assumption that air resistance is negligible all projected objects follow a parabolic path.

There are many activities (diving, jumping, and so on) in which the human body becomes a projectile and these fundamentals also apply to the human body in flight. As for any projectile, the path of the body through the air is determined at takeoff, by the height, angle and velocity of the takeoff. However, **the parabolic path is followed by the center of gravity of the total body,** not of each segment. Even though a person swings his arms and kicks his legs during flight, the **path of the center of gravity** is not altered; but the center of gravity does not necessarily remain at the same point in the body during flight. Various movements of body segments while in the air can change the relationship of the various segments about the center of gravity and alter the point where the center of gravity of the body is located, but the **path of the center of gravity cannot be altered.** LaDue and Norman explain this principle by stating "If the performer is in the air, free of support, no movement will raise or lower his center of gravity, but it may raise or lower his body around the center of gravity."[3] In other words, the height of the center of gravity **in relation to the projecting surface** cannot be changed once the individual is in the air but the position of the center of gravity within the body is changed by any motion of body segments.

As an example during a dance leap or spread-eagle jump by a cheerleader, the performer appears to "hang in air". However, the center of gravity stops only for an instant at the height of the ascent and immediately begins to fall. Is this apparent "hanging" an illusion? The answer is no! It is not an illusion. As the cheerleader approaches the high point of the jump she/he spreads the legs (abducts both hip joints). This movement tends to raise the center of gravity within the body and is executed precisely as the velocity of the center of gravity is decreasing to zero. Actually the final portion of the vertical rise of the center of gravity occurs within the body and, therefore, the trunk and head reach a certain level above the ground and remain there for a brief period as the final vertical motion of the center of gravity is completed. The performer then brings the legs together, which reverses the process so that the early part of descent of the center of gravity occurs within the body, due to the movement of the legs; this provides a second brief period when the trunk and head remain still. The combination of the spreading of the legs as the high point is reached and bringing them together at the start of descent provides a brief period of time during which the trunk and head in fact remain stationary in the air. This example points out the fact that a portion of the body such as the trunk, head and arms does not necessarily move in exact synchrony with the center of gravity of the body.

AIR RESISTANCE CONSIDERED

Up to this point in the discussion the influence of air resistance has been ignored. In many activities it is not of great importance because the object is a ball and it does not move at a great speed. However, air resistance can be a considerable factor depending on the physical characteristics of the object (its weight, size and shape), the speed with which it is moving, and any motions of the object in a direction other than the direction of flight (spin). The lighter the object and the larger its surface area, the more it is affected by air resistance; thus a shuttlecock is affected more than a tennis ball. Since air resistance increases rapidly as speed increases,[4] it is a considerable factor in the flight of high speed projectiles. While a ball may be thrown for distance most effectively at an angle of approximately 45 degrees, a golf ball, because of its great speed, must be projected at a much lower angle. The horizontal component must be enlarged to offset the tremendous air pressure built up.

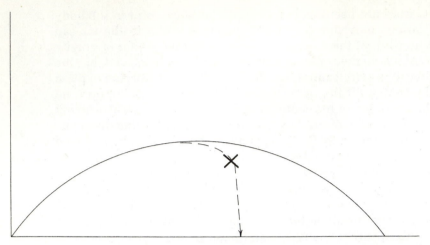

Figure 9–7.   Path of a high velocity badminton shot compared to a parabolic path.

When a football spins end-over-end, or an arrow or javelin quivers the air resistance is increased by the additional motion and greater surface area, and the flight is retarded more than would be the case if these movements were not present.

The horizontal velocity of a projectile is decelerated throughout its flight by air resistance. Because of this a projectile does not follow the true parabolic path diagrammed (Fig. 9–6). The greater the air resistance the more the flight departs from that of a true parabola. The path of a shuttlecock hit by a forceful blow departs markedly from the parabolic path. Because of its light weight, shape and speed, air resistance builds up to the extent that the horizontal force is overcome long before gravity has pulled the shuttle to the ground. When the horizontal force has been dissipated by air resistance the only force left to act is the force of gravity and the shuttle falls straight down from that point (Fig. 9–7).

SUMMARY

There are three forces that act on any object projected through the air; gravity, air resistance, and the initial force which put it in motion. Therefore, a projectile carries out two independent motions, a horizontal motion which is gradually decreased by air resistance and a vertical motion which gravity decelerates as the object climbs and accelerates as it drops from the high point.

The distance that a projectile travels depends upon the height of its release, its initial speed and the angle at which it is projected. When air resistance is not a factor, **theoretically** the optimum angle of projection for maximum distance is 45 degrees. As air resistance becomes a greater factor the angle is lowered to increase the horizontal component of the projecting force. If the purpose of projection is speed rather than distance, the angle should be as low as possible to carry the required distance. The greater the speed of projection the lower the angle can be for a given distance.

The lighter the object, the larger its surface area, the greater its speed and the more it is moving in any direction other than the direction of flight (spin), the greater the air resistance.

If air resistance were neglected, a projectile would follow a parabolic path. If projected from the ground the projectile would land at the same angle and the same speed as that at which it was projected. The greater the air resistance the more the path of flight departs from the path of a true parabola. When the human body becomes a projectile, the center of gravity of the body follows a parabolic path.

REFERENCES

1. Beiser, Arthur: *The Mainstream of Physics.* Reading, Massachusetts, Addison-Wesley Publishing Company, Inc., 1962, p. 50.
2. Miller, D., and Nelson, R.: *Biomechanics of Sport.* Philadelphia, Lea and Febiger, 1973, p. 80.
3. LaDue, Frank, and Norman, Jim: *This is Trampolining.* Cedar Rapids, Iowa, Torch Press, 1956, p. 69.
4. Rasch, Philip J., and Burke, Roger K.: *Kinesiology and Applied Anatomy.* Philadelphia, Lea and Febiger, 1959, p. 123.

ADDITIONAL READINGS

Beer, F., and Johnson, R.: *Vector Mechanics for Engineers.* 2nd ed. New York, McGraw-Hill Book Company, 1972.
Hay, James: *The Biomechanics of Sports Techniques.* Englewood Cliffs, New Jersey, Prentice-Hall, Inc., 1973.
Krause, J., and Barham, J.: *The Mechanical Foundations of Human Motion.* St. Louis, C. V. Mosby, 1975.

PART 3

APPLICATION OF THE BASIC MECHANICAL PRINCIPLES TO FUNDAMENTAL PHYSICAL SKILLS

STANDING AND LYING

10

When lying on the back or abdomen, the body's base is as large and its center of gravity as low as possible; thus balance is no problem and the muscles can relax. A side-lying position reduces the size of the forward-backward base and introduces the problem of balance. However the base is enlarged easily by placement of a bent knee, an arm or both, forward of the body. Nevertheless, the particular position assumed when lying is important to comfort and, over a period of time, to body configuration. Because the principles of effective body alignment are understood more easily when discussed in reference to the upright position, standing is considered first.

STANDING

Since everyone learns to stand as an infant, many individuals have assumed that there is no necessity for studying this skill. It has also been argued that no one stands still for any length of time, that dynamic, not static, posture is of importance.

It is certainly true that individuals move more than they stand still. Hellebrandt concluded that even standing is not static but rather that it is "movement upon a stationary base."[1] She found that individuals are constantly swaying and thus the center of gravity is constantly moving. This involuntary swaying was found to be important in that it aided the return of venous blood and assured adequate circulation in the brain.[2] Experimentation indicated that this sway was so accurately balanced that the average center of gravity always fell close to the geometric center of the base.[3]

The stretch (myotatic) reflex apparently is responsible for the balanced control which keeps the center of gravity within the limits of the base of support of the body,[4] and plays an important role in the maintenance of the upright position. When the extensor muscles, those which resist the tendency for the pull of gravity to flex the joints of the legs, trunk and neck, are stretched they are reflexly stimulated to increase tonus and thus hold the joints in extension. In the lower extremity this reflex is also elicited by pressure against the sole of the foot. The tonic neck and labyrinthine reflexes also aid in maintaining the upright position in that they cause reactions of the body in response to positions of the head.

However, these reflexes operate regardless of the particular upright position assumed by the individual. Since the body is made up of many segments joined together at the joints by muscles and ligaments, there are a great many positions that it can assume. Also, there are many variations in body build which influence position and these individual differences must be considered. As the child grows he or she develops a habit of aligning the body segments in a certain way. While it is true that he does not maintain any one position for an appreciable period of time, a characteristic pattern is observable. The habitual position is usually influenced to a great degree by the models observed most frequently as he is growing up and the importance that he attaches to those models. Observation of any typical college group indicates that the majority of students have not been fortunate in the models most readily available to them. It is only necessary to open a fashion magazine to understand one reason for many of the inefficient and aesthetically displeasing postures of young girls. Unfortunately, good models have not always been offered during instruction dealing with movement. Too frequently the parent or teacher has been a model of inefficient and uninspiring habitual posture.

While it is certainly necessary that an individual possess a certain level of strength, flexibility, kinesthetic perception, and kinesthetic memory to be able, at will, to assume and maintain a well-balanced position, these factors are not the primary causes of the poor positions of the majority of individuals. There will be some whose muscular strength or flexibility, due to such factors as physical handicap, illness, injury, and long-term extreme positions at a joint, has fallen below the minimal level. However, for the great majority, the most important factors are an understanding of an efficient position,[5] the kinesthetic perception of it, and last, but by no means least, a sincere desire to re-educate the muscular and nervous systems so that this position is assumed habitually. The understanding and kinesthetic perception can be learned in a relatively short time. Besides helping the individual to solve these problems the parent or teacher must also provide an inspiring model. However, habits are formed only with constant repetition over a long period of time and only through patient and persistent application will the gaining of the knowledge of the mechanics of standing become a valuable tool for improving position; the individual must be motivated to really **want** to develop a new habitual pattern.

Values of a Well-Aligned Position

Most people, men and women alike, are interested in the way they look and the impression they make on others. The knowledge that one looks well adds materially to a positive self-concept and thus to self-confidence. Normally, the first impression of an individual is visual and, therefore, body alignment is an important factor in the impression one individual makes on another. A drooping posture is associated by the observer with an unenthusiastic and listless personality and could be a negative factor in a job interview or other important encounter. Also, clothes are made for a balanced figure and do not hang evenly on a body which slouches.

Reason indicates that a well-aligned position should require less energy than a poorly balanced one. Electromyographic records of the muscle function of a young adult female[6] showed less activity in thigh and lower leg muscles when standing in a well-balanced position than when standing with the pelvis tilted either forward or backward. On the other hand, Tepper, Hellebrandt and Brogdon[1, 7] found that the **metabolic cost** of standing was slight, although there was considerable variation among individuals. A study by McCormick[8] has borne this out and has indicated that the metabolic cost of the well-aligned position was somewhat greater than that of the position known as the typical "fatigue posture" — a position with hips forward, upper back rounded, trunk inclined backward, and head forward. In this position all segments have been allowed to sag to the point where bone and ligament structure prohibit further movement. It is the position which, in the minds of most people, has become associated with fatigue.

In this position gravity exerts considerable rotating force on each of the weight bearing joints. Wells has characterized this position as one of "hanging on the ligaments."[9] With the ligaments and muscles considerably stretched, a great deal of adjustment is necessary before the body is in a position to move efficiently. While it is probable that this position requires no more energy than a well-aligned position, it is one which can cause pain due to stress (stretch and pressure), and it is **not** a position from which one is able to move with dispatch. Some of the joints, for example the knees, are in a position which leaves no margin of safety, since they are at the extreme position possible in one direction. Also the depression of the body segments seems to be reflected in the lack of alertness of the mind. One neither gives the impression of being alert and animated, "ready to go," nor does one feel this way. Further research dealing with the metabolic cost of various standing positions for individuals for whom a well-aligned position is habitual and for those for whom it is not, as well as study of the industrial output and energy requirement of individuals with various habitual postures, would prove interesting.

Although the metabolic cost of standing has been found to be slight,[1, 7, 8] the effect of various positions on the efficiency of movement and the psychological and aesthetic values are important considerations. In addition, the fact that faulty body mechanics (in standing or lying) can cause painful conditions "has become a well-established concept in the field of orthopedic surgery, and is one of the basic concepts in the field of physical medicine."[10] Pain is caused by pressure from some firm structure (bone, cartilage, taut muscle, and so forth) on any part of a nerve or by tension (stretch or strain) of a structure (muscle, tendon, ligament) which contains nerve endings.[11] Basic to an understanding of pain caused by faulty positions is "the concept that the accumulative effects of constant or repeated small stresses over a long period of time can give rise to the same difficulties as a sudden severe stress."[10] Wells[9] stated that the skeletal structure should be architecturally and mechanically sound so there is a minimum of strain on the weight bearing joints. These joints must be so aligned that friction is minimized, tension of opposing ligaments balanced, and pressures within the joint equalized.

Study is needed to determine the psychological implications of position and movement. It is certainly obvious that position is expressive of mental attitude. One question that needs to be investigated is the extent to which body concept and self-image are influenced by changes in patterns of position and movement.

Basic Principles of an Efficient Standing Position

Although individuals move much more than they stand, many of the basic principles that apply to the great variety of positions necessitated by voluntary movement can be more readily explained in a discussion of static posture.

Since an efficient position for any task is one which makes the best adaptation of the particular body structure to the mechanical problems involved in the task, the "correct" position varies to some extent depending upon body structure. However, despite differences in body structure there are certain principles which all individuals can apply, but application of these principles cannot be expected to produce individuals whose positions look the same.

Since the body is made up of segments, assuming an upright position can be likened to building a man of blocks (Fig. 10–1). So long as the blocks are centered one above the other the man of blocks will stand. However, if one block is moved so that its center of gravity is not over the block below, the man of blocks will fall. The human body does not fall apart as do the blocks because its various segments are held together by muscles and ligaments. However, when a body segment is out of line with the segment(s) below, gravity tends to pull the entire segment downward, the bones of the joint are out of line, pressure is exerted unevenly, and the tension of opposing ligaments is unbalanced. Since the more nearly the center of gravity of an object is centered over its base the more stable the object, total body balance is maintained with a minimum of strain when each segment is centered over the one below.

Good posture might be defined as that position in which the center of gravity of each body segment is centered over its supporting base (the segment immediately below). In this position the force of gravity is used to advantage as much as possible in keeping the alignment in the weight

Figure 10–1. Man of blocks.

bearing joints. The line of gravity of each segment is an extension of the line of gravity of the segments above and below; thus gravity actually helps to maintain the position of various segments, since it pulls each downward evenly onto the one below. The more nearly vertical the long axis of every segment, the greater the stabilizing effect of gravity. Whenever one body segment moves out of line, the center of gravity of the total body shifts in the direction of movement of that segment and another segment must be displaced in the opposite direction to bring the center of gravity of the total body back over the base, or the base must move. The greater the angle of inclination of the total body or any segment of the body from the vertical, the greater the muscular effort necessary to hold it.

When standing, balance must be maintained in both the anteroposterior (forward-backward) plane and the lateral (sideways) plane. When the segments are aligned one above the other, a line, as seen from the side, passes from the mastoid bone (just behind the tip of the ear) through the tip of the shoulder, the middle of the hip,* the front of the knee, and falls in front of the ankle over the center of the feet (Fig. 10–2A). Brunnstrom[13] stated that the line of gravity falls through the center of the base, and Hellebrandt[14] placed it at an average of five centimeters in front of the ankle in young women. Thus the body can sway forward and backward without the line of gravity falling beyond the heels or the toes. Since the body weight falls forward of the center of the knee and in front of the ankle, gravity is always exerting some forward rotating force (torque) on the body as a whole. Joseph stated that "there is general agreement that the extent of swaying is such that the line of weight almost always remains in front of the ankle joints. . ."[15] However, if the line of gravity fell **through** the ankle joints removing this torque, "the margin of posterior stability would be the short horizontal distance between the ankles and the points of heel contact with the ground."[16] Falling as it does over the center of the foot (from heel to toes), the distance from the line of gravity to the posterior edge of the base of support is increased.

Morton stated that since the direction of structual unbalance which results is forward, the muscular strain needed to maintain the erect posture is imposed entirely on the large and powerful calf muscles, while the weaker anterior group is released from any counter-balancing tension. He also pointed out that this anteriorly unbalanced position "comprises a highly important phase in the initiation of forward movement of the body."[17]

In the lateral plane the line for a well-balanced position falls from the center of the head through the spinal column, the center of the hips and falls over the center of the base (from side to side). This gives a margin of safety in balance as the body sways sideways.

Position of Feet.   This position of the body is most easily maintained if the feet are a few inches apart as they are when the legs are vertical (straight down from the hips). This gives as large a base as possible without introducing a diagonal force against the ground. When the feet are together the base

---

*The line of gravity actually passes somewhat posterior to the hip **joint.**[12] However, this would put it approximately through the center of the mass of the hip as one views it from the side.

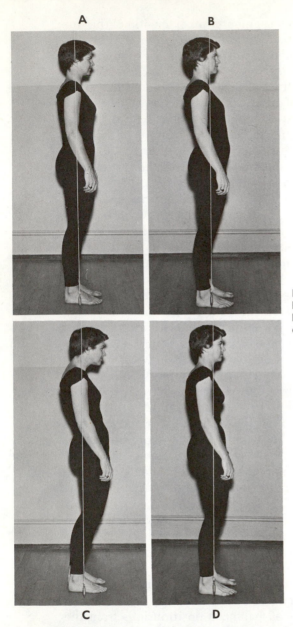

Figure 10–2. A, Well balanced position. B, Hips forward, shoulders back—strains lower back. C,D, Zigzag positions that lead to strain on all joints.

is smaller and the force is exerted down and slightly inward. When they are farther apart than the width of the hips the force is exerted diagonally outward (Fig. 10–3). If the toes are straight ahead the weight falls on the heels, the outer borders of the feet, and the metatarsal bones. If the toes are turned outward the weight of the body falls on the inner borders of the feet — on the arches (Fig. 10–4). This can be readily demonstrated by standing with the feet turned outward and consciously relaxing the muscles of the ankles and feet. The rolling inward of the ankles is immediately apparent.

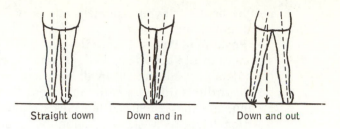

Figure 10–3. Direction of forces exerted against floor by individuals with feet in various positions.

Straight down   Down and in   Down and out

Since the outer border of the foot is flat and the inner border forms an arch, their functions differ. The flat outer border is well-designed to support weight, while the arch is extremely important in the absorption of force and thus the reduction of the jar to the body at every step. If, all the time that an individual stands, the weight of the body falls diagonally across this arch, as it does when the toes are turned outward, the bones are pushed together, nerves may be pinched, and eventually the arch may be flattened and its function lost. The position of the toes ahead is also important in that it places the feet in a position from which they can exert force directly backward when forward movement is desired. This is discussed in Chapter 11, Walking.

Position of Knees.   When the knees are hyperextended (pushed backward as far as possible) the bones of the knee joint are forced together. Should any backward force be exerted against them there would be no margin of safety. They would be forced beyond their normal limit and injury would be likely. This position of the knees tends to cause the pelvis to be tilted forward and the tension of the position is likely to be reflected in general tension throughout the body. If the knees are bent the bones of the thigh and the lower leg are placed in a diagonal relationship to each other and the force of gravity acts to pull them closer together and the body closer to the ground. Since in this position the long axes of the leg bones have departed from the vertical relationship it takes more muscular force to hold the position. The most efficient and safest position of the knees, then, is

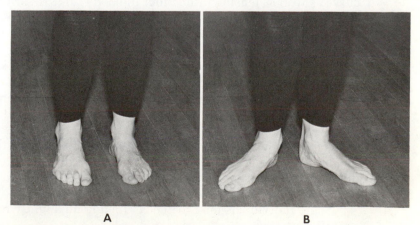

A   B

Figure 10–4.   A, Weight on outer border of feet. B, Weight on weak arch.

neither bent nor hyperextended but "easy," leaving some margin for back-ward movement.

Position of Pelvis.   Since the pelvis is the link between the entire upper structure of the body and the legs, any shifting of its position necessitates considerable readjustment in all body segments above and below. When the pelvic girdle is tilted forward* the knees are hyperextended, the lower back arched, and the abdominal muscles stretched. Habitual assumption of this position leads to weakened abdominal muscles as well as to lower back strain. The other extreme the pelvis tilted backward with the hips tucked under, results in the lower back being flattened and the knees somewhat bent. Both positions make it extremely difficult to maintain a good position of the upper trunk. Neither extreme is desirable. Only with the pelvic girdle held in a balanced position between the two extremes can the other body segments be balanced one above the other. Many individuals stand with the pelvis tipped forward and the well-balanced position may be more easily understood by them if described by the phrase "pelvis tucked **very slightly** under." Because it does link the supporting segments of the body (the legs) to the body above (the trunk, neck, and head), control of this segment of the body is an extremely important factor in the assumption and maintenance of a well-aligned position. Ability to control the pelvic girdle at will has been found to be a considerable factor in the ability to improve body align-ment.[5]

Position of Shoulder Girdle.   The shoulder girdle should be balanced above the hips with the two shoulders level and pointing directly out to the sides. If the left shoulder is carried higher than the right, the thoracic (upper) spine is curved to the left. This causes the vertebrae to be tilted and uneven pressures in the joints result. The muscles on the left side of the spine are stretched while those on the right are shortened. In the level position the pull on the two sides of the spine is equalized and the spine remains in its normal straight position. If the tips of the shoulders are carried forward the rib cage is depressed, the upper back rounded, the muscles and ligaments across the back of the shoulder girdle stretched, and the anterior muscles shortened. Throwing the shoulders backward results in a flattening of the normal thoracic (upper back) curve, an increase in the lumbar (lower back) curve as well as tension throughout the body (Fig. 10–2B). When the tips of the shoulders point straight to each side the weight of the arms is balanced, neither pulling forward nor backward on the shoulder girdle. When the shoulders are "hunched" muscles are tense and energy is wasted. The muscles soon become fatigued and strain results. The shoulders should be relaxed, not pulled upward, forward or backward.

Position of Head.   Since the head is heavy and is attached to the rest of the body by a relatively small flexible segment (the neck) it is important that it be well-balanced above the shoulders. When the chin is dropped the line of vision is downward instead of forward and, as when the chin is thrust forward, the head is overbalanced forward causing strain on the muscles of the back of the neck and shoulders. The chin should, therefore, be carried level and drawn back as far as possible without tension.

Some individuals tend to "cock" (bend and slightly rotate) the head to

---

*When the pelvis tilts **forward,** the iliac crest moves forward and·slightly downward.

one side. This not only causes tension in the shoulder and neck muscles, but also presents a vision problem since it places the eyes at different heights. This position is normally caused by a habitual sitting (to work) posture and is discussed in Chapter 15, Sitting.

Suggestions for Gaining a Concept of an Efficient Standing Position

A kinesthetic awareness of this position can be gained by experimentation with the various positions possible for each segment. If extreme positions are assumed, the effects on other segments of the body noted, and **conscious attention directed** to the feeling of strain in various areas, the contrast of the feeling accompanying the intermediate, well-balanced position is obvious.

Starting with experimentation with the feet together, then wide apart, a few inches apart, with the toes in, then out, and then straight ahead, accompanied by consideration of the effect of each position, a well-aligned position of the body can be built upward just as a man of blocks is built (Fig. 10–1).

Pushing the knees backward as far as possible (hyperextending) and then flexing them illustrates quickly the interaction of knees and pelvic girdle and the resulting effects on the whole body. Standing even for a minute with the knees bent is usually long enough to demonstrate the strain on the leg muscles caused by a flexed knee position.

In experimenting with the extreme positions of the pelvic girdle, placing one hand on the lower back and attempting to hollow the back as much as possible may aid in giving the feeling for tilting the pelvis forward. If one hand is then moved down onto the hips and the other hand is placed on the abdomen, a feeling for pulling up with the abdominal muscles and down with the hip muscles that results in the backward tilting of the pelvis can be experienced. Following the perception of these two positions, an intermediate (balanced) position of the pelvis can be ascertained more readily.

As each extreme position is assumed the effects upon other parts of the body can be consciously observed. An individual experiencing difficulty in tilting the pelvis forward and backward in the upright position may be able to arch and then flatten the lower back while lying on the floor and then, having experienced the motion, be able to carry it over to the standing position. Sometimes it is necessary to feel this movement in another person by placing one hand on the abdomen and the other on the hips of an individual who can move his pelvis from one extreme position to the other and then back to the intermediate position. Since the ability to control the pelvic girdle is so important in assuming and maintaining a well-aligned position, it is worthwhile to take time to gain this control.

Observation has indicated that many girls and young women and some young men stand with their hips forward and shoulders back of the line of gravity of the body (Fig. 10–2B). This position causes strain particularly in the region of the lower back. A **slight** straight backward adjustment of the pelvic region and forward adjustment of the shoulder region straightens the body line so that the shoulders are directly over the hips and the strain on muscles, ligaments, and joints is reduced. Since the adjustment required by most individuals is slight it is sometimes difficult to feel (kinesthetically). Exaggerating the pelvis-forward-shoulders-back position and then moving the pelvis backward as the upper trunk and shoulder region move forward may help in gaining a concept of the straight body line. Sometimes this adjustment can be perceived more easily if one hand is placed on the abdomen and the other on the back as near the shoulder blades as possible and the lower hand is pushed somewhat backward while the upper hand is brought forward.

A full-length mirror in which the individual can see himself in profile is an aid in developing the new concept. An individual who has stood habitually in the position with the shoulders back of the hips feels as if he is overbalanced forward when his body is aligned with the shoulders directly above the hips. This is undoubtedly due to the important function of the inner ear in balance. Standing habitually in a position which keeps the head back, the individual develops the concept of balance with the head back. When the upper trunk, and with it the head, is moved forward a **readjustment of concept is necessary.** This does not happen immediately and it is important that the individual realize that, for a time, because of the shift of the head position, there will be a feeling of being slightly overbalanced forward even when actually standing in a well-balanced position.

Experimentation with the shoulder region should include tilting the shoulder girdle to the left and to the right, pulling the shoulder tips forward and backward as far as possible, and hunching and relaxing the shoulders. To experience the extreme forward and backward positions of the tips of the shoulders, the tips are rolled forward as far as possible and then, by drawing the inner borders of the shoulder blades toward each other, they are pulled back as far as possible. In this way a feeling for control of the shoulders without reactions in other parts of the body can be gained. The shoulders can then be adjusted so that they point directly to each side. A feeling for relaxed shoulders can probably be gained most rapidly by hunching them upward as far as possible and then allowing them to drop. A circular motion of the shoulder may also be useful in relaxing these muscles.

The difference between moving the chin up and down and forward and backward needs to be consciously experienced. The up-and-down motion is familiar and easy. If, following this movement, the chin, while being held **level,** is thrust forward as far as possible, and then, using the muscles at the back of the neck, it is drawn straight backward as far as possible, when the tension is released the head will be left in a well-balanced position.

Effect of an Incline on Standing Position

When the surface on which an individual is standing is angled, the line of gravity is no longer perpendicular to the surface; it is thrown forward in relation to the individual's base (his feet) when the angle is downward, and backward in relation to his base when the slope is upward (Fig. 10–5). If the adjustment to bring the center of gravity back over the base is made by

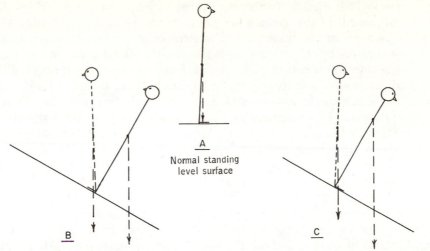

Normal standing
level surface

<u>A</u>

<u>B</u>

Adjustment of center of gravity necessitated
by upward incline

<u>C</u>

Adjustment of center of gravity necessitated
by downward incline

Figure 10–5. Adjustment of center of gravity necessitated by changes in angle of supporting surface.

increasing the angle of the ankle joint when on a downward slope and by decreasing this angle when on an upward slope, the body alignment can be maintained (Fig. 10–6).

Effect of Heels on Standing Position

Since heels on shoes elevate the heel of the foot, the body is thrown forward just as it is when standing on a downhill slope. In order to keep the center of gravity of the body over the feet the body must be adjusted

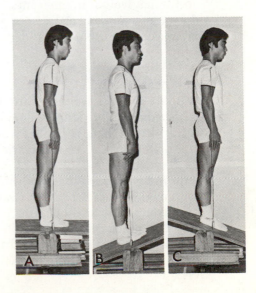

Figure 10–6. Adjustment at ankles to change in slope of supporting surface; original alignment of body segments maintained.

backward. Again, if this adjustment is made from the ankles, the relative alignment of the various segments of the body is not disturbed. The only change is at the ankle joint where the angle between the leg and the foot is increased; the higher the heels the greater the adjustment required. Extreme heels in combination with inflexible ankles can make it impossible to adjust the center of gravity efficiently. If much of the backward adjustment of the body is made from the waist, as is frequently the case, the alignment of the entire body is disturbed and many joints are put into a position of strain. Strain is felt particularly in the lower back region. The position of the foot in shoes with high heels causes the calf muscles to be shortened and the anterior muscles to be stretched. Constant wearing of high heels can result in inability to place the heel of the foot on the ground.

As a result of electromyographic studies of standing, Joseph[18] reported that wearing high heels appears to result in increased activity in the muscles of the leg and hip, and that instability was indicated by relatively large bursts of activity in both the anterior and posterior muscle groups.

Kendall[19] stated that, because of the forward shift of the weight, the proportion of the weight borne on the balls of the feet increases directly with the height of the heels and therefore, continuous wearing of high heels results in anterior foot strain. In addition, high heels tend to cause the feet to slip forward into the toes of the shoes and when this happens the toes, being wedged into too small a space, are subjected to considerable deforming pressure.

Effect of Pregnancy on Standing Position

In pregnancy the center of gravity of the body is displaced forward and again a backward adjustment of the body is necessary in order to maintain balance. Because of the added weight within the abdomen it is even more important that the adjustment be made from the ankles than in the case of high heels mentioned above. It is simply a matter of counterbalancing the additional weight in the front of the body with the **body weight as a unit.** If the adjustment is made from the waist the strain on the lower back is increased because of the added weight and lower back pain is likely to result.

When a pregnant woman wears high heels she compounds her problem. The heels throw her center of gravity **forward in relation to her base of support** and the weight of the fetus moves her center of gravity **forward within her body.** Thus a **double backward adjustment** is required. This results in loss of ankle action when walking since the ankles must be almost completely extended (plantar flexed) to adjust the body as a whole in order to keep the center of gravity centered above the feet. If the adjustment required is so great that the center of gravity cannot be kept above the base with ankle adjustment, back strain will result unless the problem is reduced by lowering the heel height.

The added weight being off-center forward also tends to tilt the pelvis forward, increasing the lower back curve and causing back strain. Contraction of abdominal, hip and trunk muscles is required to stabilize the pelvis.

Effect of the Height of Household Work Surfaces on Standing Position

Since the height of a kitchen sink, counter or workbench affects the standing position, it is an important factor in the fatigue experienced by men or women who spend considerable time during a day at a workbench, sink or counter. A sink should be of such a height that the individual who will be using it can, when standing in a well-balanced position, place the hands flat on the bottom. If it is lower, the trunk must be bend forward all the time the individual is working at the sink. Thus the lower back muscles are called on constantly to support the weight of the trunk against gravity's pull. In order to avoid this same waste of energy while working at a counter, the counter or work bench should be a few inches (approximately 5 inches) below elbow height. A small space which allows the toes to project under cabinets below a counter makes it possible to stand close to the task and thus maintain the normal, well-balanced position while working.

It is wise to use an adjustable ironing board so that it can be set at a height that makes possible a well-balanced standing position with the elbow bent sufficiently to allow free hand movement while applying downward force. Since the height of an iron (plus its handle), sander, drill, etc. raises the hand above the ironing board or workbench by some 4 to 5 inches, the ironing board or workbench needs to be somewhat lower than a counter. However, since a downward force is needed, it should be only 2 to 3 inches lower.

LYING

Even while lying down all segments of the body are being pulled downward by gravity; and when lying in a position that leaves any section unsupported it is possible to have discomfort in a relatively short time if a joint or body segment is sensitive. When ill or injured and as one gets older, this becomes an increasing problem. Discomfort can be avoided by assuring that normal body alignment (as when standing) of the various segments is maintained regardless of whether lying on the back, face or side. Some areas may need support; the areas requiring support and the amount of support required vary with body build. In any position the spine should be straight (right to left) with the shoulders and hips at right angles to it; the normal anteroposterior curves of the spine should be maintained. Where small bony prominences that concentrate force on small areas and allow for no "give" (see pp. 109–110) must support the weight of various segments, pressure can be relieved by padding which spreads the force and supplies softer surfaces.

Lying Supine (on back). Because gravity tends to pull the knee joints into hyperextension, pressure may be felt in these joints when an individual lies on the back for any period of time. Also, the weight of the legs pulling on the pelvic girdle tends to tilt it forward; the posterior edge is pulled up and forward and the pull is transferred to the lower back, resulting in backache if the individual has a back problem. There are now several adjustable beds available so it is possible to gain the same comfort afforded by a hospital bed on which the area beneath the knees can be raised. In the absence of an adjustable bed, a pillow placed so that the edge is just below the knees flexes the knees slightly and, because it lifts the knee end of the thighs, it tends to tilt the pelvic girdle slightly backward, releasing the pull on the lower back. This is the same effect gained by lifting the knee area of an adjustable bed.

Gravity and the weight of the sheet and blankets act to plantar flex (hyperextend) the feet and **over a long period of time** this position can result in a shortened tendon, making it difficult to lower the heel to the floor when standing. In any case this position can be extremely uncomfortable. The feet of an individual who must remain in bed over a period of time need support that places them in their normal (standing) relationship to the leg (approximately at right angles). This can be accomplished with a board, a box or even a pillow which fills the space between the heels and the end of the bed.

When a pillow is placed under the head, either to support the head **in line with the spine** or to eliminate the feeling that the head is low, an edge should be flattened and put under the shoulders so that the neck and head are angled upward rather than the head pushed forward out of line with the spine. Pillow size depends upon chest depth.

Lying on Side.   Hollows result from the side lying position: under the neck, at the waist and at the ankle. The size of these hollows varies greatly with body build. Placing a pillow under the head and neck can support them in line with the spine; size of the pillow depends on shoulder width. Padding the waist hollow prevents lateral curving of the spine and may be very important to comfort if backache is any problem; this also reduces pressure on the hip. The amount of padding depends upon the width of both shoulders and hips; a pillow, unless unusually small, is likely to be too much since it needs only to be **just enough to keep the spine from sagging.**

Lying on the side is not a stable position because of the small base of support in the forward-backward direction; in addition the weight of the top arm pulls forward-downward on the shoulder and the upper leg pulls in the same direction on the hip. The narrow base causes little problem for the normal healthy individual; an arm(s), leg(s) or both are automatically flexed and placed forward to widen the base. An ill individual may need assistance in flexing the upper leg. Aging individuals and persons who are ill or have a shoulder (or hip) problem may find that the pull of the top arm or leg can cause considerable discomfort in the shoulder or the hip. Using pillows to support the flexed top leg **at the height of the hip** prevents the hip strain caused by the downward pull of the leg; in the same way, strain of the shoulder can be relieved by supporting the flexed top arm with pillows so that it is raised **to the level of the shoulder.**

Lying Prone (on face).   Lying prone forces the feet into hyperextension (plantar flexion) and again, if assumed over a long period of time, can cause problems; even for a short period of time this position of the feet may become quite uncomfortable. Individuals who can move freely can move toward the foot of the bed and allow their feet to dangle over the end of the mattress. The stretch can also be relieved by supporting the ankles with a pillow high enough so that when the feet drop relaxed, the toes just clear the bed; if too high, the resulting knee flexion can cause a problem.

Shoulder tips tend to be pulled downward by gravity and, for some, this may cause discomfort which can be alleviated by placing a rolled pad diagonally under the shoulder from clavicle toward the armpit to bring the shoulder up into line; sometimes this can be accomplished by putting a corner of the pillow under the shoulder tip. A large pillow under the head usually lifts the head so far that it is out of line with the spine and thus causes strain. In a prone position the head must always be rotated to one side or the other and so, if there are any neck problems, lying prone is to be avoided.

CHANGE OF POSITION

Although the positions described are mechanically the most efficient, it must be remembered that whether lying or standing a change of position is always restful, and therefore, when it becomes necessary to stand or to lie in bed for any period of time various positions are, and should be, assumed. The more the segments of the body can be kept in good alignment, the better. However, a poor position if assumed for **a short period of time only,** will not be harmful. For example, the typical position of standing with the weight on one foot and the upper body "hung up" on the supporting hip causes a high hip on the supporting side, a low shoulder on that same side and a curve in the spine to the opposite side (Fig. 10–7). This position causes stress in joints and strain in muscles and ligaments, and if assumed habitually a misshapen body results. However, it rests the muscles of one leg and **if taken for a matter of moments, and both legs are used alternately,** no permanent harm is caused. It is important that these positions that upset the total body alignment be used **for change only** and that the well-aligned position be the basic position of the body not only when standing and lying but during activity as well.

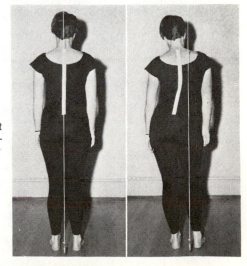

Figure 10–7. A, Well balanced position — straight spine. B, Weight on one foot. "Hung on one hip" — curved spine.

SUMMARY

Without some conscious learning experience a high percentage of individuals do not naturally stand in a well-aligned position. The characteristic posture of an individual is an important factor in the impression he makes on others, in his own feelings of well-being and self-confidence, and in the efficiency of his movements.

Whether lying or standing, in an efficient position the various body segments are aligned so that there is a minimum of friction and uneven pressure in the weight bearing joints and strain on muscles and ligaments, as well as a margin of safety in every joint so that an unexpected force will not push the joint beyond its normal limits and thus cause injury.

When standing this position is most easily maintained if the feet are a few inches apart (not wider than the hips) and the toes straight ahead, the knees "easy," the pelvis in a balanced position, the shoulders directly above the hips with the tips level and pointing directly out to the sides, and the head balanced above the shoulders with the chin level. To allow for normal body sway without loss of balance, the weight should fall near the center of the base, between the feet and in front of the ankles.

When lying, whether on the back, face or side, the spine should be straight (normal anteroposterior curves) and the pelvis and shoulder girdle should be perpendicular to it. In general, the body segments are in the same relative alignment as when standing. Strain which may develop can be relieved by well-placed pillows.

The knowledge of a well-aligned position and the kinesthetic perception of it are only the first steps in acquiring efficient habitual posture. A desire to make this a part of one's being which is strong enough to lead to persistent practice is essential for the formation of the new habit.

A change in the angle of the supporting surface or the addition of a weight to the body necessitates adjustment to keep the line of gravity falling through the center of the base. The more this adjustment is made at the ankle joint so that the body as a whole maintains its well-balanced alignment, the less the strain.

REFERENCES

1. Tepper, Rubye H., and Hellebrandt, Frances A.: The influence of the Upright Posture on Metabolic Rate. *American Journal of Physiology, 122:*563, 1938.
2. Hellebrandt, Frances A., and Brogdon, Elizabeth: The Hydrostatic Effect of Gravity on the Circulation in Supported, Unsupported and Suspended Positions. *American Journal of Physiology, 123:*95–96, 1938.
3. Tepper, Rubye H., and Hellebrandt, Frances A.: *op. cit., 122:*567, 1938.
4. Hellebrandt, Frances A.: Standing, a Geotropic Reflex, The Mechanism of the Asynchronous Rotation of Motor Units. *American Journal of Physiology, 121:*471–474, 1938.
5. Broer, Marion R.: A Study of Factors Influencing the Ability to Improve Antero-Posterior Posture. Unpublished master's thesis, University of Wisconsin, 1936.
6. Broer, Marion R., and Houtz, Sara Jane: *Patterns of Muscular Activity in Selected Sport Skills: An Electromyographic Study.* Springfield, Ill., Charles C Thomas, 1967.
7. Hellebrandt, F. A., Brogdon, Elizabeth and Tepper, Rubye: Posture and Its Cost. *American Journal of Physiology, 129:*773–781, 1940.
8. McCormick, H. G.: *The Metabolic Cost of Maintaining a Standing Position with Special Reference to Body Alignment.* New York, King's Crown Press, 1942.

9. Wells, Katharine F., and Luttgens, Kathryn: *Kinesiology.* 6th ed. Philadelphia, W. B. Saunders Company, 1976, p. 403.
10. Kendall, Henry Otis, Kendall, Florence P., and Boynton, Dorothy A.: *Posture and Pain.* Baltimore, Williams and Wilkins Company, 1952, p. 104.
11. *Ibid.,* p. 105.
12. *Ibid.,* p. 10.
13. Brunnstrom, Signe: Center of Gravity Line in Relation to Ankle Joint in Erect Standing, Application to Posture Training and to Artificial Legs. *Physical Therapy Review, 34:*114, March, 1954.
14. Hellebrandt, Frances A., Tepper, Rubye H., Braun, Genevieve L. and Elliott, Margaret, C.: The Location of the Cardinal Anatomical Orientation Planes Passing through the Center of Gravity of Young Adult Women. *American Journal of Physiology, 121:*468, 1938.
15. Joseph, J.: *Man's Posture, Electromyographic Studies.* Springfield, Ill., Charles C Thomas, 1960, p. 16.
16. Morton, J. Dudley, and Fuller, Dudley Dean: *Human Locomotion and Body Form.* Baltimore, Williams and Wilkins Company, 1952, p. 49.
17. *Ibid.,* p. 50.
18. Joseph, J.: *op. cit.,* pp. 52, 56.
19. Kendall, Henry Otis, Kendall, Florence P., and Boynton, Dorothy A.: *op. cit.,* p. 192.

11

WALKING

In standing the main concern is stability. However, stability does not always contribute to the individual's particular purpose. The act of walking is a matter of disturbing the mechanical equilibrium of the body, pushing the body forward, and forming successive new bases by moving the legs forward alternately. Walking is possible because friction between the foot and the supporting surface resists the backward component of the downward-backward force applied against the surface by the extension of the joints of the leg and foot; this keeps the foot from slipping backward and the forward-upward reaction force, equal and opposite to the downward-backward force from the foot, moves the body forward. Since the body as a whole moves forward, walking can be described as linear motion. However, this linear motion of the body is brought about by two angular motions of the legs. As the body weight moves forward, the upper end of the leg lever moves forward about the foot as an axis. This is followed by a swinging forward of the foot to establish a new base and in this movement, the distal end of the leg moves about the hip as the axis (Fig. 11–1).

As in standing there are certain basic physiological reactions which occur without conscious attention, "... the initial lifting of a foot from the ground is accompanied by a flexion at all joints in the extremity. With the resulting lengthening of the extensor muscles, stretch reflexes are initiated

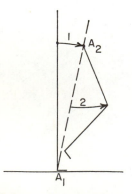

Figure 11–1. Double angular movement involved in walking.

1 Center of gravity moves
   about foot (A_1)
2 Leg moves about hip (A_2)

which operate to inhibit flexors and excite extensors. This brings about an extension at joints as the foot is thrust to the ground. A supporting reaction is present in the opposite extremity until the latter begins this process. Thus, the alternating reactions progress as walking, and do so more or less automatically, though, of course, the pattern may be modified or interrupted at will."[1]

The general body position for walking is the same as that for standing, the only difference being that the center of gravity of the body is moved forward so that gravity helps to overcome the inertia of the body and force can be applied against the floor in the direction opposite to that of desired movement (reaction force against body in direction desired).

In the act of walking each leg alternates between a supporting and a swinging phase. During a part of the supportive phase the leg exerts force to propel the body forward, but during a part of the time it exerts force that resists the forward movement of the body. Since the foot strikes the ground **ahead of the body** there is a **forward** component of force in the thrust of the foot against the ground (Fig. 11–2). This results in a **backward** counterpressure of the ground against the foot which checks the forward momentum of the

Figure 11–2. Forces involved in the thrust of the back foot against the ground and the resistance of the forward foot. A, diagonal backward-downward force produced by the body against the surface; B, downward component of force A; C, backward component of force A; D, reaction to force A effective against the body;' E, upward component of the reaction force; F, forward component of the reaction force; a, diagonal forward-downward force produced by body against the surface; b, downward component of force a; c, forward component of force a; d, reaction to force a effective against the body; e, upward component of reaction force d; backward component of reaction force d. Note: Components E and e are effective in supporting the body against gravity's pull; force F is effective in moving the body forward so long as it exceeds f, which retards forward motion.

body. This resistive force makes it possible to stop the forward movement of the body at any point in the walking sequence. Without this force, inertia could cause the trunk to continue moving forward beyond the base. The resistive force is present from the time the foot first strikes the ground until the center of gravity of the body has moved forward to the point above the supporting foot. Elftman[2] found that the horizontal component of the resistive force reaches its maximum at about the time the ball of the foot touches the ground and then decreases, at first rapidly and then slowly, to zero after the heel begins to rise and before the opposite foot touches the ground. As soon as the center of gravity of the body has moved forward of the supporting foot, the thrust against the ground caused by the extension of the hip, knee, and ankle has a backward component and, therefore, the counterpressure of the ground pushes the body forward. As the heel rises, this backward horizontal component of force increases rapidly, reaching its maximum as the ball of the foot is leaving the ground and becomes zero as the foot leaves the ground.[2] The backward horizontal component of the propelling force (back foot) must exceed the forward horizontal component of the resistive force (front foot) if progressive motion is to result (Fig. 11–2). The vertical component of the force supports the body against the pull of gravity. The farther back the weight of the body is at the time that the propelling leg is extended, the greater the vertical component in relation to the horizontal component of the propelling force. If this vertical component is too large in proportion to the force exerted by gravity and the horizontal component, a bouncing walk results.

As soon as the leg has exerted its backward push against the ground the swinging phase of the walk begins. This starts with flexion at the hip joint which is followed by flexion of the knee and ankle. This flexion of all the joints of the leg shortens the lever so that it clears the ground despite the shortened distance from the hips to the ground and also makes it easier to move the leg weight since the leg's center of gravity is closer to the axis. The swinging motion is initiated by muscular contraction (flexion of hip), but both gravity and momentum play a part in its continuance. The hip continues to flex as the knee begins to extend after the foot has passed under the body. As the foot approaches the ground, the hip extensors act to decelerate the forward movement. Since the foot reaches forward to take the weight and the ankle is flexed, the heel strikes the ground first. The weight is immediately spread over the foot (the heel, outer side of the foot, and the metatarsals), and then moves to the toes and the final push for the next step is applied. This "rolling" of the weight across the foot from heel to toe reduces the shock of impact by providing for gradual force absorption. There is a period of double support in every step. By the time that the break in heel contact has been made so that the weight stress has shifted to the metatarsals, particularly the first metatarsal and digit and the second metatarsal, the larger part of the body weight has been received by the opposite foot.[3] The slower the walk, the more the overlap of the supportive phases of the two feet.

The force exerted by the foot against the surface as the heel strikes the ground and as the toes push off is greater than the body weight due to the velocity of the body at heel strike and the thrust of plantar flexion at push off[4] (force vs. floor = W + Wa/g). Because of this force at heel strike, a narrow heel will snap if the wearer attempts to walk normally, i.e., heel to toe. Therefore, small high heels cause a flat-footed gait which requires shorter steps and leads to jarring of the body, since all the force must be absorbed suddenly rather than gradually as the weight rolls across the foot from heel to toe.

In walking, as in any motion, the inertia of the body must be overcome. This is accomplished by the force exerted by the pushing foot assisted by the pull of gravity which is effective when the weight of the body is shifted forward. Walking has been described as a series of episodes in which balance is lost and regained. The center of gravity is moved forward, disturbing the stability of the body and, as gravity acts to pull the body forward and downward, the back foot pushes backward and downward causing a reaction force against the body forward and upward. The back foot is then lifted and moved forward so that a new base is formed under the forward moving center of gravity.

The forward movement of the center of gravity increases the forward component of the counterpressure of the ground against the pushing foot and thus force is applied more in the direction of the desired movement. If there is sufficient friction between the feet and the surface, the more forward the center of gravity the greater the forward component of the reaction to the pushing force. Thus the speed of a walk is determined not only by the magnitude of the reaction to the pushing force, which in turn depends upon the force exerted by the foot **and** the resistance of the ground, but also by the direction of its application. The effect of the angle of inclination of the body on the speed of the gait can be experienced by walking with the weight well back (exaggerated) while exerting considerable force in the push of the foot against the floor and then, **keeping the same pushing force,** shifting the weight forward. The additional speed with which the body moves forward is immediately apparent. This demonstration also points up the bouncing walk which results from keeping the weight back.

Speed of walking can also be increased by lengthening the stride. However, when the stride is lengthened the up-and-down motion of the body is increased unless the supporting knee is kept somewhat flexed as the center of gravity passes forward over it. Metheny[5] suggested lengthening the stride with no additional energy expenditure by relaxing the supporting knee and allowing it to bend slightly, so that the hips are brought closer to the ground and the heel strikes farther in front of the body. This puts the back leg in position to exert its force more diagonally backward so that the reaction force is more forward, increasing the forward component, thus making the force exerted more effective for forward movement.

When walking against a high wind, the body leans well forward into the wind to increase the forward component of the pushing force. The greater the forward lean, the greater the horizontal component. The amount of lean must vary with the force of the wind. Since the farther forward one leans the more effective is gravity's pull on the body, the body must not be angled beyond the point at which the pull of gravity is balanced by the resistance of the wind. Since wind is likely to blow in gusts it is dangerous to move the center of gravity too far forward even though the push is more effective, because a sudden reduction in the force of the wind would leave the body overbalanced forward and a fall would be likely.

Any movement of the center of gravity forward is accomplished most effectively when the segments of the body are maintained in their same relative alignment, by shifting the body as a whole forward from the ankles. Frequently, individuals who are attempting to hurry lean forward from the hips. This places strain on the smaller muscles of the back which must hold the trunk up against gravity's pull, and although it does move the center of gravity forward somewhat, it does not move it as far forward as does a shift of the entire body from the ankles. Walking rapidly while leaning forward from the hips and then, keeping the same push off, bringing the hips forward (and shoulders back somewhat) to make the body a straight line leaning forward from the ankles, demonstrates that the latter position is more effective since the body moves faster with the same force.

The stability of the body in walking, as in standing, is directly related to the size of the base of support. Therefore, the lateral distance between the feet is a factor in balance. It is also a factor in the direction in which the pushing force is applied. In standing, the base involves both feet with the line of gravity falling between them (center of the base) and therefore, the position of the feet a few inches apart (width of the hips) gives greater stability. However, in walking the base shifts from one foot to the other and, in order to maintain stability, the center of gravity of the body must shift to a position over the supporting foot. If the feet are moved straight forward from their stable standing position (walk with feet apart) the weight must be shifted a considerable distance from side to side at every step. This can be

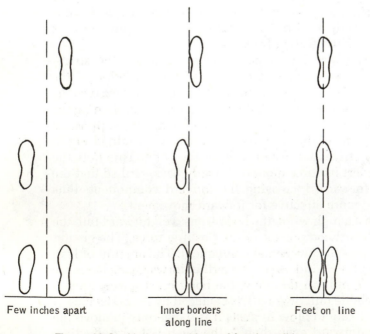

Few inches apart   Inner borders   Feet on line
                          along line

Figure 11–3.   Various positions of feet in walking.

demonstrated easily in the standing position with the feet a few inches apart by picking up the left foot, placing it on the floor and then picking up the right foot. The sideways movement of the entire body which results is immediately apparent. Thus walking with the feet apart causes a "duck waddle," in which the body sways from side to side. This is the type of walk normally used by a baby learning to walk. He spreads his feet because his balance is precarious. He also uses his arms to help maintain his balance in the same way that a tightrope walker uses a long pole.

The sideways swaying can be eliminated by placing each foot directly under the center of gravity at each step. This is accomplished by walking a line, placing one foot directly in front of the other. However, this method of walking decreases the width of the base during the period of double support and thus reduces the stability of the body and additional energy must be expended to move each foot out and around the other at every step.

The most effective position of the feet, then, is that in which they are moved in toward the center so that the sideways shift of weight is kept to a minimum and still each foot can move directly forward (Fig. 11–3). When the inner borders of the feet are placed along a line the base is wider than when the feet are placed one in front of the other, the feet can move directly forward and the movement of the center of gravity from side to side is slight. In fact, if the pelvis is stabilized the leg can be swung through with little or no movement of the center of gravity to the side. Experimentation with the three positions of the feet with the attention consciously directed to the reaction of the body, the feeling of stability, and the ease of foot movement in each, clearly points up the advantages of walking with the inner borders of the feet along a line.

When walking with the toes pointing ahead, the force is exerted in the desired direction of movement. If the feet are placed on the ground with the toes turned either out or in, the push is exerted diagonally backward-outward (away from the center of the base), sending the body forward and inward (Fig. 11–4). Since the right foot pushes diagonally right and back, the

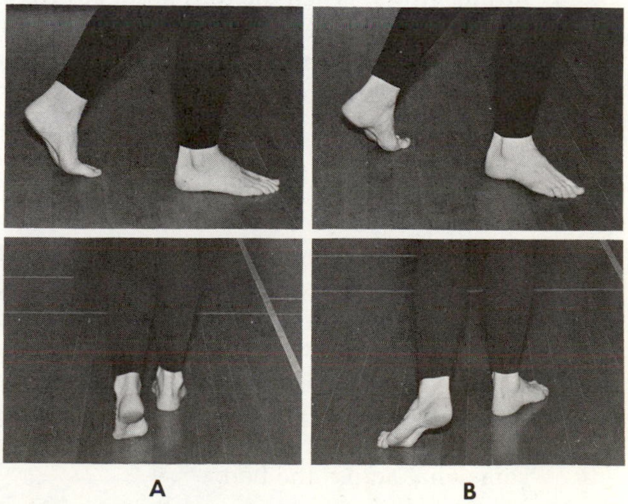

Figure 11–4. A, Push straight backward. B, Push diagonally backward.

A   B

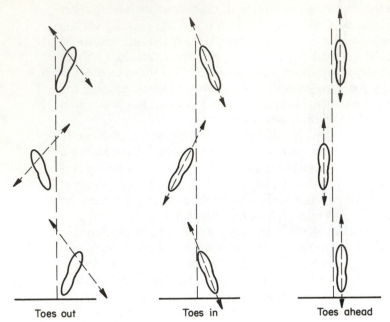

Figure 11–5. Direction of force application resulting from various foot positions.

body moves forward and to the left in response to the force exerted by it. The push of the left foot sends the body forward and to the right (Fig. 11–5). Thus, energy is wasted and a zigzag walk results. The toe-out position causes outward force because the push is made with the **inner border of the great toe** and the first metatarsal (Fig. 11–5). In the toe-in position the force is exerted by more of the toes. As in standing, the toe-out position of the feet causes the weight to fall on the inner borders of the feet putting stress on the arch, and since the push-off is exerted by the inner border of the great toe and first metatarsal, the force passes diagonally across the arch adding further stress. When the toes point approximately straight ahead, all force is directed backward and is, therefore, useful in causing movement of the body in the desired direction (forward). Also, the force passes straight backward through the arch of the foot.

The arms swing easily in opposition to the legs. This motion is reflexly controlled and when an individual has difficulty with this coordination, tension or voluntary effort is interfering with the normal response. The tendency of the body to rotate due to the off-center application of force by the foot is counteracted by the swing of the arms. The left foot push-off followed by the forward swing of the leg causes an off-center force which tends to rotate the pelvis and trunk to the right, but the simultaneous forward movement of the right arm, tending to rotate the shoulders and trunk to the left, balances this force and thus reduces the lateral rotation of the trunk. Because of the way that most persons' arms hang naturally, this arm swing is not directly forward but rather diagonally forward, being somewhat across the body.

Standing with the arms hanging naturally at the sides and simply bending the elbows demonstrates the fact that most persons' hands do not point directly forward but rather that the lower arms are in front of the body. The extent to which they cross the body varies with the individual body build; in fact for some few, the hands do not cross in front of the body. When they do, outward rotation at the shoulders would be necessary to place the arms in such a position that the hands swing directly forward. This would require unnecessary muscular tension. In ordinary walking the arm swing is largely the product of inertia and gravity acting on the weight of the arm.[6] When the gait becomes faster, voluntary swinging of the arms helps to carry the upper trunk forward. Any bending of the arm at the elbow shortens the lever and thus makes faster movement of the arm easier.

Occasionally, one sees exaggerated hip rotation used to produce momentum as an aid in swinging the leg forward. While this can be an effective procedure for someone handicapped by loss of function of the hip flexors, it is not efficient for a normal individual. Development of a feeling for stabilizing the pelvis and moving the knee straight forward helps in overcoming this tendency. Lack of stabilization which holds the pelvis **level** produces a "hip switch" in which the hip of the swinging leg drops sharply and the knee of the supporting leg tends to hyperextend. A heavy and aesthetically displeasing walk results. A heavy lumbering walk also results when an individual "collapses" through the abdomen and trunk (allows the upper body to settle down into the pelvis). This individual is also likely to stand (and walk) with his weight back toward his heels. Getting a feeling of "lift" through the trunk and moving the weight forward will lighten the walk.

Since the forward movement of the body is effected by the horizontal component of the diagonal pushing force, friction is essential for the counterpressure of the surface to be transferred to the body. If there were little or no friction the backward component of the pushing force would simply move the foot backward across the surface. The greater the horizontal component in relation to the vertical component of the pushing force, the greater the dependence on friction for efficient locomotion since more of the force is applied backward which is the direction to most effectively overcome friction. The more vertical the application of force the smaller the component in direct opposition to friction and the more effective the friction. Therefore, the less the friction, the less the force of the foot against the ground can be directed backward, and the more the weight must be kept above the pushing foot. Shortening the step keeps the center of gravity more vertically above the base and thus reduces the backward component of force.

When walking on a highly polished floor, ice or any slippery surface, the stride must be shortened to keep the center of gravity more nearly above the foot and thus to reduce the horizontal component of the force to a minimum. Wells[7] pointed out that an appreciation of the horizontal component of the force of locomotion should make individuals aware of certain dangers in the home. Wet or highly polished floors and scatter rugs should be approached at a slower pace and with shorter steps which keep the center of gravity more vertically above the base so that the horizontal component is lessened. This same problem is involved whenever friction between the foot and the counteracting surface is slight.

If the surface lacks solidity, such as soft snow, mud, sand, and the like, it gives with the push of the foot against it (see p. 101), and offers too little resistance to supply effective counterpressure. Since much of the force is dissipated in pushing the foot and the snow or sand backward more force must be exerted to achieve forward progress. When walking on the beach it is important to remember that fatigue sets in sooner than when walking on normal hard ground so that the distance to be walked up the beach will be gauged accordingly. Walking in soft sand of an ocean beach is more difficult than on the hard packed sand usually found close to the water's edge.

WALKING BACKWARD

When walking backward the center of gravity is not shifted in the direction of movement as it is in walking forward. Instead a foot is lifted and placed securely a short distance back before the weight is shifted: this is because there is little base behind the ankle. Because of the greater strength of the calf muscles over that of the anterior leg muscles, the length of the foot in front of the ankle, and the fact that the toes are in an excellent position to push the body backward if the center of gravity should move so far forward that balance is endangered, in walking forward the center of gravity can be shifted forward safely and thus advantage can be taken of the force of gravity and the more direct angle of push. However, in shifting the center of gravity backward balance is likely to be lost unless a new base is prepared **before** the shift is made. Therefore, short steps must be taken when walking backward.

WALKING ON INCLINES

As indicated earlier (p. 164) a sloping surface requires an adjustment of body position to keep the center of gravity over the base (feet). This adjustment must be forward when on an upward slope and backward when the slope is downward (Fig. 10–5). The steeper the angle of the incline the greater the adjustment of the body necessary. When this adjustment is made from the ankles, the basic well-aligned position of the body can be maintained. When the forward adjustment is made from the hips the strong gluteal muscles are brought into play giving additional muscular strength. However, the back muscles must then strain to hold the upper body up against the pull of gravity unless there is a railing on which the hand can be placed so that the weight of the upper body can be supported by the arm, or unless a cane is used. Also, the aesthetic value of leaning from the ankles as opposed to leaning from the hips cannot be overlooked.

When the backward adjustment, which is necessary in walking down an incline, is made from the hips, strain is put upon the lower back.

When walking uphill the forward lean from the ankles also makes it possible to apply the force as much as possible in the direction of desired movement which is upward and forward. In walking down an incline the problem becomes one of resisting the pull of gravity in order to control velocity. The backward lean makes it possible to apply force forward and downward in the direction to oppose gravity. Actually, walking down an incline becomes a matter of controlled resistance to gravity's pull. Thus in some circumstances it is easier, **although more dangerous**, to move the feet forward rapidly (to run) than to resist the pull of gravity at every step (to walk) when going downhill. This becomes more apparent as the incline becomes steeper.

On steep grades there is a tendency for the foot to slip because it is applying force downward as well as backward, or forward in the case of walking downgrade, and gravity is also pulling downward. The downward component of the force is added to gravity's pull; thus considerable force must be resisted by friction. Crossbars on the supporting surface reduce the possibility of slipping since they present a surface against which the foot can push more nearly straight backward (or forward).

WALKING UP AND DOWN STAIRS

The chief problem in walking upstairs is the conservation of energy while that of descending is principally safety. Karpovich and Sinning[8] stated that it takes approximately 15 times as much energy to walk up a flight of ordinary stairs as to walk a level distance equal to the vertical height of the stairs. While descending requires more energy than walking on the level, it takes only about one-third the energy of ascending.* To avoid unnecessary fatigue and strain the general body position for both tasks should be the same well-aligned position of the body segments as described for standing.

When walking upstairs the center of gravity should be shifted forward, so that the reaction force from the back leg's push is in a diagonally forward and upward direction (Fig. 11–6). This forward inclination should be from the ankles keeping the body segments in their same relative alignment. Leaning forward from the hips throws unnecessary strain on the muscles of the lower back. As in walking up an incline, the bend from the hips enables the strong gluteal muscles to work to good advantage and therefore makes more force available. Older people may need this additional muscular power but should then use the railing so that some of the weight of the upper trunk can be supported on the hand. The back leg pushes the weight up and forward over the front leg, and while this leg lifts the body and pushes the weight forward, the back leg is lifted and placed on the next step under the upward-forward moving center of gravity. Thus, a smooth ascent results from the coordination of the forces produced **by both legs** at every step, the back leg pushing the center of gravity over the forward leg so that it is in an advantageous position to add its force to that of the back leg by pushing downward against the step to move the body upward.

If the foot is placed flat on the step, energy does not have to be expended to hold the heel up against the pull of gravity. This can be demonstrated

---

*Kamon found that climbing a **ladder mill** takes four times the energy required in descending.[9]

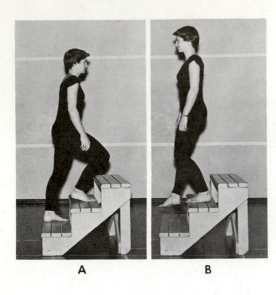

Figure 11–6. A, Weight forward. Push in direction of desired movement. B, Weight held back for safety.

easily by standing for a few seconds with the ball of one foot on a step and then placing the foot flat on the step. The extra energy required to stand on the ball of the foot over that required to stand on the entire foot is obvious. Balance is also a problem due to the small base afforded by the ball of the foot. However, normally the time during which the weight is supported on the ball of the foot is very short; also, if the step is so narrow that placing the

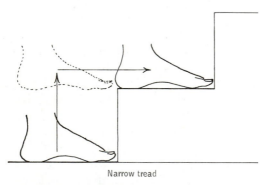

Narrow tread

Figure 11–7. Effect of various widths of stair treads on movement of foot.

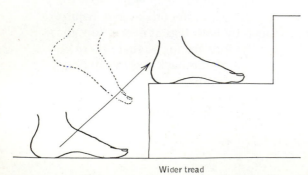

Wider tread

entire foot on it puts the toes close to the riser so that the foot must be raised straight upward, and then moved forward to be placed on the next step instead of moved diagonally forward and upward, the energy saved may be wasted in the additional movement necessary (Fig. 11–7). When placing the foot flat on a **narrow** tread there is also danger of catching the toes on the lip of the step and many stairs are constructed with a slight extension of each step over its riser.

In descending stairs the center of gravity is kept back over the center of the base, because of the danger of falling down the stairs if it should move beyond the toes. **Safety** makes it essential that the general principle concerning the placement of the center of gravity in line with the direction of movement be ignored. Actually walking down stairs is a matter of controlled "giving in" to gravity (lengthening contraction of the extensors). It involves control of the rate at which gravity pulls the body down. The weight is lowered to the next step by giving with the supporting knee. Since the center of gravity is over the supporting foot, any push exerted by that leg moves the body upward and it then has to be lowered through a greater distance. Energy is wasted in pushing up and the individual bounces down the stairs. Added force due to the dropping of the body from the additional height must be absorbed. The ball of the swinging foot makes the first contact with the step below, and the heel comes down immediately.

EFFORT REQUIRED TO WALK UP INCLINE AND FLIGHT OF STAIRS

In general, it requires more effort to climb a given height on stairs than on an incline. Walking upstairs involves lifting the body weight a certain height at every step until the desired height is reached. The effort expended can be calculated by the formula for work ($W = F \times D_v$), which means that the weight of the body is multiplied by the distance (height) that it is lifted. The effort expended in walking up an inclined plane multiplied by the length of the incline is equal to the weight lifted times the distance that it is lifted. Therefore, because the length of an inclined plane exceeds its height, it has a theoretical mechanical advantage of the ratio of these two distances.

$$\text{force} \times \text{length of incline} = \text{weight} \times \text{height of incline}[10]$$

$$\frac{\text{Force}}{\text{Weight}} = \frac{\text{height}}{\text{length}} \tag{11.1}$$

SUMMARY

In walking, the inertia of the body can be overcome most efficiently by moving the center of gravity forward so that the force of gravity assists the movement, and the pushing force exerted by the counterpressure of the ground against the foot is applied at an angle which results in a larger horizontal component and is, therefore, more advantageous for forward movement. The general alignment of the body segments follows the same principles discussed in the preceding chapter on standing.

There is a short period of double support in every step and each step has two principal phases, supportive and swinging. The supportive phase consists of two parts, one propels the body forward and the other resists the forward movement. Because of the forward diagonal position of the leg, backward force which resists the forward movement of the body is applied from the moment the foot strikes the ground until the center of gravity of the body is above the supporting foot. The propelling force exerted by the pushing foot must exceed this resistive force for movement to result.

Since it results in force being applied in the direction of desired motion with as little lateral motion of the center of gravity as possible, the most efficient position of the feet is that of the toes pointing ahead and the inner borders of the feet falling along a line.

The easy, relaxed arm swing in opposition to the swing of the legs serves to reduce the trunk rotation and helps to carry the upper body forward.

The speed of the walk can be increased by increasing the force exerted against the ground, moving the center of gravity of the body farther forward and lengthening the stride.

Because balance is more precarious when walking backward, the foot must be moved back to prepare a new base before the center of gravity of the body moves to any extent.

When walking up an incline or stairs, the force exerted by the legs and feet is made more effective by moving the center of gravity of the body forward so that the force is applied in the desired direction of movement. Since safety is the major factor in descending stairs, the weight is kept back over the center of the supporting foot. On an incline the body must lean backward from the ankles to keep the center of gravity over the base. Whether descending stairs or an incline, the body weight is lowered most efficiently by a controlled "giving in" to gravity.

REFERENCES

1. Gardner, Ernest: *Fundamentals of Neurology*. Philadelphia, W. B. Saunders Company, 1947, p. 227.
2. Elftman, Herbert: The Force Exerted by the Ground in Walking. *Ant. Z. Angew. Physiol.*, 10:489, 1939.
3. Morton, Dudley J., and Fuller, Dudley Dean: *Human Locomotion and Body Form*. Baltimore, Williams and Wilkins Company, 1952, pp. 83–84.
4. Williams, Marian, and Lissner, Herbert R.: *Biomechanics of Human Motion*. Philadelphia, W. B. Saunders Company, 1962, p. 122.
5. Metheny, Eleanor: *Body Dynamics*. New York, McGraw-Hill Book Company, Inc., 1951, p. 146.
6. Morton, Dudley J., and Fuller, Dudley Dean: *op. cit.*, p. 242.
7. Wells, Katharine F., and Luttgens, Kathryn: *Kinesiology*. 6th ed. Philadelphia, W. B. Saunders Company, 1976, p. 412.
8. Karpovich, Peter V., and Sinning, Wayne E.: *Physiology of Muscular Activity*. 7th ed. Philadelphia, W. B. Saunders Company, 1971, p. 126.
9. Kamon, Eliezer: Negative and Positive Work in Climbing a Laddermill, *Journal of Applied Physiology*, 29:1–5, July, 1970.
10. Flitter, Hessel Howard: *An Introduction to Physics and Nursing*. 2nd ed. St. Louis, C. V. Mosby Company, 1954, p. 65.

RUNNING

12

Running is a fundamental skill in a high percentage of sport activities. In addition, the increased awareness that exercise which makes demands on the heart and lungs is extremely important to well-being has made running a vital part of the daily lives of many.

In general, the mechanics of running are the same as those of walking. In some ways running is easier than walking. Babies may run before they walk. A baby normally stands with feet apart to give a wide base and thus stability in the lateral plane, but having very small feet which give a short base forward and backward, the center of gravity is likely to pass the forward margin of the base. By moving his feet forward rapidly, he may be able to maintain an upright position until he reaches a person or a piece of furniture which will support him. Also, because of the reduction or elimination of the resistive phase which is a considerable factor in the walk, a slow run takes less energy than a fast walk. This is easily demonstrated by walking a short distance **as fast as possible** and suddenly breaking into a jogging run. The relief from the strain caused by the resistive force of the walk is immediately apparent.

Running differs from walking in that the period of double support is eliminated and a period of no support, between the time that the back foot exerts its force and is lifted from the ground and the forward foot strikes the ground, is added. More force is supplied by the extensor muscles of the driving leg and foot giving both more forward and more upward velocity. The latter is important in keeping the body in the air long enough to make full use of the forward component of the driving force. The leg swings forward, then starts back and just before contact it is moving backward rapidly. The foot strikes the ground under the knee and as nearly as possible under the center of gravity of the body; thus at the instant of landing on the forward foot the reaction force from the ground is almost entirely upward giving vertical support[1] and the resistive force found in the walk is either eliminated or considerably reduced. In fact, the supportive phase is almost entirely propulsive. The greater the speed, the more they are concurrent.

Because the foot contacts the ground under (or almost under) the center of gravity of the body, it is possible to land on the ball of the foot or on the whole foot. Authorities agree that, at low speed, the runner strikes the ground with the whole foot. Bowerman and Brown[2] claimed that it is most comfortable and efficient for the foot to land flat or possibly toward the heel and roll forward across the ball of the foot, while the ball of the foot landing is used when a burst of speed is required. Ariel's studies of running which use the computer and oscilloscope show that, while it looks as though runners land on their heels, they do not. "The good ones don't."[3] Dyson[4] and Slocum and James[5] agree that the sprinter lands well up on the ball of the foot and toes; however, Dyson stated that the heel touches the ground lightly as the body passes over the foot while Slocum and James stated that the dorsiflexion of the ankle is usually not sufficient to permit the heel to touch the ground. "The trained sprinter maintains his foot in plantar flexion and carries his weight on the toes and ball of the foot throughout the support phase."[6] They pointed out that this is at a high energy cost. Bowerman and Brown[7] agreed that few runners have sufficiently limber ankles to be able to hit on the ball of the foot and then settle back onto the heel. However, they cautioned that if the runner lands on the ball of the foot and does not have this ability to give with the ankle on landing, pressure is put on the arch as well as on the bones and muscles of the leg; injury may result. Ariel's more recent studies indicate that the fast runners "flick the foot down flat at the last instant."[8]

Since, in running, the force of the push-off is greater and the body is actually momentarily free of support in the air, the force that must be absorbed on contact with the ground is much greater than in walking. If the runner's ankles are sufficiently limber, landing on the ball of the foot could make it possible to reduce the jar of landing more readily by giving with the ankle. When the contact is made with the total foot, the force is absorbed gradually by rolling forward across the foot as in the walk. Additional "give" in the knee puts this joint in an advantageous position to exert more propulsive force. Staying on the ball of the foot throughout the support phase results in the elimination of some ankle plantar flexion during the push-off and thus the force of the foot thrust against the ground may be diminished.

Given a certain propulsive force, the smaller the vertical component, the greater the horizontal component. Therefore, the vertical component of the propulsion force should be kept as small as will counteract gravity's downward pull, so that as great a proportion of the force as possible will be effective in driving the body forward, rather than be wasted in producing a bouncing run. The relative sizes of vertical and horizontal components depend upon the relationship between the body's center of gravity and the point of force application; thus the runner's **center of gravity** must be well ahead of the back foot at the time of maximum thrust against the ground, so that the forward component of the reaction force will be maximized.

However, the runner's **trunk** must be upright to keep the runner in balance. A forward lean of the trunk places the runner off-balance and, instead of propelling the body forward, the leg muscles must exert additional upward force to keep the runner from falling;[9] thus with a forward lean of the trunk, the **center of gravity** must be kept back, reducing the forward component in order to increase the upward component of the propelling force. With the trunk upright, the center of gravity can be farther forward of the pushing foot and still the runner will remain balanced (Fig. 12–1).

Figure 12–1. Force involved in thrust of foot against the ground when running; A, diagonally backward-downward force against the surface; B, downward component of force A; C, backward component of force A; D, reaction to force A effective in propelling the body; E, upward component of propelling force; F, forward component of propelling force. Note: Center of gravity well ahead of foot although trunk is upright.

"The forward-lean theory also contradicts some of the basic factors in running efficiency: (1) Maximum extension of the lumbar-to-ground lever is essential to stride length and contributes power to the forward thrust during takeoff. With the trunk in the leaning position, the pelvis is tilted forward, and the full working range of extension cannot be utilized. (2) Flexion of the hip during forward recovery swings the lower extremity forward and positions it in advance of the body. With the trunk erect, this action is rapid and the thigh in its forward position is high in relation to the ground, making it possible for the lower leg and foot to be positioned well forward, thus effectively elongating the stride. With the pelvis tilted forward in the leaning position, flexion is impeded, the thigh cannot be brought as high from the ground, and the extremity cannot advance as far ahead of the body."[10]

Since the body is moving forward faster in the run, the legs must swing faster in order to form a base under the moving center of gravity. As the leg swings forward the knee is flexed considerably more than in the walk so that the leg's center of gravity is brought closer to the hip. Since the lever is shortened by flexion of the knee, the leg's radius of gyration (moment of inertia) is reduced and its angular velocity is increased.

As in walking, the arm swing must be coordinated with that of the legs in order to balance the rotating effect of the leg swing on the trunk. Since the legs are moving faster, the arms must move faster also. Some authorities claim that the faster the arms are swung, the faster the individual will be able to move the legs. Because of the reflex alternation of arms and legs, increasing the speed of the arms may make it easier to increase the speed of the legs. In order to move the arms rapidly with as little effort as possible, they too are shortened by flexing the elbows. The swing is somewhat across (in front of) the body as in walking. It seems reasonable, however, that when maximum speed is desired, the swing should be somewhat less diagonal so that the force can be more directly backward and forward. The energy used in the outward rotation of the arms at the shoulders, necessary to point the hands more forward, is expended for the purpose of adding to the forward component of the force of the swing. Observation of pictures of Olympic runners indicates that they do tend to swing the arms more forward as they go into their final sprint near the finish line. Bunn[11] stated that a runner with heavy hips and legs in relation to his arms and shoulders must carry his arms farther from his body or increase the vigor of his arm swing to balance the force of the legs.

Since an object has inertia to any change in its state of motion (Newton's First Law), in running, as in moving any object, it takes less energy to maintain a given speed once attained than to vary the speed. The greatest amount of force is required at take-off. As the level of speed which is to be attained is reached the force required is decreased.

Speed of running is increased by increasing the propulsive force and/or the length of the stride and the two are interrelated. Increased propulsive force at a given angle results in more force both upward and forward; the greater upward component, resisting gravity, keeps the body in the air longer allowing it time to move farther, **and** the greater horizontal component drives the body forward faster and thus farther before it contacts the ground. The longer stride lowers the center of gravity and to avoid superfluous vertical motion which would detract from the forward motion, the supporting knee is flexed more. This additional flexion puts the muscles of the leg in position for more powerful extension and thus makes possible a more powerful drive and a longer stride. Lengthening the stride is effective only to a point. Reaching too far forward causes the foot to contact the ground ahead of the runner's center of gravity and a braking action is the result; the foot produces a forward-downward force against the ground and the backward component of the reaction force against the runner retards speed. In addition, Bowerman and Brown pointed out that "too long extension backward stretches the extensor muscles of the leg and hip beyond the point at which they can generate maximum forward thrust."[12]

Movements in any direction other than the desired direction of movement may detract from the efficiency of the movement. Therefore, the knees should be carried straight forward and upward and the arm swing should be inward only enough to counterbalance the rotation of the pelvis. Girls and women frequently have difficulty in running because they attempt to run with a minimum of knee lift. In order to move the foot forward without lifting the knee, the thigh must be rotated inward and the foot and lower leg thrown out to the side and around. They also tend to rotate the arms outward "hugging" the upper arms and elbows to the body and allowing the lower arm to "flap" out at the sides in response to the decided rotation of the hips. Females may have some mechanical disadvantage in running because of the angle of the femur resulting from a broader pelvis. However, lateral sway can be kept to a minimum if the knees are bent and carried straight forward.

Emphasis on **lifting** the knee forward and relaxing the shoulders while bending the elbows so that the arms can swing in their natural position will increase both the efficiency and the aesthetic appearance of the run. When the arms are flexed at the elbows in their natural position, which is with the lower arm diagonally in front of the body, it is more difficult to "hug" the arms to the body. Outward rotation tends to push the upper arm against the trunk. Practice in exercises which relax the upper arm and shoulder girdle and move the arms independently of the trunk should be helpful. Morehouse and Cooper[13] suggest holding the thumb against the tip of the second or third finger instead of making a fist in order to prevent tension in the muscles of the arm. They point out that the muscles used to press the thumb against one of these fingers are located in the forearm, while clenching the fist involves muscles of the entire arm and thus may cause tension which restricts arm action. This could be a useful device for those whose arms are tense.

Because the propulsive force is stronger and is exerted in a more horizontal direction, the friction between the feet and the supporting surface is even more important in running than in walking (p. 180). Running should not be attempted unless there is sufficient friction to prevent slipping. While tennis shoes increase the friction between the feet and the tennis court or gymnasium floor, they are not effective on a wet field. If running on wet grass is likely to be required, or when maximum results are desired on a field or track, shoes with cleats are needed. Since cleats indent grass or actually pierce the ground (depending on the type of cleats), they offer a surface which can push directly against a (more or less) vertical surface of the ground or grass rather than one which pushes **across** the surface, in which case the reaction force is entirely dependent on friction. When cleats are such that there is **no** slipping, they are said to provide a coefficient of friction of 1.

RUNNING IN A CIRCLE

The moving body, like any object, tends to follow a straight line (Newton's First Law). Therefore, if it is necessary to change direction while running, force must be applied toward the outside of the arc. In order to apply force outward, the line from the runner's center of gravity to the point where he is applying force against the surface must be downward and outward; thus, the runner leans in toward the center of the circle (Fig. 12–2). The force of the leg drive is then outward as well as backward and downward and the ground reaction force, being equal and in the opposite direction, sends the body forward and inward. Since the force is diagonal, friction is important to preventing slipping.

Figure 12–2. A, Running straight forward; B, Running in curved path. Lean places body in position so that the center of gravity is angled inward from point of application of force against floor; thus force is diagonally outward as well as backward-downward. Thus reaction force against body is inward and forward-upward causing body to turn.

If the friction force is not large enough to resist the horizontal component of the force of the runner's push against the ground, he is not able to turn. The runner can decrease the problem of slipping by increasing the radius of his turn (making a more gradual turn) or by slowing his velocity (reducing the force exerted against the ground). The designer of a track banks it to make it easier for a runner to turn without losing velocity. When a track is banked the reaction force at the runner's feet has a component towards the center of the circle, which supplies the centripetal (inward) force necessary for the turn.

STANDING START

If a fast (sudden) start is desired, a position which allows the center of gravity to be well forward without loss of balance is necessary. For maximum starting speed a crouching start is used (Chap. 24) but there are many running situations for which the crouching start is not feasible since it requires a nearly vertical resisting surface. In a standing start a forward-backward stride position with the weight on the forward foot is taken. The knees are bent so that they are in a position to extend, and thus exert force. Since the center of gravity is relatively high and over the forward edge of the base, if the stride is not too long it is easy to move the center of gravity ahead of the forward foot to a position for effective forward propulsive force.

The back foot begins the overcoming of the body's inertia by moving the center of gravity forward, but the major take-off is exerted by the forward foot. Since the desired motion is forward the toes of the feet should be pointing ahead. From this position they can exert force directly backward and downward. The tendency of some individuals to assume a standing position with the back foot pointing out to the side results in the force produced by that foot being transferred diagonally across the arch of the foot and exerted against the side of the knee. The reason most frequently advanced in favor of pushing with the inside of the back foot (toe pointing out to the side) is that it gives a larger surface with which to apply force. Since friction is dependent upon the total force pushing the two surfaces together and the material of which the two surfaces are made and **independent of surface area** (p. 76), this position does not increase friction and thus does not increase the force returned to the body.

STOPPING

In stopping, the problem is one of absorbing force gradually so that balance is regained without strain of any joint. Since the movement is forward the knee of the forward leg must flex to absorb the forward momentum gradually. This flexing of the forward knee drops the center of gravity and shifts it backward, keeping it within the forward limit of the base. This can be demonstrated by standing in a forward-backward stride position with the weight well forward and then bending the forward knee. The dropping of the center of gravity and the shifting of the weight backward is immediately apparent. If the forward knee is straight the momentum of the trunk carries the upper body forward over the foot. The giving of the knee is also important in that it puts the leg into position to extend and, since the center of gravity is behind the forward foot at this time, to push the center of gravity backward over the center of the base, reestablishing the stability of the body. It is extremely important that the foot of the leg that is to absorb the force in stopping be placed on the floor with the toes straight ahead. If they are turned in either direction, the forward momentum of the body is thrown against the side of the ankle and the side of the knee and the lateral ligament may be strained.

Forward velocity can also be stopped by jumping and landing in a stride position on both feet. A forward-backward stride gives a wide base in the direction of the momentum of the body. If a side stride jump stop is used, the jump must turn the body sideways to the direction of movement to widen the base in the needed direction. Hips, knees, and ankles must give to absorb the force of landing and keep the center of gravity over the base. The jump can be used effectively to stop in basketball, since the forward momentum frequently is not too great and this type of stop allows for a pivot on either foot.

SUMMARY

Running differs from walking in that there is no period of double support and there is a period of no support. Since the foot strikes the ground under, or almost under, the center of gravity, the resistive phase is eliminated or greatly reduced. The first contact may be made with the ball of the foot or with the whole foot; the ball of the foot landing makes it possible to absorb the additional force of the run without jar by giving with the ankle, knee, and hip if the runner's ankles are sufficiently limber. If the landing is made on the whole foot, the weight rolls across the foot to the ball. Additional flexing of the knee puts the muscles of the knee into position for more powerful extension. The center of gravity is more forward of the pushing foot, increasing the forward component of the propulsive force, but the trunk remains upright to minimize the vertical force required for maintenance of balance.

To make it easier to swing the legs forward quickly, the knees are flexed to reduce the moment of inertia and increase angular velocity as they swing through. The elbows are also bent to facilitate rapid swinging of the arms. The arm swing serves the same purposes as it does in walking.

Speed in running is increased by increasing the propulsive force and/or length of the stride up to the point at which a resistive phase is introduced. Since movements in any direction other than that of desired movement detract from the efficiency of the run, the knees should be brought straight forward and upward and the arm swing should just balance the rotating force of the legs against the pelvis.

Friction is more important in running than in walking, both because more force is exerted and because it is applied in a more horizontal direction.

When running in an arc it is necessary to apply force toward the outside of the arc to overcome the body's inertia to change of direction. Therefore, the body leans in toward the center of the arc.

When starting from a standing position the feet should be in a forward-backward stride with the toes straight ahead so that the force can be exerted straight backward and downward. The knees are bent so that the legs are in position to exert force and the weight is on the forward foot.

In stopping, the forward momentum must be absorbed gradually and the stability of the body reestablished. This can be done by giving with the forward leg while the center of gravity is still behind that foot, absorbing the force, lowering the center of gravity and moving it backward. A subsequent extension of the forward knee moves the center of gravity back over the center of the base. Jumping to a stride stop can also be successful if the stride is in the direction of the momentum and the knees, hips and ankles give on landing.

REFERENCES

1. Slocum, Donald B., and James, Stanley L.: Biomechanics of Running, *Journal of American Medical Association*, 205:11:724, September 9, 1968.
2. Bowerman, Bill, and Brown, Gwilyms S.: The Secrets of Speed, *Sports Illustrated*, 35:5:28, August 2, 1971.
3. Moore, Kenny: Gideon Ariel and His Magic Machine, *Sports Illustrated*, 47:8:57, August 22, 1977.
4. Dyson, Geoffrey H. G.: *The Mechanics of Athletics*. London, University of London Press Ltd., 1964, p. 102.
5. Slocum and James, *op cit.*, p. 726.
6. *Ibid.*
7. Bowerman and Brown, *loc cit.*
8. Moore, *loc cit.*
9. Bowerman and Brown, *op cit.*, pp. 22–24.
10. Slocum and James, *op. cit.*, p. 726.
11. Bunn, John W.: *Scientific Principles of Coaching*. Englewood Cliffs, New Jersey, Prentice-Hall, Inc., 1955. p. 113.
12. Bowerman and Brown, *op cit.*, p. 26.
13. Morehouse, Laurence E., and Cooper, John M.: *Kinesiology*. St. Louis, C. V. Mosby Company, 1950, p. 245.

HOPPING, JUMPING, LEAPING AND LANDING

13

In hopping, jumping and leaping the body is projected through the air and therefore, the laws which govern any projectile apply to it. This means that regardless of the particular activity that projects the body, the path of its center of gravity through the air is determined by velocity at take-off and the angle of projection. Once the body has lost contact with the projecting surface no movement of various body segments can alter the **path followed by the center of gravity** (Chapter 9). The positioning of various body segments around the center of gravity can be changed and this will alter the **location** of the center of gravity **within the body**, but the **path** of the center of gravity through the air is determined at take-off. Gravity, of course, begins to act immediately to draw the body toward the earth.

In addition to the necessity for overcoming the body's inertia, the pull of gravity (the body weight) must be overcome in order to lift the body off the ground. Therefore, the force required to project the body into space is greater than that required to move the body forward along the ground. The magnitude of the required force is dependent upon the weight of the body.

When the propulsive force is exerted by one foot and the body lands on the same foot the action is defined as a **hop.** If the landing is made on the other foot, it is defined as a **leap.** In a **jump** the propulsive force may be exerted by either one or both feet. The distinguishing characteristic of a true jump is that in landing both feet contact the ground simultaneously. The leaping and hopping type of projection is probably used more in daily life than is a true jump. However, jumps of various types are important in many sport and dance activities. Since the principles that apply to all of the body projecting activities are the same, they are discussed as they apply to a jump for height and to a jump to cover distance.

In all of these activities the problem is to apply the basic principles of projection (discussed in Chapter 9) to the human body so that sufficient force to overcome the body's inertia and gravity's downward pull can be applied at the angle which results in the desired flight through the air. Control of magnitude of force and angle of projection are all important in fulfilling the purpose of the particular jump; the angle of projection is determined by the direction in which the force is applied.

The force that projects the body into space must be exerted by the muscles of the body. It is produced by quick contraction of the extensors of the legs aided by a forceful arm swing. The faster the leg extension, the more force produced against the floor, and the greater the counterpressure which projects the body. In preparation for the production of this force the hips, knees and ankles must flex to put the extensors of the leg in position to exert force. Up to a point, depending upon the strength of the legs, the deeper the crouch the more the force which is obtainable. A deeper crouch puts the extensor muscles on stretch and gives a greater distance over which acceleration is possible. However, since the body must be lifted through the distance that it is lowered, more work is done when a low crouch is used, and the angle of muscle pull is also changed. The optimal depth of crouch, therefore, depends upon the strength of the leg muscles. A deeper crouch is possible if leg muscles are strong. Each individual must experiment with various depths of crouch to determine that which is most effective for him.

Immediate extension following the drop into the crouch results in more force than does a held crouch. Studies of high and long jumping, ski jumping and vertical jumping all indicate that maximum heights are obtained by pushing with very large forces for short periods of time. A muscle must be actively contracting to store energy, therefore a counter movement (downward) followed by quick extension for takeoff should facilitate the storage and utilization of elastic energy.[1] In addition, a held crouch tires the muscles so that extension force is reduced. Working with computerized data Ariel "brought about a two-inch improvement in one female basketball player whose coach had had her bending her knees too deeply before ascent."[2] The crouch of the jump can be likened to the backswing of a throwing or striking action. It is the preparation for the force producing action.

The arms also have a "backswing" action. They must swing into a preparatory position for the movement which is to aid in propelling the body. When distance is the purpose of the jump, the arms are swung backward to balance the forward lean of the body, and to put them into a position which gives maximum time to work up forward momentum that will aid in carrying the upper body forward. If the purpose is to gain height, the arms are dropped with the elbows somewhat flexed, again to allow for movement to develop momentum, this time upward. The flexion of the arms makes it possible to swing them more nearly upward in the direction of desired movement and shortens the levers, making it easier to move them rapidly.

When jumping from a stand, both legs are extended suddenly as the arms swing in the direction of desired movement. A push with both feet equally and simultaneously exerts maximum force available, and assures that the force is applied equally to both sides of the body so that strictly linear motion rather than angular motion will result, and the body will travel straight in the desired direction. Whenever the take-off is from one foot, as in the leap or a jump preceded by a run, the center of gravity is brought in line with the take-off foot at the moment of force application and the arms swing in opposition (left arm forward as the right leg swings forward with left leg take-off) to balance hip and shoulder rotation. A preparatory run which gives the body velocity in the direction in which the action is to be executed, adds force to the final projection. The force gained from this momentum is greater than that which could be produced by the second foot in a jump from a stand. In order to take off from two feet forward motion must be completely or virtually stopped.

There are many activities, for example a diving hurdle and the lay-up shot in basketball (Fig. 1—13), in which it is desirable to convert forward momentum into upward momentum. Lifting one knee forcefully not only produces upward momentum but it also raises the center of gravity **within** the body before the take-off and keeps it back over the supporting leg so that the force produced by its extension is more upward. This can be demonstrated by standing in a forward-backward stride with the weight over the forward foot and forcefully lifting the back knee forward-**upward.** The shift of the weight backward over the supporting foot is evident.

The momentum of the arm swing is transferred to the upper body and, if timed with the leg extension, adds force to the jump. When jumping for distance the arms are swung forcefully forward which is the direction of movement. When height is the objective, the arms are swung upward.

Since the effectiveness of any force produced by the body depends upon the interaction between the body and the supporting surface, friction between the feet and the resisting surface must be sufficient to prevent slipping if all of the force produced by the body is to be transferred back to it. Friction is particularly important when jumping for distance since the force has a backward as well as a downward component.

Since a projectile continues to move in the direction in which the force was applied to it, modified by the force of gravity, the angle of take-off is extremely important to the purpose of the jump. When the center of gravity is forward of the point of take-off, the force is exerted against the floor diagonally downward-backward, and the reaction force effective against the body has both a forward and an upward component (Fig. 13–1).

In jumping for height the desired direction of movement is straight upward and therefore, the center of gravity should be directly above the feet at take-off. Any forward lean of the trunk which accompanies the flexing of the legs should, therefore, be kept to a minimum. If the feet are separated **slightly** forward and backward, the base is enlarged in the direction in which balance is precarious as the body crouches and it is easier to keep the center of gravity centered over the base. As a result the force is more likely to be exerted straight upward. If used, this spreading of the feet should be slight so that the force is not exerted on an angle (forward-downward against the floor by the forward foot and backward-downward by the back foot) and is important **only** for the individual who has difficulty in keeping the center of gravity above the base with feet even. If an individual jumps somewhat forward when desiring to jump upward, this **slight** (half foot length) spreading of the feet forward-backward may help. Experimentation with crouching with the feet together and then with one slightly in advance quickly demonstrates the added stability of the second position.

The knees must flex straight forward over the toes, so that the force exerted on extension can pass straight throught the joints and not at an

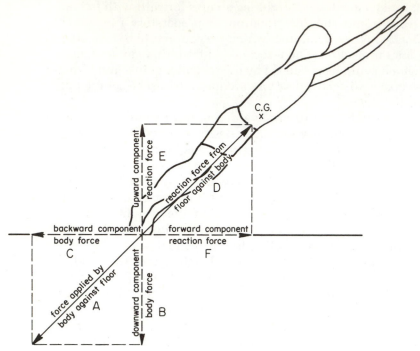

Figure 13–1. Components of diagonal force involved in the thrust of the feet in a jump for distance.

angle. Also, the toes should be straight ahead. The final force is applied by the toes and if they are turned outward, the force is applied at an angle inward. If equal, the inward force of the left foot will counteract that of the right foot and while the direction of the body will not be changed, force is wasted and strain is put on all joints, particularly arches of the feet, ankles and knees. To minimize the strain on arches, ankles and knees, this knee and toe position is important in any of the body projecting activities.

Nelson[3] has pointed out that during a leap by a dancer, ice skater or gymnast, a basketball lay-up, or a spread-eagle jump by a cheerleader, it may be observed that the performer appears to "hang in the air". This is because the final rise, and the beginning of the drop, of the center of gravity occurs **within the body** when arms and legs are lifted then lowered (p. 149).

It is more apparent in the lay-up and the cheerleading situations than in those activities that involve forward as well as upward projection such as the leap. In the latter, the center of gravity rises in the body as the performer approaches the high point because of the leg spread and arm lift causing the momentary pause in movement of trunk and head, just as in the cheerleading example. However, because one leg must reach forward to catch the forward moving body, the legs are not brought together lowering the center of gravity in the body after the high point has been reached and therefore, the second brief period during which the head and trunk remain still is not present. To attempt to obtain greater height of the head for a given projecting force by movements which drop the center of gravity **within the body,** just as it reaches its peak, requires precise timing and, therefore, does not appear to be an effective technique except for skilled performers.

When distance is the purpose of projection the center of gravity must be well ahead of the feet at take-off. Therefore, instability in the forward direction is desirable and, to keep the base small in this direction, as well as to equalize the force applied by the two feet, the feet are kept in line. They should be the width of the hips apart for stability in the lateral plane, and so that the force is exerted straight backward and downward without any inward or outward component. When the feet are placed farther apart than the width of the hips the reaction force is exerted inward against the ankles, knees, and hips as well as forward, and injury could result. Since the inward component of the force exerted by each leg is in direct opposition to that of the other leg, less distance results from a given force produced because so much of it is wasted. This can be demonstrated easily by standing with the feet in a wide stride (exaggerated) and attempting to jump forward. The difficulty of moving forward to any degree is apparent immediately.

As noted previously, the toes should point straight ahead and the knees should flex straight forward over the toes. The entire body must lean forward from the ankles in order for the center of gravity to be moved forward. Frequently individuals have the feeling that they are leaning forward when actually they are bending forward from the hips. They have moved the hips out and back to balance the upper trunk and the center of gravity remains back. To move the center of gravity forward, the pelvis is maintained in its normal well-balanced position as the legs flex and the trunk angles forward. The lean of the body forward is balanced by the backward position of the arms. The weight is over the forward edge of the base. When the arms start their forward swing the center of gravity moves beyond the base and gravity assists in carrying it still farther forward before the legs have completed their extension. The arm swing is important not only in force production, but also in the control of the angle of the body at take-off since it moves the center of gravity forward of the pushing feet.

Some individuals, rather than jumping from both feet, will "step forward." This tendency is noted as children progress through the developmental stages of learning to jump forward. Halverson and Roberton[4] reported that as the forward lean increases, it becomes progressively more difficult for children to inhibit the stepping tendency. This is, of course, caused by the feeling of instability of the preparatory position. This can be lessened by moving the arms well back to counteract the forward lean.

The forceful extension of the legs in the jump for height leaves them in a position directly below the center of gravity of the body, so that equilibrium on landing is no problem and, being extended, they are in position to flex at all of the joints on contact with the floor in order to reduce the downward velocity gradually and thus absorb the force of landing without a jar to the body.

In the jump for distance, however, the legs are behind the body at take-off and must be brought forward to catch the weight as the body falls to the ground (Fig. 13-2). The center of gravity is relatively close to the ground and the legs must be shortened by flexion of all joints in order to clear the ground as they swing forward under the body. This shortening also brings the center of gravity of the legs closer to the axis of movement (the hips), and thus it is easier to move them forward rapidly. Many individuals have difficulty in jumping for distance because they do not flex the joints of the legs to any degree following take-off and, as a result, the feet hit the

Figure 13–2. Distance traversed by center of gravity is considerably less than distance of jump; flexion of joints of legs shortens radius of rotation for faster rotation of body around feet in gaining position of balance as well as absorbing force of impact gradually.

ground almost immediately, stopping the forward motion of the body. Distance can be gained by extending the flexed legs, which have been moved forward under the trunk, as far forward as possible in landing. Thus the length of the jump is much greater than the distance through which the center of gravity must be projected (Fig. 13–2). This extension of the legs is also necessary to put them in position to give as the body lands, and thus gradually absorb the force. However, it leaves the center of gravity behind the feet. The flexing of the legs as the feet touch the ground not only absorbs the shock of landing, but also shortens the body lever and thus increases the angular velocity of the trunk around the feet, so that the forward momentum of the body can carry the center of gravity over the feet.

A backward swing of the arms while the body is in the air aids in swinging the legs forward, and puts the arms in position to swing forward and thus add momentum to carry the upper trunk forward over the feet as they contact the ground. For many this is a difficult coordination to perform in the short time available and it is questionable whether any but the highly skilled will be successful in its use. If poorly timed the arms might be swinging backward as the jumper lands, and this would keep the center of gravity back rather than aid in bringing it forward. In this case it would be better to keep the arms forward following the arm swing at take-off.

When landing from a jump, balance can be maintained or regained more easily if the base is widened to some extent (not beyond hip width). The feet should be adjusted before they contact the floor. It should be recognized that landing with the feet together as is required in the execution of many gymnastic techniques adds to the difficulty of the performance, and thus is a part of the skill which must be developed. Many activities are not performed in the easiest possible manner because their purpose is to test skill.

In any jumping activity shoes with cushioned soles which will absorb some of the force of landing should be worn. If jumping is to be practiced repeatedly, the use of mats or some other soft surface is advisable. For jumps that produce a great deal of force such as the running long jump and high jump, a jumping pit must be used so that the surface can assist the body in absorbing the force more gradually. Before practicing the more forceful jumps, drill in correct landing is essential.

For the same reasons that one cannot walk backward as efficiently as forward (Chapter 11), it is difficult to jump backward. However, whether jumping backward, sideways, forward or upward, the same principles apply. Because of the difficulties involved, the amount of force that can safety be exerted or the angle of application will have to be adjusted and distance sacrificed in favor of safety.

The various high jumps, long jumps, the hop, step and jump, leaps over hurdles, dives and many gymnastic events are a few of the activites which involve projecting the body into space. Although their purposes vary, the mechanical principles are the same. Hurdling is a combination of running and leaping. The take-off, in diving from a springboard in a pool, in a gymnasium or from a mat is mechanically the same. The amount of force produced and the angle of application vary according to purpose but the basic principles are identical. For example, the take-off for the racing dive is the same as for the long jump except that the purpose does not require upward force to keep the body in the air against the pull of gravity and therefore, the force can be applied at a flatter angle making a greater proportion of it effective in producing forward motion. At take-off the center of gravity can be more forward and lower than in the long jump. As in the jump a vigorous forward swing of the arms helps to overcome inertia and start the center of gravity moving forward, and gravity is useful in carrying the center of gravity downward to a position which allows for the most effective application of backward force against the pool edge. The vertical wall of the pool makes it possible to exert force directly backward by curling the toes over the edge. The racing dive resembles the crouching start for the run in that, in both, the projecting force can be exerted against a surface perpendicular to the direction of desired initial motion. The take-off for the running front dive is essentially the same as the jump used in the basketball lay-up shot or any other activity in which forward momentum is converted to upward momentum.

SUMMARY

Regardless of the specific purpose of an activity, the same basic principles apply to all activities which project the body into space.

The path of the center of gravity through the air is determined by the magnitude of the projecting force and the angle of its application. The projecting force is produced by quick extension of the legs aided by a forceful arm swing and deceleration. The legs must flex in preparation for the forceful extension. The stronger the leg muscles the deeper the crouch that can be used. The angle of application is determined by the position of the center of gravity in relation to the feet at the moment of take-off. Placing one foot slightly ahead of the other increases stability and makes it easier to keep the center of gravity over the center of the base. Therefore, this position can be effective in jumping for height. Since in jumping forward the center of gravity must be ahead of the feet, instability is desirable and the feet are placed in line, hip width apart. The center of gravity is moved to a position above the forward margin of the base, so that the arm swing forward moves it beyond the edge of the base where gravity can assist in moving it farther forward by the time the final force of the legs is applied. This places the center of gravity well ahead (in the direction of movement desired) of the point at which the force is applied. At any time that the feet apply a considerable amount of force, it is extremely important that the toes be straight ahead and that the knees flex straight forward above the toes, so that the force is exerted in a straight line through the joints and strain of ankles and knees is minimized.

In a standing jump more force is available when the take-off is from two feet equally. However, the momentum developed by a preliminary run adds considerable force to a jump. Forward momentum can be converted to upward momentum by the forceful lifting of one knee which, besides adding upward momentum, keeps the center of gravity back over the take-off foot and raises the center of gravity even before the body leaves the ground.

In any activity in which the body moves through the air, considerable force must be absorbed on landing. To avoid injury, all joints of the legs must give in sequence as contact with the ground is made so that the velocity can be reduced gradually. Supplying a nonresistive surface for landing is essential for the more forceful jumps.

REFERENCES

1. Nelson, Richard: personal correspondence.
2. Moore, Kenny: Gideon Ariel and His Magic Machine, *Sports Illustrated*, 47:8:60.
3. Nelson: *loc. cit.*
4. Roberton, M. A., and Halvorsen, L. E.: The Developing Child—His Changing Movement, in Logsdon, B. J., et al: *Physical Education for Children: A Focus on The Teaching Process.* Philadelphia, Lea and Febiger, 1977, p. 37.

LANDING AND FALLING   14

The only difference between landing from a jump and falling is that in a fall the equilibrium of the body is out of control. Falls account for many work injuries and are considered an important cause of accidental death in the home. If, in landing from a jump, the equilibrium becomes out of control a fall results. The physical principles which are entailed are identical in any situation when the human body must stop motion, whether of an outside object contacting some body segment (e.g., catching), or of the moving body itself contacting a more or less resistive surface (e.g., falling, landing from a jump).

The problems center around the regaining of equilibrium and avoidance of injury by the reduction of the shock of impact through increasing the distance and time over which the velocity is reduced, increasing the area of the body receiving the force, and receiving the force on the softer, more padded areas of the body.

When falling downward with little or no forward velocity, the feet should be kept under the body if at all possible so that they will contact the ground or floor first. Since balance on landing is a problem, if it is possible the feet should be adjusted to form a wide base (no more than the width of the hips sideways) before the landing is made. If wider than the hips the force of landing is exerted at an angle and causes pressure against the inside of the knee, ankle and hip joints. By landing with the ankles extended the weight can be taken first on the balls of the feet, and then in rapid succession the ankles, knees, and hips can be allowed to flex, each resisting to some extent, so that the downward motion can be slowed gradually. If a great deal of momentum must be absorbed, as when falling from a considerable height, the placement of the hands on the ground gives an added area of contact, and the giving of the wrists and elbows further increases the time and distance over which the force is absorbed. It may be necessary to tuck the body and go into roll in order to spend the force even more gradually.

When forward momentum is involved as when one trips, becomes overbalanced while running or falls from some moving object, injury can be avoided or minimized by relaxing to allow joints to give and muscles to be "soft" while curling into a ball and rolling so that the velocity is retarded gradually. Whether a forward roll, a shoulder roll or a hip roll, the area taking the force is greatly enlarged and the time for reduction of velocity is increased. If the body does fall forward onto the hands and arms, the wrists and elbows must give as they take the weight. This must be a **controlled flexion** so that the velocity is reduced gradually.

Every effort should be made to avoid landing on the head, elbow or knee, since these areas are solid and no give is possible. The head, being so vital a part of the body, must be protected even at the cost of injury to an arm. It has been suggested that, by giving with the wrists and arms and arching the back so that the body rocks forward, the force is distributed over a large area and to some extent the velocity is slowed gradually as the body rocks. This method of absorbing the force does keep the head up off the ground, but it must be remembered that the head is at the end of a long system of levers and the force is magnified as it throws the head backward. The velocity is reduced much more rapidly than when one rolls, and if it is very great a "whip lash" injury of the neck muscles may result from this method of stopping the momentum. This may also result in injury of the lower back. Therefore, if at all possible, curling into a ball and rolling is much safer than arching the back and rocking. Frequently, when one is falling in such a way that the knee would be the first part of the body to hit, a slight twist of the body will throw the weight onto the well padded buttocks. Or, when falling onto the elbow, a twist will throw the weight onto the back of the shoulders which, if rounded, allows the body to roll.

Stepping off a moving vehicle frequently results in a fall since the body has acquired the velocity of the vehicle, and because of inertia, continues to move when the feet are stopped by their contact with the ground (See Fig. 4–1). Since this is an extremely dangerous practice, it should be avoided. However, if it should happen, a fall may be avoided by running with small rapid steps in the direction in which the vehicle is moving so that the base can "catch up" to the body's center of gravity which is moving in that direction. The speed of the steps is reduced as the body gradually reduces its velocity.

When falling backward, the body should be relaxed. The weight is taken by the hands and arms which give, allowing the weight to come down onto the buttocks and, if the body is tucked and allowed to roll backward, the force of impact can be absorbed gradually.

When sliding into base in softball or baseball, as much body surface as possible should be used so that the force is distributed over a large area. The center of gravity is lowered gradually during the last steps so that the downward force is minimized.

In general, when falling the body should be relaxed and flexed so that it will roll rather than stop suddenly. When arms or legs contact the ground all of the joints give, each resisting some of the force, so that the velocity is reduced gradually.

JUMPING, DIVING AND FALLING INTO WATER

Falling into water differs from falling on a firmer surface such as the ground, floor and mats, because the water gives with force of the body, allowing the body to pass through the water. The give of the water lessens the shock of impact. The larger the area of the water contacted, the greater the water resistance. Therefore, to reduce the shock of impact, water should be approached with **as small a body area** as possible. A small area is directly resisted by an equally small area of water, and the water is pushed downward and outward. The reaction force of water is inward and upward. Thus the force of the water is not directly upward and, as a result, it is less effective in resisting the movement of the body through the water. When a large area contacts the water, as when the diver "hits flat," a large area of water exerts force directly upward resisting the body's downward movement and greater force is exerted against the body. This might be likened to pressing the flat of a knife against a piece of cheese as opposed to pressing the cutting edge against it. The former being wide is resisted but the latter being narrow passes easily through the cheese. When entering the water head first, the body should be **kept rigid as it enters the water,** as opposed to giving as it hits a more resistive surface. If, in a dive, the elbows are allowed to bend as the hands (which are leading the head) contact the resistance of the water, the hands and arms will not push the water downward and outward, and the head is resisted by an area of water equal to the area of the head. The arms, when held rigid, in effect, "cut a hole" for the body to move into. In general, when **falling** or **diving into water,** every effort should be made to present as small an area of the body as possible to the surface of the water, and to keep the body rigid. These principles are directly opposite to those which are applicable to falling on a resistive surface, because in the latter instance all of the give must be within the body itself, while in the case of water the force is reduced by the gradual giving of the water.

However, there are situations in which it is necessary to prevent the sinking of the head below the surface when **jumping** into water. In this case, water resistance must be maximized. This can be accomplished without injury by spreading the legs wide forward-backward and stabilizing the arms out to the sides at shoulder height to increase, as much as possible, the size of the area presented to the water by body segments that can withstand the resultant force.

15 SITTING

Much time is spent sitting; in general, one sits while performing various work tasks or while resting. However, it would seem that there is a third reason for sitting which is neither for concentrated work nor for rest — sitting while conversing, reading for short periods of time when one anticipates the necessity for getting up rapidly and frequently and so forth. The so-called "straight" chair is used for work, the "easy" or "lounge" chair, sofa or bed for rest and the "occasional" chair, which is between these in the support offered the body, for conversing. The more the chair supports the body the more the muscles can rest, but the less free the body is to perform various tasks which may be demanded of it. In sports one sits on a horse and in various types of boats, in a snowmobile, on a toboggan; the skier sits in a chair lift and the golfer sits in a cart. The support afforded the body varies in each of these situations but the principles involved are the same regardless of the sitting task.

Since all sitting enlarges the base of support and places the center of gravity of the body close to the base, much of the strain of standing, in which the relatively high center of gravity must be kept over a small base, is eliminated. The system of levers that must be held erect is much shorter, being only the trunk, neck, and head, and, therefore, is easier to control. However, the same basic principles of keeping the various body segments in line which apply to standing, also apply to sitting regardless of the particular purpose for sitting or the type of chair or other object used.

There are three major problems involved in sitting in a chair: getting into the chair, sitting in the chair and getting out of it. When sitting down the chief consideration is that of providing a base under the backward moving center of gravity, so that the body weight can be kept under control while the body is being lowered; when sitting in the chair it is that of economy of energy and avoidance of strain over perhaps a long period of time; and when arising from the chair, that of shifting the weight forward over the base. In all of these the aesthetic consideration cannot be overlooked.

SITTING DOWN AND ARISING

Straight Chair. Since a straight chair usually has an open space between its legs and is not as low or as deep as the lounge chair, it does not

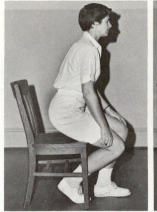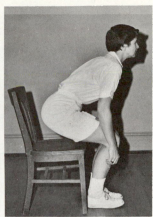

Figure 15–1. *A*, Good — base under center of gravity. *B*. Poor — center of gravity kept over base by forward lean.

A   B

present some of the problems that are encountered with the latter. The chair, being open under the seat, makes it possible for the individual sitting to place one foot back under the seat. Placing one foot back under the seat as far as possible supplies a base which is under the center of gravity of the body as it moves backward, and thus places the leg in a position to control the lowering of the body weight into the chair (Fig. 15–1). If the feet are kept **in front of** the chair either the body must bend forward considerably to balance the backward shifting hips, or the body drops into the chair with a jar since the force of gravity is unresisted. Obviously, neither is mechanically efficient nor aesthetically pleasing.

Sitting down in a straight chair efficiently involves standing with the back to the chair, placing one foot as far back under the seat as it can reach easily, and then allowing the hips and knees to flex, so that the body weight is lowered to the seat of the chair by a controlled giving in to gravity through an eccentric (lengthening) contraction of the extensor muscles. As the body is lowered the trunk is allowed to incline forward slightly. The hips are then slid back in the seat if they did not contact the chair at the rear of the seat.

Arising from the chair is accomplished by reversing the above procedure. Again, one foot is placed back under the seat so that it is in a position to apply force upward through the center of gravity of the body. If the seat is relatively deep the body will have to be shifted forward in the chair, so that the center of gravity is over the back foot before an attempt to rise is made. The trunk is inclined slightly forward from the hips since this is the direction of desired movement, and the legs are extended lifting the body upward and forward, transferring the weight to the forward foot. Because the weight is forward and the push is in a forward, as well as upward, direction it is very easy to continue movement in a walk. If this is not desired the trunk should be inclined forward to a lesser degree.

Occasional Chair. Since normally an occasional chair is also open under the seat the same procedures are followed. Usually this type of chair has arms. Most authors have stated that the arms of the chair should never be used in lowering oneself into the chair. However, it would seem that if the

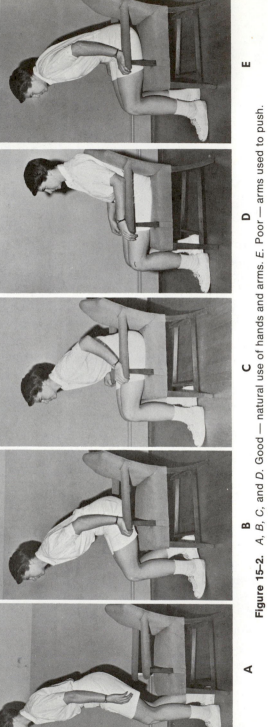

A   B   C   D   E

Figure 15-2. *A, B, C,* and *D.* Good — natural use of hands and arms. *E.* Poor — arms used to push.

hands are placed on the arms of the chair as they naturally come in contact with them and some slight amount of resistance is afforded by them as the body weight is lowered, they can be effective in aiding the process and at the same time increase its naturalness. Also, the use of the arms in rising can increase the efficiency if coordinated with the leg extension (Fig. 15–2). Since the legs are a great deal stronger they are better suited to the task of lifting the body weight and should, therefore, produce the major force. Attempting to avoid use of the arms completely results in an unnatural and stilted movement.

Easy Chair.   The great majority of easy chairs are solid from the seat to a point a few inches above the floor and thus it is impossible to place a foot under the seat. The only way that the weight can be maintained above the base while it is being lowered, is for the individual to stand more or less sideways to the chair with the feet in a forward-backward stride position. This position of the feet gives a wide base for balance. The foot nearest the chair must be forward so that, as the weight is lowered, the body can be twisted slightly toward the chair and the weight taken on that hip. (Experimentation will immediately demonstrate that it is impossible to sit in the chair if the foot nearest the chair is back.) The hips are lowered to the edge of the chair by the controlled bending of the hips and knees as when sitting down in any chair and the body is turned and slid back into the seat. Actually this turning and moving back starts as the body is lowered so that the total process is a continuous motion. Frequently the friction between the seat and the hips is considerable because of the type of material covering the chair and the clothing of the individual. Placing the hands on the arms of the chair so that some of the weight can be taken off the hips reduces the friction and makes it possible to slide into the chair more easily.

It is difficult to get out of this type of chair easily and gracefully, and the deeper the chair and the greater the friction, the more difficult the task becomes. The process of sitting down is reversed but if the chair is very deep it may be impossible to make the process continuous. The body weight must be moved to the forward edge of the chair and again, taking some of the weight on the arms aids in the process. In sliding forward the body should be turned slightly to one side, so that the weight is more on one hip and the feet should be separated to enlarge the base. The center of gravity can then be brought above the base with little forward bending of the trunk. From this position the legs are extended to lift the body from the chair. Experimentation with attempting to get out of such a chair with the hips back and the body facing straight forward will demonstrate the extreme forward flexion of the trunk, usually including extension of the arms forward, that is necessary to balance the weight of the hips so that the center of gravity is brought over the feet. If the chair is very deep it is impossible to get the center of gravity above the feet in this way. Use of the hands on the arms of the chair to give some slight aid to the legs in lifting the body is efficient, but use of the arms to **lift** the body weight is not efficient since the muscles of the legs are much stronger and therefore, more suited to the task. Only when the legs are incapacitated should the arms supply any major force.

Floor.   The problem of maintaining the balance so that the body weight can be controlled as it is lowered to the floor becomes progressively greater

Figure 15-3. Dropping to sitting position on floor.

as a child becomes taller. Since a very young child is relatively light and his center of gravity is so near the floor little momentum is developed even in a completely uncontrolled drop to the floor, and therefore the force of impact is not greater than can be absorbed by his well padded hips. The older child or adult, weighing more and having a considerable distance to drop, must control his weight to avoid the possibility of injury. There are many ways that this can be accomplished.

Those who are very flexible can be successful in squatting and then, by extending the arms forward to balance the weight, lowering the hips to the floor. Some individuals cross the lower legs and allow the knees to bend outward while gradually lowering the weight to the floor. Both of these methods take a great deal of balance since the base is extremely small. In controlling the weight with the feet in the crossed position greater pressure is exerted against the sides of the knees.

Another method is that of squatting and then placing a hand on the floor behind one hip to support some of the weight as the hips are lowered to the floor. The hand can also be placed on the floor to the side of the body and slid along the floor as the weight is lowered, first onto one hip and then adjusted to rest on both. The base is enlarged by the use of the hand and the weight can be controlled easily.

Kneeling on one or both knees enlarges the base, eliminating the problem of balance relatively early in the performance of the task, and from this position it is easy to slide a hand along the floor on the side of the bent knee and to lower the weight to that hip. This process can be modified by crossing one leg behind the other, flexing the forward leg which is supporting the weight, to lower the body to the point where the hand on the side of the crossed leg can reach the floor, and thus enlarging the base and aiding in the final lowering of the weight to the floor (Fig. 15–3). Because of the reduction in the size of the base during the first part of the process this requires more balance control than does kneeling.

Regardless of the way in which it is accomplished the center of gravity must be kept above the base if the weight is to be controlled. Enlarging the base by the use of one hand as the hips approach the point at which they, in order to reach the floor, leave their position above the feet, is the easiest method for performing this task.

To get up from the floor the problem is to move the center of gravity to a position above the feet. When sitting with the feet flat on the floor and knees bent up in front of the body it is possible to accomplish this by extending the arms forward and rocking backward and then forward, to work up sufficient momentum to carry the center of gravity of the body upward and forward over the feet. While this is undoubtedly a test of skill it is far from the most efficient method of standing up. Some individuals with strong legs can, from the crossed leg or "tailor position," lean well forward and stand. Most have neither the strength nor the balance to do this and again, as in using this method to sit down, pressure is exerted against the sides of the knees as the legs extend. If the weight is shifted to one hip, that hand placed on the floor and the lower leg on that side crossed behind the other leg, it is very easy to come to a kneeling position on one knee and then to a stand. This gives a wide base at the time that the hips are not above the feet and makes use of arm and shoulder girdle strength to start the upward motion, but the real task of lifting the body weight is performed by the stronger leg muscles. When executed as a continuous movement this method is both easy and aesthetically pleasing.

SITTING POSITIONS

Regardless of the purpose, the general principle that the sitting position should be one in which the body segments remain in the same relationship to each other as they are when in a well-balanced standing position should be observed.

Straight Chair or Occasional Chair. When sitting in a straight or occasional chair, the hips should be well back in the chair and the pelvis should be in its balanced position (neither tilted forward nor backward); the entire back should be supported. If the knees are flexed at right angles and the feet flat on the floor, some of the weight of the thighs is supported by the feet and excessive pressure on the blood vessels and nerves at the back of the knee is avoided (Fig. 15–4A). When it is necessary to move the upper body forward so that the eyes are brought closer to the work, the trunk should be shifted from the hips, in much the same way that the body is shifted as a unit from the ankles when the weight is moved forward in standing or walking, so that the well-balanced alignment of the body segments can be maintained (Fig. 15–5).

When a task is undertaken for any length of time, it is important that the position be such that both eyes are the same distance from the work. This means that the plane of the face must be parallel to the plane of the work and the midline of each must fall on the same line.[1] Angling the working surface allows for the maintenance of a well-balanced position while retaining this

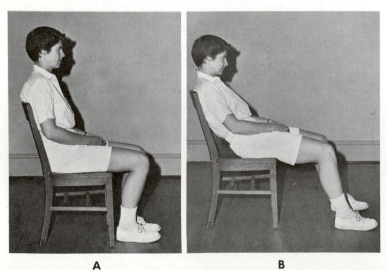

| A | B |

Figure 15–4. *A.* Good — all of back supported. *B.* Poor — lower back and thighs unsupported, pelvis tilted backward.

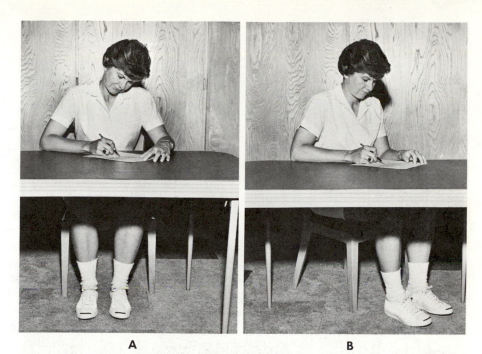

A   **B**

Figure 15–5. *A.* Poor — head cocked to bring eyes equidistant from work. *B.* Good — upper body and head well-aligned.

relationship with the work. Sitting directly facing a desk leads to "cocking" the head since the paper, because of the position of the arm as the hand is brought in front of the body, is at an angle. In order for the eyes to be equidistant from the writing, the head is tilted and slightly rotated (Fig. 15–5*A*). Therefore, it is better to sit slightly at an angle to the desk or table with the body turned away from the preferred hand (turned toward the left if right handed)[1] (Fig. 15–5*B*). This puts the eyes equidistant from the work with the head in a well-balanced position (Fig. 15–6).

Sitting with legs crossed lifts one hip and places the pelvis on an angle, causing a compensating lateral ("C") curve in the spine. This position also results in pressure on the nerves and blood vessels that run behind the crossed knee which, if continued for any length of time, causes the foot and leg to "go to sleep." However, this position will not be harmful if not maintained so long that the blood and nerve supply to the foot are cut, and if legs are alternately crossed so that the curve caused by crossing one leg is compensated by the crossing of the other. Unusual positions should not be maintained habitually but are not harmful if assumed occasionally for short periods of time for a change of position.

A complete discussion of various restful positions can be found in Metheny's *Body Dynamics*[2] and is not included here.

Easy Chair.   Since the purpose of the easy chair is to rest, the entire body must be supported so that the force of gravity simply pulls the body against the chair and the muscles are no longer called upon to support the body weight. The hips should be all the way back in the seat of the chair so

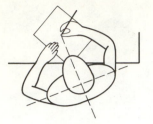

Figure 15–6. Head well-balanced, eyes equidistant from work. (Adapted from Harmon, D. B.: Eye Preference, Certain Body Mechanics and Visual Problems. Unpublished paper, 1963.)

that the hips, lower back, upper back and, if the most restful position is desired, the neck and head can be supported. When the hips are forward, the lower back is unsupported and gravity constantly acts to pull this part of the body downward. The back of such a chair should be soft so that it will take the contour of the body curves. Since most of these chairs are deep it may be impossible to sit with the hips against the back and still flex the knees and have the feet flat on the floor. When this is the case, the legs and feet must be supported by a foot stool of approximately the same height as the chair seat or slightly lower. A support of the legs which is higher than the chair seat forces the knees backward. A support under the feet only, leaves the lower leg unsupported against gravity's pull. The arms should be allowed to fall naturally from the shoulder when the lower arms are supported by the arms of the chair, the elbows being bent at approximately right angles.

Floor. While, on the whole, adults do not spend a great deal of time sitting on the floor, the time so spent by children and young adults is considerable, and it is important that they understand the advantages and problems of various positions. It is clearly evident from observation of any group that there are many different positions used in sitting on the floor.

The position of sitting with the legs straight out on the floor in front of the body poses different problems for different individuals. When some individuals sit in this position, the pelvic girdle remains in its normal position (neither tilted forward nor backward) but for others it is impossible to avoid a tilting backward of the pelvis. The only problem for the first group

Figure 15–7. Balanced pelvis, spine straight laterally, arms giving some support to back.

(balanced pelvic girdle) is that the posterior thigh muscles both extend the thigh and flex the leg and therefore, in this position, they are stretched at both joints; this makes the position uncomfortable to maintain for any length of time. This stretch can be relieved by placing the feet flat on the floor with the knees flexed up in front of the body (Fig. 15–7). This keeps the weight even on both hips and the spine straight laterally. Some of the strain of maintaining the upright position of the trunk can be relieved by the arms if they are placed around the knees. The danger in this position is that the individual may pull the shoulders forward and round the upper back.

A backward-tilted pelvis can be caused by this stretch of these two joint muscles or by a difference in skeletal structure; muscles and/or ligaments may not be long enough to allow full flexion of the hips when the knees are straight. Regardless of the cause, this position of the pelvis rolls the hips under the trunk and makes it difficult to keep the trunk erect; it tends to fall backward. When these individuals flex their knees as indicated above, they roll even farther back on the hips (Fig. 15–8) and find maintenance of balance very difficult. Observation to date has indicated that women are more likely than men to have a balanced position of the pelvis when sitting in this position; however, some women do have the problem of a pelvis which rolls under while some men have a body structure that allows the pelvis to remain in a balanced position.

Sitting "tailor fashion," that is, with the feet crossed and the knees flexed and dropped out to each side, is comfortable for those individuals who are flexible, but difficult for anyone with tight muscles along the inside of the thighs (Fig. 15–9). In fact, this position can be useful in stretching these tight muscles. It is important that the trunk, neck and head remain in the well-balanced position as when standing.

One of the most commonly assumed positions is that of sitting with the knees flexed and both feet to one side of the body. This position lifts the hip on the side of the feet tending to throw the upper body off balance to the opposite side (Fig. 15–10). To counteract this the shoulder on the side of the high hip is dropped and a "C" curve of the spine to the opposite side results. If the position is taken with the feet to the right and then to the left for an equal amount of time, the curve is compensated and no great problems arise. The problem arises when the position is assumed habitually with the feet to

Figure 15–8. Sitting with knees bent. Note: Tilt of pelvis backward; compare with Fig. 15–7.

Figure 15–9.   Spine straight, flexibility required.

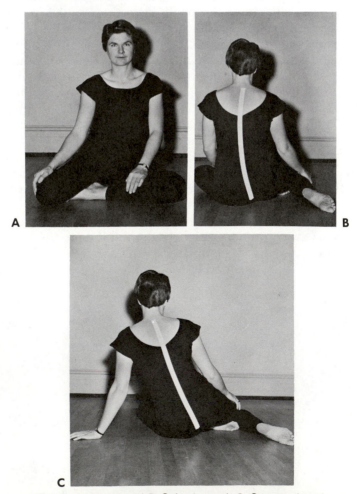

A

B

C

Figure 15–10.   *A* and *B.* Spine curved; *C,* Curve reduced.

Figure 15–11. Spine straight, pressure on knees.

the same side. Unfortunately, each individual normally has a preferred side, the position is more comfortable when the feet are on a certain side, and while he may shift briefly for a change of position, most of the time that he sits on the floor his feet are on the preferred side. Whether or not this contributes to the development of a permanent curve of the spine depends upon the amount of time this individual spends in this position. Leaders of young peoples' groups should understand the implications of such a position so that they would never insist, for the sake of the pattern of the group, that during ceremonies, some of which are of considerable length, all of the boys and girls sit with their feet to the right side. Instead, they should encourage frequent changes in position when children sit on the floor.

The curve in the spine can be considerably reduced if, instead of balancing the upper body by dropping the shoulder on the side of the high hip, the opposite arm is used to support some of the weight of the trunk (Fig. 15–10C).

Some very flexible individuals, particularly children, sit with their lower legs bent under their bodies (Fig. 15–11). This position does allow the spine to remain in its straight position but causes pressure on the blood vessels and nerves, particularly those running behind the knees and, if maintained for any length of time, cuts off circulation and nerve supply to the lower legs.

Since the back is unsupported, all of these positions are more tiring than sitting in a chair. It must be remembered that, as in standing, a change of position is restful. Several of these positions may be assumed if it is necessary to sit on the floor for any length of time. The important principle is that, as in standing, walking and running, the trunk, neck and head should be maintained in a well-balanced position, one above the other, with no joints in a position of strain. When a position which violates this principle is assumed for the sake of change, a compensatory position should be taken for an equal time. However, during the greatest amount of time the principle should be followed.

Bed. Besides sitting in bed (at various angles) when ill, many individuals read or watch television in bed before settling down for the night. Too often the position leaves the lower back unsupported. Pillows need to be placed so that they fill any space between bed and back and support the head in line with the spine. A pillow just below the knees relieves the pressure that can be caused by overextension and also lessens the pull which tends to tilt the pelvis forward, thus reducing back strain. The mechanical beds now on the market (based on the design of hospital beds) make it easier to sit in bed in a well-aligned position but they are expensive.

If the weight of the hanging arms causes discomfort in the ill or elderly, this can be relieved by supporting the flexed elbows and lower arms so that the normal height of the elbows is maintained and pull on the shoulder is eliminated.

IMPORTANT CONSIDERATIONS IN REGARD TO FURNITURE

Straight Chair.   Chairs should be chosen to fit the individual who will be using them. The height should be such that when the hips are at the back of the seat, the feet are flat on the floor and the knees flexed at right angles. The feet then support some of the weight of the thighs and reduce the pressure on the blood vessels and nerves which run behind the thigh. If the chair is chosen at a time when the individual is wearing shoes with heels it may be too high for comfortable sitting at a future time when low heels are worn. Therefore, it is wise to slip off shoes to test the height of the chair.

Too frequently individuals are not in a position to choose a chair of correct height but must use whatever is provided. In most school situations the chairs for a certain grade are all the same height, although the leg length of persons varies greatly. Placing a block of wood, a box or a book under the feet when the chair is too high makes it possible to sit properly in the chair and still have the feet supported. Because it is so uncomfortable to have the feet unsupported, the well-balanced position of the body is sacrificed in order to get the feet on the floor, unless something is put under the feet. The individual slides the hips forward on the seat of the chair leaving the lower back completely unsupported and, if continued over any period of time or assumed frequently, future back pain is inevitable.

The depth of the chair seat from its back to its front edge is just as important to comfort and the maintenance of a well-balanced position as its height. The seat should be of such depth that the front edge crosses the thighs a few inches behind the knee. Too deep a seat necessitates the moving forward of the hips to relieve the pressure against the back of the knee or even to flex the knee. Again, this leaves the lower back unsupported and upsets the alignment of the entire upper body. Too shallow a seat results in too much of the weight of the thigh being unsupported by the seat and thus its weight is pressed down on the nerves that run along the back of the thigh.

The back of the chair should support the back of the individual regardless of the type of chair. Since when sitting the hips protrude backward beyond the back, it is necessary for a chair back to be open or curved outward at its base in order to give support to the lower back. A straight chair back or one that slants slightly backward from the base leaves the lower back completely unsupported. A chair that is to be used for long hours of work should have an adjustable back so that the support can be fitted to the individual's back. The chair should also be adjustable in height.

Easy Chair. If the legs are supported at approximately the height of the chair seat (never higher) the height and depth of the seat are not important. A support which lifts the lower leg higher than the thigh tends to hyperextend the knee joint causing pressure in this joint. The chair back should be soft so that it will fit the curves of the body and give complete support. When the chair back does not support all sections of the back, pillows should be used. The chair arms should be of such a height that they will support the lower arms when the elbows are approximately at right angles and the arms are hanging naturally from the shoulders. Chair arms that are too high push the shoulders up into an unnatural position and if too low they do not give maximum support to the individual's arms and thus relief to the shoulder muscles.

Desk. A desk or other working surface at which the individual sits should be at a height just below the bend of the individual's elbow when sitting in the chair to be used with a desk. If higher, the shoulders must be hunched in order to have the lower arm on the working surface. If lower, the individual must lower the shoulders in order for the desk surface to support the lower arm. This causes a rounded back. If circumstances make it necessary to use a desk which is too low, small blocks of wood can be put under the legs to adjust it to the proper height. If the only available desk is too high, the chair should be raised either by the use of a pillow in the seat or by blocks of wood under the legs. It must be remembered that this necessitates some support which will raise the feet of the individual an equal amount, so that the basic sitting position can still be maintained.

When a typewriter is to be used, a lower desk or table is needed since the keyboard is some inches above the surface of the desk. The keyboard should be at such a height that the hands are slightly below the bend of the elbows when on the keys. If higher than this the lower arms and hands must be held up against the pull of gravity constantly. The use of a copy holder avoids the need for dropping and turning of the head.

Workbench, Counter and Stool. Since workbenches and counters are built at a height for working while standing, when it is desirable to sit to work it is necessary to use a high stool so that the arms are in the proper relationship to the surface, that is, so that the working height is a few inches below the elbow height. Since the stool is high there should be a step which supports the feet. Many benches and counters have cupboards built beneath them making it impossible to sit facing the counter because there is no space for the knees. Sitting sideways to the counter necessitates twisting the trunk and is very tiring. Use of pullout boards built into the workbench or counter makes it possible to sit in a normal position and still be close to one's work.

SITTING ON A MOVING SURFACE

There are many times when the surface on which the individual is sitting is moving rather than stationary. People sit in planes, cars, boats, golf carts, snowmobiles, on horses. The law of inertia makes it clear that, whenever the base is moving, the individual must be alert to the possibility of changes in velocity or direction. When a horse shies or refuses a jump, the unwary rider may find himself on the ground; he tends to keep moving in the direction he was moving before the horse jumped to the side or stopped before the jump.

Riding in a golf cart can lead to a similar result. Sitting in a golf cart as a passenger requires constant attention to ground contour and the possibility of change in direction. The driver knows when he is going to turn, and in addition, his hold on the steering wheel makes it easy to stabilize his position in the cart. The passenger, however, must anticipate directional change so that he is prepared to lean inward (toward the direction of the turn), just as a runner must lean inward when he wishes to turn (p. 189), to avoid the possibility of being thrown out of the cart. This tendency is experienced also when riding in a car. One only needs to close one's eyes when riding along a curved road to be conscious of it. However, unlike the golf cart, the car has sides which, except in unusual circumstances, serve to keep the passenger in the vehicle and, in addition, seat belts assure maintenance of the position on the seat. Unless a shoulder belt is used to restrict motion, the tendency for the upper body to be thrown outward is still present. With the eyes open so that the curves can be anticipated, the individual unconsciously adjusts the upper body to resist the outwardly directed force.

SUMMARY

There are three major problems involved in sitting in a chair whether one is sitting to work, to converse, or simply to rest: getting into the chair, sitting in the chair, and getting out of it.

In sitting down, the chief consideration is that of providing a base under the backward moving center of gravity of the body. In standing up the problem becomes that of shifting the weight forward over the base so that it can be lifted by the extension of the legs. Whenever possible one foot should be placed back under the seat of the chair to enlarge the base backward in sitting down or arising. The weight can then be controlled as it is lowered since it at no time passes beyond the edge of the base, and, in standing, the force of the legs can be exerted upward and forward if the trunk is shifted very slightly forward from the hips. When the chair is solid from the seat to a few inches above the floor, making it impossible to place a foot under the seat, the center of gravity can be kept over the base as it is lowered by standing sideways to the chair in a forward-backward stride position. The weight can then be lowered to the edge of the seat and the body turned as it is slid backward into the chair seat. To get up the process is reversed.

When a chair has arms, the hands should be allowed to contact them naturally and can assist in taking some of the weight in lowering and lifting the body, but should **never** be called upon to produce the major force involved unless the legs are incapacitated to some degree.

When sitting down on the floor, one hand can be used to enlarge the base as the hips approach the floor and to aid in lowering the body weight to one hip. The position can then be adjusted so that the weight is equally distributed on both hips. It is easy to come to a kneeling and then to a standing position by shifting the weight to one hip, placing that hand on the floor while crossing the leg on that side behind the other leg, pushing with the hand and then extending the legs.

Regardless of the surface upon which one is sitting or the purpose, the general principle that the position of the upper body should be such that the segments remain in the same relationship to each other as they are when standing in a well-balanced position should be observed.

The hips should be well back in any chair and the back of the body should be supported. Unless the legs and feet are supported at approximately the height of the chair (no higher), the feet should be flat on the floor with the knees flexed at right angles. When it is necessary to bring the eyes closer to the work, the entire upper body is shifted forward from the hips.

When sitting on the floor, care should be taken that no position which causes a curve of the spine is assumed habitually. In all sitting it should be remembered that a change of position is always restful, and that those positions which cause poor alignment of body segments are not harmful if taken **briefly** and compensatory positions are used for an equal period of time. However, the position assumed for the majority of time should place the body segments in a well-balanced alignment.

Furniture influences the position one is able to assume. Both the height and depth of chair seat are important factors at any time that the lower legs are not supported by a footstool. The chair seat should be of a height that allows the feet to be flat on the floor when the knees are bent at right angles, and its forward edge should cross the thigh a few inches behind the knee when the hips are well back in the chair. The back of the chair must support the individual's back, and the arms of the chair should allow the elbow to flex at approximately a right angle when the upper arms hang naturally from the shoulders. Any working surface, desk, typewriter, workbench or counter should be at such a height that the hands, in performing the particular task involved, are a few inches lower than elbow height when the individual is sitting in a well-balanced position.

When sitting in bed, pillows should fill any spaces between the back and bed and should maintain the basic alignment of trunk, neck and head.

When sitting on a moving surface, the individual must be alert to possible velocity or directional changes.

REFERENCES

1. Harmon, D. B.: Eye Preference, Certain Body Mechanics and Visual Problems. Unpublished paper, 1963.
2. Metheny, Eleanor: *Body Dynamics*. New York, McGraw-Hill Book Company, Inc., 1951, pp. 178–190.

16 PUSHING AND PULLING

In general, pushing and pulling tasks are more common in normal everyday activities, work actions and nursing-type tasks than in sports. Individuals push heavy furniture, baby carriages, carts full of groceries, lawnmowers, wheelbarrows and many other objects. They pull rakes, hoes, sleds. They open and close drawers, windows and doors. They push shovels into the earth. They may find themselves in situations in which they have to assist persons with varying degrees of incapacitation in and out of chairs and beds, as well as help them move (or move them) in the bed. These are but a few of the common tasks which involve pushing or pulling movement. While pushing and pulling are not involved in the same quantity of sport activities, an understanding of this type of movement is essential in aquatic sports, since they, with the exception of diving, are almost entirely push-pull activities. In rowing, canoeing and swimming, the movement of the boat or the individual results from the push against the water by oars, paddles, or arms and legs. Archery is a pulling activity. The push pass or shot in basketball and the shot-put in track also involve pushing movements. Essentially every movement of the human body is either caused or controlled by a pull, since movement of a body segment results either from the shortening of muscles or from gravity's action which must be controlled by a resisting muscular force (pulling). (See p. 92.)

Many pushing and pulling tasks are light, but several involve the application of considerable force and make economy of effort and avoidance of strain prime considerations. In heavy tasks, the initial force overcomes the inertia, and additional force must be applied as long as movement is desired. To accomplish successfully the particular purpose involved in pushing or pulling an object, the desired direction of movement, type of movement (linear or angular), distance to be moved, speed of movement, as well as the friction and other resistive forces must be considered. The friction between the feet of the person applying the force and the supporting surface is important also. The speed of movement and distance moved, in fact whether or not movement takes place at all, are determined by the magnitude of the force applied in relation to the magnitude of the resistive forces. The direction of movement is dependent upon both the point of application of the force and the direction in which it is applied. The point of application and resistive forces such as friction, determine whether linear or angular motion results.

PRINCIPLES INVOLVED

Magnitude of Force.   When force rather than control of direction is the primary consideration, the **strongest muscles available to the particular task should be used** in order to avoid strain. This means that the legs should supply the main pushing or pulling force. Also, when force is of primary consideration, the individual should contact the load and set the muscles for the task **before** the pushing or pulling force is exerted. Sudden application of considerable force before the setting of the arm and shoulder muscles has stabilized the joints will not result in movement of the object, but only in the giving of the wrists, elbows and shoulders. The firmer the arms and trunk, the more the force produced by the legs will be transferred to the object to be moved.

The amount of force that can be transferred to the object also depends upon the counterpressure of the supporting surface against the foot. If there is insufficient friction, the force exerted by the individual results in pushing the foot backward rather than in moving the object forward. Friction between the feet of the individual pushing the object and the supporting surface is, therefore, desirable. However, friction between the object being pushed and the supporting surface is undesirable in that it necessitates a greater force to effect and maintain motion.

Lack of firmness of the supporting surface is undesirable, both because less counterpressure is applied to the feet of the individual and, therefore, more force is necessary to attain a given result, and because greater resistance is offered to the forward movement of the object. When the surface is not firm, it gives with the weight of the object and thus forms, in effect, a series of vertical walls around the object which must be pushed down as the object moves forward.

Because of inertia to any change in movement state (Newton's First Law) **it takes more force to start an object moving than to keep it moving.** Sufficient force should be applied continuously to keep the load moving at a moderate velocity once it has started moving. Overcoming the initial inertia is the greatest problem in any pushing or pulling task.

Direction of Force.   **The force should be applied as nearly as possible in the direction of the desired movement.** There are some tasks that require the body to be placed in an inefficient position if the force is to be applied directly in the line of the desired motion. When this is the situation, more effort may be wasted in attempting to perform the task in an efficient body position than would be lost in applying the force at an angle rather than in the direct line of desired movement. However, the undesirable component of the force should be kept as small as possible. Whenever the force is applied at an angle to the line of movement, only the component of the force in the direction of movement is effective in accomplishing the desired result (Chapter 6, Force). It follows that less energy is required the nearer to the desired direction of movement the force can be applied, since a greater

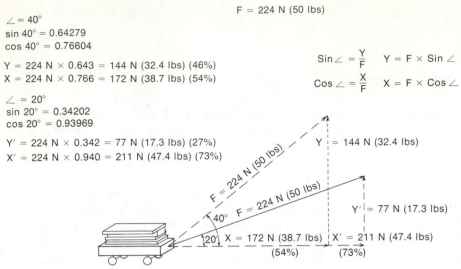

Figure 16–1. Effective horizontal and vertical forces resulting from application of force of 224 N (50 lbs) at forty and twenty-degree angles.

percentage of the force is effective in moving the object in the desired direction. For example, if in pulling a cart holding several mats, a force of 224 newtons (50 lbs) is applied at a 40 degree angle, 46 per cent of the force tends to lift the cart and only 54 per cent is effective in moving it forward. If this same force is applied at a 20 degree angle (closer to the direction of movement), 73 per cent of the force acting on the cart is effective in moving it forward (Fig. 16–1).

However, the amount of friction between the object to be moved and the surface across which it must move must be considered also. The greater the friction, the larger the upward component of force that is desirable in order to reduce this friction. When an object is free to move only along a predetermined path, for example, a window which moves up and down in its casing, force in any direction other than that of its path is not only wasted, but also adds to the difficulty of the task by increasing the friction between the window and the casing.

Point of Application of Force. The point at which the force is applied depends upon the type of motion desired. When the force is applied through the center of gravity of the object, linear motion results and the object moves in the direction of the force, if friction is not too great and there is no obstacle in its path. The greater the friction, the lower the force must be applied or the larger the upward component necessary. When force is applied away from the center of gravity of the object, the object tends to rotate. **The farther from the center of gravity or the axis of rotation the force is applied, the longer the force arm and the less force needed to rotate the object.**

If friction is not great, the application of a **single** off-center force both moves the object forward and rotates it toward the opposite end. If a force were applied right of center to a couch on casters, the couch would move forward and also turn toward the left. If friction were great enough, the left

Figure 16–2. Forces *B* and *C*, equal and applied equidistant from center of gravity, act as single force *A*.

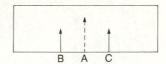

B   A   C

end would not move and only rotation would result. **Equal forces applied equidistant from the center of gravity act as a single force through the center of gravity** (Fig. 16–2). Some of each force is not effective in producing forward motion, since each has an inward component. However, more efficient control of direction is possible than with a single force through the center of gravity since each force has greater leverage to offset possible rotation. If, in attempting to apply a force through the center of gravity, it is actually applied even slightly off-center, or if the friction encountered by one side of the object is slightly more than that encountered by the other, the object turns and no force is immediately available to counteract this rotation. If, however, the force is applied at two points equidistant from the center and the object starts to turn to the left, added force at a point to the left of center (Fig. 16–2B) will counteract the tendency, while if it begins to turn to the right the force at the point to right of center (Fig. 16–2C) can be increased. Being away from the center each force is effective in producing compensatory angular motion and much greater control is possible. However, since each of these forces is applied off-center, some of each will be wasted as far as forward motion is concerned. Force is sacrificed for the purpose of gaining additional control.

EFFICIENT PERFORMANCE

Moving Objects.   If the object is not on wheels and considerable friction is involved, consideration should be given to the possibility of reducing the friction by placing the object on a dolly (a small low platform on wheels) or by putting some object that has a lower coefficient of friction between the object and the surface on which it rests. For example, the task of pushing a heavy piece of furniture across a carpeted floor can be greatly eased by placing glass coasters under the legs of the furniture. If the legs are too large for glass coasters, small pie pans or any other material that slides easily will reduce the force required and save "wear and tear" of the carpet.

When pulling an object, a longer rope reduces the upward component of force applied and increases the horizontal component. The greater the friction that must be overcome the shorter the rope should be; this increases the force's upward component, which, in effect, reduces the weight of the object on the surface (Fig. 16–3). If friction is not a problem, a longer rope is more efficient because a greater proportion of the force exerted is effective in the direction of desired movement. The rope should be attached to a point in line with, or below, the center of gravity of the object depending upon the amount of friction. The individual pulling should stand facing the direction of movement with the feet in a forward-backward stride to widen the base in the direction of anticipated movement, and with the toes straight ahead so

Figure 16–3. Component of forces involved in pulling with a long and short rope; F_h = horizontal (forward) component; F_v = vertical (upward) component.

that the force can be exerted directly backward. An inclination of the body forward from the ankles puts the center of gravity ahead of the pushing foot so that the force can be exerted diagonally forward (Fig. 16–4). The knees must flex so that they can exert force when extended. The degree to which they need to bend depends upon the force that must be exerted or upon the weight of the load to be moved and the friction involved. The muscles of the pelvis and trunk must be set so that the force produced by the leg extension will be transferred through the body to the rope.

Individuals sometimes start a heavy load moving by standing facing the load and "sitting backward" (Fig. 16–5). This does use the body weight as the moving force but can be dangerous. It must be remembered that, because of inertia, it takes more force to start an object moving than to keep it moving. Once the object starts to move, an individual who stands with feet together (Fig. 16–5B) may lose his balance, since he is not in an efficient

Figure 16–4. Using legs to pull.

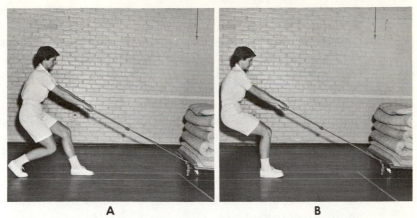

Figure 16–5. Using body weight to start momentum. A. Wide base for balance. B. Unbalanced (**dangerous**).

position to move his body rapidly. Balance backward is more precarious than forward since the base behind the ankle is so short and lacks the leverage of the toes. When this method is used the individual must widen the base to the point that one foot is well back under the body weight and should be prepared to move quickly and, when the load is on wheels, to turn and face forward once the load starts to move.

There are many tasks that require the individual to face the object to be moved but involve only a slight movement of the object. For example, if a mattress has gotten off-center on a bed, it needs to be pulled into place; while this requires movement for only a short distance, because of the weight of a mattress and the friction involved it is a heavy task and if inefficiently performed can cause strain. To apply sufficient force without back strain, the individual faces the side of the bed, grasps the cords on the side of the mattress and, standing with one foot well back, arms extended and knees well flexed, pushes with the forward leg. In this way the stronger legs are used to produce the force which moves the body, and with it the mattress, backward. A particularly heavy or a king-sized mattress requires that two individuals work together; each grasps one cord on the side of the mattress and when both are in position, a signal is needed so that both push with the forward leg at the same time.

If the mattress has slipped toward the foot (or head) of the bed, it is easier for two people to pull it into place, one on each side of the bed grasping a cord and standing with the side close to the bed and back toward the direction the mattress is to be moved, feet in a forward-backward stride and hips and knees flexed. On signal both push with their forward legs transferring their body weight backward and pulling the mattress up (or down) on the springs. One person alone pulling up or down applies an off-center force which will move only one side of the mattress and thus it rotates. It is then necessary to pull on the other side to straighten it.

In order to push an object, the hands should be placed near the point opposite the object's center of gravity so that the downward component of force, which is frequently present in a pushing task, is reduced to a minimum. While in pulling the vertical component of the force is upward and, therefore, may be useful in reducing friction, in pushing the vertical component is downward and adds to the friction, making the object more difficult to move. An upward component of force is possible only when the hands can be placed lower than the center of gravity of the object. The push should be applied through the center of gravity in the direction of desired movement if friction is inconsequential. However, if there is considerable friction, the position must be adjusted so that the force can be applied below the center of gravity to reduce the friction. The exact point for the effective application of force can be determined by experimentation using as the criterion the object's tendency to tip. If there is a great deal of friction an object may tip even when force is applied through its center of gravity, because friction keeps the bottom from moving. Therefore, force must be applied below center.

Placing the hands opposite or below the object's center of gravity may necessitate lowering the body weight. When this is done by flexing the legs rather than leaning forward from the hips, the legs are placed in position to extend and no strain is placed on the small muscles of the back. If the task necessitates a very low crouch which places the body in a difficult position to maintain or in which to move, it is more efficient to put a rope around the object and pull than to attempt to move it by pushing.

When pushing, the individual must stand away from the object so that he can incline his body toward it, and thus put his center of gravity ahead of his pushing foot in order that the force can be exerted more in the direction of desired movement (Fig. 16–6). As in all other activities, the inclination of the body forward should be from the ankles and the well-aligned position of the body should be maintained. The feet must be placed in a forward-backward stride position, so that the pushing foot can be well back and the forward foot in a position to catch the body weight as forward movement begins. The muscles of the arms, shoulder girdle, and trunk should be set **before** the force is applied, in order for the push of the legs to be transferred through them to the object with no absorption by the arms of the force produced by the leg extension. Since the body pushes by extending the legs, the strongest muscles available to the task are used.

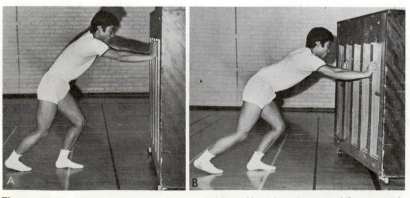

Figure 16–6. Using legs to push heavy object. Note hands spread for control in *B*.

When pushing upward or pulling downward, the body is placed under or as near to the object as possible to enlarge the vertical component of the force as much as possible. When pushing downward or pulling upward, the body weight is placed as nearly as possible over the object. Thus, in pushing a shovel straight down into the earth, one stands right next to the shovel and places one foot on it so that the force can be exerted straight downward.

In opening a tight or stuck casement window (opens upward), the most efficient method calls for standing close to the window, flexing the legs so that the heels of the hands can be placed under the middle sash with the elbows well-flexed (hands close to the shoulders), and then extending the legs. The force is exerted by the strong leg muscles directly upward and the position of the arms eliminates any possibility of force being absorbed by a give of the elbows. A window which moves easily may be opened by pulling up on the handles. Since the force available in the arms is sufficient for the performance of the task without strain, there is no need for expending the effort involved in lowering and raising the body weight. However, the individual should stand close to the window so that the force is applied straight upward in the direction of the window's predetermined pathway. When one reaches across a table to open such a window, balance is precarious and the force is diagonally up and toward the individual and thus against the inside of the casing, therefore friction is increased. Also, the small muscles of the back are brought into the task to stabilize the upper body against the pull of gravity and the resistance of the window.

Frequently is it necessary to move an object which is relatively light but difficult to move in a straight path. In such a situation force is no problem and the principle of applying the force at two points equidistant from the center of gravity of the object should be followed. For example, to move in a straight line a long light object on wheels such as the portable blackboard, pictured in Figure 16–7, one should stand close to the center of the object and grasp it as far ahead of the body as possible with one hand and as far behind as possible with the other. Being light and on wheels, the object moves easily as the individual walks and, because of the length of the force arms (distance of hand to center of gravity of board), the hands are in an effective position to exercise control over the object's tendency to swing to one side or the other.

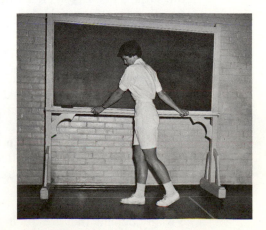

Figure 16–7. Hands spread for control — light object.

Occasional arguments arise as to whether it is easier to push or to pull. Actually no broad statement can be made. The question must be settled for each particular task. Which is easier depends upon whether a downward or an upward component of force is advantageous for accomplishing the particular purpose, whether the task is a heavy one or one that calls primarily for control, and whether linear or angular motion is desired. A downward force is advantageous, for example, in using a vacuum cleaner, a mop, or lawnmower. It is detrimental in a heavy task in which friction is a problem. If a downward force is advantageous, the object should be pushed. If it adds considerably to the forward force required to move the object by increasing the friction which is already a problem, it is easier to pull the object. As indicated earlier a pushing force with an upward component can only be applied by lowering the body, so that the hands can be placed at a point below the object's center of gravity. If this causes the body to assume a low crouch in which it is difficult to move forward, it is more efficient to use a rope and pull.

The importance of the upward component depends upon the friction involved. There are many tasks in which it does not matter appreciably which method is used. In pushing a wheelbarrow the downward component of force adds to the friction of the wheel on the ground. However, a wheel which turns easily makes this a relatively unimportant consideration. In pulling the wheelbarrow the individual loses the advantage of being able to watch the load. The slight advantage gained by the upward component of force of the pull is not sufficient to offset the disadvantage. However, when it is necessary to move the wheelbarrow up a hill or a step, the upward component of a pulling force becomes important and, therefore, the wheelbarrow should be pulled.

Many golfers use two-wheeled carts rather than carrying their clubs. Force to move the cart, applied at the handle, is diagonally downward-forward when the cart is **pushed** and upward-forward when it is **pulled.** Therefore, it requires less force to pull than to push a golf cart. Although its wheels are relatively large, the resistance of the grass surface, which is never completely smooth, is a factor even when the fairway is level. The upward component of the force applied by pulling is effective in reducing the resistance of the grass and in lifting the cart over any lumps or indentations in the surface just as it is in lifting a wheelbarrow over a curb. When walking downhill it is immaterial whether the cart is in front of, or behind, the golfer because gravity's pull is added to the golfer's force to move it down the slope. However, when walking uphill, the golfer must exert much more force to push than to pull the cart. Obviously the cart must be moved **upward against gravity** and a pull force has an **upward** component. The downward component of a push force pushes the wheels into the hill and makes it more difficult to move the cart forward-upward; much force is wasted.

When the force advantage is immaterial the question of whether to push or to pull should be decided on the basis of the ease of body position, control and so forth. If directional control is the most important consideration, pushing has an advantage if the object can be kept closer to the individual.

Many objects that are too heavy to be pushed as a whole can be moved efficiently by angular motion. An individual attempting to move a heavy couch, for example, or ⸺ ʼnk should move first one corner and then the other. Since the longer tʰᵉ ʟorce arm, the less the force required to rotate the object, the force should be applied as far from the center of gravity or the axis of rotation is possible. Moving the couch by rotation is simply a matter of pushing one end forward and then the other. Moving a wardrobe trunk or high carton is a slightly different problem. Since it is higher and has a smaller base it can be moved most easily by placing the hands against one top corner and pushing forward slightly, enough to tip the trunk so that it rests on the diagonally opposite corner. It can then be swung around with very little force. Gravity acts to assist this movement. A series of these movements, rotating the trunk or carton, first on one corner and then on the other, moves it forward. This same method can be used successfully with a heavy chair.

Moving Human Body.   Regardless of whether the task involves pushing or pulling objects or the human body, the basic principles are the same. When one is well and in good physical condition, various tasks involving moving the human body are so simple that whether or not some energy is wasted in their performance is immaterial; but when handicapped or ill, or when it is necessary to assist an ill or handicapped individual, attention to these basic principles is imperative. A few examples of such problems are included to illustrate the application of these principles.

While rolling over in bed is to most no "task" at all, there are times when this simple motion may require all of one's resources and thus it becomes necessary that all force be exerted effectively. When it is a case of pushing or pulling oneself the problem is to find a surface against which force can be exerted in a direction to cause the desired motion. Just as a backward-downward force against the floor moves the body forward when walking, a force applied by the right hand against the left side of a mattress (lying on back), which is a force applied to the right, pulls the right shoulder of the individual toward the left; since it is an off-center application of force, the body is rotated (rolled) up onto its left side.

Reaching overhead and grasping **over** the head end of the mattress makes it possible to apply force against the mattress toward the foot of the bed which results in movement of the body toward the head of the bed. If the legs can be used, bending the knees so that the feet are flat on the bed makes it possible to push the heels down into the mattress exerting additional force toward the foot of the bed and aiding in the upward movement of the body. If they cannot be used to produce force, this flexing of the knees is still helpful in that it, in effect, takes the weight of the heavy legs out of the moving task (they do not have to be pulled upward; they straighten as the body moves upward). The weight of the leg can be taken out of the rolling task above by crossing the right leg over the left before pulling with the arm; this starts body rotation also, and thus aids in the performance of this task. Possible methods of reducing the weight to be moved should always be sought.

Many persons find themselves in the position of having to assist in, or cause, the motion of others. Besides nurses, physical therapists and athletic trainers whose work requires the performance of such tasks, many people have relatives in their homes who are handicapped and require help on a temporary or long-term basis. Many who are in this situation are themselves elderly, not overly strong and may weigh considerably less than the individuals that they must attempt to help to move. To prevent injury to themselves as well as to be successful in producing the desired motion, it is essential that these persons understand and apply the principles of efficient movement.

In moving another person, the basic position is the same as that used to push or pull an object, that is, feet in a forward-backward stride and trunk angled from the ankles in the direction of desired motion to allow use of the strong leg muscles for the moving force (Fig. 16–4, 16–5A). While in pushing and pulling objects the force is more often produced by the back leg pushing the body weight forward, moving people up, down, toward the side, or to a sitting position in bed is usually a matter of pushing with the forward leg to transfer the body weight of the person performing the pulling task to his back leg since he is usually pulling the individual toward him. The first problem is to determine the most effective place to put one's hands to apply force in the desired direction. If pulling an individual from a back-lying to a sitting position, placing a hand over and **under** the individual's far shoulder results in a force, first upward and then upward and toward the one who is pulling as he transfers his weight from his forward to his back foot. If rolling an individual over in bed, hands reached over and **under** the individual's far hip and shoulder are in an excellent position to apply force up and toward the person pulling; the force is applied against the two heaviest portions of the body and the body rolls up as a unit. (Fig. 16–8).

When it is necessary to pull an individual across a bed (sideways), reaching **under** his body and placing the hands so that the fingers are pointing **up on the far side,** puts the hands in position to apply force straight toward the puller as he transfers his weight; this position (under) also reduces to some extent the friction between the individual and the sheet. However, this is a much more difficult task than rolling the individual over because of friction and because all of the weight is moved; in rolling, the weight rotates around one (the low) side. Because it is a very heavy task, the body needs to be moved in segments rather than all at once; first the head and upper body (one arm under head with fingers pointing up on the far side of the shoulder, other arm under the chest area with fingers up on far side of chest), then the hips (one arm above the other below the buttocks, both under with fingers up on far side), and finally the legs. This order can be reversed but the movement should never be started with the hips as this leaves the individual's body in an uncomfortable curve.

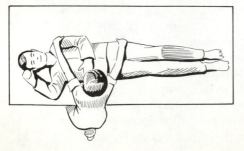

Figure 16–8. Using pull force to roll individual from back to side. Note hands over and under far shoulder and hip.

If a person needs to be moved up or down in the bed consideration must be given to whether the applied force will force the vertebrae together or pull them apart. The person being moved is much more comfortable with the pulling force than when the vertebrae are jammed together. Thus when moving someone down in bed, the simplest method involves standing at the foot of the bed, grasping the ankles and taking the position which allows use of the body weight to add to the pulling force (Fig. 16–5A). One foot **must** be placed well back to keep the center of gravity above the base (feet) as the weight is transferred backward. Pulling from the foot of the bed makes it possible to apply the force directly downward (toward the foot of the bed). However, if it is necessary to reach **over** a footboard of the bed to grasp the person's ankles the pulling position will have to be taken at the side of the bed. In this situation, the person being moved will need to be grasped by reaching **under** his hips and curling the fingers over the top of the pelvic bone. If an attempt is made to pull downward on the shoulders, which offer the best surface for grasping, the person's vertebrae will be jammed together, since friction and inertia cause the hips to resist motion.

The shoulders (actually the armpits) should be used as the surface for a pushing force to move the individual up in bed (toward the head) since the upward force tends to separate vertebrae. Upward force against the hips would push them together. Again the individual's knees should be flexed (feet flat on bed) to take the leg weight out of the pushing task. If the person can grasp the pusher's shoulders, the force will be more effective since the shoulders will be stabilized, rather than "giving" with the force of the push against them.

An individual who is heavier than the person moving him can be sat up on the edge of a bed by a well-executed push maneuver. If the individual can, he rolls to his side and flexes his knees; if he cannot, he is rolled as indicated earlier and his knees are flexed so that his feet are just off the bed. In this position his thighs form a surface against which a push force can be exerted to rotate the individual to a sitting position; if the thighs are pushed flat onto the bed, the trunk must lift **so long as the angle of the hips is maintained** (Fig. 16–9). To maintain this angle the person who is moving him, facing his thighs, places one arm (near arm) under his head and around

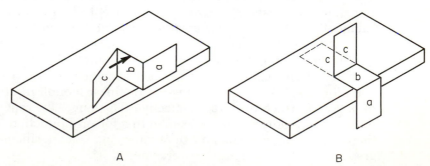

A   B

Figure 16–9. Schematic drawing of rotation of person to sitting position at edge of bed. *a,* Lower legs; *b,* thighs; *c,* trunk. Force applied to rotate thigh *(b)* from a vertical to a horizontal position (flat on bed) rotates upper trunk area *(c)* upward *so long as angle between the two segments* is maintained. If angle not maintained, trunk *(c)* flattens instead of liftine. (see dotted lines).

his shoulder while the other arm is wrapped over, around and under the lower end of the thighs. By pulling with both arms the angle at the hips can be maintained. **This is the only use made of the arms; they have no part in the force to lift the individual.** The person moving the individual then places his chest against the individual's thighs and, using the same process of weight transference described earlier, pushes the thighs to a flat position on the bed. This is accomplished with relative ease when the angle at the individual's hips is maintained at **less** than a right angle and the push of the chest against the thighs is maintained until the thighs are actually flat; the chest of the person causing the movement moves forward and over the individual's thighs.

Regardless of the direction of motion required, the individual helping a person to move, or actually causing the motion must:

1. Determine the surface of the individual's body against which force can be applied as much as possible in the direction of desired motion.
2. When forces are toward the individual's head or feet, choose the surface which will assure that the force will separate, rather than jam together, the vertebrae.
3. Place hands against this surface so that the palms are facing the direction of desired motion.
4. If possible, take the weight of the heavy legs out of the task.
5. Take a forward-backward stride position with knees well flexed.
6. Stabilize the arms, shoulders and upper body, so that force produced by the legs will be transferred through the arms to the individual to be moved.
7. Extend the leg(s) to transfer weight in the direction of desired motion.

SUMMARY

When a task involves any considerable amount of force the legs, which have the strongest muscles available for a pushing or pulling task, should be used to provide the main force. The body, in a well-aligned position, should lean from the ankles in the direction of desired motion to move the center of gravity ahead or behind the pushing foot, so that the direction of force application is backward-downward (or forward-downward), and the reaction force will have a horizontal component. To assure control of body balance the feet must be in a forward-backward stride position. The individual should contact the object or person to be moved and set the muscles for the task before exerting the pushing or pulling force.

The placement of the hands or attachment of a rope on an object determines not only whether angular or linear motion results, but also the direction in which the force is effective. The longer the rope that is used in pulling, the more the force is exerted in a forward direction. A shorter rope increases the upward component of force, and is more efficient only when a great deal of friction must be overcome.

In pushing, the more nearly the hands are placed opposite the center of gravity of the object, the more directly the force is applied in the direction of desired motion.

When pushing or pulling upward or downward, the individual should stand as close to the object to be moved as possible, so that the force can be exerted in the direction in which movement is desired, i.e., vertically.

Leverage is used when control is important. Force is applied at two points equidistant from the object's center of gravity. Leverage is also important when moving an object by angular motion. Force is applied far from the center of gravity or axis to move one side of the object, and then the other side is moved by the application of a second force.

Friction between the feet of the individual pushing or pulling and the supporting surface is essential for the force exerted by the legs to cause movement. The greater the friction between the object or person to be moved and the supporting surface, the greater the force required to move it. Whenever this friction is great it should be reduced, if at all possible, by placing some material with a lower coefficient of friction between the object and the supporting surface, or by applying a diagonally upward force so that a considerable upward component will be present. Lack of firmness of the supporting surface increases the difficulty of the task, in that there is less counterpressure against the feet and more resistance to the forward progress of the object or person being moved.

The question, whether it is easier to push or pull, must be decided on the basis of the particular task involved.

17

HOLDING, CARRYING, STOOPING AND LIFTING

Days are filled with a wide variety of stooping, lifting, holding and carrying tasks that vary from very light chores to those which require a great deal of effort for their accomplishment. These activities enter into the daily routines, work patterns and recreational pursuits of every individual. From case histories, Hilleboe and Larimore[1] reported that tasks involving lifting, carrying, moving or placing of various materials, machine parts or other objects account for 23 percent of all work injuries, and the common complaint of back ache resulting from ineffective body mechanics in the home is familiar to all. The lifting activity may be simply picking up a child's light toy, but it may be one of the stronger tasks of lifting the child himself or helping an elderly or handicapped individual into or out of a chair. In the garden one may be involved in weeding over a period of time or in transplanting a heavy bush. Sacks and heavy boxes of groceries have to be lifted and carried frequently. Heavy objects must be lifted from the floor, from tables and from, and to, high shelves. The list of such tasks is endless.

Since they involve the addition of a weight to the body, the center of gravity, which must be kept above the base, shifts and the body weight must be adjusted. Because many of these tasks involve a lowered body position and/or the moving of considerable weights, economy of effort and avoidance of strain, as well as the maintenance of equilibrium, are major concerns.

Holding involves exerting against an object or person only that amount of upward force necessary to balance gravity's pull so that the object has no vertical motion. Carrying differs only in that the object acquires the velocity of the body as it moves. Actually, an object is held while it is being carried. In lifting, an additional upward force is applied in order that the object or person will move upward in opposition to the force of gravity.

The force required to hold and lift an object depends upon its weight.

The force of gravity must be overcome if the object is to be held and moved

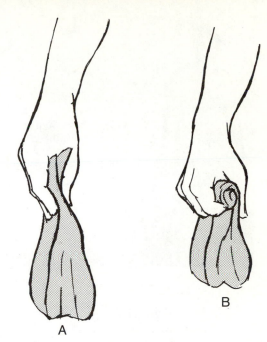

Figure 17-1. Holding sack between thumb and fingers, compared to holding *rolled* sack with fingers *under* roll.

A

B

upward. Since gravity acts in a vertically downward direction, the body force must be applied upward. As much of the hands or arms as possible should be placed **under** the object in order to resist directly the downward pull of gravity. If the object is held between the thumb and fingers (Fig. 17-1,A), the forces are exerted inward toward the object, and only friction between the object and fingers and thumb keeps gravity from pulling the object downward. Unless the fingers can be curved around some part of the object so that they form a base **under** it, the supportive force is not applied in the direction that resists gravity (the force acting on the object), and considerable force must be applied by the relatively weak muscles of the thumb and fingers; thus this is an inefficient method of holding. It is impossible to hold even a light object for any length of time when it is grasped by the thumb opposing the fingers. The object is held only as long as the inward forces creates sufficient friction to resist gravity. Therefore, the top of a sack is rolled to make a handle **under** which the fingers can be placed to exert upward force (Fig. 17-1,B).

In gymnastics, figure skating and various forms of dance, there are times when an individual is lifted and/or supported by another. However, in these activities the individual being lifted normally supplies much of the lifting force. This chapter deals with situations in which all of the force is supplied by the lifter and, therefore, the above activities are not included although the general principles that are discussed apply to them as to any lifting task.

HOLDING AND CARRYING

Whenever an object is held it becomes a part of the total body weight and the center of gravity of the body-plus-weight shifts in the direction of

Figure 17–2. Adjustment to keep center of gravity of body plus suitcase centered over base made with the *total* body; segments remain in alignment.

the weight. To maintain stability, this new center of gravity must be shifted to a position over the center of the base by an adjustment of the body. If this adjustment is made by shifting the body as a unit from the ankles, the relative alignment of the various body segments is not disturbed. Thus the body as a whole is used to counterbalance the weight of the object held, and the weight can be held with a minimum of strain on the various muscles and joints (Fig. 17–2). The nearer to the body's center of gravity a weight is held, the smaller the force which is exerted on the body and the less the adjustment of the body which is necessary to counteract it. Therefore, a weight should be held as close to the body as possible to keep the resistance arm short. The farther it is held from the body, the longer the resistance arm and the more force required to balance the weight (Chapter 5, Leverage). This can be demonstrated easily by holding a book on the flat palm close to the shoulder, and then straightening the arm and holding the book at shoulder height but at arm's length.

Carrying a heavy object at one side of the body shifts the center of gravity to that side bringing it dangerously near, or beyond, the base of support. By raising the opposite arm sideways while keeping the body in its same basic alignment, certain weights (not too heavy) can be counterbalanced so that the line of gravity again falls through the center of the base (Fig. 17–3). The extended arm with its weight farther from the line of gravity becomes a greater balancing force than the arm hanging at the side, since the reaction of a lever is in proportion to the length of its resistance arm. Although the arm is lighter than the object held, the fact that its center of gravity is farther from the line of gravity of the body while that of the weight is close makes it an effective counterbalancing force.

Williams and Lissner[2] found that when a load is carried on one side of the body (for example, on the left) the force on the opposing supporting hip (head of right femur) during walking is much greater than when the load is distributed on both sides of the body. This is true even when the total load carried on the two sides is **twice as great** as that carried on one side. In other

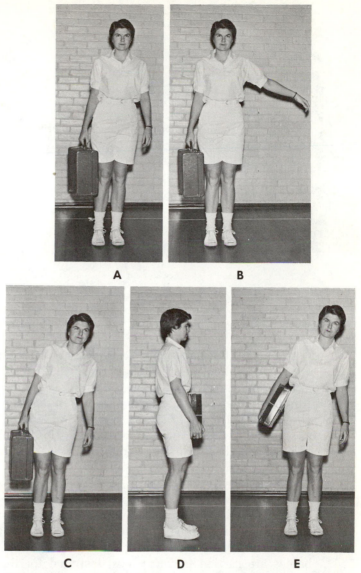

Figure 17-3. *A*, Body shift from ankles (as in Fig. 17-2). *B*, Weight balanced by arm. *C*, Strain on lower back. *D*, Holding close to body — small adjustment required is made by moving the body backward as a whole (from the ankles). *E*, Strain on lower back.

words, when a 50 pound (22.7 kg) weight is carried on each side of the body (total 100 lbs, 45 kg), there is less force on the head of the femur at each step than there is on the right femur if 50 pounds is carried in the left hand only. When the weights are equal, they balance each other and no adjustment of the body is required (Fig. 17-4).

Some loads, because of their size and shape, must be carried in front of the body. When a heavy load is carried in front of the body, it may be possible to support some of the weight by the thighs[3] if the knees are flexed. In this case the body leans backward (as a unit) from the hips to balance the

Figure 17–4. Two suitcases of approximately same weight require little or no adjustment of the body position.

weight and keep the center of gravity of the body plus the weight over the feet.

Whether the task involves carrying books, groceries, a child or any other weight, when the object is held in one arm up against the chest, the tendency is to "hug" it to the body. In so doing the shoulder on the carrying side is lifted, and therefore habitually carrying in one arm is likely to lead to a high shoulder on that side. As soon as the shoulder girdle is tilted, a compensatory curve develops in the upper spine. Carrying an object in both arms in front of the chest pulls the shoulders forward and rounds the upper back. There is a tendency for the individual to thrust the pelvis forward to make a "shelf" for the object to rest on, and this upsets the entire body alignment. A briefcase allows books and papers to be held close to the body while maintaining a well-aligned position, and makes it possible for the force exerted by the individual to be in direct opposition to gravity's pull (fingers **under** handle). Many students now carry their books on their backs and frequently babies are carried in backpacks designed for that purpose. This has the advantage of centering the weight right-to-left. Since it is off-center backward, the weight shifts the center of gravity backward within the individual's body and he must compensate with a forward lean. This is an adjustment that can be made easily from the ankles without any disturbance of body alignment; so long as the individual stabilizes his trunk and shoulders, making the adjustment at the ankle joints, this is an efficient method of carrying a weight. If the weight is carried in a sling in front of the body, total body adjustment **backward** from the ankles is necessary.

Hikers also carry weights on their backs. It is important to realize that, when climbing uphill with a weight on the back, the problem of adjustment to keep the center of gravity over the feet is increased. The hill throws the center of gravity of the body **backward in relation to the base** (see p. 165) and the weight moves it **back within the body**; thus a **double** forward adjustment is required to keep the center of gravity over the base. If the weight is sufficiently heavy, it may be impossible to lean far enough forward from the ankles and additional adjustment must then be made at the hips. Unless a stick in the hand supports the upper body, this position will result in strain on the lower back muscles which must support the long trunk with the weight against gravity's pull. Anything which restricts flexion of the ankles such as heavy boots, reduces the amount of weight that can be carried uphill on the back without strain. A weight carried in front makes the balance adjustment easier when going **uphill** since it moves the center of gravity forward in the body somewhat off-setting the hill. However, the use of the arms may be hampered and, when rock climbing, a weight in front would keep the body out from the rocks.

If objects are placed on a tray so that they are balanced, the center of gravity of the tray is the distance of approximately half of the width of the tray away from the body, and the hands must be placed at that distance from the body to keep the tray from tipping. This means that, if the tray is large, the resistance arm is long and the weight is extremely difficult to hold if carried in front of the body. If the tray is carried above one shoulder with one hand placed under the center of the tray and the other on one edge for control, the weight is brought in closer to the line of gravity of the body and is easier to carry. To balance the weight of the tray, the body weight is shifted from the ankles to the opposite side. The degree of side shift which is possible from the ankles is extremely limited, and thus when considerable adjustment is required, much of it will be made at the waist. A shift of weight from the waist causes a lateral curve in the spine and the muscles of the back are placed in a position of strain; thus carrying heavy trays should be avoided when possible.

Frequently individuals carry a baby astride one hip. This requires that the hip be moved up and out into the position seen when standing "hung on one hip" (Fig. 10–7) and the same problems of back and joint strain are involved; however, they are greatly magnified because of the added weight to which the body must adjust. In addition, when walking the high hip leg is shortened and thus the body is thrown out of alignment even farther.

It is the custom of some peoples to carry all objects on their heads. This method has certain advantages and disadvantages. It makes it possible to keep the weight directly above the center of gravity of the body. The center of gravity of the body-plus-weight is raised but not moved forward, backward or to either side. It is still on the same line of gravity and, therefore, no adjustment is required. However, if the object becomes even slightly off center, its rotating effect is great because it is so high. Since the very flexible neck is below the weight, strong neck muscles are essential to prevent any movement which would shift the center of gravity of the load away from the line of gravity of the body. Those who carry objects on their heads stand well, because it is essential that the body be well-aligned if balance is to be maintained with such a high center of gravity.

When two individuals are carrying a heavy object down an incline or stairway, the weight of the object is against the lower individual, unless the one at the upper end moves closer to the center of the object and/or pulls backward to hold some of the weight back against gravity's pull.

STOOPING (CROUCHING) AND LIFTING

Lifting tasks involve pushing and pulling movements and, therefore, the physical principles which must be applied if they are to be performed efficiently are the same as those discussed in the previous chapter. Lifting is actually pushing or pulling in a vertical instead of in a horizontal direction. In lifting a low object to approximately chest height, the action is that of pulling, and beyond chest height it becomes one of pushing.

To lower the body in order to contact the object to be lifted, a stooping (crouching) rather than bending forward motion uses the strong leg muscles instead of the weaker back muscles. The heavier the object to be lifted, the more essential the use of the leg muscles becomes. It is generally agreed that when a lifting task involves any considerable weight or repeated lifts, strain of the lower back can be avoided only by stooping. There has been some discussion concerning the efficiency of stooping as compared to bending over for lifting light objects. In support of bending over, some cite a 1955 article in *Collier's* reporting studies made by Dr. Brouha, in which the vertical force exerted against the supporting surface by both movements was measured. He found greater force was exerted while stooping than while bending and concluded that, "For a single action and for lighter weights, there's no doubt now that bending is more economical for the body."[4] It would seem, however, that only one aspect of efficiency, that of vertical force expended, was investigated. Since, in stooping, the entire body weight is lowered and then must be raised, it seems reasonable that the vertical force would be greater. However, the **total** force exerted in the bend is **not** vertical, but has a backward component as well. This conclusion, based on vertical force only, does not consider the fact that the force required can be exerted by the strong muscles of the legs in the stoop, while it must be exerted by the small and considerably weaker muscles of the lower back in the bend. Also, in stooping, the force is exerted straight upward through the center of the weight to be lifted (body-plus-weight), while recovery from a bend requires a diagonally upward and backward pull of a weight which is far from the fulcrum for the movement (the hips) and, therefore, the weaker back muscles must act under a condition of adverse leverage.

When an individual bends over to tie a shoe lace or to touch his toes, and then lifts only the upper body in order to resume a standing position, the weight to be lifted can, of course, be considered to be concentrated at the center of gravity of the upper body. The length of the resistance arm of the lever involved is the distance from the hips to this point. When he bends to pick up an object, the weight of the object is added at the hands, and the weight to be lifted is concentrated at the center of gravity of the upper trunk-plus-object (Fig. 17–5). The object, being at the extreme end of the lever, greatly lengthens the resistance arm, and thus the effect of the weight is augmented. It seems probable that the stronger muscles of the legs, acting as they do under circumstances of favorable leverage, are better able to cope with the additional vertical force found by Dr. Brouha to be required by the stoop, than are the small muscles of the back, which are required to function under conditions of adverse leverage when pulling the body-plus-weight upward and backward from a bend. It is possible that even though less

Figure 17–5. Straining the back.

vertical force is exerted, muscle strain could result even with a single action.

Some amount of bending over is desirable to exercise the back muscles and maintain flexibility of the lower back and hip region, but this should be restricted to tasks which involve only lifting the upper body or, **occasionally, very light objects.** However, constant repetition of a light lifting task can result in strain. Many people are cognizant of the dangers of heavy lifting but overlook the strain and stress associated with habitual poor body mechanics during the performance of light tasks. When a heavy object must be lifted, stooping (crouching) is always required and, for one with a back handicap, stooping **is a must regardless of the lightness of the task.** If such an individual bends forward to touch his toes in a stretching exercise, the standing position should be regained by flexing the knees and bringing the hips in under the trunk, so that the legs can be used rather than the lower back muscles to lift the long trunk lever.

An individual with a knee handicap must determine the best method for each task on the basis of the demands of the task and the relative strength of his back and his knees. In general, for light tasks, it is probably better for him to bend so that the knees are not involved in the lifting of the body weight. However, a heavy task should not be attempted in this way. If it is impossible or very difficult for him to stoop, some method of moving the object other than lifting must be employed or the lifting task left to someone else.

The advantages of stooping (crouching) are (1) the strongest muscles available to the task are used, (2) the weight can be kept close to the line of gravity of the body, and (3) the force is exerted in the direction of the desired movement, and it is completely effective in lifting the weight upward. While less **vertical** force has been found to be required by bending, weaker muscles must perform the task, the weight is considerably farther from the line of gravity of the body and the force must be exerted in a diagonally upward-backward direction, and thus only the vertical component is effective in moving the weight upward. Since, in stooping, the center of gravity is lowered directly above the base, the position of the body is more stable than in the bent position which keeps the center of gravity of the body high, moves considerable body weight forward of the base and thus requires additional compensatory backward shift of body segments.

When lifting, the knees, hips and ankles flex to lower the body and the trunk inclines slightly forward. This places the body in an easy normal position, rather than the stiff position which results when an attempt is made to keep the trunk completely upright. When the knees are flexed, it is more difficult to arch the lower back as the trunk inclines forward, and thus there is less possibility of lower back strain. Since it takes considerable energy to lift the body weight itself, the body should be lowered only far enough to assure that the hand or hands can be placed under the object to be

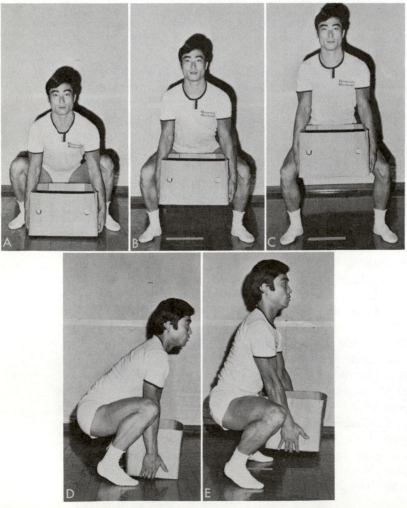

Figure 17–6. Using the strong leg muscles to lift a heavy carton. Note: small base in anteroposterior direction at beginning of the lift (D and E).

lifted. If the object has a handle, the fingers can be wrapped around the handle and the body weight does not have to be lowered as far.

Two methods for stooping (crouching) to lift a heavy object from the floor have been suggested. Both involve standing close to the object and lowering the body by flexing the joints of the legs. However, one suggests that the object be in front of the individual and the other that it be at his side.

In the first, a wide side stride is necessary in order for the object to be between the legs so that a diagonal lift of the object up over the knees is eliminated. The base is narrow in the forward-backward plane, and thus balance may be precarious. However, since the weight is to be lifted between the legs, it can be kept close to the line of gravity of the body and the force is exerted straight upward (Fig. 17–6). If the object is not between the legs but rather is in front of the knees, it must be lifted up and over the knees and any advantage of having it in front is lost. Kendall[3] suggested bracing the elbows on the thighs whenever possible, to give support to the arms at the beginning of the lift. It must be noted that this would not be possible unless there were some way to take hold of the object several inches above floor level.

The second method, that with the object at the side, allows for a more stable base, since the feet can be separated forward-backward to widen the base in the direction that the body segments will be moving, and thus increase the stability of the body. The slightly off-center application of force at the beginning of the lift becomes centered as the object is brought close to the body's center of gravity (Fig. 17–7). Because of the balance factor, this method is preferred by many over the method which starts with the object between the feet. It causes very little, if any, rotation of the spine because the forward-backward stride position, with the foot **away** from the weight forward, rotates the pelvis toward the object, and the shoulders need be rotated very little, if any, beyond the line of the pelvis. Of course, if the foot **toward** the weight is placed forward, the pelvis is rotated **away** from the object and a great deal of trunk rotation is required. Obviously, this would be an ineffective method for accomplishing the lift. Experimentation with both foot

Figure 17–7. Using the strong leg muscles (weight at side).

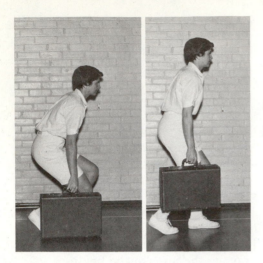

Figure 17–8.   Using the strong leg muscles.

positions makes this apparent. When an object that is to be carried at the side (such as a suitcase) is involved, there is, of course, no question. It is always more efficient to stand with the side to the suitcase, lower the body until the handle can be grasped, and then to straighten the legs and adjust the body weight from the ankles to counterbalance the weight (Fig. 17–8).

When lifting a child or helping a handicapped person (young or elderly) from a chair, the same procedure applies.* The only difference involves that of hand placement. In lifting an object, the hands are placed **under** the object or its handle so that the force can be applied **upward;** in lifting a person, the armpit offers a surface against which it is possible to apply upward force and, since it is close to the head, it has the advantage of affording control of that important segment of the human body. Thus when lifting a child from the floor, the lifter squats **close to the child** (straight upward force), feet in a forward-backward stride (large base for balance), and placed his hands **under** the two armpits (upward force), thumbs in front and fingers behind for control. Stabilizing the pelvis and trunk, the child is lifted by extending the joints of the legs. Once motion is underway, it is easier for the weaker arm muscles to continue the motion to bring the child to the position in front of the chest.

When a situation requires assisting a young or elderly adult from a chair, it is difficult to grasp under both armpits, since this requires the lifter to stand in front of the chair and to reach across the individual's thighs to his armpits. However, the task can be accomplished easily by standing at the side of the chair in a forward-backward stride which rotates the hips slightly toward the chair. The lifter must face the same direction as the person to be lifted faces. The elbow of the near arm of the lifter is completely bent (upper arm along ribs, hand near his own shoulder), so that the force from his leg extension will pass through this arm with no "give," to the shoulder of the

---

*If the baby is in a playpen, it is important that the lifter reach through the bars of the pen and pull the child to the edge before attempting a lift so that the resistance arm of the weight is reduced and so he can get into a better position for using the legs to supply the lifting force.

individual being helped to stand. This position also places the lifter very close to the person to be lifted so the resistance arm of the weight is as short as possible. The shoulder of the person to be lifted is grasped **under** the armpit as indicated previously. As the legs are straightened, the weight must be transferred to the forward foot so that the force against the individual's shoulder is **upward** and **slightly forward.** This is necessary since his feet are in front of the chair and thus his center of gravity must be moved forward to a position above his feet. To make all of the lifting force effective in moving the individual, the shoulder against which the force is applied needs to be stabilized; this can be done by the lifter grasping the person's upper arm with his own free hand and pulling down on it as he extends his own legs and transfers his weight forward. This is actually a "push maneuver" and, except for the fact that this force must have some forward component, could be likened to the problem of opening the stuck casement window discussed in Chapter 16 (p. 227). This technique assumes that the individual being lifted has no shoulder problem.

Even heavy persons can be assisted in this way. If the weight does prove to be too much for the lifter, a second lifter can apply force in the same way to the other shoulder; a signal should be given so that the leg extension of the two lifters will be coordinated. Of course, if the individual being assisted has some strength in his legs, a signal should be used so that he can coordinate his own effort with that of the lifter(s) and thus simplify the task.

In lifting a heavy tray from a table to a position above one shoulder, the tray should first be slid to a point at which a few inches extend over the edge of the table, the body should be turned sideways to the table and lowered by flexing the joints of the legs. One hand grasps the edge of the tray and the other is placed under it palm up so that, as the hand at the edge pulls the tray outward on the table, it can be placed under the tray's center. The tray needs to be pulled outward only far enough for the supporting hand to be placed under its center before it is lifted by the extension of the legs. The hand on the edge of the tray, having a long force arm (from hand to the center of gravity of the tray), is effective in controlling the tray, while the one under the center supports it against gravity's pull. To put the tray down onto a table, the individual stands with his side to the table and stoops (crouches) until one side of the tray rests on the table. It can then be pushed completely onto the table as he stands.

If a mattress must be turned, the "pull maneuver" (Chapter 16) can be used to move it well over toward one side of the bed; by standing close to the mattress with one foot well forward of the body, flexing the knees, stabilizing the arms and trunk and then extending the knees, the mattress can be lifted to stand on its side on the bed; if it is slightly overbalanced, gravity will complete the turn. It can then be pulled into place by again using the legs to produce the pulling force as described earlier (p. 230). A heavy or king-sized mattress requires two people, one holding each of the two cords on one side of the mattress; a signal is needed so that both exert force at the same time.

Some heavy lifting tasks can be performed effectively by the use of the body weight to overbalance the weight to be lifted (Fig. 17–9). A heavy

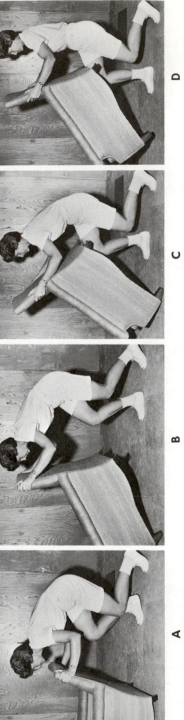

Figure 17-9. *A, B,* Force applied at chair top makes rotation easy — legs supply force. *C, D,* Weight transference lifts chair.

Figure 17-10. Weight of chair balanced by body weight.

overstuffed chair is both difficult to grasp and heavy to lift. However, it is easy to tilt it forward by pushing forward against the top of its back. Since the force is applied far from the chair's center of gravity, it takes relatively little force to tilt it. If it is tipped far forward so that when the individual stands in a wide forward-backward stride position, the thigh of the forward leg can be placed against the bottom of the chair, and the arms take a firm hold around the chair back; the chair can be lifted from the floor by a transference of body weight from the forward to the backward foot. As in any pushing or pulling task, the arm, shoulder girdle and back muscles should be set before the lifting force is exerted.

By rocking the weight well backward so that the forward foot can be lifted momentarily from the floor, the chair can be moved. Once the chair is off the floor, the second thigh can be brought under the chair bottom while the body weight balances the weight of the chair. If a chair is so low that it is difficult to get the thigh very far under the bottom for the lift (Fig. 17-9C, D), better control will be gained by placing the second thigh under the chair (Fig. 17-10). With the chair off the floor, this second thigh can be placed well under the chair bottom. By rocking the weight toward that leg, the weight on the first thigh can be reduced so that it can be moved farther forward under the chair bottom. With both legs supporting the chair and the body weight balancing it, it is possible to walk forward slowly by very slightly rocking from side to side. In this way the weight of the chair is used to help lift each foot in turn. The weight of the body simply balances the weight of the chair and, although this is a heavy object and all trunk muscles are called into action to stabilize the trunk, there is no strain on the small muscles of the back.

Before the chair is put down onto the floor, one leg must be placed backward. The chair is then put down by transferring the weight to the forward foot, lowering the front legs of the chair to the floor and then tilting it backward until all four legs again rest on the floor. In this way, the body weight can be used as the lifting force for any object which weighs less than the individual lifting it and which can be grasped by the arms and rested against a thigh. Besides being applicable for lifting very heavy objects, this technique is useful with large objects that are not easily grasped in the normal lifting position.

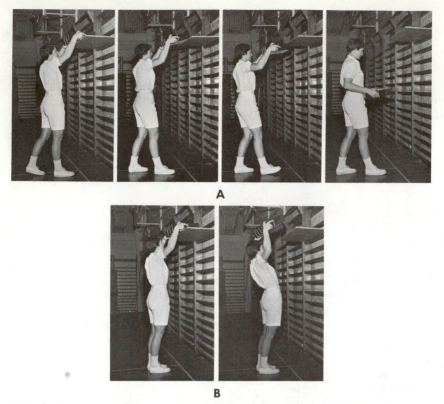

Figure 17–11. *A*, Weight transference takes box from shelf. *B*, Strain on lower back.

In lifting an object from a high shelf, balance is always a problem. Since the force to start the task must be applied outward in order that the object can clear the shelf, the original velocity of the object is outward and since it is applied against the body at a high point it tends to tip the body backward (Fig. 17–11). Therefore, it is important to have a wide base in the forward-backward direction, so that balance will not be lost. To avoid excessive reaching the forward foot should be close to the shelf, **the other foot well back.** The body weight is on the forward foot as the hands contact the object. The object is pulled slowly to the edge of the shelf by some weight transference. This original force must be applied carefully to avoid having the momentum of the object carry it off the shelf before the individual is ready to control its weight. It is important to remember that, because of inertia, it takes more force to start an object moving than to keep it moving (Chapter 4, Motion).

After the object has been moved to the edge of the shelf, the individual should get set for the lifting task. The object should be grasped so that force can be applied directly in opposition to gravity's downward pull. This means that a good part of the hands must be under the object, either centered or on both sides. If it is flat enough (like a suitbox) that it can be grasped over both ends and have the fingers well under, and is not too heavy, it can be controlled well in this way. However, removing a suitcase or briefcase from an overhead storage area of a bus, plane or train or from a shelf presents another problem. A suitcase is too thick for such a grasp but has a handle. In this case one hand grasps the handle for control and the other is placed in such a position that, as the suitcase is pulled slowly outward, the palm of the hand will be under its center. A carton with a heavy cord or rope can be handled in a similar way.

All of these objects are pulled outward off the shelf by transferring the body weight from the forward to the backward foot. This uses the strong leg muscles to do the work, the back muscles being called upon only to stabilize the trunk. Weight transference places the body far enough from the shelf that there is space for the object to drop straight down in front of the body. As soon as the object is clear of the shelf, the arm and shoulder girdle muscles resist the pull gravity just enough to assure a controlled lowering of the object to a point where it can be carried most easily. In the case of the suitbox, this might be in front of the body while the suitcase would be lowered to a position at the side. This is a controlled "giving in" to gravity (eccentric contraction) by the muscles of the arms and shoulders, just as walking downstairs is a controlled giving by the muscles of the legs.

To put the object up onto the shelf the opposite movement is executed. The box is lifted upward while the weight is on the back foot and the transference of body weight moves it onto the shelf. In the case of an object with a handle, such as a suitcase, the upward force required can be reduced by the use of momentum created by swinging the object forward and upward. One hand is then placed under the object and the body weight is transferred from the back to the forward foot to move the object onto the shelf or rack (Fig. 17–12). This method of swinging an object to gain upward momentum can be very useful in putting a heavy suitcase or a spare tire into the trunk of a car. Momentum should be used whenever possible to augment the lifting force.

Standing on a chair or stool to reduce the distance of the reach is dangerous when an object of any appreciable size and weight is involved, since the base is small and allows no transference of weight backward. If the chair is close to the shelf so that the force of the body weight is straight

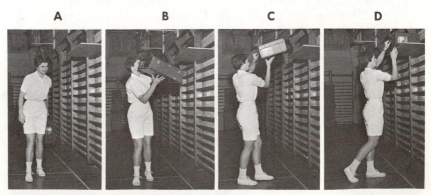

Figure 17–12. *A, B,* Momentum from swing starts the lift. *C, D,* Weight transference puts suitcase on shelf.

downward to reduce the possibility of the chair slipping, there is no space between the individual's body and the shelf for an object of any size to be lowered. To make space, the individual must lean backward from the waist. Since the base is small and the weight high, balance is precarious and this backward leaning may overbalance the body. In any event, it puts strain on the muscles of the lower back; not only must they support the upper body in this off-balance position but the weight as well. If, on the other hand, the stool or chair is placed far enough out from the shelf to allow space for the object to drop in front of the individual, he must lean toward the shelf to contact the object. This causes a diagonally backward force against the chair and unless friction is great, it is pushed out from under the individual. This practice has resulted in many falls.

If the reach from the floor causes strain, a low footstool placed under the forward foot while keeping the other foot back will relieve it to some extent. Even though one foot is lifted off the floor during the forward reach, it must be kept **back** in position to drop to the floor to take the body weight as it moves down and back. The force of the forward foot against the stool is straight downward so that slipping is not as great a problem, but the weight can be transferred to the back foot as the object comes off the shelf. It may be advantageous to stand on a stool close to the shelf to move the object close to, or slightly out over, the edge of the shelf where it can be reached more easily from the floor. The stool should then be removed and a wide stride assumed before the object is actually removed from the shelf.

Some lifting tasks, such as lifting a shovel full of dirt, involve long handled implements. In such a case the individual stands so that the load is to his side and slightly ahead, in a position where the shaft of the shovel is in front of his body. As in all lifting tasks, the body is lowered by flexing the hips, knees and ankles and slightly inclining the trunk forward. One hand is placed well down the shaft in order to shorten the weight arm while the other grasps the handle of a short shovel or the shaft of a long shovel as far up as can be comfortably reached. The hand closer to the weight is used as the fulcrum and the other, having the advantage of a long force arm, produces the major part of that lifting force which is exerted by the arms (first class lever). Extension of the legs, plus this leverage action of the arms, lifts the load. Some force is usually supplied by the lower hand also, making the shovel a combination of first and third class levers.

If the lifting task calls for the cooperation of two or more persons, they should lower their bodies so that they can place their hands under the heaviest parts of the load in such a way that the weight can be divided equally, set their muscles for the task and, on signal, all exert force at once. In this way the load is distributed evenly and all parts of the load move upward uniformly. If one person applies force before another, the load is tilted and more weight rests on the person who is in the lower position. When several persons are involved, the load is lifted first to their knees and then, on a second signal, all stand. If any readjustment of weight is necessary, it can be made before they attempt the major part of the lift. This procedure also is more likely to result in unified movement. This is the technique used in first aid when a person is lifted from the floor by four or five individuals.

When any amount of forward lean of the body is required by a lifting task, the lower back "should not be allowed to arch but should be flattened by 'tucking the hips'."[5] Kendall[6] stated that a person with tightness in the muscles of the lower back has difficulty in tucking the hips (tilting the pelvis backward) and therefore is more susceptible to strain from lifting than is the person with normal flexibility.

Regardless of the lifting task, whether it involves a box, a child or an adult from a chair, whenever the individual finds that the load does not move **as the legs begin to straighten** but that the hips push out behind leaving the upper body low, he **must stop any attempt to lift** the object and seek help. Further effort will simply strain the back. If he continues until he feels some strain in the back it is too late, the harm has been done. **AT ANY TIME THAT THE HIPS CANNOT BE KEPT UNDER THE TRUNK AS THE LEGS EXTEND, THE LOAD IS TOO HEAVY.** If this were understood, there would be fewer back strains from attempting tasks beyond the strength potential of the individual.

When possible, pushing or pulling a heavy object or rotating it around its corners is preferable to lifting and carrying it. However, friction may make pushing inadvisable or even impossible, unless something with a lower coefficient of friction can be placed between the object and the surface across which it is to be moved. Sometimes the object is too low to be pushed or rotated efficiently; sometimes steps are involved. The method to be used in moving any object or person must be determined after consideration of **all** factors which pertain to a particular situation.

SUMMARY

Holding, carrying and lifting all involve a pushing or pulling effort in a vertical instead of in a horizontal direction. Therefore, the principles of efficient performance are the same as for a pushing or pulling task.

Although various tasks may be executed somewhat differently because of the size, weight and shape of the object to be moved and the objective of the movement, any heavy lifting or carrying problem must be approached with five basic questions. (1) What position must be assumed, so that the parts of the body (hands, arms, thighs, etc.) which are to exert force directly against the object are **under** the object (or some surface of the object) in a position to oppose directly the force of gravity? (2) How can body balance be maintained without the loss of the basic body alignment? (3) Does the preliminary position make it possible to exert the lifting or supporting force vertically upward rather than on a diagonal? (4) Will the major lifting or supporting force be exerted by the strong leg muscles? (5) Can momentum be used to augment the lifting force?

To avoid back strain in lifting, any attempt to lift must be stopped immediately when the hips cannot be kept under the upper body as the legs extend. The load is too heavy for the strength of the individual and he should seek help.

The most efficient method for moving any given object — lifting, pushing, pulling or rotating — can be determined only after consideration of all factors which pertain to the particular situation.

REFERENCES

1. Hilleboe, Herman E., and Larimore, Granville W.: *Preventive Medicine*. 2nd ed. Philadelphia, W. B. Saunders Company, 1965, p. 21.
2. Williams, Marian, and Lissner, Herbert R.: *Biomechanics of Human Motion*. Philadelphia, W. B. Saunders Company, 1962, p. 111.
3. Kendall, Henry Otis, Kendall, Florence P., and Boynton, Dorothy A.: *Posture and Pain*. Baltimore, Williams and Wilkins Company, 1952, p. 190.
4. Davidson, Bill: Stoop or Bend. *Collier's*, *135*:11:30, May 27, 1955.
5. Kendall, Kendall, and Boynton, *op. cit.*, p. 191.
6. *Ibid.*

THROWING AND CATCHING

18

THROWING

Throwing and striking differ from other methods for moving objects in that a maximum velocity is reached, the object is released and it then continues to move without further impetus from the body. Throwing is primarily a sport activity. In a variety of sports, balls of all sizes and weights are rolled or thrown by one hand or two. Nor is the object thrown always a round ball. The javelin, discus and beanbag are also thrown. While given the name of "ball" the football is not round. However, regardless of size, shape or weight, whether rolled or thrown, the essential mechanics remain the same. Motion is transferred from the body to the object thrown. The object is held in the hand or hands, or as in the case of lacrosse, in another object which is in turn held in the hand. The hand (and with it the object) is moved and the object is released.

Since an object acquires the motion of any object to which it is attached (Chapter 4, Motion), the object held in the hand acquires the speed and direction of the hand and, when released, continues to move **at this velocity** and **in the same direction** until acted upon by other forces, such as air resistance, gravity or friction (Law of Inertia). In throwing, then, one must consider the methods for developing speed and for controlling direction of the hand. Control of direction involves adjusting the angle of release in both the vertical and horizontal planes. This is the point at which rolling differs from throwing. The mechanics of rolling are the same as those for the underhand throw with the exception that, since the ball is rolled along the floor or turf, the hand must be lowered, the verticle angle of release is not involved and friction becomes an important consideration.

Factors Influencing Speed. The faster the hand is moving at the moment of release, the faster a given thrown or rolled object will travel. The longer the backswing of the hand, the more time there is to develop velocity. The backswing can be increased by turning the side opposite to the throwing arm toward the direction of the throw, by rotating the body away from the direction of the throw and by placing the feet in a stride position with the foot opposite to the throwing arm forward. The wider base thus afforded increases balance by enlarging the base in the direction of the movement, and increases the length of the backswing by making possible a backward transference of weight and by allowing maximum rotation, since the hips are rotated toward the throwing side.

Experimentation with throwing as far as possible with the feet together, with the feet in a side stride, with the right foot forward and finally with the left foot forward demonstrates the importance of a wide base in the direction of the force and the restriction of body rotation caused by the position which places the foot on the same side as the throwing arm forward. The added backward rotation which is possible when the opposite foot (left for right-handed thrower) is forward is obvious when, after standing with the same foot as throwing arm forward while attempting to rotate the body as far as possible, this foot is moved backward. When the foot on the side of the throwing arm is forward, the pelvis is rotated away from the direction of the backswing and the backswing is restricted. If the right-handed thrower understands that the left foot forward increases equilibrium by enlarging the base **without restricting** body rotation to the right, he will realize when it is necessary to assume this position. An understanding of the direction of the pelvic rotation resulting from different foot positions is very important to the efficient solution of a variety of movement tasks.

The more contributing body segments that are brought into the action, if they are timed in sequence, the more speed obtainable. For maximum speed, each body segment must come into action at the time the segment below has reached its maximum speed. Body rotation and the shifting of the body weight forward with the throw both put more body segments into the throw and increase the length of the backswing, and therefore add doubly to the speed of the hand. An experiment with two female physical educators in which the various joints were immobilized while throwing a tennis ball indicated that, for these subjects, approximately 50 per cent of the velocity of the overhand throw resulted from the body rotation and step. Since it was impossible to immobilize the fingers as this prevented grasping the ball, the finger action was involved in every item measured. In both subjects, the total shoulder, elbow, wrist and finger action accounted for approximately one-half of the force produced (53 per cent and 51 per cent) and the body rotation, step and fingers, the other half. It is little wonder that those who attempt to throw with their arms alone and overlook the importance of their trunks and legs are relatively unsuccessful in throwing overhand.

Any movement of the body in the direction of the throw adds force to the throw. The transference of weight, a run or hop all give the body velocity which is transferred to the throwing arm and thus to the object to be thrown. Transference of weight is used in any throw in which speed is a factor. If, in transferring the weight, the individual steps forward onto a straight leg, the forward momentum is restrained just as it is in walking, from the time the forward leg takes any of the weight until the center of gravity of the body is over the forward foot. When the forward knee is allowed to flex as the weight is transferred, there is no resistance to the forward motion. However, at the time of the final motion of the upper body and arm before release, the leg must be straight to give a solid base for a forceful throw. It has been stated that attempting to throw while flexing the knee is "like trying to throw from a trampoline or shoot a cannon from a canoe."[1]

When rolling a ball it is necessary to lower the body so that the hand can reach to, or close to, the ground. Since leaning over places the body in a precarious state of equilibrium, the center of gravity being high and the weight of the trunk forward, and also puts strain on the small muscles of the back, the body should be lowered by flexing the legs. Therefore, if rolling is practiced before throwing, a pattern of bending the forward leg during weight transference can be established and then carried over into the throwing pattern. A run preceding the roll adds even greater speed just as it does to the throw. This is the principle applied in the approach in bowling. The velocity of the body gained through the approach is added to the velocity of the arm swing.

A throw executed on a moving base (run, slide) requires perfect balance and, therefore, in order to control the weight over the base, relatively small steps are taken. In order to transfer the weight from the foot on the side of the throwing arm to the opposite foot at the instant required for maximum sequential action, a hop on the back foot (right foot for a right-handed thrower) may be needed. This hop also makes it easy to rotate quickly to the throwing side for maximum backswing.

The faster the muscles which contribute to the throw are contracted, the faster the hand will be moving at the moment of release. It is possible to go through the motions of a forceful throw in slow motion and, although the backswing is long, the trunk rotated, and the weight transferred, still the hand will not be moving with any speed at the middle of the arc of the movement.

The more nearly the release coincides with the instant of maximum speed of the hand, the faster the throw. Human muscles are incapable of stopping motion suddenly without jerk or strain, and so the velocity of the hand must be reduced gradually. The hand is moving fastest at the center of the arc of the throw. If an attempt is made to stop at, or immediately following release, the arc of the throw is shortened and the speed of the hand must be slowed before the object leaves the hand. A jerking back to stop the motion actually produces force that counteracts the forward velocity of the throw. A follow-through places the point of release at the center of the arc, and the maximum speed developed by the particular movement can be transferred to the object thrown. Strain of the arm and shoulder is also avoided.

If all the force produced by the body is to be transferred to the object, there must be a firm surface for the feet and sufficient friction to prevent slipping. Whenever the purpose of the throw demands sufficient force to require a wide base for balance and the use of weight transference, a considerable proportion of the force exerted by the body against the supporting surface is backward. Therefore, the friction between the feet and the surface is extremely important in causing the reaction force of the surface against the feet and through the body, and thus in producing a firm base for trunk, shoulder, arm and hand action.

The more the internal resistance is reduced before the throw, the less

the possibility of injury. Warming up the muscles by throwing easily before attempting an all-out effort may add to the efficiency of the throw
and certainly reduces the possibility of muscular strain.

Whether or not maximum force is desirable depends upon the purpose of the particular throw. Frequently the certainty of the catch of a
relatively short throw is more important than speed. Less force must be
used when throwing to an individual who is running toward the thrower
since this not only decreases the distance of the throw, but also adds the
receiver's momentum to the force of the impact, and thus increases the
possibilities of a fumble of the catch. Whenever the purpose does not demand maximum distance or maximum speed, the pattern of movement is
adjusted so that the ball is thrown with less speed. Not every throw demands as long a back-swing as possible. It is not even always necessary to
have the feet in a forward stride, or the opposite foot forward. These are
important only in that they contribute to the speed of the hand and of the
thrown object. The important consideration is the relationship of these,
and other factors discussed earlier, to the speed that the body can produce
and the magnitude of the force desired. The most suitable speed for the
purpose must be determined and adjustment of movement pattern made
accordingly.

The most efficient throw for a given situation may be made with a
short swing which, in a particular situation, may be accomplished most
efficiently with the feet almost together. If the situation calls for a toss to
a player standing nearby in which the certainty of the catch is important,
the small amount of force that is needed may be produced more efficiently by using the arm alone rather than by going through the whole "throw
pattern." Since little force is involved, balance is not a problem and,
therefore, foot position is unimportant. Too frequently the pattern of maximum force is thought of as **the** "throwing pattern" and this foot position,
etc., is insisted upon for every throw. When the contribution of each part
of the movement to speed and angle of release is understood, the individual is in a position to make judgments according to purposes and more
efficient movement can result in situations which call for less than maximum force. Too frequently "form" is judged according to the "maximum
force pattern," rather than the movement which can accomplish the purpose with the least expenditure of effort and strain.

Factors Influencing Direction. An object continues to move in the
direction in which it was moving at release until acted upon by some
other force. If the hand is traveling in an arc, the thrown object moves in
a line which is tangent to that arc at the point of release. This means that
there is only one point on the arc at which it can be released if it is to
move in a given direction. The more nearly the arc approaches a straight
line, the less divergent the tangents at various points on the arc (Fig.
18–1). Therefore, the flatter the arc through which the hand travels, the
greater the probability of accuracy. One way that the path through which
the hand travels can be flattened is by moving the center of the arc in the
direction of the movement and in the direction of the circumference of
the arc.

For example, in the underhand throw, since the movement is in the
vertical plane, the arc can be flattened by moving the shoulder (the center

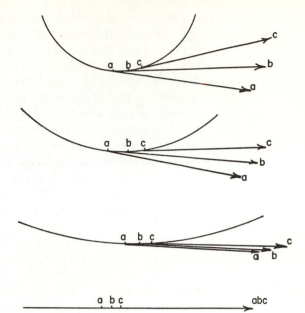

Figure 18–1. Effect on divergence of various tangents as arc is flattened.

of the arc) forward and downward (Fig. 18–2). Flexing the forward knee as the weight is transferred and a follow-through in a forward direction accomplish this. In the overhand throw, the arc is flattened by a sequential extension of the joints of the arm as the throwing shoulder moves forward due to the rotation of the spine and the transference of weight. This is an example of various levers working together to produce a more linear motion of the hand. The rotation of the trunk which moves the shoulder forward and out to the side of the throwing hand is a factor in flattening the arc (right-to-left) of the sidearm throw.

The longer the throw, the more important is control of direction since any deviation from the desired direction becomes magnified the farther the object travels. This is an important consideration in many activities, as, for example, in bowling in which the lane is approximately 60 feet long and a high degree of accuracy is essential to success.

Many of the factors that contribute to speed are likely to decrease control of direction. For example, it is easier to control fewer body segments but maximum speed results from the use of all segments that can

Figure 18–2. Schematic representation of the flattening of the arc of the underhand throw accompanying a forward and downward movement of the shoulder.

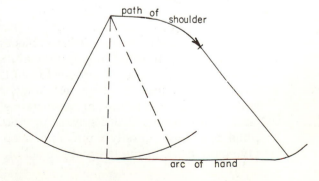

contribute to the movement. It is easier to control a relatively slow motion but speed results from fast muscular contraction.

Once the object has left the hand, its path is influenced by any other forces which act upon it. The more accurate the allowance for these other forces (gravity, wind and spin), the more accurate the throw. Since the object moves in the direction in which the air is moving, it should be aimed somewhat into a cross wind rather than straight in the direction of the desired movement. The stronger the wind, the more it should be aimed upwind. Since a ball with right spin curves to the right and one with left spin to the left, a destination which is straight ahead can only be reached by a ball with right spin if aimed to the left of the desired destination. Since gravity always acts in a downward direction, it alters the path only in a vertical direction and thus affects the **distance** that the object travels.

Factors Influencing Distance.   The distance an object will travel depends upon the speed with which it is released, the angle at which it is released and the action of outside forces.

Other things being equal, the faster the object is moving at release, the greater the distance it will travel. Since gravity begins to act on the object at release, distance also depends upon the angle at which the object is thrown. The general principle that, **in the absence of air friction**, the greatest distance for a given speed results from a projection at a 45 degree angle has been discussed in Chapter 9, Projection. (See Fig. 9-6.)

Angle of release as well as speed must be adjusted to the purpose of the particular throw. The speed of most thrown balls is not great enough to cause the building up of considerable air resistance against their forward progress and, therefore, if the objective of the throw is to gain the greatest possible **distance**, a ball should be thrown at approximately a 45 degree angle. Experimentation with throwing a ball with as much force as possible at a low angle, a high angle, and a 45 degree angle demonstrates the importance of angle to the distance of the throw. Various rafters or points on a gymnasium ceiling or, if outdoors, tree limbs and points on buildings or hills in the distance which will guide the release at the approximate angle desired can be utilized as targets for the various throws. If the purpose is to have a ball **arrive as fast as possible** at a given point which is **not** maximum for the speed obtainable by the thrower, the angle should be flattened. How much it can be flattened depends upon the speed which the individual can muster. The faster the ball travels, the less time gravity has to pull it toward the earth and the lower it can be thrown.

When wind is involved, the angle must be adjusted. A head wind resists the forward progress of the object and, therefore, decreases the distance an object travels. To gain maximum distance, the angle of release is flattened so that a greater proportion of the force applied is directed horizontally to combat the wind resistance. Since the force of a tail wind is added to the force of the throw, distance can be gained by increasing the angle of release so that a greater proportion of the **throwing** force is applied to combat gravity's pull and keep the object in the air longer, to give more time for the tail wind to act on it.

Spin on a ball builds up air pressure which affects the distance that it travels. Since forward spin causes a ball to drop faster than it would normally, less distance is obtained from a given initial speed and angle of release. Back spin, causing a ball to remain in the air longer, may result in greater distance. However, any spin increases air resistance. Spin is discussed in detail in Chapter 7.

Since a heavy object has a greater inertia than a lighter one, it takes more force to develop a given speed in throwing it, but, given a certain velocity, it travels farther than a light object because of its ability to combat air resistance. As the surface area which is presented in the direction of movement increases, the distance the thrown object will travel decreases (given the same projecting speed) due to the additional air resistance created. Thus, a small ball will travel farther than a large one of equal weight and both will travel farther than an irregularly shaped object of the same weight. A rough surface on an object also increases air resistance and can cut distance.

Throwing Patterns.   There are three basic throwing patterns; which will be most efficient depends upon the size, weight and shape of the object to be thrown and upon the purpose of the throw. The **factors** which contribute to speed and accuracy are identical for all. The **method** in which they are applied varies.

In the **overhand** pattern the segments of the arm are brought into the movement in sequence, giving a "whiplike" action at the distal end of the system of levers. Because this movement allows for the longest backswing possible and the use of more body segments in sequence, more speed can be developed with this type of throw than with the underhand. Thus it is used for speed and distance. The elbow is flexed on the backswing to shorten the lever and make it easier to move rapidly, as well as to place it in a position for sequential extension. It also makes reversal of direction to start the forward movement easier. It is more difficult to reverse the direction of the straight arm because of the greater backward velocity de-

Figure 18–3.   Elbow angle at time of ball release.

veloped at the end of the longer lever. Many sources have indicated that the ball is released at the point of full extension of the arm. Pictures taken during electromyographic studies[2] of a skilled young woman show clearly that the ball is released well before the arm reaches full extension (Fig. 18–3). In fact, there was an angle of approximately 105 degrees at the elbow as the ball was leaving the fingers. This agrees with the finding reported by Gollnick and Karpovich[3] who, in a study of joint action of young men throwing a baseball, found an elbow angle of 102 degrees at the time of release. Actually, this situation should have been anticipated since, as pointed out by Gollnick and Karpovich, it takes some distance to decelerate an arm moving at this speed. Undoubtedly injuries would have resulted if students had followed instructions and actually released at the straight arm point. The human body has many protective mechanisms that man is just beginning to understand.

Girls and women frequently have difficulty in developing the whip-like action of the overhand throw. They tend to throw with the arm, ignoring the body, and to drop the elbow close to the side of the body, from which position a pushing action results since the hand is forward of the elbow and shoulder. In many ways this throw pattern resembles that of a child in the early stages of development, although the child usually elevates the elbow. In discussing the developmental stages of the throw, Halverson and Roberton[4] stated that the trunk acts first as a passive non-moving stabilizer and that, when first used, it is moved only in a forward-backward direction; rotation comes later. They also stated that the arm leads the forward movement in the early developmental stages. This type of movement allows very little backswing and thus little time to develop velocity before release; sequential action of step, trunk, shoulder, elbow and wrist is impossible.

These individuals need to understand the contribution of backswing and the rest of the body to the force of the throw. They need to experiment with the arm position with the elbow down close to the body and with the elbow up and away from the body, so that they can determine for themselves the difference in the speed of a hand "pushed" forward and one which is "whipped" forward by the sequential extension of all joints possible when the elbow is up. Forward rotation starts in the pelvis and moves through the trunk. The shoulder comes into the action followed by the elbow and wrist. The hand, since it is the end of the whip, is the last body segment to be brought forward.

Holding the end of a four or five foot rope which is behind the body and throwing the far end out and forward demonstrates the different results obtainable from the "pushing" and "whipping" motions, and is frequently a successful method for gaining the feeling for the throwing motion. When the hand is pushed forward, the rope is simply pulled against the back, but when the whiplike action is used, the rope is snapped forward over the head. Going through the motions with something heavy in the hand may also help individuals develop a kinesthetic perception of a throw. A tennis racket in its press is excellent for this purpose, and advantage can be taken of this situation to point out similarities between throwing and striking activities such as the tennis serve and smash, badminton overhead clear and smash, and volleyball spike (Fig. 1–11). Sometimes the kinesthetic concept can be transmitted by standing close behind the individual, holding his throwing hand, and, after assuring that his arm is relaxed, actually throwing his hand. Repetition of this movement while the individual concentrates on how it feels is often helpful.

The true overhand throw can be used only with an object which is small enough and of such a shape that it can be gripped by the fingers, and light enough that it can be controlled at a considerable distance from the body. If a ball is too large to be grasped, it will roll off the hand as the motion of the backswing is reversed, since there are no fingers behind the ball to overcome its tendency to continue to move backward. The pattern must be adjusted to a push which puts the hand behind the ball. Heavy objects necessitate an underarm pattern in which gravity assists the thrower at those times when the object is far from the body, or a push shot in which the object is held close to the shoulder, inertia is overcome by total body motion, and then all arm and shoulder muscles come into the action simultaneously. The shot put delivery, because of the weight of the shot, is actually a pushing action rather than a throw.

The **underhand throw** pattern allows for the use of more varied objects. Because the object is closer to the body and the arm is straight, a heavier object can be controlled. The only times that the object is far from the body are at the beginning of the swing and at the top of the backswing. The momentum gained by the pull of gravity during the drop at the early part of the back-swing aids the arm in lifting the ball on the backswing. To initiate the movement all the thrower must do is push the heavy object forward away from his body. Gravity then aids in dropping the ball and in moving it backward. Since this throw is in the vertical plane, gravity assists the thrower in producing the forward movement of the object. A relatively large object can be controlled when this pattern is used because the palm of the hand can be placed under the object and it can rest against the lower arm.

This position eliminates the whiplike action of the arm and limits the usefulness of the wrist in the production of speed and, since both back-swing and body rotation are more restricted than in either the overhand or sidearm throw, this throwing pattern is not effective for the production of maximum speed or distance. However, because the throwing hand can follow a straight path throughout the swing, greater right-left accuracy is possible. Accuracy becomes mainly a matter of controlling the vertical angle of release.

An understanding of, and feeling for, this pattern can be acquired rather quickly by rolling a ball along a line to a partner at a distance of some four or five feet. The importance of having the backswing and follow-through follow the line is immediately obvious. By moving to a point 25 or 30 feet from the partner and again rolling the ball so that it will reach him, the factors which increase speed and distance, such as lengthening the backswing, transference of weight, and so forth, can be discovered by each individual. As the need for force is introduced, balance will become a problem if the center of gravity is kept high as the ball is rolled.

The importance of flexing the knees to lower the hand to the floor can be made obvious by experimentation with a **forceful** delivery, first while bending over with the knees relatively straight, and then while stepping forward onto a well flexed knee. Thus, the factors which contribute to speed and accuracy in the horizontal plane can be determined without having to be concerned with control of the vertical angle. The next step, obviously, is to consider the difference between rolling and throwing, and the added control which this difference necessitates if one is to throw successfully. The fact that, **when throwing,** the forward knee should extend before release to afford a firm base must be emphasized. The path which is followed by a ball when released at various points along the arc of the swing can be determined experimentally. If, when standing with the feet together, the arm is swung through a vertical arc and a ball is released early in the swing, near the center of the arc and then toward the end of the swing, the importance of flattening the vertical arc becomes apparent. The methods for accomplishing this have been discussed previously in the section dealing with the control of direction.

The underhand throw is used in many activities such as softball — particularly the pitch — horseshoes, deck or ring tennis and bowling. It is the throwing pattern which is chosen whenever a relatively short, well controlled throw is desired. The same pattern is also extensively applied in striking activities. The volleyball serve, the badminton serve (Fig. 1–10) and underhand clear, and underhand or pick-up tennis shot are a few examples of such application.

The **sidearm** throw pattern allows for the use of body rotation and for a longer backswing, even while throwing objects which are too large to be grasped by the fingers. Large objects eliminate the whiplike action of the arm, since the palm must hold the object against the lower arm and the arm acts as one lever rather than as a series of levers. Since a longer backswing is possible and more muscles contribute to the throw, more force is obtainable than in the underhand throw. Because the arc of the swing is more horizontal, left-right accuracy is a greater problem than in either of the other throwing patterns. When small objects are thrown, the pattern is the same as the overhand throw in all of the factors that develop velocity. Since the hand moves through a more horizontal arc, accuracy is not as easily controlled.

This pattern is most useful in throwing large objects for distance. The forehand drives in tennis and badminton, and the batting action of baseball and softball in general employ this same movement pattern (Fig. 1–12).

CATCHING

In catching, rebound can be prevented and the shock of the impact reduced by effecting a gradual loss of the kinetic energy of the ball through using as much distance as possible to reduce its velocity, increasing the time over which the force is absorbed, increasing the area which receives the force of impact and making use of all of the "shock absorbers" which are built into the body — the wrists, elbows, shoulders, hips, knees and ankles.

In preparation for receiving the force of an oncoming ball, the feet should be separated in a forward-backward stride position to enlarge the base of support in the direction of the force that must be resisted and thus improve stability. A crouch position lowers the center of gravity and further increases stability. The necessity for this depends upon the speed and height of the approaching ball. Every attempt should be made to place the body in line with the approaching ball so that the force can be taken close to the center of gravity of the body. When a ball is caught high above the head or far out to the side, the force is taken at the end of a long lever arm and its rotary effect on the body is amplified.

A padded glove both increases the area over which the force is absorbed and supplies an absorbent surface which reduces the force to some extent before it is transferred to the hand. The distance and time over which the force is reduced can be increased by pulling the hands in toward the body as they contact the ball and transferring the weight to the back foot or, if considerable force is involved, taking one or more steps backward. When the catch is to be followed by a throw, the momentum of the oncoming ball can be used to effect the backswing in preparation for the throw. By giving toward the side of the throwing arm, the give becomes the backswing for the throw that follows.

The position of the hands in catching is the most important single factor in avoiding injury. Since the area of the end of the finger is very small and any force taken on the end of a finger simply jams one bone back against the next, it is essential that the tips of the fingers should **never** be pointed toward an approaching ball. The position of the hands with the fingers pointing either upward or downward places the palms of the hands, which present a much larger and more absorbent surface, toward the oncoming force. Because of their anatomical structure, the fingers must point upward when the hands are above waist height and downward when below waist height, if the palms are to face forward. Only when a ball is dropping from above should the fingers point forward. In this case pointing the fingers forward faces the palms of the hands upward facing the approaching ball.

Catching an individual who is falling presents a somewhat different problem from catching a ball. The armpits offer an area which is small enough to grasp and a surface against which an **upward** force can be exerted. In addition, force applied to the armpits is applied close to the individual's head, the most important segment to protect. Every effort should be made to grasp him under his shoulders so that his head is kept from hitting the ground. If a hand, arm or leg is grasped the individual simply rotates around the point of contact and the head, being far from this fulcrum, may hit with considerable force. The individual who is attempting to make the catch must move in close to the falling person to shorten his arm lever and to apply his force more directly upward against gravity. As in any catching task, a wide stride in the direction of the force makes it possible to resist the force with less probability of loss of balance. The weight can be transferred as contact with the falling individual is made, thus giving time and distance for the gradual reduction of velocity.

SUMMARY

In throwing, an object held in the hand acquires the speed and direction of the hand and, when released, continues to move at this velocity and in the same direction until acted upon by other forces. Therefore, the faster the hand is moving when a ball is released, the greater is the velocity of the thrown ball. Maximum speed results from the use of all of the body segments that can contribute to the movement when timed in sequence, fast muscular contraction, the longest backswing possible, full body rotation, follow-through, transference of weight in the direction of the throw and a straight knee at release to provide a firm base. Friction between the feet and the supporting surface is essential if the force exerted by the body against the surface is to be transferred back through the body to the ball. A step, run or hop preceding the throw adds speed because the velocity of the body is added to that of the throwing movement. Follow-through is essential in that it makes possible a release which coincides with the instant of maximum velocity of the hand. The extent to which these various factors are employed depends upon the amount of speed called for by the purpose of a particular throw.

Flattening the arc through which the hand moves increases the possibilities for accuracy. In the underhand throw, the arc is flattened by moving the shoulder forward, by flexing the knee as weight is transferred and following-through as far as possible in the forward direction. The sequential extension of the joints of the arm as the shoulder moves forward effects some flattening of the arc in the overhand throw. The rotation of the trunk which moves the shoulder forward and out to the side of the throwing hand is effective in the sidearm throw.

The distance which an object travels depends upon the velocity and angle of its release and the action of outside forces. When maximum distance is desired, all factors which contribute to velocity should be employed and the ball thrown at an angle of approximately 45 degrees. If air resistance is a considerable factor, this angle must be modified downward. If the purpose involves having the ball reach a certain destination in the shortest possible time, the angle should be flattened as much as possible. The degree to which the angle can be flattened depends upon the velocity that can be produced by the thrower. Both velocity and angle depend upon purpose.

A head wind resists the forward movement of an object and the angle of release should be flattened to increase the forward component of force in order to combat it. A tail wind adds its force to the velocity of the ball, making it advantageous, if distance is the objective, to keep the object in the air longer and, therefore, the angle of release is increased so that a greater proportion of the force is effective in resisting the pull of gravity.

There are three basic throwing patterns. The overhand pattern, because it utilizes all of the factors of maximum velocity to advantage, is the most effective for high speed and long distance. It cannot be used if the object to be thrown is too large to be grasped by the hand or too heavy to be moved rapidly far from the body. Because the throwing hand follows a straight path, the underhand pattern is most effective for throwing tasks involving a high degree of accuracy. However, in order to follow the straight path, many factors leading to maximum velocity are omitted and speed is sacrificed to accuracy. The sidearm pattern uses many of the factors which develop speed and at the same time makes it possible to throw large objects which, because they cannot be grasped by the fingers, cannot be thrown overhand. However, since the hand moves through a more horizontal arc, left-right accuracy is more difficult to control. The pattern is most useful in throwing large objects for distance. All three patterns are used extensively in many striking activities.

Since balance is a problem in receiving force, the feet should be separated forward-backward (in the direction the object is moving) in catching. Every attempt should be made to place the body in line with the approaching ball to reduce the leverage of the force as the object contacts the hand or hands. A padded glove increases the area over which the force is taken and presents a more absorbent surface. Giving with the arms and body, even taking steps in the direction of the force increases the distance and time over which the velocity is reduced and lessens the shock of impact. This give can be used to effect the backswing of a throw that is to follow the catch.

The position of the hands is important in avoiding injury. The hands should be placed in such a position that the palms, which present a relatively large area, face the direction of the approaching ball so that they, rather than the very small area of a fingertip, will receive the initial force. In order for the palms to face forward, the tips of the fingers must be pointing upward when the hands are above waist height, and downward when below waist height. If the ball is approaching from above the palms should face upward.

REFERENCES

1. Moore, Kenny: Gideon Ariel and His Magic Machine, Sports Illustrated, 47:8:56, August, 22, 1977.
2. Broer, Marion R., and Houtz, Sara Jane: Patterns of Muscular Activity in Selected Sport Skills: An Electromyographic Study. Springfield, Charles C Thomas, 1967.
3. Gollnick, Philip D., and Karpovich, Peter V.: Electrogoniometric Study of Locomotion and of Some Athletic Movements. Research Quarterly, 35:3, (Pt. 2):369, October, 1964.
4. Roberton, M. A., and Halverson, L. E.: The Developing Child — His Changing Movement in Logsdon, Bette, et al.: Physical Education for Children: A Focus on the Teaching Process. Philadelphia, Lea and Febiger, 1977, p. 51–53.

19

STRIKING

While there are some household tasks that involve striking, such as swatting a fly and hammering, this is a much more important skill in the field of sports. Various sports encompass striking a ball with the head, shoulder, knee (soccer); with foot (soccer, football); with the hand or hands (volleyball, handball); with a racket (badminton, tennis, racquetball, squash); with a stick, club, or bat (hockey, golf, softball and baseball); and one object striking another, as happens in basketball when the ball strikes the backboard, or in bowling when the ball strikes the pins which in turn strike other pins.

In some of these activities a stationary ball is hit by a moving object, in others a moving ball hits a stationary object (the floor, backboard or bowling pin) and in still others a moving object (ball or shuttle) is struck by a moving object (racket, bat, hand, etc.). In some the striking surface is flat, in others it is rounded. Regardless of these differences, the problem for the player is to produce the required force and to apply it to the object directly or through the use of an implement, at such an angle that the particular purpose will be accomplished.

A stationary object when struck will move only if the force applied to it is of sufficient magnitude to overcome its inertia (Newton's First Law of Motion). The force must be great enough to overcome not only the inertia, due to the object's mass and speed, but also all restraining forces (friction, air resistance and other forces) as well.

The direction of an approaching object is changed and the object moves in the general direction of the movement of the striking implement or rebounds from a surface only if sufficient force is applied to overcome the force of the object. A ball striking a canvas which is hanging loosely does not rebound because the surface gives, absorbing the force, and thus does not supply sufficient resistance to produce a reaction force against the ball. The floor, on the other hand, supplies a force sufficient to resist completely the force of the ball and the ball rebounds.

The **law of conservation of momentum** states that when two or more objects collide with each other, momentum is conserved. The total momentum after the impact is equal to the total momentum before the impact. In other words, when a bat meets an oncoming ball, the total resulting momentum is the sum of the momentum of the bat (the mass of the bat times its velocity) and the momentum of the ball (the mass of the ball times its velocity). The difference between the two determines the direction of the resulting motion; it is in the direction of the greater momentum. If the momentum of the bat is greater than that of the ball, the forward momentum of the bat is decreased, and the ball is given reverse momentum equal to the sum of the two original momentums minus the momentum which the bat still has. Dissipating forces such as energy lost in friction and heat will, of course, reduce this somewhat.

It must be remembered that the **law of action and reaction** (Newton's Third Law of Motion), when applied to striking, means that during impact there are two equal and opposite forces set up between the two objects. One force is exerted by the striking implement on the object struck and the other by the struck object on the striking implement. The reaction of the object against the striking surface is just as great as the force which projects the object. As noted, this force depends not only on the force produced by the striking implement, but also on the force exerted by the struck object. In both cases, the force involved depends on the mass of the object and the speed with which it is moving. While the badminton racket has less **inherent** force than the tennis racket because of its lighter weight, this deficiency can be overcome by the added velocity with which it can be moved at the moment of impact.

Because of this action-reaction force, the striking surface must be firm if maximum projecting force is to be applied to the object. If some of the momentum of the contact goes into pushing the surface backward (striking surface gives), the projecting force will be correspondingly decreased. Direction may also be changed by this giving of the striking implement. Projection force and direction may be changed by the give of the object struck, the striking surface, or both. The reduction of projection force due to the give of the object struck is obvious when the bat meets a fleece ball which is soft and not elastic and does not bounce back into shape.* When the strings of a tennis racket become loose, some of the force is dissipated by the give of the strings as the ball hits the racket. When a forceful hit with the hand is desired, if the flat, open palm is used, some of the force is absorbed because the hand, being constructed of many small bones and muscles, cannot be kept completely firm.

There are various methods for making the hand a more solid striking surface and these are used in volleyball. The fingers can be curled into the palm and the ball hit with the curled fingers or with the heel of the hand. Some individuals make a fist and hit with the thumb side of this fist. This provides a surface which is solid but which is relatively small since the hitting area is only the side of the index finger and the lower segment of the thumb. Since the hitting surface is small a more accurate contact with the ball must be made, if results are to be as anticipated. If the force is not applied through the center of gravity of the ball in the direction of desired flight, the ball will go off at an angle. The somewhat larger area of the fingers or the heel of the hand which is available as a solid striking surface when the curled fingers are turned forward makes it easier to apply force through the center of gravity of the ball in the desired direction.

---

*See discussion of coefficient of restitution, pp. 126.

Discounting such restraining forces as friction and air resistance, the speed of a struck object, then, depends upon the degree of restitution of the object and of the striking surface, the mass and velocity of the object, and the mass and velocity of the striking implement.

FACTORS INFLUENCING THE MAGNITUDE OF THE FORCE APPLIED

When striking with the hand or an implement held by the hand, or hands, the body movement patterns are basically the same as those used in throwing. Figures 1–9 through 1–12 illustrate this similarity. Even though other parts of the body (principally the feet) may be used in striking, the factors involved in producing the velocity of the striking implement are the same as those involved in producing the velocity of the hand in throwing. Since these have been discussed in Chapter 18 they are simply mentioned here.

It is not surprising that researchers have found several similarities in the stages through which a small child passes in the development of forceful one-handed overhand and sidearm patterns and the one- and two-handed striking patterns.[1]

As in throwing, the speed of the striking implement depends on the length of the backswing or the time available to develop velocity, the number of contributing muscles which are brought into play, the sequence of contraction of these muscles and the speed with which they are contracted. To apply maximum striking force, the impact must be close to the instant of maximum velocity of the striking implement, just as in throwing the release must coincide with the instant of maximum velocity of the hand. In striking, the segment moving the striking implement must begin deceleration just before impact in order to stabilize the joints for resisting the force of the impact.[2]

In both throwing and striking, a follow-through prevents the slowing down of the hand or striking implement before release or contact, as the release or impact can then be at, or very close to, the center of the arc of movement, which is the instant of greatest velocity. The racket is slowed by the force of the impact as well as by muscular action; when the object being struck is missed, the muscular force required for deceleration is much greater than when hit. When kicking, knee injury can result from missing the object because the lower leg is moving toward its limits of extension.[3] Regardless of whether throwing or striking with the upper or lower extremity, if maximum force is to be imparted, there must be a firm surface for the supporting feet (or foot) and sufficient friction to prevent slipping.

In striking, however, a few additional factors are involved. One, the firmness of the striking surface, has been discussed previously. The firmer the striking surface, the greater the force imparted to the struck object. Since momentum is proportional to the mass of the object, it is obvious that the heavier the striking implement, up to the point of loss of control, the greater the momentum possible. If a bat is so heavy that it cannot be controlled, speed of swing is lost and the resulting momentum is decreased rather than increased by the weight.

Another factor influencing speed is the length of the striking implement. The longer the striking implement, again up to the point of loss of control, the faster the distal end will travel if a given force is applied, and the more force that can be imparted. However, the longer lever is more difficult to control. Also, it may be impossible to withstand the force of impact so far from the fulcrum and accuracy of impact may also be affected.

In addition to the above factors that involve the striking implement, the degree of restitution is also a factor. Because the object is flattened at impact and then retakes its shape, it moves away from the striking implement at a greater speed than the velocity with which the striking implement was moving at impact. The reaction force caused by the object pushing against the implement as it recovers its shape is added to the force of the striking implement. When a **moving object** is to be struck, the magnitude of the force produced by the impact depends also upon the momentum of the **object;** in other words, its mass and velocity.

In any striking situation, the more nearly the force is applied to the object being struck in line with its center of gravity, the greater the force transferred to the object in the desired direction. The "topped" golf ball is familiar to all. The ball being contacted above its center of gravity is hit more down into the ground than it is forward.

As in throwing, the purpose of striking does not always require the production of maximum force. At times it is advisable to conserve energy by adjusting the movement pattern. At other times it may be expedient to go through the maximum force pattern and reduce the force just before impact by contracting opposing muscles, **for the purpose of deception.** In this case energy is sacrificed to strategy. The purpose of the energy expenditure, though not to hit the particular object with as much force as possible, is just as important to the game situation. In order to deceive one's opponent successfully, it is necessary to understand the mechanics that are effective in producing maximum force.

FACTORS INFLUENCING THE TYPE OF MOTION IMPARTED TO THE STRUCK OBJECT

Force applied in line with the object's center of gravity results in linear motion of the object. The object moves straight in the direction of the resultant of the forces applied to it with little or no spin. However, some spin may be caused on various objects by air resistance or by friction. When a ball lying on the ground is hit with a vertical surface through its center of gravity, it **rolls** forward because friction resists the movement of the bottom of the ball, but its center of gravity moves forward freely. If the force is applied off-center, angular motion always results. When a ball is hit off-center, when the striking surface is not perpendicular to the direction of the striking implement's motion or when the striking surface moves across the back of the ball, spin results. When forward force is applied to the object above its center of gravity, top spin results. When this impact is below the center of gravity, back spin is imparted.

If the striking surface moves upward across the back of the ball forward, (top) spin is imparted; if downward, or if the club is opened (angle upward) as it moves forward, back spin; if it moves from right to left (outside-in), right spin; and from left to right, right spin. Since in most golf shots the ball is contacted below the center of gravity, it is given back spin. A slice (curve in the flight of the golf ball to the right) results from hitting with the face angled right, causing the force to be applied off center on the left, which starts the ball spinning right (p. 103). In most tennis drives the racket passes somewhat upward across the back of the ball, starting the top of the ball rotating forward. Since a ball with forward (top) spin drops more quickly, this aids in keeping a forceful drive within the court.

FACTORS INFLUENCING THE DIRECTION OF THE STRUCK OBJECT

The direction of the struck object depends upon the angle at which it leaves the striking surface, just as the direction of a thrown ball depends upon the direction that the hand, and therefore the object, is moving at release. In both cases, gravity begins to act on the object immediately and alters its path downward. In both, spin alters direction as the object moves through the air. Striking differs from throwing in that in the former, usually more than one force is involved in determining the angle at which the ball leaves the striking surface. When there are two or more forces, the object moves in the direction of the resultant of these forces.

Moving Ball and Stationary Surface. When a moving ball with no spin strikes a resistive stationary surface, only one force is involved and, as has been stated (Chapter 8), theoretically it rebounds at an angle equal to that at which it strikes. If either the ball or surface absorbs some of the force of impact, that is, the surface is soft or the ball's coefficient of restitution is low, this angle is modified downward. When the surface is vertical, as is the basketball backboard for example, and a ball approaches at an angle from above, the rebound force is diagonally downward and, when the ball approaches from below, the rebound force is diagonally upward (see Fig. 19–1). Obviously the path of the ball will not be in a straight line as the diagram indicates, since gravity begins pulling the ball down as soon as it leaves the board. Also, the rebound angle will be affected by friction, by the coefficient of restitution and by any spin on the ball.

When spin is involved, a second force is introduced and the effective force against the ball is in the direction of the resultant of the spin force and the rebound force (Chapter 8). The speed of the spin determines the degree to which the normal rebound is altered. The faster the spin, the more the bounce is altered.

The effect of spin on rebound from a **horizontal** surface is discussed in detail in Chapter 8. Since the friction resisting the spin force caused by the **front** of the ball moving downward results in upward force against the ball, forward spin on a ball approaching a **vertical** surface on a horizontal path

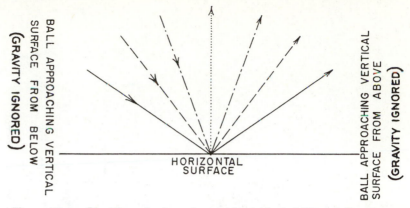

Figure 19–1. Direction of rebound — moving object striking stationary surface. (Assuming perfect restitution, no friction, no spin).

(90 degrees) causes a higher than normal rebound; back spin causes a rebound lower than normal since the front of the ball is moving upward and thus the friction force against the ball is downward (Fig. 19–2A, D). When a ball spinning to the right **around a vertical axis** approaches a vertical surface at a horizontal path (at right angles to the surface), the rebound is more to the left than normal (Fig. 19–2C), and when it approaches with left spin, the rebound is to the right (Fig. 19–2F).

The direction of the movement of the **front** of the ball determines the direction of the spin force against a **vertical** surface. If one holds a ball lightly against a vertical surface and starts rotating it as it would rotate with the various spins, the effect of the friction force is clearly seen. The ball started rotating with top spin will begin to climb the wall; the one rotated so its front moves right (right spin) will move left. The similarity between top spin on a ball approaching vertical and horizontal surfaces and right spin around a vertical axis on a ball approaching a vertical surface, and between back spin on a ball approaching vertical and horizontal surfaces and left spin around a vertical axis approaching a vertical surface, can be easily seen in Figure 19–2. If a ball approaching the vertical surface at right angles is spinning around its **horizontal axis,** the rebound is not affected and the ball rebounds straight out. The same principles operate as when a ball spinning around the vertical axis approaches a horizontal surface from directly above (Chapter 8). Right or left spin around a horizontal axis is rarely involved in striking activities.

A ball with top spin that approaches a vertical surface at an angle from below rebounds higher than if it had no spin. This means that it will rebound closer to the surface, while the ball with back spin rebounds farther from the surface (Fig. 19–3A, E). The reaction is the opposite when the ball approaches a vertical surface from above, one with top spin rebounds farther from the surface and one with back spin rebounds closer than normal (Fig. 19–3B, F). Back spin on a basketball approaching the backboard from above will, therefore, keep the ball closer to the backboard and improve the chances of the ball falling through the basket.

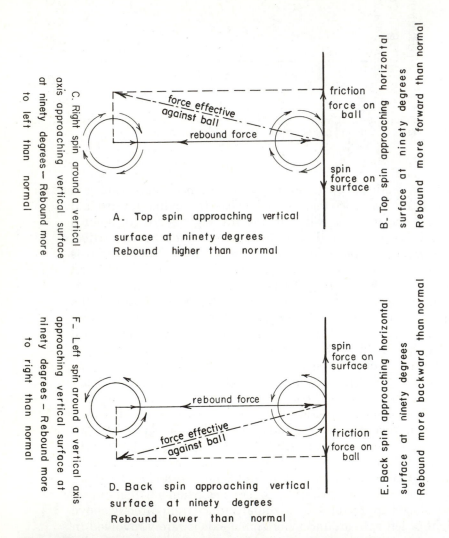

Figure 19–2. Effect of spin on rebound of balls approaching stationary surfaces at ninety degrees. (Looking at side of ball in A, B, D, and E and looking down on top of ball in C and F.) (Assuming perfect restitution, no friction, no spin.)

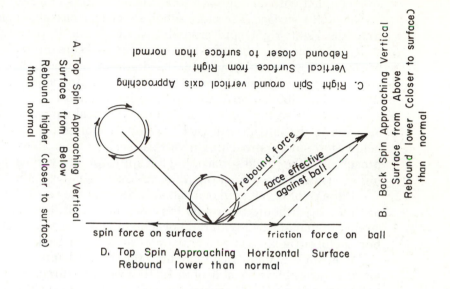

A. Top Spin Approaching Vertical Surface from Below Rebound higher (closer to surface) than normal

B. Back Spin Approaching Vertical Surface from Above Rebound lower (closer to surface) than normal

C. Right Spin around vertical axis Approaching Vertical Surface from Right Rebound closer to surface than normal

D. Top Spin Approaching Horizontal Surface Rebound lower than normal

rebound force

force effective against ball

spin force on surface

friction force on ball

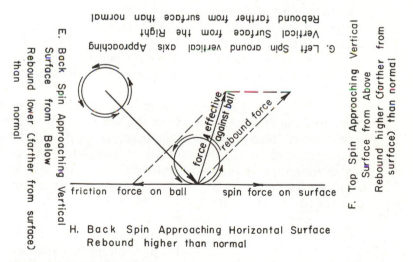

E. Back Spin Approaching Vertical Surface from Below Rebound lower (farther from surface) than normal

F. Top Spin Approaching Vertical Surface from Above Rebound higher (farther from surface) than normal

G. Left Spin around vertical axis Approaching Vertical Surface from the Right Rebound farther from surface than normal

H. Back Spin Approaching Horizontal Surface Rebound higher than normal

force effective against ball

rebound force

friction force on ball

spin force on surface

Figure 19–3. Effect of spin on rebound of balls approaching stationary surfaces at forty-five degrees. (Looking at side of ball in all except C and G, looking down on top of ball.) (Assuming perfect restitution.)

When a ball is spinning around its **vertical axis,** right spin on a ball approaching a vertical surface from the right causes a rebound which is closer to the surface than normal, and left spin causes the bounce to be farther out (Fig. 19–3C, G). If the ball with right spin approaches the surface from the left, the rebound will then be farther from the surface, while left spin coupled with an approach from the left results in a bounce closer than normal to the surface. Therefore, when shooting a basketball backboard shot from the right, right spin around a vertical axis is desirable and when shooting from the left, left spin, in order to keep the ball closer to the backboard. Figure 19–3 indicates the similarity between a ball with top spin approaching a vertical surface from below, back spin approaching a vertical surface from above, top spin approaching a horizontal surface, and right spin around a vertical axis approaching a vertical surface from the right. It also shows that a ball with back spin approaching a vertical surface from below, top spin approaching a vertical surface from above, back spin approaching a horizontal surface, and left spin around a vertical axis approaching a vertical surface from the right, follows a similar path.

If the right or left spin of a ball approaching the vertical surface at a left or right angle should be around the **horizontal axis,** the reaction would be similar to that of a ball with right or left spin around a vertical axis hitting a **horizontal surface.** Against a horizontal surface, the back of a ball approaching at an angle is depressed more than the front (Chapter 8), while against a **vertical** surface it is the **side** of the ball toward the direction from which the ball approaches that is depressed most — that is, the right side if approaching at an angle from the right and the left side if from the left. Thus, the direction of the motion of the back of the left or right spinning ball hitting a **horizontal** surface determines the effect of the spin on the bounce, **but** it is the direction of motion of the **side** of the ball in the direction from which the ball approaches the **vertical surface** which determines the effect of side spin.

The left side of a ball spinning left around a **horizontal** axis and approaching the vertical surface from the left would be moving downward. It would exert force downward against the surface and the friction force against the ball would be upward, causing the bounce to be somewhat higher than normal. Since the right side of the left spinning ball approaching from the right would be moving upward, the friction force would be downward and the bounce would be somewhat lower than normal. Right spin around the horizontal axis of a ball approaching from the left also would result in a lower than normal bounce, since the left side of the ball would be moving upward. Right spin around this axis of a ball approaching from the right would move the right side of the ball downward and the bounce would be higher. As stated previously, the type of right and left spin normally used in striking activities is that about a vertical axis.

Chart 4 summarizes various effects caused by different spins when a ball strikes a stationary surface.

This chart points up the fact that the effect of right spin around a **vertical** axis on a vertical surface is the opposite to that on a horizontal surface. This is because the spin force of the ball against the horizontal surface is caused by the **back** of the ball which, since it is moving to the left,

CHART 4. EFFECTS CAUSED BY VARIOUS SPINS WHEN BALL STRIKES STATIONARY SURFACE

Type of Spin	Effect on Bounce	
	Horizontal Surface	Vertical Surface
Forward (Top) Spin Always around a horizontal axis	longer, lower angle* and faster (closer to floor) (forward)	higher approach from above — farther from surface approach from below — closer to surface
Back Spin Always around a horizontal axis	shorter, greater angle and slower (farther from floor) (backward)	lower approach from above — closer to surface approach from below — farther from surface
Right Spin (clockwise) Around a vertical axis	approach from directly above — no effect approach at angle — to right	to left approach from right — closer to surface approach from left — farther from surface
Around a horizontal axis (used infre- quently)	to right	approach from 90° angle — no effect approach from right — higher approach from left — lower
Left Spin (counterclockwise) Around a vertical axis	approach from directly above — no effect approach at angle — to left	to right approach from right — farther from surface approach from left — closer to surface
Around a horizontal axis (used infre- quently)	to left	approach from 90° angle — no effect approach from right — lower approach from left — higher

*See discussion of fast tennis ball with top spin; p. 132.

exerts force to the left against the floor and the friction force of the floor against the ball is to the right. However, the spin force of the ball against the vertical surface is caused by the **front** of the ball since that is the part hitting the surface. Since it is moving to the right, the spin exerts force to the right against the surface and the friction force against the ball is to the left. This action of right and left spin around a **vertical** axis against a **vertical** surface is the same as that of top and back spin against a horizontal surface.

Moving Striking Implement and Stationary Ball. The direction of the force applied to a ball by a moving implement is determined by the direction of motion of the striking implement and by the angle of rebound from the striking surface. In this case, the theoretical angle is equal and opposite to

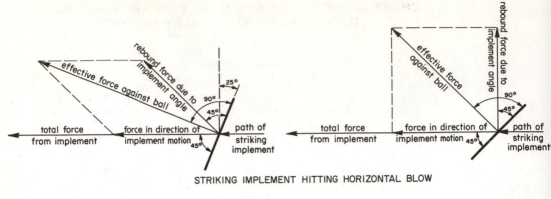

STRIKING IMPLEMENT HITTING HORIZONTAL BLOW

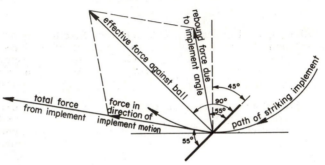

STRIKING IMPLEMENT HITTING SLIGHTLY UPWARD BLOW

Figure 19–4. Angle of rebound of stationary ball from moving striking surface. Effective force is at right angles to striking surface. (Assuming perfect restitution.)

the angle between the striking surface and the direction of implement motion. An off-center hit not only gives the ball spin, but also can change direction. However, for purposes of this discussion, a clear contact and perfect restitution are assumed.

When a moving implement such as a golf club, hockey stick or baseball bat (when using a batting tee) strikes a stationary ball all force effecting motion comes from the implement. The direction of the force against the ball depends upon the direction of motion of the implement and the angle of the striking surface. The angle of rebound of the ball is equal and opposite to the angle between the line of force (motion of implement) and the striking surface. Half of the force is effective in the direction of the implement's motion and half in the direction of the rebound angle. Since these two forces are equal, their resultant is halfway between them, or at right angles to the face of the striking surface. Figure 19–4 illustrates this fact. Variations in ball compression and firmness of striking surface can alter this somewhat.

Just as a thrown ball is given linear force in the direction which is tangent to the arc through which the hand is moving at the point of release, a ball struck by an implement moving in an arc is given linear force in the direction which is tangent to the arc of the implement's motion at the point of contact (Fig. 19–4). The direction of flight of a stationary object, then, depends upon the direction in which the striking implement is moving, the

Figure 19–5. Striking surface of a rounded implement.

angle of its surface and the relationship of the point of contact to the center of gravity of the object.

If an implement moving forward is angled upward, the ball is hit below center and thus given back spin; if angled to the right, it is hit left of center and given right spin; and when angled left, it is hit right of center and left spin results.

When the striking implement is rounded, as is a bat, the actual striking surface is a line tangent to the curve of the implement at the point of contact with the ball (Fig. 19–5).

Moving Striking Implement and Moving Ball, No Spin.   When a moving surface such as the hand, foot, a racket, bat or hockey stick strikes an approaching ball several factors must be considered: the angle of approach and momentum (velocity and mass) of the ball, the angle and momentum of the striking implement, the direction of movement of the striking implement and the point of contact in relation to the ball's center. The firmness of the striking surface and the degree of restitution of the ball are also factors.

The following discussion assumes a firm striking surface and a ball with normal elasticity. The force from the implement is divided so that one half is effective in the direction of the striking implement's motion and one half at an angle equal to the angle between the direction of the motion of the implement and its striking surface. The **effective force from the implement** is at right angles to the striking surface just as it is when a stationary ball is struck. However, the **rebound force from the ball's momentum** must be considered also when a moving ball is involved; the force of the ball against the implement causes a reaction force against the ball at an angle to the striking surface which is equal and opposite to the angle of the ball's approach. The **final force** against the ball is the sum of these two forces, the effective force from the implement and the rebound caused by the ball's approach (Fig. 19–6A, B).

If a ball approaches the striking surface horizontally and the striking surface is vertical and moving in a horizontal direction, the ball rebounds in a horizontal direction. All forces acting on the ball are in the same direction (Fig. 19–7A). If the ball approaches from above, as it does when it is hit on the down bounce, the racket must be open to have horizontal movement of the striking implement result in a horizontal path. The degree to which it must be opened depends upon the angle at which the ball approaches the striking surface (Fig. 19–7B, C). The greater the angle of approach from horizontal, the more the striking surface must be opened if a horizontal hit is desired. This also varies with the relative momentum of ball and implement.

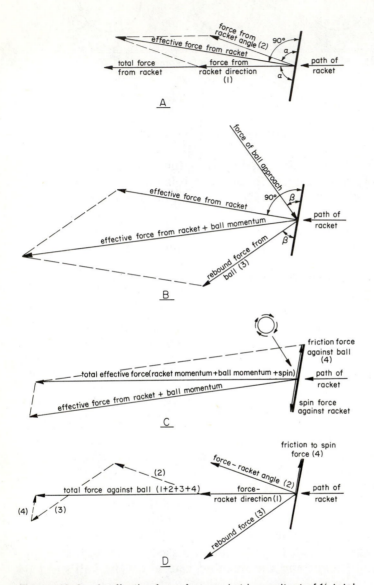

Figure 19–6. A, effective force from racket is resultant of ½ total force in direction of racket motion and ½ total force in direction of angle equal and opposite to angle between direction of total force and striking surface. B, resultant of effective force from racket and rebound force from ball's momentum. C, resultant of force from racket + ball and friction force from spin. D, resultant of all above forces added together in one diagram. Note: the final force against the ball in D is equal (in direction and magnitude) to final force in C. (Perfect restitution, no spin assumed.)

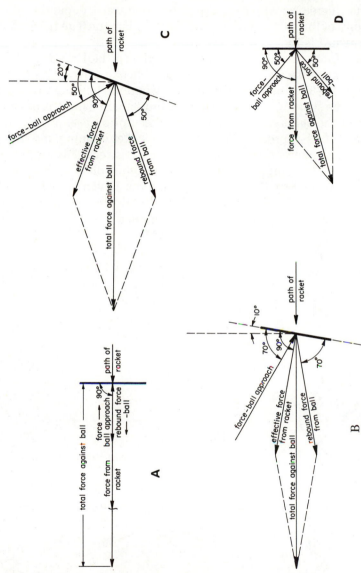

Figure 19-7. Force against ball resulting from various combinations of ball approach and angles of striking surface. (Perfect restitution and no spin assumed.)

The greater the speed of the **ball** in relation to that of the implement, the greater the effect of the rebound angle on the direction of the total force effective against the ball, and thus the more the striking surface needs to be opened to bring the ball up; the greater the speed of the **implement** in relation to that of the ball the less important is the angle of the ball's approach (and thus rebound) to the direction of the total force. A vertical racket and a horizontal path result in a downward path of the ball (Fig. 19–7 D). Again the degree to which the path is downward depends upon the relative velocity of the ball and of the striking implement. The harder the hit, the less downward is the path of the ball.

If upward force on the ball is desired when a ball approaches from above, the striking surface can be opened and either an upward or horizontal blow used (Fig. 19–8). When the upward blow **and** the ball's approach are at right angles to the striking surface, all of the implement's force is effective in the direction of the ball's rebound and all forces unite to send the ball back in the direction of its approach. The degree of racket opening and the angle of racket motion depend on the height of the hit desired. This also depends upon the angle of ball approach. With a horizontal blow a greater racket force is required to achieve the same effective force. Given the same speed of ball approach and the same racket speed, the total force against the ball is less when a horizontal blow is used. (Compare Figs. 19–8A and C; B and D).

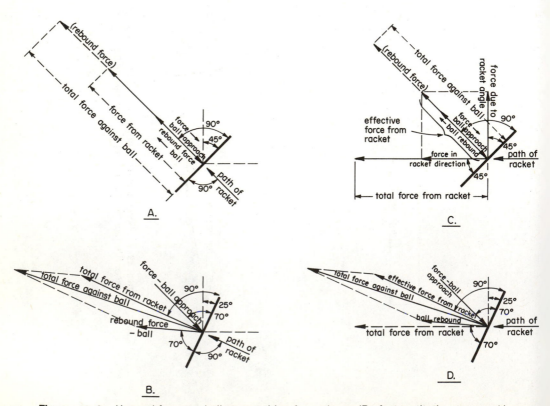

Figure 19–8. Upward force on ball approaching from above. (Perfect restitution assumed.)

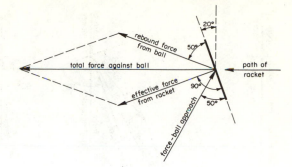

Figure 19–9. Force on ball approaching from below. (Perfect restitution assumed.)

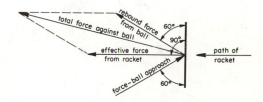

This is because the racket force is divided between the direction of racket motion and the direction dependent upon the angle of the striking surface (shown in Fig. 19–6).

When a ball approaches from below, that is, it is taken on the up bounce, the striking surface must be closed somewhat if a horizontal blow is to result in a horizontal path of the ball. If the striking surface is vertical and the path of the striking implement horizontal, an upward path of the ball results (Fig. 19–9). Again, the degree to which the path is upward depends on the relative magnitudes of the velocity of the ball and of the striking surface.

In striking, the right and left angle of approach must be considered, as well as whether the ball is approaching from above or from below. Obviously, a ball approaching from straight in front can be returned straight by keeping the striking surface facing straight ahead and the implement moving straight ahead (Fig. 19–10A). It can be sent to the right either by turning the face of the striking implement toward the right (Fig. 19–10B), or by moving the implement toward the right. This, in effect, is what happens when a ball is hit before the center of the arc of the swing has been reached.* Since the implement moves in an arc, it is moving somewhat from left to right until the center of the arc of the swing is reached (Fig. 19–10D). Also, if the striking surface is perpendicular to the direction of movement, the angle of the striking surface is constantly changing and the path of the ball is angled to the right by both the direction of movement and the rebound angle (Fig. 19–10E). If the ball is hit late in the swing, after the center of the arc has been passed, the face of the implement is traveling toward the left and a hit to the left results. A hit to the left with the implement moving straight ahead can also be accomplished by turning the striking surface to the left (Fig. 19–10C).

Just as flattening the arc through which the hand travels aids accuracy

---

*Assuming a right-handed stroke.

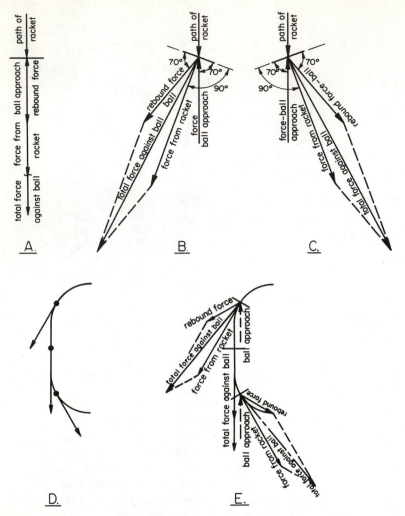

Figure 19–10. Rebound of balls approaching from straight ahead. (Perfect restitution assumed.)

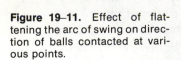

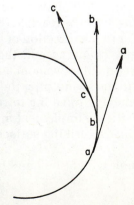

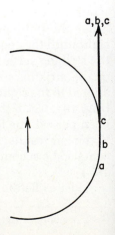

Figure 19–11. Effect of flattening the arc of swing on direction of balls contacted at various points.

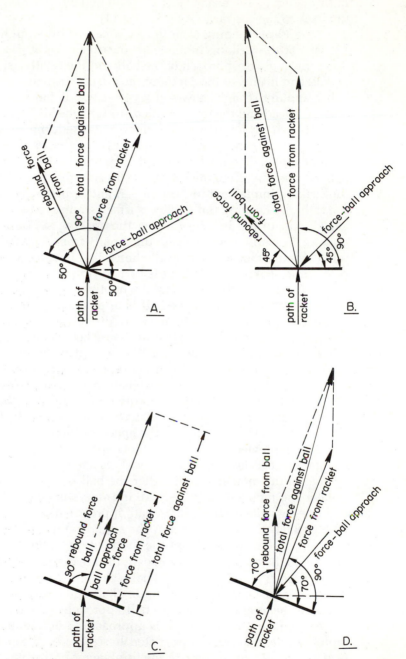

Figure 19–12. Force on balls approaching from right resulting from various directions of movement and angles of striking surface. (Perfect restitution assumed.)

in throwing, flattening the arc through which the striking implement moves makes it easier to hit straight ahead. The arc is flattened in the same way as in throwing, by the use of body rotation and by transferring the weight from the back to the forward foot (Fig. 19–11).

A ball approaching from the right can be hit straight ahead by turning the face of the striking implement toward the right (the degree depending upon the angle of approach of the ball and the relative speed of the ball and racket) and hitting at the center of the arc of the swing which results in force being applied straight ahead (Fig. 19–12A). If the striking surface is kept straight ahead and the force applied straight ahead, the ball will go to the left (Fig. 19–12B). If a return to the right is desired, the striking surface can be turned more to the right (Fig. 19–12C), or the implement can be moved through a path diagonally from left to right (Fig. 19–12D). In the same way, a ball approaching from the left can be hit straight ahead by turning the face of the striking implement toward the left and applying force straight ahead; to the right, by keeping the striking surface straight ahead and hitting straight ahead; and to the left, by turning the striking surface more to the left or moving the implement in a path diagonally from right to left. In other words, if a hit straight ahead is desired when a ball is approaching at an angle, the face of the striking implement is turned (to some degree dependent on the angle of approach of the ball and the relative speed of ball and racket) toward the direction from which the ball is approaching. The greater the angle of approach from the straight forward direction and the faster the ball is moving in relation to the speed of the racket, the more the striking surface must be turned. It must be remembered that whenever the striking surface does not face squarely in the direction of motion, spin will result.

Whether the angle of approach is from above or below or the right or the left, when the effective force from the racket and the rebound force are both applied at the same angle, the relative magnitude of the two forces does not change the direction, but only the speed of the ball as it rebounds from the striking implement. However, whenever these two forces are applied in different directions, direction, as well as speed, of the ball is altered by any change in the momentum of either the ball or the striking implement. The **greater** the momentum of the striking implement in relation to that of the ball, the less effect the angle of ball approach has on its path (the more the path of the ball is determined by the angle and direction of movement of the striking implement); the **less** the momentum of the striking implement in relation to the momentum of the ball, the greater the influence of the angle of ball approach on the path of the ball. Therefore, the less forceful the hit and the greater the speed of the oncoming ball, the more important it becomes to consider the angle at which the ball approaches the striking surface.

In summary, a ball which is approaching horizontally (a ball hit at the top of the bounce) can be projected horizontally, if the striking implement face is vertical and the path of the implement horizontal. It will be projected upward if the face is open and the path horizontal, and downward if the face is closed. A ball hit on the down bounce (a ball approaching the surface from above) can be projected horizontally by opening the face of the striking implement and keeping the path horizontal. The degree to which it is opened depends upon the angle of approach of the ball and the relative speeds of ball and racket. If the face is vertical and the path horizontal, the ball rebounds downward. The downward angle depends upon the relative magnitudes of the rebound force and the force supplied by the momentum of the striking implement. The ball can be projected upward by opening the face, hitting an upward blow, or both. When hit on the up bounce (a ball approaching from below), the face of the striking implement must be closed somewhat if the path of the implement is horizontal and a horizontal path of the ball is desired. A vertical striking surface moving in a horizontal path results in an upward rebound of the ball.

A ball approaching from the left or right can be projected straight ahead by turning the striking surface toward the direction from which the ball is approaching and applying force straight ahead. The degree to which the face must be turned depends upon the angle of approach and the relative velocities of racket and ball. The greater the angle of approach and the faster the ball's approach, the more the striking surface must be turned. If the face is kept straight ahead and the force applied straight ahead, the ball will go off in the direction opposite to that from which it approached. When the surface of the implement is at an angle to its direction of motion, the ball will be given spin.

Moving Striking Surface, Moving Ball with Spin. When a moving ball is spinning, three forces are effective in determining the ball's path: force from the implement,* rebound force from the ball's momentum, force

---

*This is actually the resultant of the half of the force effective in the direction of implement motion and the half effective at the angle caused by the angle of the striking surface (p. 277).

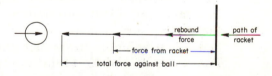

NO SPIN – APPROACHING VERTICAL SURFACE

Figure 19–13. Effect of spin on force against ball struck by moving implement — ball approaching at right angles to striking surface. (Looking at side of ball for top and back spin and looking down on top of ball for left and right spin.) (Perfect restitution assumed.)

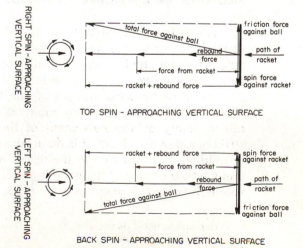

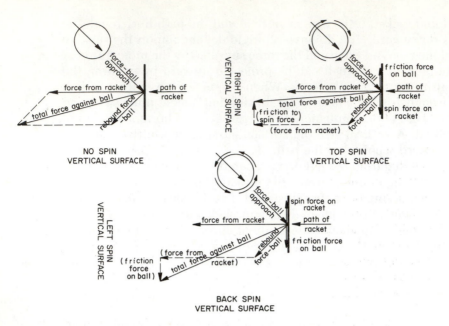

Figure 19–14. Effect of spin on force against ball struck by moving implement — ball approaching at angle to striking surface from above or from angle to the right. (Looking at side of ball for top and back spin and looking down on top of ball for left and right spin.) (Perfect restitution assumed.)

caused by the ball's spin (Fig. 19–6C, D). The rebound from a moving striking surface is changed just as it is from a vertical stationary striking surface. Top spin causes the ball to rebound higher than normal and back spin causes a lower rebound. Right spin around a vertical axis causes it to rebound from the striking surface more to its left than it would if no spin were involved, and a ball spinning to the left rebounds more to its right than normal. Figures 19–13 and 19–14 illustrate this.*

FACTORS INFLUENCING DISTANCE

The factors that determine the distance a struck object will travel through the air are the same as those that influence the distance of a thrown object: force of the impact, angle at which this force is applied to the object, spin on the object and the outside forces of gravity and air resistance.

Just as in throwing, the more force, the greater the distance of the struck object, all other things being equal. While in throwing the force is determined solely by the movement of the individual making the throw, in striking a moving object, it is determined by both the force produced by the individual and imparted to the object either directly or through an implement, and the force of the oncoming object. This has been discussed under factors involved in magnitude of force.

---

*It should be noted that these right and left reactions are from the direction of ball approach. Right spin causes rebound more to **right of player striking ball.** Also see discussion on pp. 129–133, as well as that concerning addition of forces on pp. 94–97.

In general, the rule that, disregarding air resistance and variation in ball restitution, a 45 degree angle of application of force gives the greatest distance applies also to striking. While air resistance is not a great factor in many activities involving throwing a ball, it becomes a decided factor in some of the striking activities in which the object is moving at a great speed, because air resistance increases so rapidly as speed increases. As speed doubles, air resistance quadruples. The greater the air resistance, the more horizontal force necessary to combat it. Therefore, the angle of application of force must be lowered to enlarge the horizontal component of the force applied when distance is the objective. A distance club in golf does not project at a 45 degree angle but at a much lower one, because the golf ball traveling at a high speed meets great air resistance.

A head wind decreases distance since this increases air resistance, and again the angle of application of force should be flattened so that a greater proportion of the force applied is directed horizontally to combat the wind resistance. A tail wind increases distance since the force of the wind is added to the force of the strike. If the angle of the strike is increased so that more force is applied vertically to combat gravity's pull, the ball remains in the air longer, giving more time for the wind to act on the ball and more distance can be gained. The ball should be projected lower against a head wind and higher in a tail wind to gain maximum distance.

Since forward spin causes a ball to drop faster than normally, and back spin causes the ball to remain in the air longer, a given amount of force produces less distance for a forward spinning ball and more distance for a backward spinning ball, all other things being equal. However, any spin does cause more air resistance which slows the speed of the ball.

REFERENCES

1. Roberton, M. A., and Halverson, L. E.: *The Developing Child — His Changing Movement* in Logsdon, Bette, et al.: *Physical Education for Children: A Focus on the Teaching Process.* Philadelphia, Lea and Febiger, 1977, p. 51.
2. Plagenhoef, Stanley: *Patterns of Human Motion.* Englewood Cliffs, New Jersey, Prentice-Hall, Inc., 1971, p. 69.
3. *Ibid.*

PART 4

SAMPLE APPLICATIONS OF THE BASIC MECHANICAL PRINCIPLES TO VARIOUS ACTIVITIES

INTRODUCTION TO PART FOUR

It is impossible in one volume to include complete mechanical analyses of the vast number of physical activities participated in by the general public. In fact, a complete mechanical analysis of even one activity would require an entire book. In this section **some sample** applications to a **selected group** of activities are discussed. Certain activities are treated in greater detail than are others. Since they all use various basic skills which are discussed in Part Three, repetition is avoided by reference to previous material. Golf has been analyzed in somewhat more detail and can serve as an example for further application of principles in other areas.

The applications of mechanical principles in the analysis of various activities included in this section are presented for the purpose of **suggesting ideas as a point of departure for further thinking** along these lines by the participant, teacher or coach of movement. The following material is presented, then, **not** as a complete analysis of any activity, but rather with the hope that it will spark interest in approaching the study of movement experiences from the standpoint of the mechanical aspects of the specific purposes, and that the reader, then, will complete the analysis of those activities of greatest interest and concern to him.

At the end of each of the following chapters, suggestions for further reading and study are given. The activity enthusiast will find that many of the references cited will provide important elaboration and extension of the basic mechanical principles and applications presented here. Sources of additional information can be determined readily by consulting the bibliography of biomechanics literature developed by James G. Hay which is listed with the references for each chapter.

20

GOLF

Golf is a striking activity that seems to fall into the side-arm pattern of movement. Since the ball is on the ground, the swing is essentially vertical rather than horizontal as in so many other sports (e.g., tennis, softball). Because of this, it seems that golf should be classified as an underhand movement pattern. However, if the position of address is taken and the club swung to full backswing and then, maintaining the same relationship of arms to body, the trunk position is adjusted to that of batting, it will be seen that the club is in much the same position as the bat would be at full backswing. Electromyographic records of batting and the golf swing of one individual indicate that there is more similarity in the muscle function of these two activities than between golf and any of the underhand activities studied (underhand throw, badminton serve, volleyball serve, bowling).[1] In both golf and batting, two hands must be used to control the long heavy lever. While the golf club is not as heavy as the bat, it is longer and is weighed at the extreme end of the lever.

The problem in golf, as in any striking activity, is to produce the desired amount of force and apply it by means of the clubhead through the center of gravity of the ball in the direction of desired movement of the ball. It is possible to produce considerable force because of the length of the lever used. Since golf clubs are considerably longer than most other striking implements, the speed of movement of the clubhead which results from a certain amount of force supplied by the muscles is much greater than that of shorter implements used in other sports. This extra length, however, makes control of the clubhead much more difficult. Without the help of gravity, which is gained in a vertical swing, this length of lever would be extremely difficult for many would-be golfers to control. Added to this is the fact that the striking surface is small, making accuracy of contact a major concern.

However, golf is one sport in which the manufacturer of the equipment has adjusted the vertical angle of the striking surface. Therefore it is possible for the player, through choice of implement, to vary the vertical angle of the shot without appreciably changing his swing. Since the ball is stationary, the player also has the advantage of having all the time he needs to make a decision concerning the desired angle and to get into position for the shot. Reaction time is not a problem. In tennis, as in most striking activities, the adjustment of the vertical angle of the striking surface must be made by the player during the swing following a split second decision. In golf, the vertical angle of projection can be controlled by the implement chosen without changing the swing **to any great extent**. So long as each club strikes the ball squarely with its face in its natural position (as when the club is soled), each will project the ball at a different angle. Advanced players, having greater control of the club, do adjust the swing as well as choose different clubs, and thus have available many more possibilities for ball flights.

Besides supplying the golfer with adjusted angles of striking surfaces, the manufacturer has also varied the length of the clubs. Thus, he has made it possible to reduce the length of the swing by choice of club. Therefore, the golfer can vary the velocity imparted to the ball without changing his body movement to any extent since, given the same rotary force produced by the body, the linear velocity at the end of the shorter club is less than that of the longer club. Since the golf ball is stationary, the force applied to it must be developed entirely by the player; no force is available from momentum of the ball as is the case in tennis. The force applied is dependent upon the momentum of the clubhead at impact and upon the time and accuracy of the contact, that is, whether the force is applied through the center of gravity of the ball. In order to contact the ball through its center of gravity, the body and club must, at impact, be in the same position relative to the ball as when the ball was addressed (assuming that the ball is addressed with the club soled behind the ball perpendicular to the desired line of flight). If the distance from shoulder to clubhead is shortened by flexing the arms or the distance from shoulder to ball is lengthened by raising the upper body, the ball is hit above center or may be missed entirely.

The beginning golfer has been told to "keep your eye on the ball," "keep your chin pointed at the ball," "keep the left heel down on the ground," "keep the left arm straight," "keep the right elbow close to the side," and so on. He or she has been given so many directives that an attempt to give attention to all of them has frequently resulted in tension which interferes with the smooth sequence of the movement so necessary to both force and accuracy. Actually, none of the above directives is, **of itself,** important. They are only devices which various individuals have found helpful in assuring that, at impact, the body and club position in relation to the ball will be the same as at address, so that the clubhead will hit through the center of the ball. For example, it is not important that the left arm be straight at the top of the backswing, it is only important that it be straight at impact. **If** the golfer is relaxed in his swing, centrifugal force and gravity will pull the arms straight at the center of the arc of the swing which should be the point of impact. Too frequently concentration on a straight left arm throughout the swing leads to so much tension in that arm that the golfer actually pulls it in as he swings through and tops or misses the ball. In other words, the correction is **sometimes** the actual cause of the fault that it was intended to correct. It must be recognized that the suggestion to "keep the left arm straight" may be helpful with some individuals in assuring a straight arm at contact, but that it is simply a device, not a necessary part of the form of the golf swing which everyone must follow.

Keeping the eye on the ball is a device for keeping the head steady which in turn aids in maintaining the same distance from shoulder to ball until after the ball has been contacted. Actually, once the swing has become "grooved," the ball **can** be hit with the eyes closed. Many variations in the suggested placement of the thumb on the club appear in the books dealing with golf. Stanley has pointed out that:

There is no such thing as a 'right' place for thumbs on the shaft. Some players grip with thumbs along the top of the shaft, others down the side, or around it. An ex-Open champion takes his right thumb off the shaft completely. Another professional is a first-class shotmaker in spite of having his left thumb amputated as the result of an accident.[2]

Stanley does suggest that placing the right thumb straight down the top of the shaft can be used as a device for correcting the fault of overswinging.* This places the thumb under the shaft at the top of the backswing and acts as a check on overswinging. A person having difficulty bringing the clubhead through perpendicular to the line of desired flight of the ball because of overswinging might be advised to put the right thumb down the top of the shaft. This does not mean that this is necessary for all golfers. The problem in learning golf is that a great many devices for correcting faults have been suggested (devices which are successful with some, but not with others) and some teachers, instead of using these devices one or two at a time as a need becomes evident, have lumped them together and made from them a stereotyped "form" which has been demanded of all students. These instructors have taught devices instead of the basic mechanics involved in accomplishing the purpose of a powerful, smooth flowing movement pattern.

Perhaps it is because so many people have written about golf and all have had their own devices for correcting their individual errors that this sport has become so enmeshed in detail — detail which often hinders rather than aids learning because of the tension which it produces.

Essentially there are only two strokes to be learned — the "driving" stroke and the putting stroke; the same mechanical factors are involved in both, and it becomes a matter of applying principles according to the different purposes involved. Because of this and the facts that the ball is stationary and the design of the clubs makes it possible to control vertical angle and to adjust to a degree, speed of clubhead by choice of club, it may appear that golf should be a relatively easy sport to learn. However, the length of the lever and the smallness of the area of contact as well as of the final target (the cup), make it a sport requiring a great deal of control, and thus, a sport of considerable difficulty.

FACTORS INFLUENCING SPEED

Because the club is relatively light, the speed with which it is moving at impact is the important factor in the force imparted to the ball. Thus **when the purpose of the hit demands maximum force,** all of the factors

*Overswinging — taking such a long backswing that the golfer is unable to move the clubhead forward to the ball by the time the hands are above the ball. Discussion assumes right-handed player.

that can contribute to speed at the distal end of the arm-club lever are employed. The longer the club and the golfer's arms, the greater the velocity of which the clubhead is capable, since the clubhead travels through a longer arc in a given time and therefore moves faster. However, at the same time that the limbs and clubs become longer, their moment of inertia (resistance to angular motion) also increases. Therefore, it is more difficult to produce the high angular velocities; a person with long arms and long clubs must have a greater degree of strength to take advantage of the potentially greater clubhead speeds. The length of the arc is also determined by the length of the backswing. Since the longer this arc, the more time available to develop velocity, when maximum force is desired, the backswing should be **as long as possible without loss of control**. If the backswing is so long that the clubhead drops below the horizontal, it must be raised **against** the force of gravity as the downswing begins. The clubhead is likely to lag behind the hands and unless the golfer has strong wrists which, despite this lag, can bring the clubhead into line at impact, the face of the clubhead will be angled to the right when contact with the ball is made. This will cause the ball to spin to the right (clockwise) and thus to curve to the right. (See discussion of slice, p. 298.) The long backswing also brings into play more muscles which can contribute to the swing and allows those muscles that contribute to the downswing to be maximally stretched in order to produce a greater strength of contraction. If the additional muscular strength is effectively transferred to the club, a faster clubhead speed is developed. The principal muscular force available when a short backswing is used is that of the arms and shoulder girdle. As the backswing is lengthened by pelvic and spinal rotation, the strong lower extremity and trunk muscles are put in a better position to contribute substantially to the movement. In golf, as in other sidearm throwing and striking activities, a long backswing necessitates a positioning of the body sideways to the intended line of flight of the ball. This body position also places the ball at the center of the arc of the swing which is the point at which the clubhead should be moving the fastest. Cochran and Stobbs reported computer studies of a two-lever model which "suggest that the clubhead is moving fastest at, or possibly just before, the point where it catches up with the hands."[3] For maximum transfer of momentum to the ball, the clubhead should be moving its fastest at contact.

Follow-through is important to speed in any throwing or striking activity (Chapters 18 and 19); a good follow-through is one of the best indicators of an effective sequence of movement pattern. Because the ball has already left the clubhead, the follow-through can not **directly** contribute to the speed or direction of the golf ball. However, it is impossible to be moving with maximum speed at contact and stop, or greatly slow, the movement immediately after impact; thus a faulty or incomplete follow-through indicates an ineffective swing **prior** to contact.

The speed with which the muscles involved in the movement contract is also a considerable factor in the speed of movement of the clubhead. The faster the muscular contraction, again up to the point of loss of control, the greater the velocity of the clubhead at contact. It is certainly possible to swing so fast that control is lost. Here again, the hands may be brought through well ahead of the clubhead because the club moment of inertia (resistance to angular motion) and the air resistance against the clubhead increase rapidly as speed increases, and being applied so far from the fulcrum, make it difficult to snap the wrists through and bring the striking surface in line with the hands at impact. This does not mean, however, that the beginner should practice the golf swing at a slow tempo. It has been shown experimentally that skill in activities involving both accuracy and speed is developed more readily when the activity is practiced from the beginning at the speed (or approximate speed) at which it will be performed.

Stance plays an important part in the speed of the clubhead in that it makes possible use of the entire body in the swing through weight transference from the back to the forward foot. It is also important from the standpoint of equilibrium. Since the force is moving from right to left (right-handed golfer), it is important to widen the stance in that direction. If equilibrium were to be maintained on a narrow base the length of the swing would have to be cut considerably. If the feet are placed farther apart than the width of the hips, rotation on the backswing and follow-through is restricted and thus loss of length of swing, and consequent loss of force, results. Beyond the width of the hips, the farther apart the feet are placed, the greater the curtailment of the swing. Thus a hip width stance contributes the maximum stability possible without restriction of rotation in either direction (backswing or follow-through).

Transference of weight, besides contributing to force by putting the body weight into the stroke, moves the center of the arc (the shoulder), slightly forward and thus flattens the vertical arc of the swing, giving more time in the swing during which the clubhead can hit through the ball in the direction of desired movement. Only if the ball is contacted squarely is all the force available imparted to the ball. If the ball is hit above its center, some of the force pushes the ball into the ground rather than sending it forward. When the ball lies on a hard surface and a wood is used, it may be difficult to get the club low enough to contact the ball squarely. The driving tee is important in that it lifts the ball, making it possible to hit slightly under its center of gravity and thus impart backspin. (See discussion of distance factors, p. 300). If the ball lies on grass, the clubhead can get down into the grass for a clear contact.

The degree to which the force produced by the body is effective in moving the ball depends upon the firmness of the grip and the wrists at impact. The final link between the body and the golf club is the golfer's hands. Ultimately, it is the hands that must transmit to the club the force developed by the body during backswing and downswing. Firmness of wrists and grip during development of club velocity prevents unnecessary dissipation of forces and contributes to efficient transference of all available force to the ball.

Various grips have been suggested: the overlapping, interlocking and the "baseball" grip. Bunn analyzed the striking movement of the hands as a pushing back of the top hand as the bottom hand pushes forward, the fulcrum being halfway between the hands. This action can be more effectively executed with the hands spread as in the "baseball" grip because the force arm is lengthened. He stated that this "split-second action of the wrists at the moment of contact gives the needed extra force which produces distance."[4] Other authors[5, 6, 7] have indicated that the greatest force which can be developed with a given amount of body power is centrifugal in nature. This is best accomplished with the hands acting as a unit rather than applying a leverage action. The overlapping grip, because the hands are in contact, makes this easier. It is possible that while one individual may be able to control the leverage action of the hands suggested by Bunn and take advantage of any extra force thus produced, another might find that the "baseball" grip leads to loss of control and that he is able to generate more **controlled** force through the use of centrifugal force uninterrupted by the leverage action.

The degree to which the force produced by the body is transferred to the ball also depends upon the reaction force from the ground against the feet. Any slipping of the feet means a loss of force against the ball, since some of the force goes into moving the foot or feet. For this reason, cleats on golfers' shoes aid in imparting force to the ball. Since the cleats indent or actually pierce the ground, they offer a surface which can push directly against a vertical surface of the ground rather than an area which pushes across a horizontal surface, in which case the reaction force has a greater dependence on friction. If the feet are directly under the hips as they are when the stance is widened only to the width of the hips, the pressure of the feet is more directly downward and slipping is less likely to occur. When the feet are placed apart farther than the width of the hips a more diagonal force is applied and the outward component of this force makes slipping more likely unless cleats are worn.

The speed imparted to the golf ball, as to any other ball, is also dependent upon the coefficient of restitution of the ball and the clubhead. If the ball has lost some of its ability to retake its original shape after being flattened by contact with the clubhead, some of the force is dissipated in the change of shape and does not contribute to speed.

Weaker hitters should use low compression balls;[8] the club makes more impression on contact and thus there is a greater rebound of the ball added to the speed imparted by the club. Those able to produce high speeds at the clubhead gain a greater distance from a high compression ball but weaker hitters lose distance because the force of impact is insufficient to flatten a high compression ball. **In general,** women have more success with low compression balls.

Plagenhoef[9] reported velocities of average golf drives made by male professionals as 160 mph and by women, 125 mph. The fastest velocity achieved by the men studied was 185 mph and that for women, 158 mph. He found that men moved the clubhead 24 mph faster than women before impact and that the greater grip strength of men resulted in an 84 gram advantage in striking mass. He felt that the greater variation found in mass as compared to clubhead velocity emphasizes the importance of grip position and firmness.

FACTORS INFLUENCING DIRECTION

Since the ball must eventually drop into a very small hole, and golf balls travel long distances making slight angles of deviation (right-left) in hits result in wide variations in the spots where the balls land, control of direction must be a major purpose in every shot. The direction of the flight of a golf ball is influenced by the direction in which the clubhead is moving at impact, the angle of the face of the clubhead (law of rebound), the relationship of the clubhead to the ball's center of gravity, the firmness of the grip and of the wrists at impact, any outside force acting on the ball (the wind, friction, grass resistance and so on), and spin.

When the clubhead hits directly through the center of gravity of the ball, the direction of the force which is effective against the ball depends upon the direction of the club momentum and the angle of the club face; the relationship between these two determines the angle of rebound. This rebound angle is equal and opposite to the angle between the striking surface (club face) and the direction of the club's momentum force; it is the same as the angle that would result if the ball were rolled along the path of the club's momentum force into a stationary surface angled as the club face is angled. If the club is moving in an arc, the club's linear momentum is in the direction tangent to the arc at the point of contact. The total momentum is divided equally between the direction of the club's motion and the rebound angle; thus one half of the club's total force is applied in the direction of the tangent to the arc at the instant of impact and one half in the direction of the rebound angle; therefore the ball departs approximately at right angles to the face of the clubhead (Fig. 19–4, p. 276). Variations in ball compression will alter this somewhat.

It follows, then, that the more nearly the face of the club is at right angles to the desired path of the ball at impact, the nearer to the desired path the ball will travel. This means that if a ball is to go straight ahead, the clubhead must be moving straight forward and must face straight ahead at impact, be perpendicular to the direction of club motion. To assure this, the stroke is begun by placing the clubhead in this position and taking a stance with the toes along a line parallel to the desired flight of the ball (square stance). Having a straight forward path of the clubhead with the face perpendicular at impact is more easily accomplished if the clubhead follows a path along the line of the desired direction of the shot both before and after impact. The square stance aids in keeping the swing along this path. If the left foot (right-handed golfer) is forward (closed stance), the path of the swing tends to move toward the right instead of straight ahead since the follow-through straight ahead is restricted. If the right foot is forward (open stance), the opposite is true. The backswing being restricted, the path of the swing tends to be more toward the left (Fig. 20–1).

Just as in rolling a ball or executing an underhand throw, where the arm is swung back along the line of the intended flight of the ball, the golf club is brought straight back from the ball as far as possible before being lifted up and around the body. This flattens the arc of the swing so

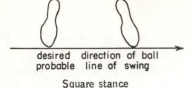

desired   direction of ball
probable   line of swing

Square stance

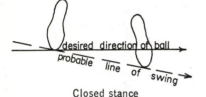

probable line of swing

desired   direction of ball

Open stance

Figure 20–1. Probable effect on direction of swing of various stances.

desired direction of ball

probable line of swing

Closed stance

that there is more time in which the clubhead can contact the ball with the face moving in the straight forward direction.

The force of impact causes the club to turn in the hands if the grip is not firm, or causes the face of the clubhead to turn if the wrists are not firm, when the ball is contacted. When this happens the direction the ball will take is unpredictable. Only when both the grip and wrists are firm does the face of the clubhead remain perpendicular to the path of the clubhead as the ball is contacted.

Since the golf ball moves through the air at a high velocity, air pressure builds up rapidly. Therefore, changes in air pressure around the ball caused by spin modify the flight of a golf ball considerably.

When the clubhead is swung straight through with its face angled toward the right, rather than perpendicular to its path, the ball is given off-center force on the left which starts it spinning to the right (front of the ball spinning to the right). This type of spin can also result if the forward moving club **slides** across the back of the ball from right to left (outside-in) during contact. Right spin curves the flight of a fast moving ball to the right (a slice) (Fig. 20–2). If the ball is hit with an outside-in force **with the clubface perpendicular to this direction of motion**, no spin will result; the ball is pulled to the left. Because of the restriction of back-swing, this outside-in movement is facilitated by an open stance, though it is possible even with a square stance if the clubhead is thrown away from the body on the downswing. This can be corrected by placing a piece of paper or a handkerchief between the right upper arm and the trunk and attempting to hold it there until the ball is contacted. A slice

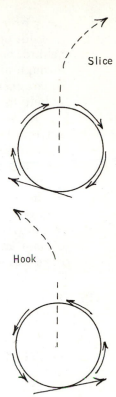

Figure 20–2. Direction of curves in flights of balls hit straight ahead with club face angled, or pulled across the back of the ball "outside-in" or "inside-out."

can result from a lag of the clubhead behind the wrists which causes the clubface to be angled right at impact; this may be due to over-swinging, snapping the wrists through too late or to a lack of sufficient wrist strength to control such a long lever. Many individuals are never success-ful in using a number one wood for this reason. If the sequence of move-ment does not flow from the center of the body out to the extremities, but rather starts with the arms and the body rotation is retarded, the clubhead tends to be pulled **across** the back of the ball.

If the clubhead is angled **left** as it swings **straight** through, the off-center force is applied to the right side of the ball and left spin results (hook). Sliding the clubface across the back of the ball from the inside-out (left to right), with its face square to the line of flight, can also result in left spin. If the face is open (angled to the right), and **the club swung from left to right** (inside-out), the ball is pushed to the right with no spin. This inside-out movement is facilitated by a closed stance since the follow-through is restricted, but it may result from hugging the right arm too close to the body on the downswing and then throwing it outward immediately before impact. If the sequence of movement is interrupted or if the arms lag behind the body rotation, the clubhead will also be pulled across the ball from the inside-out.

At times, it is desirable to produce left or right spin on the ball. On a "dog-leg" hole, a stroke may be saved by producing sufficient spin on the ball to cause its flight to follow the curve of the fairway. However, nor-mally right or left spin causes loss of strokes because it takes the ball well away from the straight line to the hole. Placing two pieces of paper on the ground, one a few inches in front of the ball and the other a few inches behind, but both along the line of desired flight, and attempting to swing through all three, the two pieces of paper and the ball, with the clubface square (perpendicular to the direction of the club's motion), will frequently help to straighten the arc of the swing and avoid side spin.

In determining the desired direction of a shot, the wind must be considered. Because the golf ball travels well up in the air, a cross-wind has considerable effect upon the direction of its flight; the ball is carried with the wind. If the wind is blowing from the left to the right, the ball must be aimed left of the hole, and if blowing from right to left, to the right of the hole. In other words, it should be aimed into the wind. How much the angle of the path of the ball needs to be adjusted depends upon the force of the wind. If it is forceful, it may be expedient to sacrifice some length of shot and play the ball closer to the ground where the wind tends to have less velocity.

Allowance must also be made for various contours of fairways and greens. Since a ball rolls down slope due to the pull of gravity, a shot must be aimed uphill of the green or the cup.

FACTORS INFLUENCING DISTANCE

As the distance purpose of the shot changes, various factors affecting the distance a projectile travels must be considered. As with any projectile, the distance a ball travels depends upon the force imparted to it by the clubhead, the angle at which the force is applied and the spin imparted to the ball. The first, the force imparted, has been discussed.

The vertical angle of application of the force depends upon the inclination of the clubface. The greater the angle of inclination of the face of the clubhead, the smaller the forward component and the greater the upward component of the force applied by it. Since the ball is projected at a right angle to the striking surface, the more vertical the clubface the more distance and the less height obtainable. Owing to the strong air resistance created by the great speed of the golf ball, the optimum angle for distance is considerably less than the theoretical 45 degrees. A larger horizontal component is needed to overcome the air resistance. A club with a more nearly vertical face should be chosen when maximum distance is desired, and as less distance and more height are desired, clubs with progressively more open faces should be used.

According to Hicks,[10] a given club will loft the ball less when the clubface is in a closed position (angled to the left relative to a line perpendicular to the direction of motion of the clubhead) than when it is opened (angled right); thus a lower trajectory results from a hook than from a slice with the same club.

Spin affects the distance a ball travels since top spin makes a ball drop faster and back spin keeps it in the air longer against gravity's pull (Chapter 7). When a ball is contacted below its center, back spin results. The dimples on the golf ball help get it into the air and keep it there,

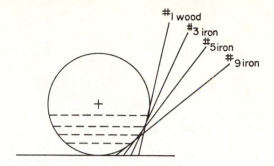

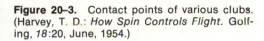

Figure 20–3. Contact points of various clubs. (Harvey, T. D.: *How Spin Controls Flight.* Golfing, *18*:20, June, 1954.)

because they give the surface roughness which produces a turbulent boundary layer (layer of air) around a spinning ball. A turbulent boundary layer "sticks longer to its associated surface than a laminar surface"[11] (air that flows smoothly across a surface); thus the lift effect from the back spin lasts longer with a dimpled than a smooth ball.

Even the driver, which has the most vertical face of all the clubs (with the exception of the putter), has enough loft so that the ball is contacted slightly below center and imparts back spin to the ball. Some back spin is essential to stabilize flight in the vertical plane and to keep the ball in the air longer. As the club loft increases, the point of contact on the ball is lower (Fig. 20–3). Harvey[12] clearly explained the way spin is imparted to the golf ball. He stated that only up to a point does the golf ball follow the rule that the lower the ball is contacted, the greater the spin. Since the ball leaves the clubface quicker and flattens less as the angle of divergence between the path the clubhead is traveling and the line of flight of the ball increases, with the more lofted clubs there is less flattening of the ball, less contact time and thus less spin. He stated further that the number five iron imparts the most back spin because the angle of inclination of its face is the greatest at which there is enough flattening to permit the grooves of the clubface to hold the ball from slipping. On the clubs with greater loft, the grooves on the face become narrower and shallower as far as their effect on the ball is concerned and they do not hold the ball, contact time is less and back spin is less.[12]

Back spin can also be produced by hitting downward across the back of the ball. When the ball is hit at the center of the arc of the swing with the club in its natural position, it is hit a horizontal blow which results in some back spin, because the ball is contacted below center. The amount of spin depends upon how much below the center the ball is contacted, the length of time the grooves of the club keep the ball in contact and the amount the ball is flattened. When the golf ball is played back of the center of the stance, it is hit a downward blow, the club passes downward across the back of the ball and back spin results. The farther back the ball is played, the more downward is the hit and the more back spin is imparted to the ball. Harvey[12] also pointed out that, if the ball is played on a hard surface, a downward hit pinches the ball between the ground and the clubhead, increasing back spin. However, if the surface is heavy grass, the pinching effect is not as great because of the give of the soft surface,

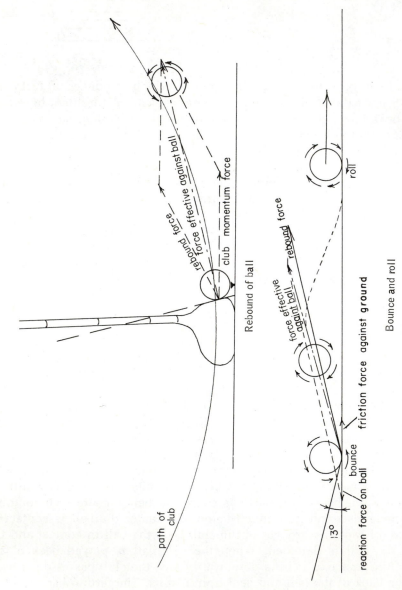

Figure 20–4. Number one wood.

and less back spin results. Although the surface of a sand trap gives, the sand increases the friction between the clubface and the ball, preventing slipping and increasing contact time, and thus more back spin than is normal for a particular club is imparted. This is not true when an explosion shot, in which the sand taken during the shot keeps the clubhead from actually contacting the ball, is used.

Spin also affects distance in that it stabilizes flight. It is also an important factor in the roll of the ball after it lands. The more the back spin, the less the roll, since the force of the spin against the ground is opposite to the direction of movement of the ball. Therefore, for distance shots, only enough backspin to stabilize the flight and to keep the ball in the air longer is desirable. The back spin should be minimized, as it is when clubs with a more vertical face are used, so that when the ball lands and friction slows or stops the bottom of the ball, its forward momentum will be able to overcome the back spin and move the top of the ball forward, reversing the spin and allowing the ball to roll forward. A great deal of back spin is desirable on approach shots to the green, in which little or no roll is desired. Therefore, the ball is played farther back so that it will be hit a downward blow. However, the farther back the ball is played, the more open (angled to the right) is the face of the club at contact and, therefore, the toe of the club must be moved forward to keep the face perpendicular to the line of flight. This moving of the toe forward reduces the vertical angle of the face of the club and as a result less loft, although more back spin, results.[13] In general, for maximum distance, a long club with a more vertical face is chosen and the ball is placed near, or somewhat forward of, the center of the stance, so that the ball is given a horizontal blow and very little back spin (Fig. 20–4). A shorter club with a more open face is chosen and the ball is moved gradually back toward the right foot, as less distance and less roll are desired, until in playing a minimum roll pitch shot, it is placed almost opposite the right heel (Figs. 20–5 and 20–6). If a high shot with less back spin is desired, as when the golfer needs to play the ball over the branches of a tree but desires to have it roll on landing, a club with an open face is chosen and the ball is placed forward of the point that would normally be used for the particular club. In this case, unless the toe of the club is moved back, the clubhead tends to be closed at contact (angled to the left). Moving the toe back increases the vertical angle of the club face and thus results in more loft, although less back spin, all other factors being equal.[13] In this way back spin, which would prevent roll on landing, is minimized.

The density of the air is a factor in distance gained by a given hit. Density varies with altitude and with temperature; the higher the altitude and the higher the temperature (for a given pressure), the lower the density.[14] While less density means less resistance to the ball's flight, it also results in less lift effect from back spin. Thus in thin air a ball may fly off the club face very fast and then dive. A club with a more open face might be chosen in order to increase the upward component of the force given the ball, since there will be little lift effect from the back spin and less air resistance to be overcome by the horizontal component of the force given the ball.

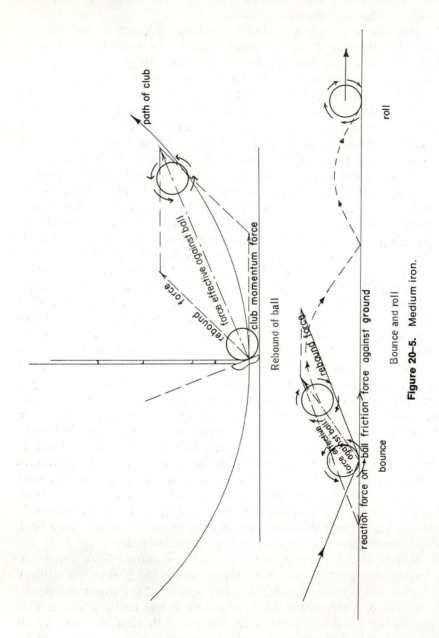

Figure 20-5. Medium iron.

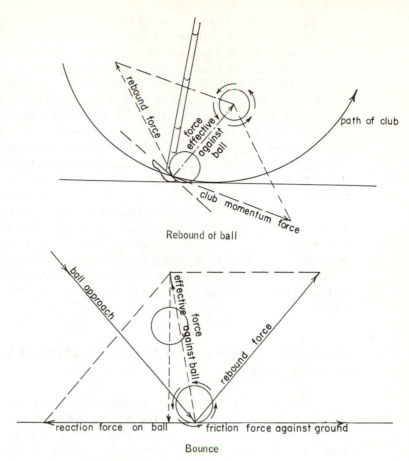

Rebound of ball

Bounce

Figure 20–6. Lofted iron (downward hit).

The contour and condition of the ground also affect the distance of a shot, in that they are important factors in the bounce and roll of the ball. When the ground is hard, it absorbs little or no force of the ball as it lands; most of the force is transferred back to the ball and the ball bounces and rolls. Hard ground does not give with the weight of the ball as it rolls and, therefore, offers little resistance and the ball rolls farther for a given force than it does on soft ground. In the case of soft ground, a great deal of resistance is offered to the forward roll of the ball, because the ground gives with the weight of the ball, in effect, forming a series of vertical walls in front of the ball which must be pushed down with each turn of the ball. Bounce and roll are also less, because a great deal of the force of the ball is absorbed when the ball first strikes the ground. The longer the grass, the softer the surface, the more force is absorbed on landing and the greater the resistance to the forward roll of the ball. Wet grass offers more resistance to a rolling ball than dry grass and, all other factors being equal, a ball rolls farther on dry than on wet grass. In putting, the longer and wetter the grass, the longer the backswing and follow-through must be to roll the ball a given distance to the cup.

Choice of club is also affected by various lies on the fairway. While it may seem that an uphill lie demands a club with a more open face to lift the ball up the hill, the opposite is actually the case. Since the golfer is standing on an uphill slope, the swing of the club is in an uphill direction and therefore imparts upward force, and so a club with a less angled face than would be normally chosen is needed. This is not to be confused with a flat lie at the foot of the hill, in which case the golfer does not stand on the hill and so the swing is forward, not upward, and a club with an open face would be needed. When standing on a downward slope (downhill lie), the swing is downward and in order to lift the ball to send it out from the slope and straight ahead, a club with a more open face is required. Side-hill lies affect the length of the club chosen. When the ball which must be hit across a hill lies below the golfer, the distance from shoulder to ball is farther than usual and a club with a longer shaft needs to be used. When the ball lies above the golfer the opposite is true, the distance from shoulder to ball is reduced and either the grip on the club must be shortened or a shorter club must be chosen. If the ball is played farther away, the swing is changed; it must be less vertical and more horizontal.

SUMMARY OF SOME OF THE MORE IMPORTANT APPLICATIONS*

Driving. Soling the clubhead behind the ball with the face perpendicular to the desired flight of the ball as the grip is taken helps to insure the clubhead being in the proper relationship to the ball at impact. The feet should be placed approximately the width of the hips apart to make it possible to add force to the stroke through the use of weight transference and body rotation without a loss of balance. If the feet are placed farther apart than the width of the hips, rotation of the body is restricted. Rotating the body lengthens the backswing, giving more time to work up velocity, and also adds force to the shot since the strong muscles of the legs and trunk are added to the movement. Many less skillful golfers execute a "false pivot" by keeping the weight on the left foot and bending the knees straight ahead rather than in toward the opposite leg. This gives the feeling of pivoting but does not put the trunk muscles into the swing and transfers the weight in the direction **opposite** to that of the swing, thus taking force away from the hit.

Carrying the clubhead straight back and low to the ground as far as possible flattens the arc of the swing and thus aids accuracy of contact. An attempt to throw the club as far as possible down the fairway before allowing it to come up and around, is one device for further flattening the arc and giving added time for an accurate contact. Since accuracy at impact is dependent upon both the position and angle of the clubhead, and at address, this position is adjusted so that force can be applied through the center of gravity in line with the desired flight of the ball, the height

---

*For further information, see reference 15.

of the shoulders and their distance from the clubhead must be the same at impact as at address. Bending at the hips or knees during the swing shortens the distance from the shoulders to the ball, while straightening the angle at the hips or pushing up with the left foot increases this distance.

Whenever the arm is flexed at the moment of impact, the distance from shoulder to clubhead is shortened. Also, general tension can cause a pulling of the club toward the body which also shortens this distance. There are many devices that can be suggested to those who pull up away from the ball during the swing. Looking at the ball is perhaps the most commonly used. An individual may profit from practicing twisting his body to the right about an imaginary rod running down through his body with a plate fastened against the head so as to prevent the head's sliding up and down on the rod, and then "untwisting" to the left. Another may be helped to develop a feeling for maintaining this distance by having a partner place a club on his head as he addresses the ball and hold this club in the same position as he swings. If the club is held steady, it applies pressure to resist any upward movement of the head and if the head moves downward, the club is no longer felt against the head. He is thus made aware of changes in body position that affect the distance from shoulders to ball. Sometimes swinging while facing one's shadow and noting the position of the head during the swing aids in developing a feeling for maintaining a constant height of shoulder girdle during the swing.

Swinging the club rather than attempting to **hit** the ball can be one of the greatest contributing factors to a clean impact. Better results are obtainable with a below optimum speed and a square contact than with a very forceful swing and an off-center impact. In general, the club best adapted to the purpose of the particular shot should be chosen and then swung naturally, allowing the angle of its face to take care of the angle of projection. If a shot with less force is needed, both the backswing and follow-through should be reduced equally so that the ball is still contacted near the center of the arc of the swing.

While both force and accuracy are extremely important in every golf stroke whether driving, approaching or putting, the **major** concern of the longer hits might be considered to be force and that of putting, accuracy. As compared to putting, the directional accuracy of the long shots is important within a **relatively** large area, and, compared to the long hits, the force of the putt is relatively small. However, many a putt sent toward the cup does not drop either because of insufficient force to reach the cup or too much force which causes it to jump the cup. The force problem of the long shots is that of developing maximum speed of the clubhead. The shorter the distance to be covered, the more the golfer is required to **control** the magnitude of force, that is, to generate only the speed of clubhead required for that particular purpose. In approaching and putting, this force control becomes a very important consideration.

Putting. The putter, having a vertical surface, contacts the ball just about at its center. Since the force is applied forward through the center of gravity, the ball stays on the ground and, because of the friction between the ground and the ball, it starts rolling immediately (Fig. 20–7).

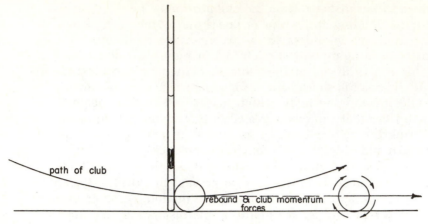

Figure 20–7. Rebound of ball from putter.

There are almost as many putting styles as there are golfers; this is understandable since there are so few principles that must be followed in order to have success and there are so many ways that putting can be accomplished. Whether the golfer stands with a wide or a narrow stance is unimportant because, in most instances, the force needed is not great enough to require transference of weight. The only thing that is important is that the golfer feel well-balanced.

Accuracy is a major problem in putting, and therefore, it is important that the stroke be smooth, with equal backswing and follow-through. Only in this way is it possible to judge the amount of force that will be imparted to the ball. The amount of force can be regulated by changing the length of the swing. It is impossible to judge the force that will be imparted to the ball by a jerky stroke — one with a sudden stop. In this case, the follow-through must be cut by muscular force opposing the forward movement, and accurate judgment of the degree of contraction that will reduce a given forward velocity a specific amount is improbable. On the other hand, practice will soon show the length of stroke necessary for a putt of a certain distance if a smooth stroke is used. The stroke can be duplicated almost exactly.

Accuracy is aided by utilizing all of the aids that insure the clubface moving in a straight line along the line of putt or this line extended. Moving the clubhead straight back and then straight forward along the line of putt with the face perpendicular at all times insures contact at the desired angle in the right direction. This is exactly the same as moving the hand straight back and forward along the line of the intended flight of the ball in the underhand throw or of the desired path of the bowling ball. A sudden stopping of the forward momentum causes jerking of the muscles which, besides making it impossible to judge the amount of force imparted, is likely to turn the face of the club from its perpendicular relationship to the line of putt and the ball goes off at an angle. A low backswing and follow-through along the line of putt insure this smooth stroke and flatten the arc, giving more distance over which the ball can be contacted and sent in the desired direction.

Pointing the left elbow toward the hole aids some individuals in keeping the clubhead moving in the forward path rather than being pulled around to the left. It is a useful device for one who has difficulty because of a tendency to swing the clubhead in an arc to the left. Any method for immobilizing parts of the body not needed for the stroke aids in accuracy because some of the possibilities of error are thus removed. Some individuals immobilize the elbows and putt with a pendular swing from the shoulders. Others rest the right arm on the right thigh and putt with the wrists. Style is not important so long as it facilitates, rather than hinders, a smooth stroke that follows the line of putt.

The putt can be no better than the judgment of the line of putt. If the line of putt is incorrectly visualized in the mind, the putt, no matter how accurate, will not go to the hole. In lining up the putt, it is important to squat behind the ball; this lowers the eyes closer to the line of the putt and makes it possible to sight over the ball to the hole. When standing above the ball in position to putt, the eyes are not in line with the hole and the ball, but rather see the hole at an angle. Just as in spot bowling, putting across a spot on the line of putt relatively close to the ball (chosen while sighting over the ball) can aid in accuracy because the ball and spot are within the line of vision at the same time and angle of sighting is not a factor in attempting judgment.

With the ball on the ground, judgment of contour and surface of the green is much more important to putting success than to driving success. Contour and surface affect both the direction of the putt and the amount of force to be imparted to the ball. More force is needed for a given distance if the putt is uphill, and the greater the slope of the green, the more the force must be amplified. Therefore, the backswing and follow-through need to be longer. Conversely, the backswing and follow-through normally used to putt the ball a given distance need to be cut if the line of putt is downhill, because gravity is added to the force of the putt to help move the ball downward.

When putting across a slope, the putt must be aimed uphill of the cup to allow for the rolling downward caused by gravity. The greater the slope of the green and the farther the putt has to travel, the higher above the cup the putt must be aimed. As the green angles more, gravity's pull becomes more direct and more forceful. The farther the ball has to roll the longer the time gravity has to work on it. Less force is used for a putt across a hard, dry, closely cut green. When the green is wet or the grass is long, the backswing and follow-through must be lengthened to produce more force to overcome the resistance encountered by the ball as it rolls. If the grass grows in the direction of the putt, less force is required than if the grass grows away from the cup: when putting across the direction of grass growth, the aim must be slightly to the right of the cup when the grass grows from right to left, and to the left, if it grows from left to right (as the player sights over the ball).

HANDLING GOLF EQUIPMENT

In addition to mechanical problems associated with playing the game of golf, golfers must avoid strain which could result from poor body mechanics when lifting, pushing or pulling. Golf bags holding heavy clubs must be lifted into and out of car trunks or onto and from golf carts (motor driven or hand powered). While many golfers who walk push-pull two-wheeled carts, some players prefer to carry lighter bags with fewer clubs. Golfers who use two-wheeled carts would do well to understand the forces involved in pushing and pulling tasks (Chapter 16) and it is important for all golfers to have an understanding of the mechanics of lifting (Chapter 17).

When a bag of clubs is carried by its strap over the shoulder, it is wise to shift the shoulder bearing the weight from time to time in order to balance both strain on muscles and the tendency to lift the carrying shoulder which causes a lateral curve in the spine (p. 162).

When the bag must be lifted from the ground, it is important to use the muscles of the lower extremities to produce the lifting force. This is done by standing close to the bag and flexing the knee, hip and ankle joints to lower the body to grasp the handle and to place the legs in position to exert an upward force. The heavy bag with its load of thirteen or more clubs can cause considerable strain if the relatively weak lower back muscles are required to do the lifting; these are the muscles involved when a golfer bends forward from the hips rather than crouching to reach the bag. Even the lighter carrying bag with fewer clubs, when lowered and lifted more than fifty times while playing eighteen holes on a regular length course, presents a possibility of strain that should not be ignored. Repetition of a lesser strain can cause as much difficulty as one severe strain.

If a bag must be placed in a car trunk, it should be lowered to the area just inside the trunk (nearest the person putting the bag into the trunk). If it then needs to be moved back farther in the trunk, it can be pushed or rolled. It follows that when taking a bag out of the trunk, it should be pulled or rolled to the near edge **before** its weight is taken by lifting. If an individual reaches well into the trunk and lifts a bag, a great deal of strain is placed on the muscles of the lower back; these muscles must support the forward leaning trunk, neck and head plus the weight of the clubs which is magnified because it is applied to the body at the far end of the body lever (Chapters 5 and 17). When moved to the edge first, the weight is actually taken close to the body, the resistance arm is shortened and the force to be resisted is lessened; in addition, the legs can be used for the lift.

Too frequently golfers who use two wheeled carts tend to push rather than pull the carts. Study of the forces involved clearly indicate that, with the possible exceptions of walking downhill or on a hard level surface such as concrete, it requires less effort to pull than to push a golf cart. The diagonally forward-**upward** force of a pull reduces the resistance offered by the grass and any irregularities of the surface while the forward-**downward** force of the push increases this resistance (Chapter 16). Again, while the additional effort required by pushing over a flat fairway may not appear to the golfer to be very great, over the distance of eighteen holes, many of which may not be flat, a great deal more energy is required. It is particularly important to **pull uphill** because the cart must be moved upward against gravity and a pull force has an **upward** component. The downward component of a push force pushes the wheels **into** the hill making it more difficult to move the cart uphill (p. 228).

REFERENCES

1. Broer, Marion R., and Houtz, Sara Jane: *Patterns of Muscular Activity in Selected Sport Skills: An Electromyographic Study.* Springfield, Charles C Thomas, 1967.
2. Stanley, Louis, T.: *How to be a Better Woman Golfer.* New York, Thomas Y. Crowell Company, 1952, p. 20.
3. Cochran, Alastair, and Stobbs, John: *The Search for the Perfect Swing.* Philadelphia, J. B. Lippincott Company, 1968, p. 58.
4. Bunn, John W.: *Scientific Principles of Coaching.* Englewood Cliffs, New Jersey, Prentice-Hall, Inc., 1955, p. 230.
5. Morrison, Alex, J.: *Better Golf Without Practice.* New York, Simon and Schuster, 1940, p. 32.
6. Jones, Ernest, and Brown, Innis: *Swinging Into Golf.* New York, Robert M. McBride and Company, 1946, pp. 22–25.
7. Hicks, Betty: *Fundamentals of Golf.* Chicago, J.A. Dubow Mfg. Co., 1948, pp. 5–6.
8. Hagen, Howard: An Exercise in Aerodynamics, Science Tees Off on Golf Balls. *The San Diego Union,* Friday, June 14, 1974, p. C-3.
9. Plagenhoef, Stanley: *Patterns of Human Motion.* Englewood Cliffs, New Jersey, Prentice-Hall, Inc., 1971, p. 61.
10. Hicks, Betty: What Makes a Golf Ball Fly. Unpublished paper received in personal communication, 1969, p. 8.
11. *Ibid.,* p. 6.
12. Harvey, T. D.: How Spin Controls Flight. *Golfing,* 18:20–23, June, 1954.
13. Hicks, Betty: personal communication, 1965.
14. Hicks, Betty, *op. cit.,* 1969, p. 8.
15. Broer, Marion R.: Golf, in *Individual Sports for Women,* ed. Broer, Marion R., Philadelphia, W. B. Saunders Company, 1971, pp. 185–213.

ADDITIONAL READING

Hay, James, G.: *A Bibliography of Biomechanics Literature,* 3rd ed. Iowa City, University of Iowa Press, 1976 (54 references, Section T16).

21 BADMINTON AND TENNIS

Badminton and tennis are two of the most popular striking activities. The application of the laws governing equilibrium, the production and application of force, and rebound, to throwing and striking activities is discussed in detail in Chapters 8, 18, and 19. A specific application to golf has been treated in Chapter 20. Therefore, this chapter deals only with a **few** of the problems specific to tennis and badminton. Because there is much in the movement patterns that is similar they are discussed together. The few variances in movement which exist are necessitated, in large part, by the differences in the equipment used in the two sports.

The tennis racket and ball are considerably heavier than the badminton racket and shuttle. The lighter badminton racket lacks the potential force inherent in the heavier tennis racket. Compensation for the lightness of the badminton racket is secured by increasing its speed. This is done by the use of wrist snap just prior to the moment of impact. The lighter weight makes it possible for the smaller wrist muscles to be used effectively and, therefore, the racket can be manipulated at a greater speed. Flexibility of the wrist allows the racket to swing in a greater arc, the backswing is lengthened, and there is more time to develop velocity. Wrist snap just before impact moves the racket through a long distance very rapidly (Fig. 21–1). The momentum of the shuttle is so much less than that of the tennis ball because it is so much lighter, that the force of the shuttle against the racket is less. Both the lighter racket and the lighter object to be contacted make greater use of the wrist muscles possible without loss of control.

Many tennis players, particularly girls and women, lack the forearm and grip strength necessary to control the heavier tennis racket unless the wrist is kept locked throughout the stroke. The heavier ball exerts considerable force against the racket and unless the wrist is set to withstand this force at impact, the racket gives and not only is less force transferred to the ball, but also the direction of application is changed since the give of the racket changes the angle of its face. Therefore, beginners in tennis are usually more successful if they maintain a set wrist throughout the stroke. Squeezing the racket at impact aids in resisting the force of the ball against the racket because it tightens the wrist muscles.

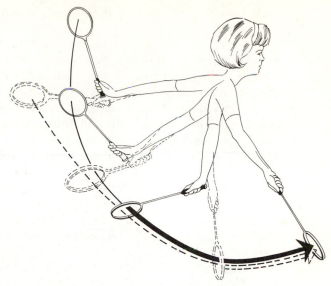

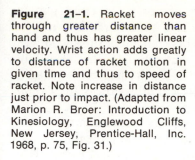

Figure 21-1. Racket moves through greater distance than hand and thus has greater linear velocity. Wrist action adds greatly to distance of racket motion in given time and thus to speed of racket. Note increase in distance just prior to impact. (Adapted from Marion R. Broer: Introduction to Kinesiology, Englewood Cliffs, New Jersey, Prentice-Hall, Inc. 1968, p. 75, Fig. 31.)

Plagenhoef[1] stated that firmness of grip at impact is the single most important element in hitting a tennis ball. In a rather sophisticated series of experiments and mathematical modeling, Hatze[2] determined that a tight grip in tennis increases the impulse imparted on the ball and thus the power of the stroke. However, he warned that high magnitude vibrations may result from off-center hitting and that a tight grip increases the magnitude of vibrations transmitted to the hand and forearm, and thus is a significant factor in the development of tennis elbow. Since it takes considerable practice for a beginner to develop the velocity that would produce vibrations of this magnitude and, by this time, he may well also develop the control required to avoid frequent off-center hits, it would seem that the contribution of a tight grip to racket control during the early learning period is the more important factor. However, he should understand the contribution of a tight grip during off-center hits to the possibility of tennis elbow so that he will be alert to the beginning of any discomfort. The advanced player who can avoid off-center hits obviously should use a tight grip. The player who has the grip and forearm strength to use the wrist successfully in tennis will be able to apply more force, but with insufficient strength, an attempt to use wrist snap leads to loss of both force and control. Because of the lighter equipment in badminton, this is less of a problem. Therefore, one essential difference between the two sports is the degree to which the wrist can be used in the production of force and this difference stems from the relative weights of the equipment.

Another major difference between badminton and tennis is in the flights of the shuttle and the ball. Because of the light weight and the shape of the shuttle, air resistance has a greater effect upon it, and it does not follow the parabolic path of the tennis ball. When a shuttle is hit with a great deal of force, air resistance to its flight through the air builds up to the point at which it overcomes the horizontal momentum of the shuttle long before the force of gravity has brought it to the ground. It follows a more or less normal path for a few yards and then slows down and drops almost vertically (Chapter 9).

Because of the greater effect of air resistance, the shuttle falls more slowly than the tennis ball, and thus difficulty in timing the hit is encountered by a player who expects it to fall at the rate of most balls. Time spent by a beginner in hitting a shuttle straight upward and watching it drop may be well invested since it can help him to readjust his concept of the speed with which different objects fall, and thus reduce, or eliminate, the frustration that otherwise frequently accompanies early attempts at service. Most beginners swing too fast because the shuttle drops slightly slower than other objects with which they have had previous experience.

It sometimes is helpful to hold the shuttle by its feathers out, over the spot where it is to be hit, and to hold the racket back ready for the forward swing. If the player then says to himself, "Drop, swing," and responds in that order, his swing will be delayed long enough to give the shuttle time to fall.

His difficulty may be due to a lack of a concept of the length of his reach when holding the racket. Being used to the distance of his reach with his hand alone, he fails to judge how far toward the floor the shuttle must actually fall. Discussion and observation of the distance that the reach is extended by the racket is helpful in building the new concept necessary in both tennis and badminton. As has been discussed earlier (Chapter 2), lack of this spatial concept can cause considerable loss of force in any stroke, since it leads to pulling in the arm and subsequent shortening of the striking lever.

Mason[3] has suggested a progression for tennis of hitting with the palm of the hand, a paddle, a short or choked racket and finally the full racket. This progression has two possible advantages. First, it makes possible a gradual spatial adjustment to the longer reach. In addition, the force of the ball that must be resisted at impact is very close to the wrist in the beginning and the resistance arm becomes progressively longer, and the force to be resisted progressively greater, as the beginner moves from hand to paddle, to choked and to full racket.

In both badminton and tennis, the racket is an extension of the arm lever. If one were to strike with the hand, the flat palm would be used. To maintain the normal striking movement, the racket is held so that, when striking on the forehand side, it is facing in the direction that the palm would be facing if the hand were flat. If the hand is held out in striking position, the racket turned so that it faces the same direction as the palm of the hand and the shaft placed against the palm, when the fingers close around the shaft, the racket simply extends the hand. This is the position described by most authors as "shaking hands with the racket." Since the wrist extensors are not as strong as the flexors, for the backhand strokes in tennis, the hand moves somewhat in a counterclockwise direction (right-handed player) on the grip to place the thumb **behind** the shaft for added control. Those with weak wrist muscles are better able to resist the force of the ball against the racket when the thumb is placed along the shaft in position to resist directly the force of impact. This causes a rigidity in the wrist, and while it helps to prevent give at impact, it can also eliminate fast wrist action. Therefore, the thumb up the shaft can be detrimental to a forceful backhand stroke in badminton. Because of the lighter weight of the equipment, it is not as necessary to sacrifice the force which comes from the wrist action.

The body position of readiness is the same for both sports. The player stands with his feet apart in a side stride, his knees are slightly bent and his weight is forward on the balls of the feet. This somewhat unstable position makes it possible to start the body moving quickly. The side stride also gives a more advantageous angle of push. It is possible to push the body in any direction by extending one of the bent knees. Time is not lost in having to bend the knee in preparation for its extension.

In moving around the court, small steps are taken so that the weight is balanced over the feet at all times and the direction of movement can be shifted rapidly. Large steps leave the body weight back during a part of each step and introduce a large resistive phase (Chapter 11, Walking). Tennis shoes increase the friction between the feet and the court surface so that the component of the force applied by the body (foot) horizontal to the surface of the court is resisted, and thus all of the force applied by the body against the ground is returned to the body. None is lost in slipping.

Except for the wrist action the strokes used in the two games are the same. Both sports employ the underhand, the overhand, and the sidearm patterns of movement discussed in Chapters 18 and 19.

The service in badminton is underhand by rule and the pattern is essentially the same as for the underhand throw (Fig. 1–10). It is sometimes performed with the same, rather than the opposite, foot forward. Since the distance to be traversed by the shuttle is short, all of the force necessary for a short service can be supplied by the wrist and arm muscles. Weight transference is not needed and balance is not a problem when little force is required. This stance (same foot forward) restricts backswing but increases the distance that the racket can follow through and, therefore, may increase accuracy of placement. A long service may require the use of the full pattern. However, since it is important that the opponent be kept uninformed as to the type of service to be delivered as long as possible, strategy dictates that the player use the same movement pattern (and stance) for both even at the expense of some force potential.

The service in tennis is, on the other hand, a very forceful stroke. It follows a pattern very similar to the overhand throw (Fig. 1–11). Gravity is useful in aiding the backswing or "downswing" of the racket. Some have suggested that the learning of the tennis serve be started with a "halfswing," that is, by lifting the racket forward and upward, and then dropping it to the position from which the forward motion begins. The force available with the full service (circular backswing) is so much greater than with a "half-swing" serve that there appears to be little argument for its use. Like the flat drive (p. 320), it is easier to use but the loss in effectiveness is much greater. The suggestion that beginners start with the "half-swing" serve is questionable in light of research concerning learning a skill by parts as opposed to as a whole. To reach the point at which the forward motion of the racket begins the "half-swing" serve requires a completely different movement pattern than the full service. Thus, when changing from this to the full serve, a new movement pattern must be learned. Since the "half-swing" pattern **is** used in the smash in tennis and badminton and the overhead clear in badminton,[4] it might be argued that both skills are needed in the game and thus the time spent on a "half-swing" serve in tennis is not wasted. The full circular backswing may be used in the smash and overhead clear because of its greater force potential, but it is more often sacrificed for the sake of making the hit very rapidly.

All of these strokes (tennis serve and smash, badminton smash and overhead clear) use a similar movement pattern for the forward swing. The arm and racket are fully extended at contact in order to take full advantage of the longest lever possible and thus produce maximum linear speed. Hitting the ball at as high a point as possible also allows more leeway for gravity's action, since it will take longer for the ball to be pulled down to net height.

Various devices for suspending the tennis ball at the full reach of the player are useful in aiding the development of a kinesthetic perception of this movement pattern without the additional problems involved in the tossing of the ball for service. Since the body weight has been transferred to the forward foot at the time of contact, the center of the arc of the swing is above this foot and, therefore, this is the point at which the racket is traveling its fastest and can be facing directly forward, so that it can strike a horizontal blow. It has been suggested that if the ball is tossed slightly **ahead** of the forward foot, the arc of the swing before impact is lengthened. Also, to maintain the flat arc longer, the server **must** rise onto the ball of his left (right-handed server) foot and allow the right foot to leave the ground; it swings through automatically and this has the advantage of starting the motion of the server toward the net.[4] Thus, the ball must be tossed straight upward, either above or slightly ahead of the forward foot. Perhaps it would be advisable to give the beginner the concept that this motion is more of a "push" than a "toss." The beginner frequently allows his hand to follow the normal arc, and thus tosses the ball back over his head instead of straight upward. Whatever the words used to explain the toss, the importance of a straight upward application of force and follow-through must be understood.

Many textbooks indicate that, in teaching the tennis service, the student should be instructed to hit **down** on the ball. If a ball is hit at a point eight feet above the ground and at a downward angle of only eight degrees, it cannot clear the net. **Even without the action of gravity** this angle places the ball only two and one half feet above the ground at the point 39 feet from the server (distance to net). Since the net is three feet high, this point is one half foot below the top of the net (Fig. 21–2). Actually, gravity's action causes the ball to hit considerably lower than this.

An angle which is only five degrees downward places the ball four and one half feet above the ground at the point above the net, without considering the force of gravity (Fig. 21–3). This means that gravity can pull the ball downward less than one and one half feet if it is to clear the net. Since gravity pulls an object downward one and one half feet in 0.306 second, this ball would have to be above the net 0.3 second after service. Therefore, the

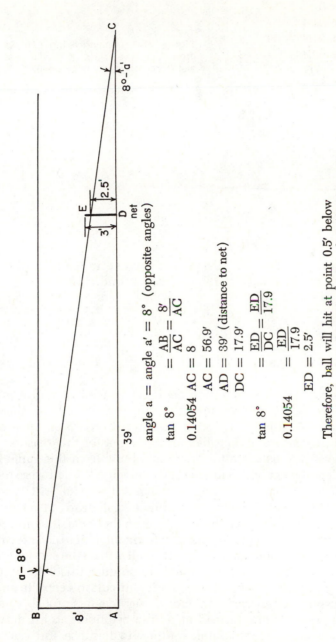

angle a = angle a' = 8° (opposite angles)

$$\tan 8° = \frac{AB}{AC} = \frac{8'}{AC}$$

0.14054 AC = 8

AC = 56.9'

AD = 39' (distance to net)

DC = 17.9'

$$\tan 8° = \frac{ED}{DC} = \frac{ED}{17.9}$$

$$0.14054 = \frac{ED}{17.9}$$

ED = 2.5'

Therefore, ball will hit at point 0.5' below top of 3' net, without any action of gravity.

Figure 21-2. Point of contact on tennis net of ball traveling path 8° downward from 8' high starting point (force of gravity neglected).

$$\tan 5° = \frac{8}{AC}$$

$$0.08749 = \frac{8}{AC}$$

$$0.08749AC = 8$$

$$AC = 91.4'$$

$$DC = 91.4' - 39'$$

$$DC = 52.4'$$

$$\tan 5° = \frac{ED}{52.4}$$

$$0.08749 = \frac{ED}{52.4}$$

$$ED = 4.58'$$

Figure 21–3. Ball traveling path 5° downward from 8' high starting point will pass 1.5' above net (force of gravity neglected).

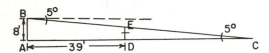

ball has to travel 39 feet, the distance to the net, in 0.3 second or have an **average** horizontal velocity of 130 feet per second.

$$D_v = \tfrac{1}{2}gt^2$$
$$1.5 = 16t^2$$
$$t^2 = 0.0937$$
$$t = 0.306$$

$$\overline{V} = \frac{D_v}{t}$$

$$\overline{V} = \frac{39}{0.3} = 130 \text{ ft /sec}$$

This is an improbable velocity for a beginner to achieve, and it is doubtful whether he would be able to keep the downward angle as small as five degrees if he were attempting to hit downward on a ball. Most beginners serve a high percentage of their balls into the net for this reason.

If, however, the ball is hit a horizontal blow from this same height (8 feet) it can clear the net with a much lower velocity. If a ball were to clear the net by 0.2 foot, gravity could pull it down 4.8 feet (8' − 3.2' = 4.8') by the time it got to the point above the net. Since a ball drops 4.8 feet in 0.55 second and since it would need to travel 39 feet in this time, it would require an average velocity of 71 feet per second for a horizontal hit to clear the net. A ball traveling at this speed and angle will land well within the service court. This is a more realistic goal. Beginners unable to produce this velocity will need to hit slightly upward. However, since it is difficult to keep the angle small when attempting to open the racket face on service, it is probably not wise to suggest an upward angle. Instead of telling beginners to hit down on the ball, which is practically impossible for them to do successfully, a horizontal blow or straight outward hit should be suggested and the reasons for the suggestion explained. The higher the ball can be contacted and the faster the racket is traveling at impact, the flatter or more downward (up to a point) the angle that can be used and still have the ball clear the net.

In making any type of shot, the vertical angle of the flight of a ball or

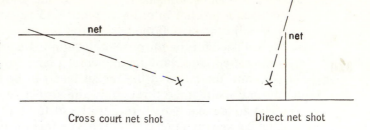

Figure 21–4. Vertical angles necessary to clear badminton net with cross court and direct return of low shuttle.

Cross court net shot   Direct net shot

shuttle which is necessary to clear the net depends upon the distance between the player and the net, the height of contact and the initial velocity of ball or shuttle. A sharp downward angle is possible only when the object is hit high and close to the net. A smash from center court is likely to result in the struck object falling on the striker's side of the net. An object contacted at net height must be given some upward force to counteract the pull of gravity. The farther from the net the hit is made and the slower the hit, the more time gravity has to act and the more upward the angle must be. If the object has fallen below the top of the net, the flight must be upward; the closer to the net, the more sharply upward. Particularly in badminton, which presents the problem of a higher net, a low shuttle contacted near the net can be played most successfully by a shot which angles it across the court. Since the shuttle can climb to the height of the net over a longer distance, it does not have to be hit at such a sharp vertical angle in order to clear the net. If hit straight forward over the net, it must travel so directly upward that it is set up for a smash return by the opponent (Fig. 21–4).

The angle of the flight of a ball or shuttle following impact depends upon the direction of movement of the racket, the angle of the face of the racket, the angle at which the ball or shuttle approaches the racket, and the relative momentum of racket and object struck (Chapters 8 and 19).

Because the lighter weight shuttlecock has less momentum than a tennis ball and the velocity of the approaching lightweight shuttlecock has been dissipated by air resistance to a greater degree than that of the heavier tennis ball, the direction of the shuttlecock's approach to the racket has less effect on the angle of its flight after impact than does the angle of approach of the tennis ball. (See p., 267.) Thus the angle of approach to the racket is a more important consideration in tennis than in badminton. There is little, if anything, that the player can do to "guide" the ball during the actual time that the ball and racket are in contact. Hatze[2] found the average ball–racket impact time to be 0.004 second. This time of actual contact is so short that it is imperative that a player set his grip and adjust angle and motion of the racket prior to the instant of contact; if he waits until contact occurs, it is too late to affect the motion of the ball.

In many throwing and striking activities, the arm or implement must stop to reverse direction at the end of the backswing. In tennis and badminton, this can be diminished by the use of a circular backswing. The circular backswing adds considerably to the time available for the development of velocity of the racket. However, it increases the difficulty of timing the stroke and of controlling the angle of the hit. The direction of movement of the racket must be adjusted as the racket moves forward. Since the racket is carried backward flat in order to reduce air resistance, the angle of its face must be adjusted also. If the backswing is separated from the forward swing and is not used for the purpose of developing additional velocity, the racket can be carried backward in the same plane in which it is to be brought forward and the angle of the racket face can be adjusted before the stroke begins and maintained throughout the stroke.

The advantage gained in additional force possible through the use of circular backswing must be balanced against the added difficulties of timing and control. It is probably advisable for beginners executing a drive to carry the racket straight back with the face perpendicular, since this presents fewer problems than the circular backswing. If, however, a beginner naturally uses a circular backswing and is successful, it should be recognized that this stroke has a greater force potential. Too frequently students are required to follow the particular pattern presented by the instructor.

Talbert has likened the tennis volley to the catching of a baseball. He stated that the volley is started with the head of the racket where the mitt would be. "Then, taking a short step forward with the left foot, the arm and racket as one lever make their short, sharp movement into the oncoming ball."[5] Since there is little, if any, backswing in a volley, the speed of the shot is largely dependent upon the speed with which the ball approaches the racket.

Tennis and badminton differ in the use of spin in the two games. Spin can be applied easily to a ball but usually is unsuccessful with a shuttle. Since top spin causes a ball to drop, it is useful in keeping a rather flat drive within court limits. Side spin both changes the direction of a ball's flight and its bounce, and makes it more difficult for the person returning the object to judge the reaction of the ball to his hit and, therefore, it contributes to tennis strategy.

Several tennis serves, among them the slice service and the American twist, make use of spin to increase the difficulty of returning the ball. For the slice serve, the outside (right side for a right-handed player) of the racket leads slightly, and thus the racket face is angled left and contacts the ball right of center, giving the ball left spin. This serve curves left (in relation to the server).[6] This can be likened to the hook shot in golf. In both, the implement face is angled left while it **moves forward**; the face is not perpendicular to the line of motion, the ball is hit off-center, and thus side spin results.

In the American twist service, the racket passes across the back of the ball from the southwest to the northeast[7] (Fig. 21–5), and thus starts the top of the ball moving forward in a diagonally right direction. This spin might be classified halfway between top and right spin around a horizontal axis. Because of this diagonal spin the reactions of the ball occur in a somewhat unusual combination. Since most balls that are spinning right or left are moving around a **vertical axis** they both curve and bounce in the same direction (Chapters 8 and 19). In the case of this **diagonally top-right** spin, the air moving with the ball as it spins, and the air resisting the forward motion of the ball, come into conflict at the top of the right side of the ball, increasing the pressure at this point and causing the ball to **curve left**

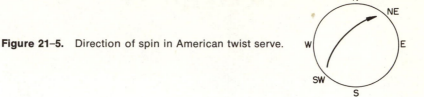

Figure 21–5. Direction of spin in American twist serve.

through the air. As the ball approaches the ground, it is moving diagonally to the left and might be expected to bounce left. However, because the ball is spinning diagonally forward-right around a **horizontal** axis, when it hits the ground the **entire bottom** of the ball is moving backward-left; the ball pushes backward-left against the ground, which pushes forward and right against the ball. Thus the ball **bounces right** of its anticipated position. Because the bounce force from the ball's momentum has a **left** component and the spin force against the ball has a **right** component, and these are in opposition, the ball tends to bounce more upward than normal. (Note: Left and right are in relation to the server.)

The reaction of spinning balls has been treated fully in Chapters 8 and 19. To avoid repetition, the reader is referred to Chapters, 8, 18 and 19 for further material applicable to these two activities. Also relevant is the application of the principles of striking to golf (Chapter 20).

REFERENCES

1. Plagenhoef, Stanley: *Fundamentals of Tennis.* Englewood Cliffs, N.J., Prentice-Hall, Inc., 1970, p. 1.
2. Hatze, H.: Forces and Duration of Impact, and Grip Tightness During the Tennis Stroke. *Medicine and Science in Sports,* 8:88–95, 1976.
3. Mason, Elaine: New Tennis Progressions. *Journal of Health, Physical Education and Recreation,* 39:24–28, April, 1968.
4. Laing, Diann: Personal communication, 1970.
5. Talbert, William F.: Tennis, Now You Can Play it Better. *Sports Illustrated,* 6:23:61, June 10, 1957.
6. Berendsen, Carol A.: Tennis, in *Individual Sports for Women,* ed. Broer, Marion R., Philadelphia, W. B. Saunders Company, 1971, p. 356.
7. Driver, Helen Irene: *Tennis for Teachers.* Philadelphia, W. B. Saunders Company, 1941, p. 43.

ADDITIONAL READING

Hay, James, G.: *A Bibliography of Biomechanics Literature,* 3rd ed., Iowa City, University of Iowa, 1976. Badminton — Section T2 (4 references). Tennis — Section T36 (30 references).

22

BOWLING

The problem in bowling is one of applying force which will give the ball sufficient velocity in an effective direction to knock down all of the pins.

Bowling uses the underhand pattern of movement, and the general mechanics for the production of force and the control of direction are similar to any rolling or underhand throwing activity. Since they have been discussed in detail in Chapter 18, Throwing and Catching, only a few specific considerations are included here.

APPLICATION OF FORCE

Because of the length of the lane, a bowler must be accurate to a fine degree. A deviation of one degree in the path of the ball results in changing the ball's location by more than a foot after it has traveled the 60 feet from the foul line to the head pin (Fig. 22–1). Therefore, while sufficient force is needed to roll the ball 60 feet with enough speed so that its momentum will knock over pins and throw them against other pins, the control of direction is more important to success than is the production of considerable force.

Production of Force. As explained in Chapter 18, the underhand pattern does not produce maximum force because of restrictions on body rotation. However, it allows for maximum use of gravity in the production of ball velocity. This advantageous use of gravity is important with the heavy ball. Since the effectiveness of a given force producing rotary motion (torque) is dependent upon its perpendicular distance from the line of force application to the fulcrum (p. 80), the ball must be pushed away from the body to increase the force potential. The greater the distance from ball to shoulder, the greater the moment of force. When the ball is pushed away

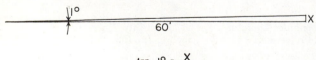

$$\tan 1° = \frac{X}{60}$$
$$0.01746 = \frac{X}{60}$$
$$X = 1.05'$$

Figure 22–1. Distance a ball will angle-in after traveling 60 feet when bowled at an angle of one degree.

from the body, the arm and ball form a pendulum on which gravity acts as it does on any pendulum. Since the force of gravity acts straight downward, the velocity with which the ball is traveling at the bottom of the arc of the swing is dependent upon the height of the swing.

$$V = \sqrt{2gh} \qquad (22.1)$$

This formula is derived directly from two basic formulae which have been explained previously (p. 49 and p. 63).

$$V = at \qquad \text{or } a = \frac{V}{t}$$

$$D_v = \tfrac{1}{2}gt^2 \quad \text{or} \quad D_v = \tfrac{1}{2}at^2 \text{ since the}$$
$$\text{acceleration is entirely}$$
$$\text{due to gravity}$$

To determine the relationship of velocity to distance these two equations can be combined. The second is first solved for "t".

$$D_v = \tfrac{1}{2}at^2$$
$$t^2 = \frac{2D_v}{a}$$
$$t = \sqrt{\frac{2D_v}{a}}$$

Substitution of this formula for time in the velocity formula gives:

$$V = at$$

$$V = a\sqrt{\frac{2D_v}{a}} = \sqrt{2aD_v} \qquad (22.2)$$

Because gravity is the accelerating force and the distance over which it is effective is the height of the swing, this formula, in the case of a pendulum, becomes $V = \sqrt{2gh}$. Therefore, gravity being a constant value, the velocity varies with the height of the swing.

The height of the backswing depends on the height at which the ball is held and pushed away from the body, since the last half of the backswing is caused by the momentum built up by gravity's pull on the ball during the first half of the backswing. The higher the push away, the greater the momentum which must be controlled, since gravity acts on the ball over a longer distance. Therefore, more strength of trunk and shoulder muscles is required to stabilize the shoulder position when a higher push away is used.

The distance that the hand can be raised straight backward is limited by the bony structure of the shoulder joint. A forward lean of the trunk is used to increase the height of the backswing without causing the swing to deviate from its straight path.[1] This forward lean of the trunk is also useful in balancing the weight of the ball at the top of the backswing.

In bowling, additional momentum is produced by the use of the approach. Since the velocity of the body can be transferred to any object held by the body, the forward velocity which the bowler acquires through the use of the approach, if timed with the swing of the ball, is transferred to the ball and augments the velocity produced by the arm swing. Since the effective summation of velocities requires that the second be added to the first, when the first has reached its peak (p. 254), the forward swing should coincide with the slide. Velocity can be gained whether the bowler takes three, four or five steps. An uneven number of steps is more difficult for most individuals to time with the arm swing. With a three-step approach, the bowler is more likely to arrive at the foul line before the ball is ready to be released. In this case, the velocity of the approach is lost before release and so is not transferred to the ball. This can be likened to stopping the circular backswing of a tennis serve to wait for a late toss of the ball. The velocity gained by the backswing is lost since the racket must start from rest at a position close to the point of ball contact. The bowler might as well start in a forward-backward stride position at the foul line if he arrives at the foul line before he is ready to release the ball.

When using a five-step approach, the bowler may not arrive at the foul line soon enough and thus the swing must be slowed. Most individuals find it easier to time four steps with the swing of the ball so that they go into their slide as the ball swings forward. All forward velocity is thus effective at the same time. The use of three or five steps is more likely to result in an uneven approach which appears as a "hoplike" movement than is the use of four steps. This upward movement detracts from the forward velocity of the body as well as interferes with the smooth arc of the swing. Because the first of four steps is taken on the right foot (right-handed bowler), the four-step approach has an added advantage of providing a base of support under the ball at the moment it is pushed away from the body to start its swing.[2] If a bowler is able, with three or five steps, to control the ball at the beginning of the swing and to time his swing with his steps and thus gain sufficient velocity without upsetting the smoothness of the arc of his swing, there is no reason for change; the approach is accomplishing its purpose. Most individuals find it easier to time four steps with the swing and to keep the approach smooth so that it does not interfere with the normal arc of the swing; therefore, the four-step approach is recommended for beginners.

Regardless of the number of steps used, the approach should be in a straight line with the desired direction of force application. Any sideways movement detracts from the forward velocity and interferes with accuracy. It is important that the bowler toe straight ahead, so that the force exerted by the push of the toes against the floor will result in straight forward motion (Chapter 11, Walking). Sometimes an individual lacking the muscular strength to adjust to the weight of the ball at the right side of the body toes out with the right foot. This is an unconscious adjustment to widen the base to the right (under the weight) and thus reduce the amount of body adjustment necessary. It results in a zigzag approach. This individual should be taught to let the free hand and arm swing away from the body to help balance the weight of the ball. He should be given a lighter ball and taught exercises which will strengthen his muscles, particularly those of the trunk.

In rotary motion, the maximum force is at right angles to the radius; thus the ball should be released when the arm is perpendicular to the floor. The hand must be lowered close to the floor. Lowering the body by flexing the knees and hips results in a well-balanced position, since the center of gravity of the body is low and remains over the center of the base (p. 54). The final forward step onto a well bent left leg and the slide both flatten the forward arc and contribute to a smooth release. The slide also allows for a gradual decrease of the momentum of the bowler. If the ball is dropped or thrown rather than released close to the floor, the downward vertical velocity of the ball may be relatively high as a result of the effects of gravity plus any vertical component of the velocity imparted to the ball at release. Besides causing the ball to hit the floor with considerable force, there may be a reduction in forward momentum or in accuracy.

Control of Direction.   As in any underhand throw the angle of force application is dependent upon the arc of the swing and follow-through. It has been suggested[3] that before starting the swing, the ball be moved to the right so that the right arm is close to, and parallel with, the right side. This position allows the ball to drop backward in a straight line without brushing the leg or forcing the body to twist. Any twisting of the body may interfere with the straight path of the swing. If held in front of the center of the body as the swing begins, unless the body twists, the ball must be dropped diagonally outward and backward and, as a result the forward swing, tends to be forward and inward. Thus the path of the swing must be straightened by the bowler while the ball is moving. This calls for greater control than simply keeping the ball in a straight line from the start of the movement to the release.

A circular swing of the ball around the body is normally due to lack of strength. Because of insufficient strength to control the ball at the top of the backswing when it is far from the body, the individual adjusts the swing to keep it close to his center of gravity. As a result, he swings the ball in a semicircle, around the body. Since the ball continues to move in the same direction as it was moving at the moment of release, a ball moving in an arc travels along a path which is tangent to that arc at the point of release (p. 256) (Fig. 22–2). This means that there is only one point at which a ball

Figure 22–2.   Path of ball released at various points on an arc.

swung in a semicircle around the body can be released and still travel in the desired direction. If released early it will go into the right channel (gutter), and if released late it will roll to the left, probably into the left channel. Again, the individual needs to be given a lighter ball until exercises and practice are effective in increasing the muscular strength of his arm, shoulder girdle and trunk.

Don Carter uses a bent elbow throughout his swing[4] to shorten the lever and thus reduce the difficulty of control at the top of the backswing. Because of this, his form has been criticized. If a bowler has sufficient strength of the arm flexors to maintain a **consistent** angle at the elbow when holding the heavy bowling ball against the pull of gravity, the bent arm may be a useful device for gaining control at the top of the backswing; since the lever is shortened, the weight is closer to the fulcrum and, therefore, the torque at the shoulder joint is reduced. If the angle of bend in the elbow is consistent throughout the swing, it does not interfere with the arc. However, it must be remembered that because a straight arm does give a longer lever, the arc of the swing with a straight arm is longer and greater speed of the ball (end of the lever) results from the same speed of motion of the upper arm. A straight arm also reduces the muscular tension necessary in the arm as well as the distance that the body must be lowered for release. Because of the arm flexor strength this device for gaining control of backswing demands, it is doubtful that girls or women would find it usable since they may be unable to maintain a consistent position. It is simply a device that one individual has found useful. There is no question of form involved since the mechanics of the movement are not affected, except that the length of swing is slightly shortened.

Spin depends on off-center application of force at release. If side spin is not desired (bowling a straight ball), the hand must be kept in the same position throughout the swing. Because a bowling ball is heavy, it is easier to control if the hand is under it with the thumb up. The hand is then in a position to oppose gravity directly as the ball drops and is behind the ball as it swings forward. If the "V" of the hand is up, the ball must be held by opposing inward pressures of thumb and fingers. This can be likened to carrying a box by holding the tops of the sides between the thumbs and fingers instead of with the hands under the box. Gravity tends to pull the sides of the box down between the thumb and fingers. If, with this position of the hand, an individual is able to hold the ball, keep the hand in exactly the same position throughout the entire swing and release smoothly, there is no need to change to the thumb-up position.

If a person who is in the habit of holding the ball with the "V" of the hand up attempts to change to the thumb-up position, he is likely to revert to habit during the end of the swing and thus impart left spin to the ball. Any twist of the wrist at release causes a side spin of the ball. Rather than attempt to change the hand position of an individual who is holding the ball with the "V" up, it is advisable to teach him to bowl a hook ball from the beginning. The important considerations in the hand position for bowling a **straight** ball (one with no spin) are that the position be one that the individual can control, that it remain the same from the start of the swing through release and follow-through, and that the thumb and fingers be withdrawn so that no off-center force is applied. In his grip Carter[5] uses an unusual device for reducing off-center force at the moment of release. He suggests eliminating the little finger from play by curling it back under itself against the ball. This might be a useful device to suggest to an individual who is applying off-center force with the little finger at release and causing right spin of the ball.

Top spin increases the speed of the ball since the spin force pushes backward against the floor, causing a reaction force which pushes the ball forward and combines with the forward force given the ball at release. It has no effect on the direction of the ball. When releasing the ball with the palm upward, top spin can be produced by first removing the thumb and then the two fingers simultaneously. Back spin decreases the speed since the spin force pushes forward against the floor. The forward force given the back spin ball at release causes it to slide along the floor until friction overcomes the back spin and the ball can roll forward. Thus, the speed of the ball is reduced. A ball with left spin curves to the left and one with right spin curves to the right. The faster it is spinning left or right, the more the ball is deflected from a straight path. The greater the speed of the ball, the farther down the alley the ball will be before its path is altered by any spin imparted to it at release. The greater the spin imparted to the ball, the sooner it takes effect.

A hook ball results from the application of an off-center force which starts the ball spinning to the left as it is released. This spin can be caused by swinging the ball with the "V" of the hand rather than with the thumb upward. In this position, the thumb comes out of the ball before the fingers and, since the fingers are on the right side of the ball, an off-center force is applied causing the ball to spin left. "If the hand is cocked upward at the point of release, a hook will be assured as the force exerted by the fingers on the right side of the ball will be made greater."[6] This lifting action of the fingers causes the ball to roll forward, and since it is applied to the right of the center of gravity of the ball, it increases the right to left spin. This lifting action can be caused by wrist action which lifts the hand at release. Because the forward momentum is great in comparison with the speed of the spin, the ball travels in a straight path for some distance down the lane before curving to the left. For this reason, the hook ball approaches the one-three pocket at a greater angle than does the straight ball, and therefore is more likely to contact directly a greater number of pins (Fig. 22–3).

Many bowlers and bowling instructors argue about the relative merits of "pin" and "spot" bowling. As in so many similar discussions concerning form, it is assumed that one is correct and the other incorrect. Mechanical analysis of the situations indicates that this is not true. The accuracy of the roll is dependent upon the arc of the swing and the release of the ball. It is only as the swing and point of release are affected by the judgment of the bowler as he sights his target that the **type** of aim is important.

The center of the head pin is 21 inches from the side of the alley; thus a straight ball placed on the alley 6 to 8 inches from the right edge can angle in only 7 to 9 inches if it is to enter the one-three pocket (Fig. 22–4). A one degree angle results in a straight ball, after traveling 60 feet, being one foot to

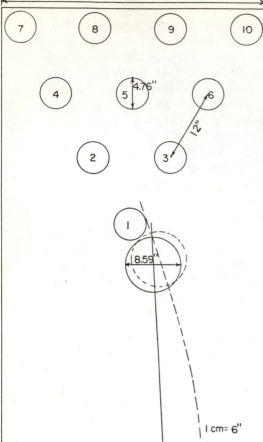

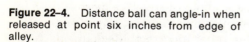

Figure 22–3. Approximate angles at which straight (bowled at one degree angle) and hooked balls enter one-three pocket.

Figure 22–4. Distance ball can angle-in when released at point six inches from edge of alley.

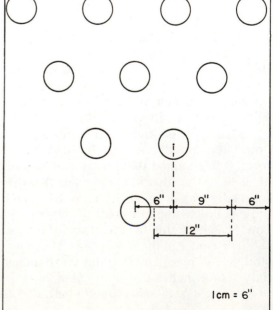

328

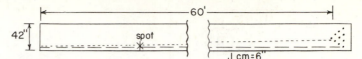

Figure 22–5. Slight angle necessary to bring straight ball into one-three pocket.

the left of the point directly opposite the point of release (p. 322). Thus, to enter the one-three pocket, a straight ball must be bowled at an angle of less than one degree.

Normally, several lanes are side by side and the total lane space is large in width as well as in length. This tends to foreshorten the length of the lane as viewed by the bowler and, when looking at pins 60 feet away, it is extremely difficult to judge the desired path of the ball. Many individuals find it easier to use a spot considerably closer to the point of release since a truer judgment can be made of the direction to the target when it is closer. When aiming for the spot (see Fig. 22–5), it is clear that the swing must be practically straight forward. However, when looking at the head pin, there is a tendency to judge that the swing must be angled to bring the ball into the pocket. Consequently, the swing may be angled too much, resulting in the ball's hitting to the left of the head pin, sometimes missing the pins altogether. Some individuals argue that spot bowling is more difficult because such a small spot must be crossed by the ball that any slight error will result in a wide deviation by the time the ball has traveled the additional distance to the pins. The point which this argument overlooks is that, **regardless of the type of aim used, a straight ball must roll over the same spot if it is to enter the one-three pocket.** If it does not, it will not enter the pocket whether the bowler was aiming for the spot or the pins.

It seems reasonable that it is easier to roll a ball across a spot when looking at it than when looking at pins some 60 feet away. There may, however, be a psychological problem connected with spot bowling. Since the bowler is interested in hitting the pins, there is a great temptation to look up at the pins at the last moment. This change in point of aim is likely to be disastrous. A bowler who finds that he is unable to discipline himself to concentrate on the spot until he has completed his follow-through may be more successful with pin bowling. If the bowler is successful in judging the angle of swing when looking at the pins there is no reason for changing to spot bowling. The use of the closer target is simply a device for eliminating the necessity for a judgment made extremely difficult by distance. It is frequently a very useful device for beginners. However, it must be remembered that it is essential that the point of release be consistent. Any change in point of release changes the angle of the line to the spot, and thus the angle of the ball down the alley. This same device is used by many golfers to assure accuracy in putting (p. 309). Since eye focus is important to balance (p. 55), the eyes should be focused on the point of aim from the time the bowler takes his stance until after the ball has been released whether spot or pin bowling is used. The eye focus also assists in maintaining a straight line of movement.[7]

Second Ball.   When the pins left standing after the first ball has been

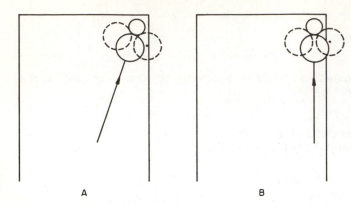

Figure 22–6. Balls varying same degree. *A.* Center of gravity still above alley. *B.* Center of gravity over channel (gutter).

A   B

rolled are in the center of the lane (strike area), the same starting position and point of aim are used as when bowling the first ball. However, when the pins left are on either side of the alley, a cross-alley ball will have a greater chance for success. The ball approaching the number ten pin on an angle to the right can vary more than one rolled straight for the pin and still have its center of gravity over the alley (Fig. 22–6). When rolling cross-alley balls, the starting point and the point of aim must be adjusted depending on the pins left standing. Kidwell and Smith[8] discussed this problem in detail and their diagram has been simplified by Culver (Fig. 22–7).[9]

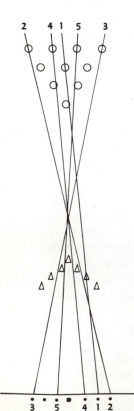

Figure 22–7. The pathways of diagonal straight balls rolled from the various starting positions across the corresponding points of aim. (From Broer et al.: Individual Sports for Women, 5th ed., p. 137.)

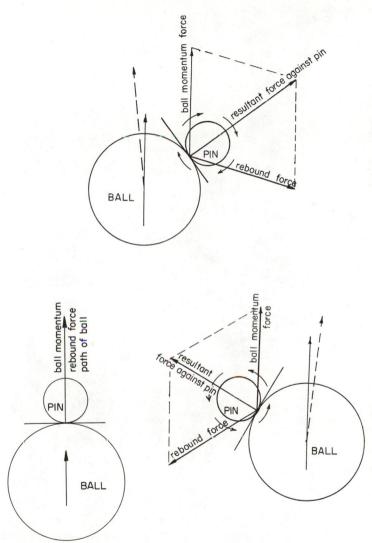

Figure 22-8. Direction of pin rebound from bowling ball with no side spin.

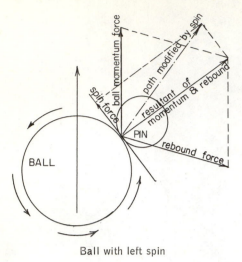

Ball with left spin

Figure 22–9. Change in path of pin rebound caused by spin of ball.

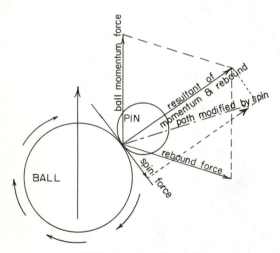

Ball with right spin

REBOUND

The ball is deflected somewhat by contact with a pin, but since it is moving and is so much heavier, the force exerted by the ball against the pin is much greater than the force exerted by the pin against the ball (p. 267). The heavier the ball and the faster it is traveling, the less its path is altered by contact with the pins. For this reason, it is best to bowl with as heavy a ball **as can be easily controlled**. The amount of ball deflection also depends upon the angle at which it strikes the pins. Because it is impossible for a ball to contact all of the pins, a strike is dependent upon some pins being struck by other pins. The angle at which the pins are thrown by the ball is extremely important.

The center of gravity of a pin is higher than the point at which the ball contacts it. Therefore, the bottom of the pin is more or less knocked out from under it and the pin begins an end-over-end rotation. The angle of rebound from a ball with no right or left spin is perpendicular to the tangent on the circumference of the ball at the point of contact (Fig. 22–8). A pin hit on the left is given right spin since the ball passes across its left side. A pin hit on the right is given left spin. A ball spinning to the left as it approaches a pin causes the path of the pin to be to the left of its normal rebound path for the particular angle of contact, while one spinning to the right rebounds the pin to the right of normal (Fig. 22–9).

SUMMARY

McKee[10] summed up the conclusions that could be drawn from an application of mechanical principles to bowling as:
1. The desirable speed of the steps is related to the length of the arm. The time taken by the swing is constant for every bowler of a given arm length regardless of length of backswing.
2. Greater velocity can be obtained by increasing the length of the back-swing. Since the swing will take place in a given time, the longer swing results in greater velocity (greater distance is covered in a given time). The most advantageous height depends upon the strength of the individual, since the longer swing generates more centrifugal force which must be overcome by the bowler.
3. The minimum muscular effort for successful bowling is that effort necessary to walk to the foul line, grip the ball and push it away from the body into a position enabling gravity to act upon it effectively. The anti-gravity muscles and those that stabilize the trunk, arm and shoulder girdle must function throughout the swing.

REFERENCES

1. McKee, Mary Ellen: The Mechanics of Bowling. *Official Bowling-Fencing-Golf Guide,* June 1956-June 1958. Washington, D.C., American Association for Health, Physical Education and Recreation, 1956, p. 15.
2. Barnet, Nan: Mechanical Principles of Bowling. Unpublished paper, University of Washington, Seattle, 1959.
3. Carter, Don: 10 Secrets of Bowling. *Sports Illustrated,* 7:21–28, November 18, 1957.
4. *Ibid.,* p. 31.
5. *Ibid.,* p. 26.
6. Culver, Elizabeth J.: Bowling, in *Individual Sports for Women.* ed. Broer, Marion R., Philadelphia, W. B. Saunders Company, 1971, p. 129.
7. McKee, Mary Ellen: *op cit.,* p. 20.
8. Kidwell, Kathro, and Smith, Paul: *Bowling Analyzed.* Dubuque, Iowa, William C. Brown Company, 1960, pp. 40–44.
9. Culver, Elizabeth J.: *op. cit.,* p. 137.
10. McKee, Mary Ellen: *op. cit.,* p. 21.

ADDITIONAL READING

Hay, James G.: *A Bibliography of Biomechanics Literature.* 3rd ed. Iowa City, University of Iowa Press, 1976. Bowling — Section T6.

23

BASKETBALL

The game of basketball involves the skills of throwing and catching, running, stopping, dodging, jumping and landing, and striking. The rebound principles of striking are involved in the dribble and in the use of the backboard when shooting. Since all of these skills are discussed in detail in Part Three, only a few specific applications are included in this chapter.

In basketball, speed in moving the body about the court and control of body and ball are of primary importance. Since the ball is large, greater control is possible through the use of two hands and a grip which holds the ball in the fingers rather than in the palms of the hands. The force can then be applied over a large area and the ball can be more easily directed. When this large ball is held in, and projected from, one hand, the hand must be under and behind the ball.

The various methods of throwing to another player or to the basket utilize all three basic throwing patterns: underhand, overhand and sidearm, and variations of these patterns. Since for the chest pass, the ball is held in two hands in front of the center of the body it is easy to control. However, the position does not allow for the usual type of backswing. A circular movement of the ball in front of the body gives time to develop velocity before release.

Many girls and women lack the strength to shoot for a goal from the free throw line with one hand. In fact some, particularly younger girls, can be successful only with the two-hand underhand shot which allows for a long backswing and makes greater use of the strong muscles of the lower extremity.

The two-hand overhead throw can be likened to the overhead volley in volleyball. Even more than normally, weight transference is important since the backswing is limited. The movement of the hook pass (or shot) is essentially a sidearm pattern adjusted to a vertical instead of a horizontal arc. The trunk movement is, therefore, a side bend rather than rotation.

In getting the body off the floor for a lay-up shot, the same basic movement pattern is employed as is used in the volleyball spike[1] and in the hurdle of a running front dive (Fig. 1–13, p. 23). In teaching the dive to a basketball player, Kilby[2] found that, when she suggested that he go out on the end of the board and "do a lay-up-shot," the student, who had been having a great deal of difficulty with the hurdle, was successful immediately. He was able to apply a familiar movement pattern to the new situation when the similarity was pointed out to him.

In dribbling, it is important to coordinate the angle at which the ball is pushed against the floor with the distance to be covered. A ball pushed to the floor at a large angle allows for little change in body position on the floor, while one pushed to the floor at an acute angle may bounce so far ahead as to make recovery impossible. Back spin on a ball bounced to oneself cuts down the distance that must be covered, while forward spin increases it and may put the ball beyond recovery, depending on the angle used.

Since spin makes catching more difficult, it should be used sparingly in passing. However, it is very important in shooting and can be used effectively in a bounce pass whether to self to move around an opponent or to a teammate. This is an instance in which right or left spin around a **horizontal** axis can be effective in changing the direction of the bounce. Since the whole bottom of a right spinning ball is moving toward the left, the reaction to the spin force against the floor causes the ball to deflect to the right. A lay-up shot (that does **not** use the backboard) given spin in the direction of the basket (when shot from the right side of the basket given left spin) is carried toward the basket. Also, spin can be used on a **rebound shot** to reduce the angle of rebound and thus keep the ball closer to the backboard. This is discussed in detail in Chapter 19. Whether or not it is desirable to reduce the angle of rebound depends on the spot where the ball hits the backboard. If it hits near the basket, the spin that reduces the angle of rebound (right spin if approaching from the right) may keep the ball so close to the backboard that it rebounds between the backboard and the basket. When the ball hits near the basket it is important that the force of rebound be very light.

With little regard for the mechanics of the situation, some authors have made suggestions as to the location on the backboard of a spot, or spots that should be used for rebound shots. The spot on the backboard that will rebound the ball into the basket varies with the point on the floor from which the shot is taken, the height of the arc, the velocity of the ball and spin on the ball. A ball with no spin rebounds approximately at an angle equal to that at which it approaches the backboard. If the shot is made from a point on the right side of the court at a 45 degree angle from the spot on the backboard it hits, the spot must be at a 45 degree angle from the center of the basket or at a point 15 inches to the right of the middle of the basket if no spin is involved (Fig. 23–1). Since gravity is constantly acting on the ball, it must also be

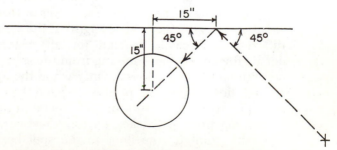

Figure 23–1.   Angle of rebound from backboard.

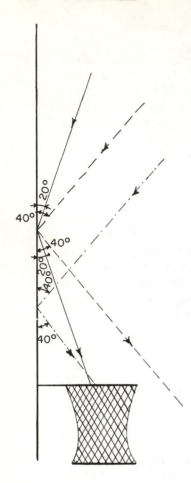

Figure 23–2. Theoretical vertical angles of rebound of basketballs hitting backboard above basket (gravity not considered).

above the basket. How much above depends upon the downward (or upward) angle at which the ball strikes the backboard. If the ball strikes at an acute downward angle, it rebounds close to the backboard, while if it strikes at a wide downward angle, it rebounds out away from the backboard and may be beyond the basket by the time gravity has pulled it down to basket height (Fig. 23–2). Actually, gravity will cause the ball to drop closer to the backboard than the diagram indicates. A ball striking at an upward angle tends to rebound upward at an equal angle. Gravity immediately alters the angle but the ball curves upward before dropping.

By varying the arc of the shots, spots of **various heights** can be used with successful results when shooting from the same point on the floor. Spots at **different distances** to the right (or left) of the basket cannot be used with equal efficiency when shooting from the same point on the floor unless the condition of spin is altered. Only when the angles between the backboard and the line to the point on the floor and the line to the center of the basket are equal, will a ball with no spin rebound over the basket. As the spot is moved out from the basket, the angle between the backboard and the line from the point on the floor to the spot becomes greater, but the angle

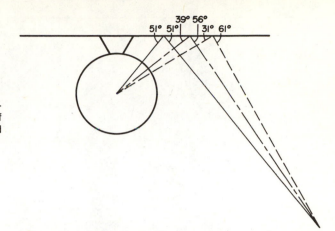

Figure 23–3. Variation in angle between backboard and line to center of basket as the spot is moved outward on the backboard.

between the backboard and a line from the spot to the center of the basket becomes smaller (Fig. 23–3). When shooting a ball with no right or left spin from a given point on the floor, only one spot can result in a rebound that causes the ball to pass over the center of the basket (Fig. 23–4). Therefore, the location of the spot contacted can vary little if the ball is to drop through the basket.

The same spot on the backboard can be used effectively from those points on the floor which are at approximately the same **angle** from the backboard (Fig. 23–5) provided the arcs of the shots are such that the ball approaches the backboard at approximately the same vertical angle. Some slight variation is possible because a ball need not pass directly over the center of the basket in order to drop through. In general, as the player making a shot moves toward the sidelines, the rebound spot must be moved farther out from the basket; as he moves in toward the center of the floor, the spot must be moved in closer to the basket. If he is not directly in line with the basket, as he moves his position on the floor straight backward away from the end line, the spot must be moved in toward the basket; and as he moves closer to the end line, the spot must be moved out on the backboard. When spin is used, the point on the floor from which the shot is made or the spot on the backboard, or both, must be changed.

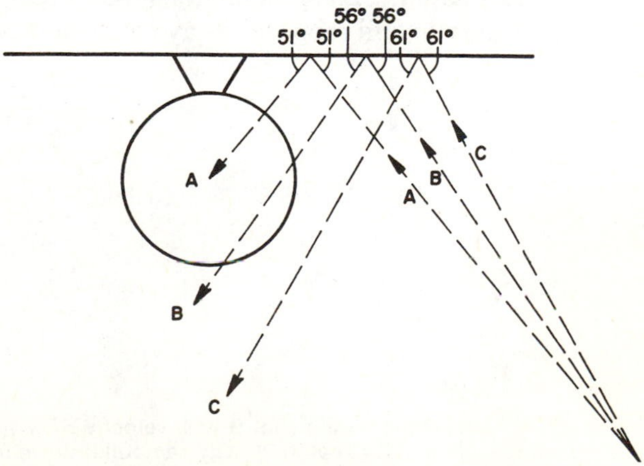

Figure 23–4. Rebound angles of balls shot from the same point on the floor, but hitting different spots on the backboard (no right or left spin involved).

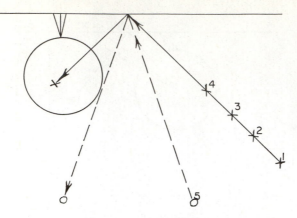

Figure 23–5. Rebound angles of basketballs shot from different points on the floor and hitting the same spot on the backboard.

The velocity with which the ball should be shot depends upon the angle of its approach to the backboard. If the ball hits at an acute right (or left) angle, it must hit farther out from the basket; thus a greater velocity is needed to carry it to the basket before gravity pulls it down to basket height. In this case, the lower the spot, the more the velocity needed since the ball will drop to basket height faster from the lower spot. When it hits close to the basket, excessive velocity may carry it beyond the basket before gravity can pull it down to basket height (Fig. 23–6). Therefore, when the ball strikes the backboard near the basket it must hit with little velocity so that the rebound will be dissipated quickly and gravity can pull the ball into the basket. Since in the lay-up shot the ball is always played close to the basket, whether or not the backboard is used, it cannot be given much velocity. To keep the ball velocity at a minimum, the ball is released at the height of the jump, when the momentum of the body has been overcome by gravity.[3]

Because the basket faces directly upward, the largest opening is available to a ball approaching directly from above. As the angle of approach becomes more acute (the arc of the shot becomes flatter), the size of the goal available to the ball becomes smaller. This can be seen clearly by looking up at the bottom of the goal from various points on the floor. When standing directly below the basket the entire width of the opening is visible. As one moves backward away from the basket the visible opening becomes smaller and smaller. Thus it is obvious that a ball, shot at a flat arc, is more likely to hit the rim and rebound away from the basket than is a ball approaching at a

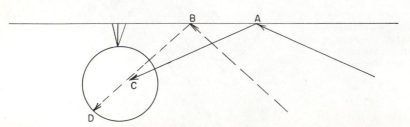

Figure 23–6. Basketball hitting spot B with velocity BD equal to velocity AC may rebound beyond basket before gravity can pull it down to basket height.

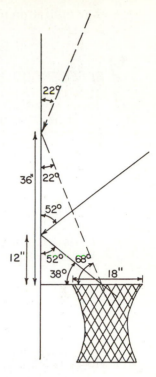

Figure 23–7. Change in angle of approach of basketball to basket as rebound spot is raised (gravity not considered).

greater angle. Therefore, it appears that a shot that does not use the backboard has a greater chance for success when arched so that the ball approaches at a large angle; this is true up to a point. Mullaney[4] pointed out that the highly arched shot has two disadvantages. In the first place, it is a longer shot and therefore any initial error in accuracy is magnified. Secondly, in dropping from the greater height the highly arched shot gains considerable velocity because of the acceleration of gravity and, if it should hit the rim of the basket, the rebound will be high.

When playing a rebound shot, the use of a higher spot results in the ball approaching the basket at a larger angle. A spot one foot above the basket has been suggested frequently. A ball rebounding from the backboard at a point 12 inches above the basket approaches the center of the goal opening at an angle of approximately 38 degrees (Fig. 23–7). Actually because gravity is constantly acting, the ball approaches the goal at a slightly larger angle. In general, the lower the spot, the smaller the angle of approach and the narrower the opening of the goal available to the ball. However, back spin can be used to reduce the angle of rebound and thus increase the angle of approach to the basket. The front of a ball with back spin pushes upward against the backboard which in turn pushes downward against the ball, and this force added to gravity makes the ball fall faster and thus rebound closer to the backboard.

A discussion of the application of mechanics to basketball involves considerable repetition since essentially the game of basketball is made up of several basic skills. For further information applicable to this game, the reader is referred particularly to Chapters 12, 13, 18, and 19 which deal with the application of physical laws to the skills of running, jumping, throwing and striking.

REFERENCES

1. Broer, Marion R., and Houtz, Sara Jane: *Patterns of Muscular Activity in Selected Sport Skills: An Electromyographic Study.* Springfield, Charles C Thomas, 1967.
2. Kilby, Emelia-Louise: personal correspondence.
3. Barr, George: *Young Scientist and Sports.* New York, Whittlesey House, McGraw-Hill Book Company, Inc., 1962, p. 116.
4. Mullaney, Dave: Free Throw Technique. *Athletic Journal,* 38:3:53, November, 1957.

ADDITIONAL READING

Hay, James, G.: *A Bibliography of Biomechanics Literature.* 3rd ed. Iowa City, University of Iowa Press, 1976. Basketball — Section T4 (69 references).

TRACK AND FIELD

24

Running, jumping and throwing are fundamental movements inherent in numerous sports and other physical activities. The principal reason for these basic movements in most sports, however, is generally utilitarian in nature. The outfielder in baseball may run extremely fast to catch a fly ball, but the main reason for his running is to catch the ball for the out and not just to run as fast as possible. The basketball player who is going up for a rebound is using the jump to increase his reach; the height of the jump may be important in determining who gets the rebound, but the motivation for the jump is not simply to jump high. Being able to throw a baseball or a football long distances may be an important attribute for a player, but in many cases the maximum displacement of the projectile is not the overriding objective. Track and field events, by comparison, are directly involved with the "how fast, how high and how far" results of fundamental movements. The sprinter and the marathon runner are equally concerned with decreasing the times in their respective events. Both the pole vaulter and the high jumper are ultimately interested in optimizing their movement patterns to achieve maximum possible height. For throwers, whether of the discus, shot put, javelin or hammer, there is a constant quest to increase the distance the object travels. Perhaps more than any other sport, track and field events challenge a person to the maximum limits of performance in the basic movement patterns of running, jumping and throwing.

The potential activities that may be analyzed in track and field are indeed diverse. Running comprises the sprints, middle and long distances, relays, hurdles and steeplechase, while jumping includes the pole vault and high, long and triple jumps. The shot put, discus, javelin and hammer constitute the implements that may be thrown in field events. A complete analysis of each of these events would require considerably more space than this chapter allows. To limit the scope of this chapter and yet examine important diverse mechanical influences in track and field activities, the following events have been selected for discussion: starts, high jump, pole vault and shot put. Sprint starts were chosen to illustrate principles in running and in accelerating the body in an essentially horizontal direction. The high jump discussion presents factors important in the projection of the human body without any external implement, while the pole vault demonstrates the potent interplay between potential and kinetic energies. Object projection is highlighted in a discussion of the putting of the shot.

Because only the most basic principles can be presented here, those seeking additional information are strongly encouraged to examine the numerous sources listed at the end of the chapter.

STARTS

The mechanics of running sprints, middle and long distance, have been discussed[1] and reviewed[2] in detail in other sources. Chapter 12 provides an analysis of the skill of running: the progression from walking to running, running on a straight course versus a curved one and the essential elements of starting and stopping. Further elaboration of starts, both standing and crouching, is presented here to emphasize the important applications of horizontal momentum and acceleration of the body and the effects of impulse and force on running velocity.

The **standing start** generally is used by middle and long distance runners and in instances where starting blocks may not be available. The mechanics of a standing start have been discussed in Chapter 12 (Running). Although the crouch start is used almost exclusively for sprint starting in major track and field competition, Short[3] has reported a significant advantage in favor of the standing start (0.2 to 0.3 sec in 50 m) for junior athletes. This advantage may have resulted because these young athletes were able to apply effective mechanics for the standing start, but not for the crouch start; however, the advantages and disadvantages of both types of starts need further elaboration.

The **crouch start** is used principally today in any race where the acceleration of the body over the first 10 to 20 yards is critical. The crouching start enables the runner to exert maximum horizontal force at takeoff, the time when the maximum inertia must be overcome. The center of gravity of the body is lowered and moved well forward of the feet (weight supported on hands) so that the drive of the legs is considerably more forward than upward. Because of the extreme forward position of the center of gravity, the body is in a position of marked instability. Therefore, at take-off, short rapid steps must be taken in order to keep the runner from falling forward.

Three types of crouch starts are the bunch, medium and elongated; the criterion that is generally used for classification is the relative position of the two starting blocks. In the bunch start, the toe of the back foot is positioned even with the heel of the front foot. When the runner is in the "on your marks" position, the space between the fronts of the blocks is about 10 to 12 inches (the length of the runner's shoe times the cosine of the starting block angle). The medium position finds the runner with the knee of the back limb even with the middle of the front foot when the "on your marks" position is assumed (toe-to-toe distance is usually about 16 to 21 inches). The knee of the back limb is aligned evenly with or farther back than the heel of the front foot in the elongated starting position (about 24 to 28 inches from toe-to-toe).

The relative effectiveness of these different starting positions has been studied frequently in the past, but major work in this area has been done by Henry.[4] He reported that a sprinter gets "out of the block" fastest with the

TABLE 24–1.   TIME AND VELOCITY CHARACTERISTICS OF CROUCH STARTS FOR VARIOUS BLOCK SPACINGS*

| | BLOCK SPACINGS | | | |
	Bunch *(11 in)*	Medium *(16 in)*	Medium *(21 in)*	Elongated *(26 in)*
Time on Blocks (time from gun to front foot leaving)	0.345 sec	0.374 sec	0.397 sec	0.426 sec
Block Velocity (horizontal velocity of athlete leaving the blocks)	6.63 ft/sec	7.41 ft/sec	7.50 ft/sec	7.62 ft/sec
Time to 10 yd	2.070 sec	2.054 sec	2.041 sec	2.049 sec
Time to 50 yd	6.561 sec	6.479 sec	6.497 sec	6.540 sec

*Adapted from data in Henry[5] and cited in Hay.[6] All values are means.

bunch start (Table 24–1). At the same time the sprinter's horizontal velocity, as he leaves the blocks, is directly related to the block spacing; the longer the spacings, the faster his horizontal velocity. However, this advantage of the longest spacing (26 inches) is lost when the sprinter reaches the 10 yard mark and the 50 yard mark. For the most important time, that at 50 yards, the medium start holds the advantage.

At first glance, it seems incongruous that the ability to get out of the starting blocks faster does not result in a faster time for the bunch start. A key to the seeming disparity lies in the **impulse-momentum relationship** (Chapter 6): the **impulse of a force** (product of a constant force and the time during which it acts) **is equivalent to the change of momentum** ($mV_i - mV_f$) that it produces. Although the sprinters using the bunch start were able to get out of the blocks faster, the "getting out of the blocks faster" meant that they had less time to effect a change in their horizontal momentum. Because their initial velocity (V_i) and therefore their initial momentum, were zero, the change in horizontal momentum can be noted directly from their horizontal velocity as they left the blocks. The bunch start has been found to result in the smallest amount of time and the smallest block velocity of any block spacing. The relationship between impulse and momentum dictates that if the sprinter wants to increase his velocity (and momentum) as he leaves the blocks while he simultaneously decreases the time during which force is applied, he **must** be able to effectively **increase the amount of force** he applies. Because sprinters using the bunch start were not able to develop the force necessary to offset the shorter time in the blocks, their momentum, as they left the blocks, and their times to 10 and 50 yards suffered (Table 24–1).

The slight advantage in block velocity that was found with the elongated spacing was lost by the 50 yard mark. In a series of mechanical trade-offs, the medium spacing seemed to emerge as the most effective crouch starting position.

Some coaches and researchers have intimated that the back limb's sole purpose is to pull out of the starting blocks in preparation for the first step and that the back limb contributes little to the forward propulsion from the blocks. Force data[7] recorded from instrumented starting blocks that measured force parallel and perpendicular to the surface of the blocks and the torques applied to the blocks, clearly show a high proportion of the impulse is provided by the **rear foot, as well as by the forward foot.** However, the front foot results do suggest that a late and inconsistent application of force by the front foot is most noticeable in a poor start.[8]

In the study of four track starting positions, Stock[9] found that a "medium high hip position" resulted in the most effective start. As the hips are raised during the "get set" phase of the start, the body's line of gravity moves toward the front of the base of support (feet and hands). When the hands are lifted after the gun sounds, the runner is in a precariously unstable position; the line of gravity falls far in front of the perimeter of his base. Stock[9] pointed out that the rear foot must move forward rapidly in order to establish the runner's balance as he drives his center of gravity forward with the extension of the forward leg. This means that an important function of the rear leg is flexion and therefore, it is advantageous that the knee be essentially extended when in the starting position. This position of the rear leg places the flexors "on stretch" and also is effective in moving the center of gravity well forward in the starting position.

As the sprinter begins to move down the track, his velocity is rapidly increasing and the horizontal component of the propulsive force starts to decrease as the forward inclination of the trunk becomes more vertical (to the point at which balance can be maintained) and the stride lengthens. Henry and Trafton[10] indicated that most of the horizontal acceleration of the body is accomplished in the first 15 yards after the start and that by 22 yards up to 95 per cent of maximum horizontal velocity has been reached.

HIGH JUMP

The general considerations in jumping have been presented in Chapter 13 (Hopping, Jumping, Leaping and Landing), and a synthesis of research about jumping (standing long, vertical, long and high jumps, and pole vault) can be found elsewhere.[11] The following discussion serves only to highlight a few selected elements of high jumping mechanics.

Cooper stated that "a high jumper is first a runner and then a jumper."[12] His statement explicitly and concisely summarizes the movement demands placed on someone who is high jumping. During the approach horizontal velocity and momentum are developed; to a substantial degree, the jumper's horizontal momentum must be converted to vertical velocity. Once the jumper loses contact with the ground his angular momentum and the path of his center of graivty are set. Hay emphasized the importance of takeoff for the high jump when he stated, ". . . it is now generally conceded that the approach run and takeoff fix not only the height to which an athlete's center of gravity is raised but also the general form of the jump (i.e., the disposition of his body parts relative to one another during flight)."[13] If the jumper has not developed sufficient angular momentum or generated sufficient vertical velocity at the instant of takeoff, no amount of body contortions will generate additional angular momentum or vertical velocity **during** the flight phase of the jump.

Numerous techniques for clearing the bar have been developed, including a scissoring of the lower extremities, the Eastern cut-off, the Western roll, the straddle and the Fosbury flop. Of these many styles the straddle and the flop are the most frequently seen in competition today. One reason for the popularity of these two techniques is the potentially small distance above the bar that the jumper's center of gravity must travel during the flight. Because the center of gravity may move to a point outside the body itself, if the jumper can maneuver his limbs around the bar effectively (Fig. 24–1A) as he passes over the bar, the center of gravity does not have to be raised to the same level as if he did not effectively position his body segments.

Hay[14] emphasized the importance of three separate distances in the final height that the athlete reaches in a jump: (1) the height of the jumper's center of gravity above the ground at takeoff, (2) the distance between the height of his center of gravity at takeoff and its maximum height during the jump and (3) the distance between the maximum height of the center of gravity and the bar height. Each jumper must try to maximize distances (1) and (2) and to reduce distance (3) to clear the highest bar height.

The height of the center of gravity is related to the jumper's physical characteristics and to the positioning of the body segments. A tall high jumper has a slight advantage over a short jumper; his center of gravity, even in normal standing, is closer to the bar. Also, with his longer upper and lower extremities, the taller jumper is able to raise the height of his center of gravity within his body by swinging the extremities upward before takeoff. The importance of the first of Hay's distances can be seen in an analysis of a jump by Pat Matzdorf (U.S.A., former world record holder). For a seven foot high jump, Matzdorf's height of center of gravity at takeoff was already 67.7 per cent of the total bar height (4 ft 8¾ in of the bar height of 7 ft).[15]

The jumper approaches the bar with a certain horizontal velocity and converts this to a velocity which is principally vertical both by increasing the backward inclination of the trunk and by flexing the knee of the take-off leg in preparation for extension to produce downward force against the ground.[16] There must be sufficient friction available between the takeoff foot and the jumping surface to prevent the loss of effective force through slipping. The amount of vertical velocity that the jumper is able to generate

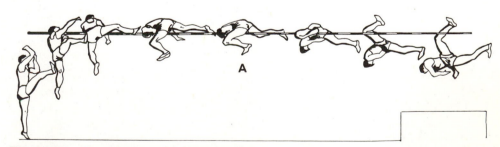

A

Figure 24–1. The straddle style of high jumping.
The effective positioning of the jumper's limbs helps to decrease the height that the center of gravity must be raised to pass over the bar. At position A the jumper has decreased the distance between his center of gravity and the bar. By reducing the distance between the center of gravity and the bar, the jumper is able to jump higher bar heights without actually raising the height that the center of gravity reaches.
(From Hay,[15] p. 440.)

during the takeoff phase of the jump is directly related to the magnitude of the **vertical impulse** that he can generate.[17] The same impulse–momentum principles indicated for sprint starts apply to the high jump takeoff.

While the jumper is in the air, and particularly while he is passing over the bar, it is important to consider the effects of "action–reaction". If a jumper has sufficient angular momentum, it may be possible for him to roll around the bar and not have his trailing leg hit the bar (Fig. 24–2A). Sometimes, however, when a jumper is having trouble with the trail leg hitting the bar, curling around the bar only aggravates the problem. Because of action–reaction, the jumper must cause the trunk or an upper extremity to move in a direction to cause an equal and **opposite** reaction in the trail leg (Fig. 24–2B). Abduction of the left arm tends to rotate the shoulder girdle back and to the left, and the reaction in the pelvis is to rotate back and to the right; this lifts the right leg over the bar. If the trunk is twisted away from the bar, the trail leg is effectively lifted over the bar. In the Fosbury flop, prevention of the trailing legs hitting the bar can be effected by vigorously flexing the neck and the upper trunk just before the legs are about to hit the bar.

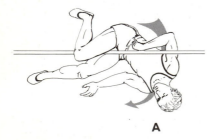

A

Figure 24–2. Interaction between body segments during jumping. In situation "A", the jumper has sufficient angular momentum to allow him to roll over the bar. In "B", it is necessary to forcefully abduct the left arm to cause the trail leg to be lifted over the bar — action-reaction principle. (Adapted from Hay,[15] p. 451.)

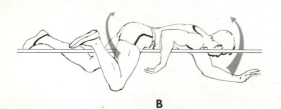

B

POLE VAULT

With the advent of the fiberglass pole, the pole vault event experienced dramatic increases in heights cleared and marked changes in the styles of vaulting. As with high jumping, a major concern in the pole vault is the conversion of horizontal velocity to vertical velocity. However, when the high jumper's feet leave the ground, the flight path of his center of gravity is set; in the pole vault, when the vaulter's feet leave the ground there is still a complex set of interactions that take place between the vaulter and the pole. The interrelationships between kinetic energy and potential energy of both position and deformation form an integral part of a successful vault.

Dillman and Nelson[18] provided quantitative information about some of the energy conversions that occur during a vault with a fiber glass pole. For their analysis, energy transformations that occurred during the vault were divided into three phases: (1) takeoff to maximum pole bend, (2) maximum bend to straight pole and (3) straight pole to the time the vaulter's center of gravity reached the highest point above the ground. A large percentage of kinetic energy was lost during the time between takeoff and maximum bending of the pole (about 71 per cent), while relatively small increases were seen in potential energy (31 per cent). While the pole was straightening in Phase 2, the kinetic energy of the system remained relatively constant and a 46 per cent increase in potential energy occurred. In Phase 2, the vaulter was able to **maintain** his energy of motion while taking advantage of the potential energy stored in the pole during Phase 1.

Films of the vaulters indicated that the effective vaulters "rode" the pole as it began to uncoil. As the energy from the pole began to increase the vaulter's vertical velocity during the uncoiling, the more successful vaulters began their pulls. The combination of the pole uncoiling and the vaulter pulling himself up resulted in the good vaulters reaching a maximum vertical velocity just as the pole assumed a straightened position.

At the time the vaulter reaches the high point of the flight, the kinetic energy of the vaulter is zero and his potential energy is maximum. The magnitude of the potential energy at the high point is a direct result of the vaulter's position above the ground.

While adequate horizontal approach velocity is necessary for a successful vault, it is interesting that Dillman and Nelson[18] reported that vaulters who attained excessively high takeoff velocities demonstrated less efficient energy patterns. The increased speed was detrimental to the effective interplay of kinetic and potential energies.

SHOT PUT

The throwing events in track and field include the shot put, javelin, discus and the hammer throw. The throwing motion associated with the javelin throw is more closely related to the overarm pattern (Chapter 18) than are the other three events. The discus throw is one of the purest of the sidearm patterns in sports. The tremendous transfers of momentum that take place during the turns prior to discus release and the aerodynamics of the discus flight have received deserved attention by many authors; useful references for all the throws in the field events are cited at the end of this chapter (see Additional Reading). The shot put has been chosen, however, as an example of the wide application of mechanical principles to the throwing events.

The actual putting motion of the shot put tends to be more of a pushing than a throwing action. As with any projectile, the shot's flight follows a parabolic path. Since the shot is a small heavy sphere air resistance can be neglected with little reservation in the analysis of the shot flight. Chapter 9 (Projection) presented many of the laws of motion that apply to the mechanical analysis of the shot in flight. The final distance that a released shot travels is a function of its location at the time of release and the speed and angle of release. The location at the time of release has two important components: (1) distance that the shot is released in front of the toe board, and (2) the height of the release above the ground. Both of these distances are influenced by the height of the individual throwing and the person's upper extremity length. Hay[19] indicated that the first distance, the horizontal distance between the inside of the toe board and the position of the shot release, may be "as much as 1 ft in some cases."

The interrelationships between the angle, speed and height of release of the shot clearly indicate that variation in the **speed of the shot at release is the most influential effecter of horizontal distance.**[20] To increase the distance of the throw, the athlete should concentrate principally on increasing the speed of the shot at the moment of release, rather than worrying too much about altering the angle of release. As with any projection skill, the impulse–momentum relationships are important in the effectiveness of the development of shot velocity. At the release the force should be applied directly through the center of the shot **in line with** the release angle desired. If application of force is not through the shot's center of gravity and totally in line with the shot path, only a component of the total force generated affects the flight of the shot; the rest causes the shot to rotate around its axis (to spin) as it moves through the air. Regardless of shot projection angle, a component of the force generated by the body will never be as effective in moving the shot forward as the total force would be.

During the put, the athlete attempts to develop a movement pattern that maximizes the distance and time over which effective forces can be developed. The styles of shot putting have progressed from a sidefacing with a hopping motion across the circle to gain velocity, to the O'Brien style (Fig. 24–3), which uses a back-facing start combined with a turn and glide across the ring that increases the time available for the development of velocity. The shot putter begins facing the rear of the circle and, in preparation for the glide across the circle, lowers his center of gravity, thereby increasing the distance over which effective upward force can be applied[21] (Fig. 24–3A). The backward glide across the circle allows gravity to begin the motion of the center of gravity across the ring and, when the motion of the body has been initiated, the putter forcefully extends the knee and ankle of the supporting limb and hyperextends the non-supporting hip (Fig. 24–3B). The vertical component of the reaction to his force produced by this extension of knee and ankle and the horizontal force against the ring surface combine to propel the body across the circle.

Figure 24-3. The "O'Brien style" of shot putting. (From Rasch and Burke,[21] p. 527.)

As illustrated in Figure 24–3, C and D, when the right foot contacts (right-handed throw), the putter must be certain to maintain the momentum of the shot across the ring; if he is too slow or stops the motion of his body and the shot, the preliminary glide is useless. As the left foot contacts the inside of the toe board, the left lower extremity must provide an essentially rigid base for the effective transfer of force through the body to the shot.

Forces must be transferred through the body by means of lower extremity extension, pelvic rotation, spinal rotation, arm extension and wrist flexion (Fig. 24–3E). Payne and his associates[23] have recorded the actual forces during the **glide** portion of the athlete's motion. When the athlete is pushing (Fig. 24–3B) against the surface of the ring, he is adding directly to the momentum of his body and the shot. When the putter's left foot contacts the front toe board, the forces are found to be acting in a direction opposite to the forward motion of the body. These forces decelerate the lower extremities; this deceleration of the lower extremities helps to accelerate the next segment in the body. As with any effective throwing motion, momentum is transmitted and added from segment to segment until at the final link, the hand in the case of putting, the momentum is transferred to the shot. In skilled throwing of the javelin, discus, baseball, football or any other object for which maximum speed or distance is desired, the sequential deceleration and acceleration of successive segments plays an integral role (see p. 254).

After the shot has been released, the athlete must dissipate the momentum of his body gradually. Frequently a "reverse" is used in which the right foot (right-handed throw) replaces the left at the toe board, while the left lower extremity swings backward toward the center of the ring to keep the center of gravity over the right foot (Fig. 24–3F). Swinging back the left leg produces an opposite angular reaction that helps to move the athlete's center of gravity back from the front of his base of support[24], and the weight of the leg extended backward balances the weight of the forward leaning trunk and the right upper extremity.

REFERENCES

1. Hay, J. G.: *The Biomethanics of Sports Techniques.* Englewood Cliffs, New Jersey, Prentice-Hall, 1973, pp. 395–415.
2. Dillman, C. J.: Kinematic Analyses of Running. In Wilmore, J. H., and Keogh, J. F. (eds.): *Exercise and Sport Sciences Reviews,* Vol. 3, New York, Academic Press, 1975, pp. 193–218.
3. Short, J.: Standing Start Modernized. *Track Technique,* 39:1227–1228, 1970.
4. Henry, F. M.: Force-Time Characteristics of the Sprint Start. *Research Quarterly,* 23:301–318, 1952.
5. *Ibid.* p. 306.
6. Hay, J. G.: *op. cit.,* p. 406.
7. Blader, F. B.: The Analysis of Movements and Forces in the Sprint Start. In Wartenweiler, J., Jokl, E. and Hebbelinck, M.(eds.): *Biomechanics I.* New York, S. Karger, 1968, pp. 278–281.
8. *Ibid.,* p. 281.
9. Stock, M.: Influence of Various Track Starting Positions on Speed. *Research Quarterly,* 33:608–609, 1962.
10. Henry, F. M., and Trafton, I. R.: The Velocity Curve of Sprint Running. *Research Quarterly,* 22:412, 1951.

11. Hay, J. G.: Biomechanical Aspects of Jumping. In Wilmore, J. H. and Keogh, J. F. (eds.): *Exercise and Sport Sciences Reviews*, Vol. 3, New York, Academic Press, 1975, pp. 135–162.
12. Cooper, J. M.: Kinesiology of High Jumping. In Wartenweiler, J., Jokl, E., and Hebbelinck, M. (eds.): *Biomechanics I*. New York, S. Karger, 1968. pp. 291–302.
13. Hay, J. G.: *Biomechanical Aspects of Jumping. op. cit.*, p. 147.
14. Hay. J. G.: The Hay Technique — Utimate in High Jump Style?, *Athletic Journal, 53*;46, 48, 113–115, 1973.
15. Hay. J. G.: *The Biomechanics of Sports Techniques. op. cit.*, p. 438.
16. Dyatchkov, V. M.: The High Jump. *Track Technique, 34*:1059–1061, 1968.
17. Hay. J. G.: *The Biomechanics of Sports Techniques. op. cit.*, p. 439.
18. Dillman, C. J., and Nelson, R. C.: The Mechanical Energy Transformations of Pole Vaulting with a Fiberglass Pole. *Journal of Biomechanics, 1*:175–183, 1968.
19. Hay. J. G.: *The Biomechanics of Sports Techniques. op. cit.*, p. 471.
20. *Ibid.*: p. 38.
21. Rasch, P., and Burke, R.: *Kinesiology and Applied Anatomy*. 5th ed. Philadelphia, Lea & Febiger, 1974, p. 527.
22. Ward, P.: The Putting Style of Al Feuerbach. *Scholastic Coach, 43*:12–13, 102, 1974.
23. Payne, A. H., Slater. W. J. and Telford, T.: The Use of a Force Platform in the Study of Athletic Activities. A Preliminary Investigation. *Ergonomics, 11*:123–143, 1968.
24. Hay, J. G.: *The Biomechanics of Sports Techniques. op. cit.*, p 479.

ADDITIONAL READING

Bunn, J. W.: *Scientific Principles of Coaching*. Englewood Cliffs, New Jersey, Prentice-Hall, Inc., 1962.
Dyson, G. H. G.: *The Mechanics of Athletics*. 5th ed. New York, Dover Publications, 1970.
Hay, J. G.: *The Biomechanics of Sports Techniques*. Englewood Cliffs, New Jersey, Prentice-Hall, Inc., 1973. (Chapter 16–Track and Field: Running; Chapter 17–Track and Field: Jumping; Chapter 18 — Track and Field: Throwing)
Hay. J. G.: *A Bibliography of Biomechanics Literature*. 3rd ed. Iowa City, University of Iowa, 1976. (Track and Field — Section T38, 534 references)
Hopper, B. J.: *The Mechanics of Human Movement*. New York, American Elsevier Publishing Company, 1973.

25

SWIMMING AND DIVING

SWIMMING AND DIVING

Although the human body is not particularly efficient in its locomotion through water, swimming and diving are both popular sport and recreational activities, and swimming has a life-saving potential. Application of basic mechanical principles to these activities affords the participant an opportunity for enhancement of performance and enjoyment. As in other chapters of Part IV, the following discussion deals only with selected aspects of both swimming and diving; those particularly interested in these activities are encouraged to extend the material through reference to the numerous sources listed at the end of the chapter.

SWIMMING

Swimming, like walking and running, is a means of locomotion resulting from the body pushing against a surface and the surface exerting an opposite force against the body. The body as a whole is given linear motion as a result of angular motion of its extremities. Swimming differs from walking and running in that the surface against which the push is made is not as resistive as the usual walking surface, and the surrounding medium offers a great deal more resistance to the movement of the body; it offers resistance to body progress and to the motion of body segments in the direction **opposite** to that of desired motion, and also affords the surface against which the body applies its force. Also, for the most part, the body is in a horizontal, rather than vertical, position and the effect of the force of gravity is greatly minimized — in some cases eliminated.

Because water is not as dense as the ground or floor it is less resistive, and thus "gives" as pressure is applied against it. Therefore, all of the force exerted by the swimmer is not effective in moving him; some of it is dissipated in moving the water. Progress is slower and requires more effort, However, the swimmer normally uses both upper and lower extremities to push against the water instead of the lower extremities only as in movement on land. In walking, one moves **through** air which, because of its relatively low density, normally offers little resistance to the progress of the body. The swimmer moves through water which is considerably more dense, making the **minimizing** of the resistance of the water to motion **in the direction the swimmer desires to move,** one of his major concerns. At the same time this same medium which resists his forward progress is the substance that supplies the force to move the swimmer and, therefore, another basic concern is that of **increasing the resistance** of the water to movements of body segments **in the direction opposite** to that in which the swimmer desires to move. Thus, swimming is a problem of minimizing the resistance of the water to movements in the direction the swimmer wishes to progress and increasing, to its maximum, the resistance of the water to movement in the opposite direction.

Because of its density, water exerts a supporting force against the body and removes the necessity for withstanding the pull of gravity that is ever present in standing, walking and running.

Drownproofing

While aquatic sports provide recreation and enjoyment, the fact that thousands of people of all ages and swimming expertise drown every year is well known. **Basic survival** is indeed one of the most important aspects of swimming.

The principal elements of flotation and buoyancy were discussed in Chapter 7, Fluid Dynamics, but it is worthwhile to examine these elements as they relate to aquatic survival. In a survival situation, treading water, floating on the back or doing a crawl stroke can lead to exhaustion and panic. In open water, considerable effort is required to keep the head above water for longer than a half-hour and in rough water, back floating can be useless.

In 1939, Lanoue originated drownproofing and currently Wetmore[1] is one of the leading proponents of, and experts in, the technique. In contrast to exhaustively treading water to lift the head out of the water so that the individual can breathe, or attempting to float on the back when many individuals' body builds are not such that the body masses above and below the center of buoyancy are balanced, the drownproofing technique employs relaxation in the position that maximizes buoyancy; it uses the vertical float position with the head forward in the water. Because most people displace a volume of water that weighs more than the body, they float with the head and neck close to the surface. In order to take a breath periodically, the head must be raised out of the water; this reduces the buoyancy of the body (less volume of water displaced) and the body tends to sink. To counteract this some downward force against the water (which results in upward force against the body) must be produced. The drownproofing experts suggest that this can be done most easily by folding the arms in front of the face and lifting the legs in preparation for a scissors kick. A thrust of the arms sideways and downward produces upward force against the body at the same time that the legs are brought forcibly together; this leg action, taking

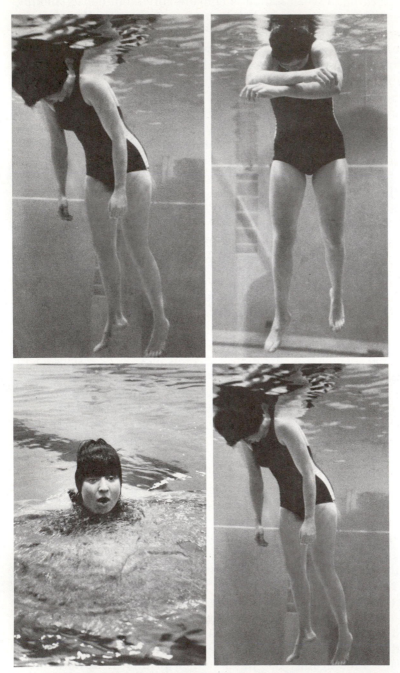

Figure 25–1. Drownproofing technique. (Adapted from Whittemore.[2] © Parade Publications Inc., 1977.)

place below the trunk, neck and head, also produces upward force (Fig. 25–1). A "travel stroke" immediately follows to make maximum use of the lung full of fresh air that has just been inhaled.

To travel forward, force must be exerted backward against the water. As the head is replaced back into the water, one foot reaches for the surface behind the swimmer and a second kick puts the body into a horizontal position, making it possible for the arms to apply the required force against the water by sweeping the arms outward-backward much as in the breast stroke. The swimmer then relaxes before repeating the cycle. The time between breaths should be about 6 to 10 seconds.

Wetmore[2] reported rather astonishing survival rates for people who found themselves in life-threatening situations and used the drownproofing technique. This procedure capitalizes on buoyancy of the body to keep the swimmer from sinking or exhausting himself by working too hard.

Water Resistance to Forward Progress

A horizontal position is easier to maintain when the body is moving through the water than when it is motionless, since the resistance of the water planes the body.

A body moving through the water in a diagonal position causes greater resistance than one which is horizontal because it presents a greater surface area against which the water acts. The larger the surface area, the greater the resistance to the movement of the body through the water. Therefore, the body position in swimming should be such that the smallest area possible is presented to the water in the direction of desired movement. Keeping the body planed on the surface of the water reduces resistance to forward progress, since the surface presented to the water is only the distance of the thickness of the body from front to back. When the hips and legs drop a very large area resists forward progress. The size of the resistive surface varies with the sine of the angle that the feet drop (Fig. 7–5, p. 119). Burying the head in the water when swimming the crawl stroke presents the entire back of the head to the water. When the face lies on the water a much smaller area resists forward progress. This head position is important also in that it maintains the basic alignment of body segments (Chapter 10) and facilitates breathing during the stroke without a lift of the head that leads to a sinking of the feet and thus to greatly increased resistance. Uneven force exerted on the two sides of the body results in a zigzag path through the water and increases the frontal area which resists forward progress (Fig. 25–2). Up and down movement in the water should also be kept to a minimum since this also increases surface area and causes waves which further resist progress. Heusner pointed out that, when a swimmer causes waves, some of his energy is spent in lifting the water and so this energy is not available for propulsion. Wave action also varies with speed; therefore, the speed at which the least wave action results is the "speed of maximum efficiency."[3]

To further accomplish a reduction in resistance, the body is streamlined as much as possible, especially during the recovery and gliding phases of

Figure 25–2. Increase in frontal area caused by zigzag path through the water.

the stroke. When the swimmer wishes to move forward, the problem is to determine how to maneuver the extremities forward into a position from which they can exert force backward without presenting a large surface which resists the desired forward movement. If, in the elementary back stroke, the legs were simply drawn apart and then pulled together, the surface area in both directions would be equal and movement through the water would depend entirely on any difference in the speed of the two actions. It may seem that when recovering the legs in the wedge kick of the elementary back stroke a large surface area is presented. However, when the legs are kept together as they are flexed, the hips sink and thus the entire surface of the back resists the forward movement of the swimmer. By bending the knees outward, the legs are shortened so that only the thighs resist the water and the surface area of the thighs is not as great as that of the back of the body. In all strokes, the arms are kept close to the body as they move forward in order to keep the body as streamlined as possible. Having the fingertips lead also reduces the surface area resisting forward movement. This can be demonstrated easily by running the flat hand through the water with the fingertips leading and then facing the palm in the direction of the movement of the hand and pushing it through the water. The marked difference in resistance is easily perceived.

In general, above the speed of 1.6 meters per second, there does not seem to be a significant difference between the drag resistances to prone and side positions when the body is at an angle of approximately 45 degrees.[4] The side position was standardized with one arm extended above the head, the other along the body, straight legs together, ankles extended and head held so that the water level was approximately through the midline of the face.[5] Although Counsilman[6] found the opposite to be the case with one swimmer, results of Clarys and Jiskoot[7] showed that, for 93 per cent of 43 swimmers, the side position offered less total resistance at slower velocities (less than 1.6 m/sec). The transient side position in the crawl may decrease the total resistance to the forward motion of the swimmer using that stroke. At velocities of 1.7 and 1.8 meters per second (approximately 58.5 to 55.5 sec/100 m), the total resistance of the side position was found to be even less, although the difference was not statistically significant. At a faster speed (1.9 m/sec; 52.6 sec/100 m), the prone position caused slightly less resistance than did the side position; again this did not prove to be a significant difference.

Since resistance increases approximately with the square of the velocity[8] any quick movement under water **in the direction of the desired movement** of the body should be eliminated. Karpovich[9] reported finding that the relationship of water resistance to speed is somewhat different for the prone and the back positions.*

Water resistance for prone position = speed^2 × .65
Water resistance for back position = speed^2 × .75

When the recovery phase of any stroke is under water, pressure is exerted in a direction that tends to send the body backward. Therefore, it is important that these movements be performed slowly as well as be kept as close to the body as possible to reduce surface area. Since the resistance of the air is considerably less than that of water, recovery of the arms out of the water reduces resistance to forward progress. The out-of-water recovery of the crawl arms reduces resistance to a minimum. Therefore, the efficient manipulation of a long extremity above the water, rather than resistance, is the problem in arm recovery of the crawl stroke. Bending the elbow greatly reduces the length of the lever (decreased moment of inertia) and makes it easier to move the arm forward. Lifting a bent elbow and carrying it forward before reaching with the hands makes it possible to relax the muscles of the lower arm during a part of each stroke and thus reduces the effort necessary.

Just as the type of shoe worn influences the degree of friction between the feet and the floor, the material of the swimming suit is a factor in water friction. Karpovich[10] found that a woolen suit offered more resistance to progress than a silk suit. Also, a loose suit, especially when relatively tight around the legs, adds to resistance. Since the space between the suit and body fills with water, the area of the body is, in effect, enlarged.

A low pressure area which causes a suction force is created immediately behind the body moving rapidly through the water; this tends to pull the body backward.[11] The faster the swimmer is moving the greater is this cavitation effect.

All movements of the body or any of its segments tend to create swirls and eddies, which cause low pressure areas around the body of the swimmer that have a retarding effect. Therefore, all movements that do not contribute to progress in the desired direction should be kept to a minimum. When water encounters curves in the swimmer's body, eddies are also produced; this is another reason for streamlining the body. The basic well-aligned

---

*These figures apply when skin surface area is 19–24 sq. ft.

position of body segments that is most efficient in standing is also most effective in streamlining the body in the water, except that, since vertical balance is not a problem, the feet should be together. Streamlining the body during the gliding phase of any stroke results in gaining the most distance for a given amount of force applied, since resistance is reduced to a minimum.

Production of Force

The body is propelled through the water by a pushing and/or pulling motion of the arms and a thrusting and/or pincer action of the legs. Since the body moves in the opposite direction to that of force application, backward pressure sends it forward, downward pressure lifts it, upward pressure sinks it, pressure to the right moves it left, and pressure to the left moves it right. The fastest motion results from reduction of resistance to the body in the direction the swimmer wishes to progress and the production of the **greatest** resistance possible to the movement of the body segments in the opposite direction.

The **important factors** in increasing the propulsive force of any stroke are the opposite to many of those discussed in connection with the reduction of resistance to progress. Maximum force is attained by presenting **as large a surface** as possible in the direction opposite to that of desired movement and by moving this surface through the water as fast as possible. Counsilman[12] pointed out that inertia (the tendency of water put into motion to keep moving at the same speed in the same direction) negates the theory that a swimmer should push straight backward over a long distance to gain forward force. He stated that "maximum efficiency in water is achieved by pushing a large amount of water a short distance rather than pushing a small amount of water a great distance."[13] He suggested zigzag pull patterns in which the hand, tilted at an angle, is pulled through the water with the direction and the tilt of the hand being changed after a short distance; he likened this pattern to a boat propellor or fan. With this type of pull, the water encountered is not already moving backward and thus offers greater resistance (a greater reaction force) to send the swimmer forward. According to Counsilman, the two problems the swimmer must solve to gain effective propulsion are: "(1) how to evolve a stroke pattern that, once he has started the water moving backward, will allow him to get away from that water and work with still water and (2) how to pitch his hands so they will serve as propellers and not as paddles."[14]

Observation of zigzagging patterns and changing hand tilts during arm-pulling motions of skilled swimmers has led to re-analysis of the influence of lift and drag forces (Chapter 7, Fluid Dynamics) in the propulsive phase of swimming strokes. In the past, drag forces were thought to be the sole contributor to forward propulsion of a swimmer. However, there is increasing evidence[15-19] indicating that the **resultant propulsive force for a highly skilled swimmer is comprised of both lift and drag forces.**

While, during recovery, the arms and legs are flexed to shorten the levers and reduce surface area, they are extended to differing degrees at

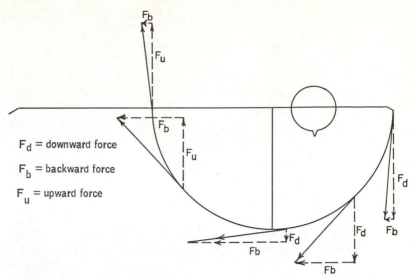

Figure 25–3. Direction and magnitude of components of equal forces applied at various points on an arc.

various points during the drive to present as great a surface as possible and to take advantage of the extra leverage. Fingertips lead during recovery, but the palm of the hand pushes through the water during the drive.

Although an outstanding swimmer uses a series of arcs and sculling motions during an arm pull, the straight arm pull, employed by most beginners, illustrates some basic interrelationships between swimming efficiency and fluid dynamics.

Since, in a straight arm pull, the extremities move in an arc, relatively direct pressure opposite to the direction of desired movement is exerted only during the middle portion of the action. Pressure applied at the extremes of the arc may introduce undesirable forces. For example, if in the straight arm pull in a crawl stroke, the hand starts pulling forcefully at the surface of the water and pulls all the way to the side of the body, the force produced during the early part of the stroke is downward and lifts the upper body, while that produced at the end of the stroke is upward and, because it is applied approximately at the center of gravity, sinks the entire body. The result is an up-and-down motion of the body that increases resistance and wastes energy.

Figure 25–3 illustrates the components of the forces applied at various points on an arc. Because, in the crawl stroke, the center of the arc (the shoulder) moves forward as the hand moves backward, the arc is actually considerably more upright than this diagram indicates. In fact, as the arm approaches the body, the arc is upward and slightly **forward** (Fig. 25–4). If, instead of pulling through the full arc, the fingers cut into the water a few inches before complete extension of the arm, when the arm is extended ready to pull, the hand is a few inches below the surface of the water and the part of the arc causing the greatest lift is eliminated. If the elbow bends when the hand passes below the body, all upward force which would sink the

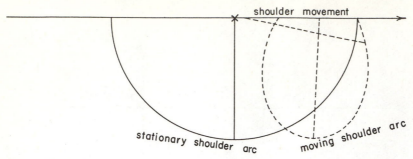

Figure 25–4. Comparison of arcs resulting from movement about stationary and moving fulcrums.

body is eliminated. If the arm and hand were one straight lever, the backward component of the force produced would be greater than the downward (or upward) component only from a point 45 degrees downward in front of the shoulder to a point 45 degrees downward in back of the shoulder. However, wrist flexion makes it possible to place the palm of the hand in a position to exert considerable force backward before the 45 degree angle position is reached.

Figure 25–5 illustrates the direction that the palm can face at various points on the arc. The actual force produced would be the resultant between a force in that direction and the force tangent to the arc at the particular point. Since both are produced by the same movement, they would be equal in magnitude and the effective force would be at an angle half way between the direction the palm is facing and the direction tangent to the arc. Wrist action is not effective in increasing the backward force beyond the vertical, but bending the elbow keeps the palm facing backward (Fig. 25–5). The straight arm pull, therefore, should be from a point a few inches below the surface of the water to just beyond the point vertically downward from the shoulder. Beyond this point as the elbow bends and begins to lift the hand, some additional backward force is produced since the palm of the hand is facing backward. Pulling too far with a straight arm introduces a great deal of upward force because of the uprightness of the arc and sinks the body. It also places the shoulder in a forward position, making a lift of the elbow difficult.

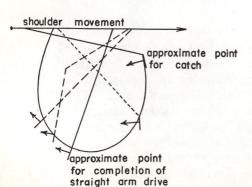

Figure 25–5. Direction palm of hand can face at various points on arc of the crawl drive.

Reaching high overhead during the arm recovery of the elementary back stroke increases the distance over which force can be applied, but the first part of the drive is wasted in producing forces that tend to send the body to the right and left. If the forces applied by the two arms are equal, the straight direction of movement of the swimmer is not affected but a great deal of energy is wasted. The last part of the arc has a pincer action, the water is forced backward as the arms approach the body, and thus aids in moving the body forward. The arc of the arms, therefore, should be from a point at approximately 45 degrees above the shoulder to the sides of the body.

In the down beat of the crawl kick, backward force can be produced by the top of the hyperextended foot as the leg moves downward as a result of hip flexion. Bending the knee slightly puts the top of the foot into position to apply the force more directly backward. During the up beat, the sole of the foot applies backward force as it moves from a flexed to an extended position. Since the application of backward force is so dependent upon foot position, flexible ankles are necessary for success in the crawl kick. Because of the forward component of the force exerted by the thigh on the down beat and the additional effective force that can be exerted by the whip of the foot on the up beat, more force is obtainable on the up beat of the kick (Fig. 25–6). Therefore, this is the portion of the kick that should be emphasized.

A kick that is wider than the depth of the body (approximately 15 to 18 inches) increases the resistance of the water to the forward progress of the body. As the kick becomes wider, the forward component of the force exerted by the movement of the thigh on the down beat also is increased. This component is greater if the leg is completely straight at this time. Thus it is possible to move the body backward by a wide straight leg kick that emphasizes the down beat, since a large forward component of force is produced. The general action of the legs in the crawl kick is very similar to walking. The central action of both is at the hip; both begin with some bend of the knee; there is a resistive component to the first part of the action; ankle action is very important. The action of the swinging phase of the walk is the same

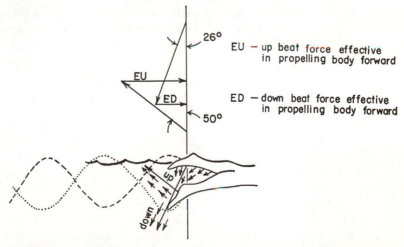

Figure 25–6.   Relative value of up and down phases of the crawl kick. (Modified from Cureton, Thomas K.: Mechanics and Kinesiology of Swimming, *Research Quarterly*, 1:4:101, 1930.)

as that of the down beat of the kick, while the propulsive phase is like that of the up beat.

In the drive of the wedge frog kick, the first backward pressure against the water is applied by the front of the lower legs but the soles of the feet, if the ankles are flexed, are almost immediately brought into position to push directly backward. Flexing the ankles gives as large a surface area as possible to exert effective force. The final force of the kick results from squeezing the water backward as the legs come together. Because, during the recovery phase of this stroke, the thighs exert forward force that tends to stop forward momentum, it is extremely important that this movement be executed slowly. The forceful movements should be reserved for the drive phase of the kick. The ankles are extended during the first part of the recovery to reduce the surface area moving forward as much as possible. (When the ankles are flexed the entire top of the foot is presented to the water in the direction of movement and thus progress is retarded.) They then flex so that the toes can lead, reducing the resistive surface as the feet reach outward, and so that they are in position to extend on the drive.

Since resistance increases with the square of the velocity, and the progress of the swimmer is dependent upon the resistance of the water to his movements, greater progress results from faster movements of those body parts in position to apply force against the water in the direction opposite to that in which the swimmer wishes to progress. While movements in the direction of progress impede the desired motion of the body through the water and are made slowly to reduce resistance, movements in the opposite direction are responsible for the swimmer's progress and are made rapidly to increase resistance.

Best results from a given application of force can be gained by the advantageous use of momentum. Since more force is needed to start an object moving than to keep it moving, the timing of the gliding strokes is extremely important to efficiency. If one stroke is executed immediately after the other, the swimmer does not gain the advantage of a short period of relaxation between strokes which is possible since the momentum of the stroke planes the body for a considerable time. If, on the other hand, the swimmer waits for his second stroke until the momentum of the first has been dissipated by the resistance of the water, he must overcome inertia on every stroke. In addition, since most individuals do not float horizontally, his feet will start to sink into a position which presents a broader surface, and thus increases resistance to progress, and requires that more force be exerted to move a given distance through the water. Since it takes time to go through the motions of the recovery phase of the stroke to prepare to exert the force, the second stroke should be started ahead of the time that it is desirable to apply the second force.

One might assume that in speed swimming, the speed that could be gained from a complete stroke would be the sum total of that which could be produced by the arms alone, plus that which could be produced by the legs alone. However, Karpovich reported finding that, for the crawl stroke, "the square of the maximum speed of the whole stroke is equal to the sum of the squares of the maximum speeds developed with the arms and the legs separately."[20]

$$V_w{}^2(\text{crawl}) = V_a{}^2 + V_l{}^2$$

This means that the total speed is considerably less than the sum of the speed of the arms plus that of the legs. If a swimmer were able to swim at 5 ft/sec with the arms alone and 4 ft/sec with the legs alone, the total speed that would result when swimming with both would be the **square root** of 41 ($5^2 + 4^2$) or 6.40 — much less than the sum of 5 + 4 (9).*

MacDonald and Stearns[21] found that in both the breast and butterfly strokes, there is an even greater loss of speed when arms and legs are combined.

$$V_w{}^2 \text{ (breast)} \quad = 0.75 \ (V_a{}^2 + V_l{}^2)$$
$$V_w{}^2 \text{ (butterfly)} = 0.90 \ (V_a{}^2 + V_l{}^2)$$

There is little information available which directly compares stroke length, stroke frequency and swimming velocity. East[22] has published some data for these relationships. In studying champion swimmers, he found improvements in performance of men's freestyle were characterized by a marked increase in stroke frequency and slight decrease in stroke length. However, in men's backstroke and butterfly, he found that a better performance resulted almost entirely from an increase in stroke length. He attributed differences in performances of men and women competing in the same swimming style to the differences in stroke length as he found frequencies to be similar.[23] Nelson and Pike[24] reported similar results and, in addition, indicated that as the distance of a race increased the stroke rate increased, regardless of the type of stroke being performed.

A great many examples of the manner in which physical principles apply to various swimming strokes could be cited.[25] However, space does not permit such a discussion here. The important point is that, regardless of whether a beginning stroke, a racing stroke or a synchronized swimming stunt is involved, the swimmer must determine how the body can be manipulated in the water so that: (1) as large an area as possible can be moved as directly as possible, in the direction which is opposite to that in which the swimmer wishes to progress; (2) the areas that must move in the direction of the desired progress can be kept as small as possible; (3) the movements in the direction of desired progress are executed slowly and those in the opposite direction relatively rapidly, the degree of speed being dependent upon the purpose of the stroke; and (4) maximum advantage can be taken of momentum and buoyancy.

DIVING

Diving comprises a wide range of activities, from cliff diving to scuba diving and from three meter springboard diving to swimming starts. Both

---

*Hypothetical figures chosen for clarity of illustration.

swimming starts and springboard diving, as well as some differences between springboard and platform diving, are discussed in this section.

Swimming Starts

In contrast to springboard and high dives, the purposes of which are aesthetic and/or acrobatic, the objective of swimming starts is entirely utilitarian. In a swimming or racing start, the swimmer is interested in getting into the water as fast as possible with an effective angle of entry. In racing events, particularly at the shorter distances and at the higher levels of competition, small fractions of time may be significant to the swimmer. In fact, at a recent Olympic competition, less than 0.01 second separated the gold and silver medalists in some races; at such levels of competition, even the smallest improvement in a racing start would be welcomed.

In a conventional swimming start, the swimmer assumes a comfortable stance, with feet about 6 to 12 inches apart for good balance and the toes wrapped firmly over the front edge of the starting block. With the toes wrapped over the edge there is a vertical surface to resist the backward component of the force exerted at takeoff, and thus there is less chance of slipping on the wet surface of the starting block. As the swimmer "takes his mark" the line of gravity is brought forward within the base of support; the closer to the front edge of the base the line of gravity falls, the less distance the center of gravity must travel during the force production phase of the dive.

During a conventional start, to develop maximum angular velocity the extended arms swing through a full circle. The increased range of motion permits a longer time to reach the highest velocity that the swimmer can achieve. As the arms are accelerated, they rapidly develop a high angular velocity and angular momentum. As the arms complete the full circle, they rapidly decelerate. At this time the angular momentum of the arms is transferred to the trunk and assists in the acceleration of the rest of the body. Even though the arms are only a small portion of the total body mass, their ability to develop a relatively high angular velocity enables them to develop the angular momentum level needed to significantly influence the momentum of the rest of the body. For a conventional swimming start, the full circular backswing technique is more effective than a simple straight backswing or a starting position with the arms back,[26] because the greater distance over which the swimmer may apply torque to the upper extremities permits a greater development of angular momentum.

Evidence has been emerging in the past few years that a **grab start** may enable the swimmer to get into the water faster and thereby begin the swimming stroke sooner[27-32] In a grab start, the swimmer grabs the front edge or the lip of the starting block, either inside or outside of his feet. The swimmer pulls with his arms while trying to extend his lower extremities so that the muscles of the lower extremities are able to develop higher levels of tension prior to the initiation of extension, and the line of gravity can be moved farther forward in the base of support; the stabilizing effect of the upper extremities can help to decrease the chance of a false start. The swimmer's velocity at takeoff seems to be similar to that of a good conventional start, but in the grab start the swimmer spends less time in contact with the block and, therefore, is able to enter the water sooner. The ability of a swimmer to tense the muscles of the lower extremities in preparation for the powerful extension in the grab start, helps to decrease the normal reaction time and movement time and enhances the resultant impulse that can be developed during contact with the starting block.[33]

An optimal angle of takeoff for both the conventional and grab starts is 13 degrees below the horizontal.[34] If the angle of projection is higher, the swimmer develops an excessive vertical velocity. Extra vertical velocity increases the time of flight; the swimmer spends too much time in flight and loses valuable time that could be spent more productively in applying propulsive forces in the water. If the angle of projection is too low, the swimmer loses time because he enters the water too soon; instead of travelling at a constant horizontal velocity for a longer flight, he is decelerated too soon by the water's resistive drag on his body. At the optimal angle of projection, these positive and negative trade-offs are balanced.

When the body enters the water, the swimmer must be able to sense that point when his horizontal momentum, the result of his horizontal velocity during flight, decreases to the forward speed that he is able to develop with his stroke. No decrease in momentum should occur as he begins his stroke. If he hurries the start of the stroke, he does not take full advantage of the momentum that he developed from the start; and if he waits too long before starting the stroke, he loses horizontal velocity. It is more difficult to regain maximum momentum once it is lost than to maintain it (inertia).

The angle of body entry into the water may vary slightly with the different demands of the various strokes.[35] The butterfly and free-style strokes have a slightly smaller angle of entry (approximately 15°) than the breast stroke (approximately 20°). With the breast stroke, the swimmer may take one arm pull and one kick before surfacing. The swimmer enters at a steeper angle so that he goes deeper, making it easier to stay under water during the completion of the first stroke; under water he experiences no wave drag and, therefore, has less total resistance to the forward motion of his body through the water.

Springboard Diving

In contrast to the utilitarian racing starts, the purpose of springboard diving is aesthetic and/or acrobatic. An outgrowth of aerial acrobatics and tumbling, springboard diving was developed in Europe and became a recognized competitive sport in England in 1905.[36]

In springboard diving, the diver takes full advantage of the energy storing capacity (potential energy) of the board to obtain the necessary velocity to project him high enough to allow time to perform the desired maneuvers before hitting the water.

As the diver approaches the end of the diving board, he performs a hurdle or jump which permits him to increase his vertical momentum. Both arms are swung forward and upward as the hurdle is performed. As in a racing dive, the angular momentum of the extremities is transferred to the trunk. The upward acceleration of the arms and the non-supporting leg adds to the stored energy in the board by causing the board to be depressed further. The arms are rapidly decelerated just before the powerful extensor thrust of the supporting leg occurs. During the deceleration of the arms and the non-supporting leg, angular momentum is transferred to the diver's trunk.

The extra height gained from the hurdle increases the kinetic energy possessed by the diver at the time of board contact and thus results in greater deformation of the board (more potential energy stored in the board). The combined extension of the lower extremities, deceleration effects of the swinging upper extremities, and the conversion of the board's potential energy to kinetic energy produce the diver's velocity at takeoff. The mechanical energy conversions between the board and the diver are similar to those already discussed for a gymnast bouncing on a trampoline bed (Chapter 6).

A diver's **center of gravity** follows a parabolic path during flight, but the location of the center of gravity may shift in reference to his body segments. If the diver goes into a layout position, without excessive hyperextension, the center of gravity is still located within the limits of the body. In a pike position, however, the center of gravity is located outside the limits of the body (p. 48). Once the diver is in the air, whenever he moves one part of his body in a certain direction, an equal and opposite reaction takes place in another part of his body to counterbalance the original motion. If a diver throws his right arm across his chest while in flight, his body rotates to his left.

Once the diver leaves the board, he is not able to change the **total** angular momentum of his body. It is possible, however, to change either or both the angular velocity and the moment of inertia during flight. Because the total angular momentum of the diver is conserved during the flight, an increase in moment of inertia is always accompanied by a decrease in angular velocity of his rotating body, while a decrease in moment of inertia results in an increase in angular velocity. The moment of inertia can be decreased by bringing the concentration of weight closer to the axis of rotation and increased by moving body segments farther from the axis. Thus, during a dive, the angular velocity of a diver increases as he goes from a layout to a pike to a tuck; the body moment of inertia decreases with each successive position, but the **total** angular momentum of the body is conserved.

Because a diver cannot create additional angular momentum during flight, all angular momentum must be developed during the time he is in contact with the board. The direction of forces from the board in relation to the body's center of gravity affects the amount of angular momentum imparted to the diver. At takeoff, the farther the line of the projection force deviates from passing through the diver's center of gravity, the greater the **angular momentum** of the diver during flight. Ideally, in an elementary **standing or running front jump dive (layout),** little or no angular momentum is transmitted to the diver at takeoff (Fig. 25–7). Thus the line from the point of takeoff through the diver's center of gravity must be in the direction of the applied force. In the front jump dive (layout), the diver leaves the board in a vertical

Figure 25–7. Standing or running front jump dive (layout). (From Armbruster et al,[36] p. 274.)

position, with arms forward and upward, and enters the water in that same vertical alignment, but with arms at his sides (Fig. 25–7). If even the slightest excess of angular momentum is given to the body at takeoff, the diver tends to pitch forward and does not enter the water in perfect vertical alignment.

In more complex dives requiring a greater component of backward force against the board so that effective angular force can be applied to the body to initiate twisting, it is important to have sufficient friction between the diver's feet and the board. Visualizing the three principal axes of body rotation helps to simplify the twisting and spinning movements of the body required in complex dives. The principal axes are: (1) **vertical axis** (head-to-toe direction) — whenever the body is doing a twist, it is rotating around the vertical axis, (2) **dorsoventral axis** (front-to-back) — this axis is involved when the body is doing a cartwheel, (3) **transverse axis** (side-to-side) — while doing a backward, forward, inward or reverse spinning dive the body rotates about a transverse axis.[37] The diver rotates about each of the three principal axes at some time during a **forward one and one-half with double twist** (Fig. 25–8). He rotates around the vertical axis (head-to-toe) during the twists (Fig. 25–8, I), around the dorsoventral (front-to-back) as the arms are circled (II), and around the transverse (side-to-side) as the diver's body is tipped off the forward spinning axis (III).

Whenever twisting occurs, it means that a torque was applied to the body as the diver left the board. Whenever spin or a somersault occurs, it

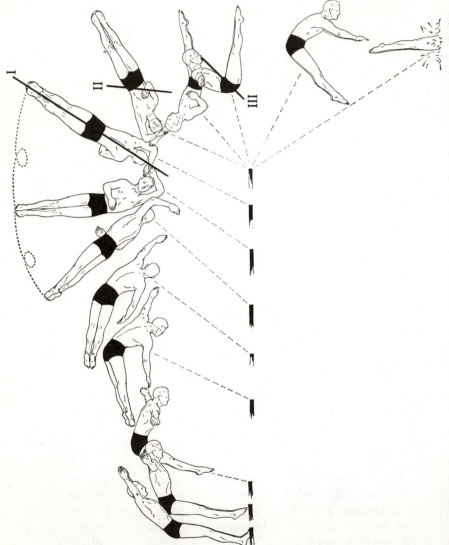

Figure 25-8. Forward one and one-half somersault, double twist. Rotation occurs around all three principal axes at some time during the dive: (I) vertical axis (head-to-toe), (II) dorsoventral axis (front-to-back), and (III) transverse axis (side-to-side). (Adapted from Armbruster et al.,[36] p. 339.)

indicates that angular momentum was imparted to the body prior to the diver's loss of contact with the board.

With higher takeoff surfaces, more time is available for the flight phase of the dive so there is a greater probability of completing complex maneuvers before contacting the water. An important difference between platform diving and springboard diving is the rigidity of the takeoff surface of the platform. No potential energy of deformation of the surface is available to help the platform diver to attain height in the dive. Many of the complex dives that can be performed from a high platform can be accomplished from a low springboard but not a low platform. The most complex require a high springboard or a very high platform.

Basic principles of mechanics are useful in simplifying the analysis of even the most complex of dives. A sound understanding of these principles should prove helpful in developing progressions of dives and in examining faults in diving techniques. The sources listed at the end of this chapter provide elaboration of the application of mechanical principles to diving.

REFERENCES

1. Wetmore, R. C.: Teaching Aquatic Survival. *Journal of Health, Physical Education and Recreation.* 43:77–78, 1972.
2. Whittemore. L. H.: Drownproofing: How to Stay Out of Trouble in the Water. *Parade.* San Diego Union, July 17, 1977, pp. 16, 20.
3. Heusner, W. W.: Mechanics and Its Relationship to Kinesiology. Paper presented in Kinesiology Section, A.A.H.P.E.R. Convention, Dallas, March 20, 1965.
4. Clarys, J. P., and Jiskoot, J.: Total Resistance of Selected Body Positions in the Front Crawl. In Lewillie, L. and Clarys, J. P. (eds.): *Swimming II.* (International Series on Sport Sciences, Vol. 2), Baltimore, University Park Press, 1975, pp. 110–117.
5. *Ibid.*, p. 111.
6. Counsilman, J.: Forces in Swimming Two Types of Crawl Strokes. *Research Quarterly,* 26:127–139, 1955.
7. Clarys and Jiskoot., *loc. cit.*
8. Bowen, W. P. and Stone, H. A.: *Applied Anatomy and Kinesiology.* 7th ed. Philadelphia, Lea & Febiger, 1953, p. 418.
9. Karpovich, P. V. and Sinning, Wayne E.: *Physiology of Muscular Activity.* 7th ed. Philadelphia, W. B. Saunders Company, 1971, p. 117.
10. Karpovich, P. V.: Water Resistance in Swimming. *Research Quarterly,* 4:3:26, October, 1933.
11. Wells, K. F. and Luttgens, K.: *Kinesiology.* 6th ed. Philadelphia, W. B. Saunders Company, 1976, p. 128.
12. Counsilman, J.: The Role of Sculling Movements in the Arm Pull. *Swimming World,* 10:12:6–7, 43, December, 1969.
13. *Ibid.*, p. 17.
14. *Ibid.*
15. Barthels, K.M.: Three Dimensional Kinematic Analysis of the Hand and Hip in the Butterfly Swimming Stroke. Unpublished Doctoral Dissertation, Pullman, Washington State University, 1974.
16. Brown, R. M., and Counsilman, J.: The Role of Lift in Propelling the Swimmer. In Cooper, J. M. (ed.): *Biomechanics,* Proceedings of the C. I. C. Symposium on Biomechanics, Chicago, The Athletic Institute, 1971, pp. 179–188.
17. Miller, D. I.: Biomechanics of Swimming. In Wilmore, J. H. and Keogh, J. F. (eds.): *Exercise and Sport Sciences Reviews.* Vol. 3, New York, Academic Press, 1975, pp. 219–248.
18. Scheuchenzuber, H. J., Jr.: Kinetic and Kinematic Characteristics in the Performance of Tethered and Non-Tethered Swimming of the Front Crawl Stroke. *Dissertation Abstracts International 6498-A,* 1975.
19. Schleihauf, R. E.: A Biomechanical Analysis of Freestyle. *Swimming World,* 15:89–96, 1974.

20. Karpovich and Sinning: *op. cit., p. 108.*
21. MacDonald, F. W., and Stearns, W. J.: A Mathematical Analysis of the Dolphin-Butterfly and Breast Strokes. Master's Thesis, Springfield College.
22. East, D. J.: Swimming: An Analysis of Stroke Frequency, Stroke Length and Performance. *New Zealand Jounral of Health, Physical Education and Recreation,* 3:16–27, November, 1970.
23. *Ibid.,* pp. 22–23. (Reported in Hay, J. G.: *The Biomechanics of Sports Techniques.* Englewood Cliffs, New Jersey, Prentice-Hall, Inc., 1973, p. 361)
24. Craig, A: Reported by Nelson, R. C. and Pike, N. L.: Analysis and Comparison of Swimming Starts and Strokes. Paper presented at the 4th International Congress on Swimming Medicine, Stockholm, Sweden, June 10, 1977.
25. Counsilman, J.: *The Science of Swimming.* Englewood Cliffs, New Jersey, Prentice-Hall, Inc., 1968, pp. 133–142.
26. Maglischo, C. W., and Maglischo, E.: Comparison of Three Racing Starts Used in Competitive Swimming. *Research Quarterly,* 39:604–609, 1968.
27. Ayalon, A., Van Gheluwe, B. and Konitz, M.: A Comparison of Four Styles of Racing Start in Swimming. In Clarys, J. P. and Lewillie, L. (eds.): *Swimming II* (International Series of Sport Sciences, Vol. 2), Baltimore, University Park Press, 1975, pp. 233–240.
28. Bowers, J. E., and Cavanagh, P. R.: A Biomechanical Comparison of the Grab and Conventional Sprint Starts in Competitive Swimming. In Clarys, J. P. and Lewillie, L. (eds.): *Swimming II.* (International Series on Sport Sciences, Vol. 2), Baltimore, University Park Press, 1975, pp. 225–232.
29. Cavanagh, P. R., Palmgren, J. V. and Kerr, B. R.: A Device to Measure Forces at the Hands during the Grab Start. In Clarys, J. P. and Lewillie, L. (eds.): *Swimming II.* (International Series on Sport Sciences, Vol. 2), Baltimore, University Park Press, 1975, pp. 43–50.
30. Hanauer, E. S.: The Grab Start. *Swimming World,* 8:5, 42, 1967.
31. Hanauer, E. S.: Grab Start Faster than Conventional Start. *Swimming World,* 13:8–9, 54–55, 1972.
32. Roffer, B. J.: A Comparison of the Grab and Conventional Racing Starts in Swimming. Unpublished Master's Thesis, The Pennsylvania State University, 1971.
33. Cavanagh. P. R., *et al., loc. cit.*
34. Groves, R., and Roberts, J. A.: A Further Investigation of the Optimum Angle of Projection for the Racing Start in Swimming. *Research Quarterly,* 43:167–174, 1972.
35. Counsilman, J., *The Science of Swimming op. cit.,* p. 140.
36. Armbruster, D. A., Allen, R. H. and Billingsley, H. S.: *Swimming and Diving.* 6th ed. St. Louis, C. V. Mosby, 1973.
37. Batterman, C.: *The Techniques of Springboard Diving.* Cambridge, Massachusetts, The M.I.T. Press, 1968, pp. 3–6.

ADDITIONAL READING

Armbruster, D. A., Allen, R. H. and Billingsley, H. S.: *Swimming and Diving.* 6th ed. St. Louis, C. V. Mosby, 1973.
Batterman, C.: *The Techniques for Springboard Diving.* Cambridge, Massachusetts, The M.I.T. Press, 1968.
Counsilman, J.: *The Science of Swimming.* Englewood Cliffs, New Jersey, Prentice-Hall, Inc., 1968.
Hay, J. G.: *The Biomechanics of Sports Techniques.* Englewood Cliffs, New Jersey, Prentice-Hall, Inc., 1973. (Chapter 15 — Swimming)
Hay, J. G.: *A Bibliography of Biomechanics Literature.* 3rd ed. Iowa City, University of Iowa, 1976. Swimming — Section T34 (252 references): Diving — Section T12 (42 references)
Miller, D. I.: Biomechanics of Swimming. In Wilmore, J. H. and Keogh, J. F. (eds.): *Exercise and Sport Sciences Reviews.* Vol. 3, New York, Academic Press, 1975, pp. 219–248. (113 references)

GYMNASTICS

26

In recent years, the featuring by the world's mass media of the sport of gymnastics in Olympic competition and other international meets has highlighted both the beauty and grace as well as the strength and power associated with skilled gymnastic performance. This widespread exposure coupled with the discovery by many of the enjoyment and challenge of gymnastic participation has kindled much new interest in this sport.

The demands on, and rewards for, the performer of gymnastics are somewhat different and more varied than those of most other sports. The projection of the body required in the gymnastic mounts and dismounts, side horse and trampoline performance and floor exercises is also important in other sports such as diving, some track and field events and even basketball and volleyball; angular motion of the body while free of support during performance on the bars, trampoline and in floor exercises constitutes a major challenge in diving. However, the effective use of gravity and inertia in the angular motion of the body required by bars and flying rings, the degree of the balance demands of the beam, still rings and bars are all considerably greater in gymnastics than in other sports. While highly skilled performance demands a high level of balance, strength, control and understanding of the application of mechanical principles, even young children can profit from participation in the elementary techniques by gaining valuable experience in exploring problems and principles of balance, force production and body rotation.

A complete mechanical analysis of each of the gymnastic activities would yield sufficient information to constitute a book. This chapter, therefore, presents only **selected examples** of applications of basic mechanical principles to tumbling and floor exercise, the vault, uneven bars and parallel bars. The bibliography at the end of the chapter cites numerous additional sources for information.

TUMBLING AND FLOOR EXERCISE

Some balance stunts involve only one individual (e.g., handstand) while others may require several (e.g., pyramids). A firm grounding in the essentials of center of gravity and equilibrium (Chapter 3) greatly facilitates the learning of any of these balance activities; the difficulty of balance tasks is related to their mechanical demands. A knowledge of basic mechanical principles can help in the development of a logical sequence for skill learning and assist in the diagnosis of performance faults. Some stunts are difficult because of the small base required (e.g., any activity on a balance beam), and others because of a high center of gravity (e.g., handstand).

Balance Stunts.   The **head stand** is an excellent example for the application of the principles of equilibrium and affords experience in the problems associated with an inverted position of the body: the effects on the semicircular canals, blood flow, labyrinthine reflexes. The hands and head form a tripod base of sufficient size to allow some sway of the trunk and lower extremities in any direction without the line of gravity of the body falling outside its perimeter. If the hands are placed in line with the head, the base is wide from side-to-side but is narrow forward-backward, the direction of flexion or extension of the vertebral column, hips or knees. Thus any movement of trunk or lower extremities causes instability in the head stand when the hands are positioned to the sides of the head. A triangle formed by the head and hands widens the base in both the lateral and forward-backward directions, and thus provides greater stability.

When the center of gravity is approximately centered above this tripod, the hands are in an excellent position to apply force diagonally upward and backward should the legs begin to fall forward. If the center of gravity should sway backward and approach a point above the back edge of the base, it is more difficult to re-adjust it toward the center since the head and neck do not have the leverage for the production of forward force that the hands do for backward force. Therefore, it may be wise to keep slightly more weight on the hands than on the head. This means that the center of gravity is very slightly forward of the center of the base and more sway can be anticipated forward than backward.

Two methods are commonly used to raise the lower extremities to the position above the head, (1) forcefully kicking them upward, and (2) drawing the knees into the chest and **then** extending the legs upward. A third but

Figure 26–1. Momentum of kick-up tends to carry center of gravity beyond base.

much more difficult technique involves raising the lower extremities from a piked position. This is difficult both because of the strength required to lift the long lever and the necessity to balance the weight of the legs that are forward of the base by movement of the hips backward, and to adjust the hip position as the leg position shifts toward the vertical.

The first common method, often attempted by beginners, uses a push off by the foot and a forceful extension of the hips to provide the momentum to carry the limbs to a vertical position. A frequent problem lies in stopping the momentum when the legs reach the position above the center of the base (Fig. 26–1). The long leg levers have a relatively high angular momentum (moment of inertia times angular velocity) which tends to carry them on beyond the base. Since this momentum is in the backward direction, the head and neck with their relatively ineffectual leverage are called upon to resist it. It is difficult to judge the exact amount of force necessary to produce enough momentum to carry the legs up into position but which will be neutralized by gravity by the time the limbs and trunk reach the point above the center of the base. When the knees are brought in to the chest and the lower extremities are then extended upward, the weight is centered above the base with the center of gravity low and it remains over the base as the center of gravity moves upward with the leg extension. Essentially no momentum other than that directed straight upward is involved (Fig. 26–2). Greater abdominal and erector spinae muscle strength is required at the beginning of this second technique but the problem of keeping the center of gravity over the base is minimized and thus success is much more likely. Most overbalancing tendencies during this movement are in a forward direction since the legs are in front of the body, and the hands and arms of the performer are in a good position for control. Sometimes a beginner tends to straighten the hip joints and lower back before starting to extend the knees. This places the lower legs well back of the base and overbalances the performer backward (Fig. 26–3). It is important that all joints of the hips and legs be extended simultaneously so that all parts of the legs are kept over the base as they move upward.

Just as it is possible to balance a forward hip thrust in standing by a

Figure 26–2. Head stand from tuck—center of gravity over base throughout.

Figure 26–3. Over balanced—hips extended before knees.

backward lean of the upper body, the person standing on his head can keep the center of gravity of the body over the base in an arched position. The diagonally forward body is balanced by diagonally backward lower extremities. Because the various body segments are not balanced one above the other, additional effort is needed to maintain this position. Strain of the lower back is caused in the same way as when standing with the hips forward and the shoulders back. The lumbar vertebrae and intervertebral disks may be stressed excessively. Because a more exaggerated position is frequently assumed in the head stand, the strain is even greater than in standing. While the arched head stand may be desired for the sake of line in a given event, the most **efficient** position is that in which the various body segments are aligned just as they are in standing (Chapter 10).

The base of support for the **front scale** is one foot regardless of whether the stunt is performed on the balance beam or the floor; however, on the beam the foot must be placed carefully to take full advantage of the width available and, if the foot is wider than the beam, the base of support is narrower than when on the floor. There is little margin for any sideways displacement of the center of gravity; the base is only four inches wide. In addition, the psychological effect of knowing that there is no base beyond the edge of the beam is a factor for many individuals. Maintaining the line of gravity within the **width** of the base is a greater challenge than keeping it within the base's **length;** the foot is longer than it is wide and the forward-downward motion of the trunk and one arm is counteracted by the backward movement of the free leg, the hips and the other arm to keep the center of gravity of the body over the supporting foot.

The hips must be thrust backward farther in the **straddle stand** on the balance beam because both arms as well as the trunk are forward and a leg is not available as a counter-balancing mass since both feet support the body. The side stride position of the feet gives a wide base sideways (the feet and the area between them) and thus balance sideways is not the problem that it is in the front scale; however, the base is smaller in the forward-backward direction since the body faces sideways to the beam and the beam is not as wide as the foot length.

Rotary Activities. In some rotary stunts the body simply rotates around an axis passing through the center of gravity of the body. Somersaults and twists executed while the body is free of support are examples of this type of stunt. In others, such as the forward roll and cartwheel, the body rotates around a point of support at the same time it is rotating around a moving axis that passes through its center of gravity. The principles of angular motion that are discussed in Chapter 4 are particularly applicable.

Speed of movement of the body is dependent upon the force produced and the direction of its application. In angular motion the radius of rotation is an additional factor because it affects the moment of inertia. During free flight, the angular velocity of a body increases as its moment of inertia decreases; this decreases as the radius of rotation is shortened (Chapter 4). Thus a given angular momentum results in faster rotation of the body when in a tuck than in a lay-out position. Because the moment of inertia is so much larger, resistance to angular motion is greater for the body in an extended than in a tuck position. Therefore, to achieve the same level of angular velocity, a larger force must be applied to the extended body than to a body in a tucked position.

The **forward roll,** one of the basic tumbling stunts (Fig. 26–4), can be executed on a mat or on the balance beam. This stunt involves rotation around a constantly shifting point of contact with the floor at the same time that the body rotates around its own center of gravity. The beginner may start the forward roll in a squat position. Since the object of the stunt is to roll forward, he pushes with his feet and legs backward and downward against the floor to displace his center of gravity forward and somewhat upward until it passes beyond the forward edge of his base (his toes). This is more easily accomplished if the base is narrow in the forward-backward direction. Therefore, the toes should be in line. This position also makes it possible to apply force evenly to both sides of the body and reduces the possibility of an off-center application of force that would cause a roll to be at an angle rather than straight forward. An angled force application would be particularly disastrous when performing a forward roll on the balance beam.

As the center of gravity passes over the forward edge of the base of support, the force of gravity is added to the force produced by the legs and the body is pulled downward. Because the body is well rounded (tucked), it rolls forward. As long as the body is kept in the tucked position, the moment of inertia (about an axis passing laterally through the body) is relatively low and, therefore, resistance to rolling forward is relatively small; the principal force retarding the body's forward motion is friction. Grasping the lower legs is one method of resisting the tendency of centrifugal force to extend the body during a fast roll (Fig. 26–5). When the performer has rolled to the point where the feet are on the mat, extension of the body greatly lengthens the radius of rotation (increases moment of inertia) and slows the angular velocity, making it possible to stop the center of gravity above the feet and regain a standing position (Figs. 26–4 and 26–6).

As the performer becomes more skilled and begins his roll on a mat from a stand or a run, the rotary force becomes greater and the speed of the roll increases. The sudden increase in the moment of inertia by extension of the

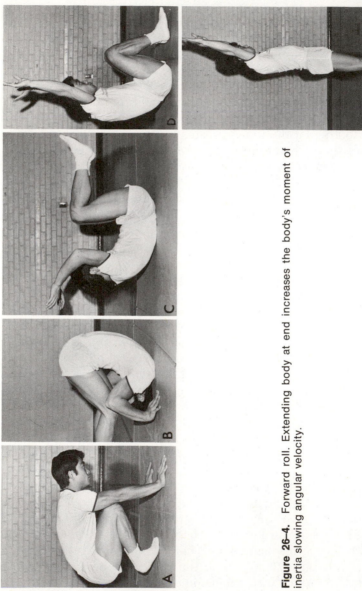

Figure 26-4. Forward roll. Extending body at end increases the body's moment of inertia slowing angular velocity.

Figure 26–5. Forward roll. Legs grasped to resist centrifugal force.

body at the end of the roll may not slow the momentum sufficiently to allow the performer to maintain his balance. The momentum can be stopped gradually either by running forward a few steps or by converting the forward momentum to upward momentum by a jump, and by absorbing the downward force by allowing the ankles, knees and hips to flex as the feet return to the mat. Because of the small base involved a roll on the beam must be slower and more controlled; the performer may contract trunk flexors to maintain the tucked position while abducting the arms directly out to the sides during the roll. When the arms are stretched out to the sides, the greater moment of inertia of the body about the axis running from head to toe increases the resistance to angular motion off either side of the beam. Therefore, abducting the arms during a forward roll on the beam gives the gymnast more lateral stability.

At the beginning of the roll on the mat, after the center of gravity has passed beyond the feet, the weight is taken momentarily by the hands and sufficient upward force is exerted by the arms to hold the body high enough to allow the head to clear the mat and gradually lower the shoulders. The literature indicates a difference of opinion as to the most effective position for the hands for a roll on the mat. Some authors suggest that the hands be placed on the mat with the fingers pointing toward each other (hands sideways), since this position reduces the resistance to forward movement caused by the fingers when facing forward. Others feel that the hands are important in adding force to that applied by the lower extremities and the effect of gravity to give greater angular force to the body and, therefore, the hands should be placed on the mat with the fingers pointing ahead so that they are in a position to apply downward and backward force to help send the body upward and forward. Since most girls and women do not have great strength in the arm and shoulder girdle muscles, it is advisable for them to place their hands in the most effective position for applying force so they are able to support the body weight long enough to allow the head to clear the mat and to control the lowering of the shoulders to the mat.

In the **backward roll,** as in the forward roll, the body must be placed in an unstable position so that gravity can act to cause rotation around the feet. In this case the center of gravity must be moved back of the base. This is done by flexing the knees and hips. Gravity pulls the body downward and

Figure 26–6. Backward roll. Extending body slows momentum.

backward and if the body is well tucked the torque (angular force from gravity) develops the momentum that causes it to roll. Bunn[1] stated that some straightening of the body and drawing in of the lower extremities as the buttocks become the base put the center of gravity back of the hips causing an additional torque to increase rolling momentum. The tucking of the body not only curves the body so that it will roll but also shortens the radius of rotation and increases the angular velocity. As in the forward roll, the body rotates around two axes, its own center of gravity and an ever-changing point of contact with the mat (Fig. 26–6). The buttocks, various points along the back and finally the hands are successive axes for the rotation around the point of contact with the supporting surface. After the center of gravity of the body has moved forward of the hands, any force exerted by the arms is applied upward and in the direction of movement. Thus it is effective both in lifting the body to allow space between the mat and shoulders for the head and in adding to the angular momentum. Again the angular velocity is rapidly decreased by extending the body, thus lengthening the radius of rotation and increasing the moment of inertia.

When the performer wishes to go into a **head stand from a backward roll,** the body extends so that the momentum is decreased as the hips approach the position above the head. The hands must be shifted as far as possible forward of the head to widen the base in the direction of the moving force and to place them in position to apply force diagonally backward and upward to stop the forward momentum of the body.

The **forward tuck somersault** is essentially a forward roll completed in the air, free of support. The body rotates around its own center of gravity. In all stunts that involve rotation of the body around its center of gravity when the body is free of support, the principles of projection must be applied. Time is important because gravity is constantly pulling the body downward. The time available to the performer for the execution of the stunt depends upon the height of projection which, in turn, depends upon the force and angle of projection. The higher the body is projected the more time that is available to complete the rotations in the air. Greater height is possible when jumping from a trampoline than from the floor because of the release of potential energy involved in the deformation of the bed of the trampoline.

Once the body is free of support, change in the position of the extremities and the head can cause the body to revolve or twist around its center of gravity but cannot change the path of the center of gravity through the air. The center of gravity follows the same path as that of any other projectile of equal mass projected with an equal velocity and at an identical angle. Force applied by the body is effective for its own movement through space only when it can be applied against a surface which then exerts an opposite force against the body, causing it to move. It is important that the gymnast land in the center of the trampoline bed so that the forces from the bed will be equal in all directions.

In all rotary events the body must be in an unstable position at takeoff. If the center of gravity is directly above the base at takeoff, no angular momentum is imparted to the body. Thus the principles of stability are applied in reverse. The loss of stability is used to advantage; that is, the body is placed in such a position that the force of gravity is effective in aiding the rotation and, if the takeoff force is not applied directly through the performer's center of gravity, rotation of the body results during flight.

Although a gymnast cannot increase the amount of angular momentum once he or she is in the air, he can change his **speed** of rotation (angular velocity) by shortening or lengthening his radius of rotation, effectively changing the moment of inertia. Because the moment of inertia is less in the tuck position than when extended, the body rotates faster and it is possible for the performer to complete the turn with less height, or complete more turns with a given height, in the tuck than in the layout position. Also, the torque necessary to cause rotation of the body in the tuck position is less. Heidloff[2] pointed out that centrifugal force (Chapter 4) is involved in all rotary motion and this force tends to cause the body to straighten out from the tucked position. The force produced by the flexor muscles must balance the tendency for the lower extremities to straighten (centrifugal force) if the body is to remain tucked, to keep the moment of inertia at the lowest possible level. The arms holding the flexed legs close to the body overcome the tendency for the body to straighten caused by centrifugal force and thus prevent the lengthening of the radius of rotation and the increasing of the moment of inertia.[2] The forward rotation is slowed or stopped at the completion of the turn by releasing the legs and extending the body, thus greatly increasing the moment of inertia.

The acceleration caused by gravity and the increase of angular velocity with the shortening of the radius of rotation (decreasing the moment of inertia) are used to advantage in many events (See discussion of Bars).

VAULTS

The **vault,** performed over a horse, consists of a run-up, hurdle step, takeoff, preflight (flight to the horse), support, flight (flight off the horse) and landing. During the run-up phase, the performer develops relatively high horizontal velocity and linear momentum. In the hurdle step, which in many ways is similar to the hurdle step of springboard diving, some of the horizontal momentum is converted into vertical momentum. Vaulters gain additional height in their approach flight to the horse by using a Reuther board.

Kreighbaum[3] investigated the effect of use of the board by eight women and found that the positions of their centers of gravity were definitely affected by the potential energy (energy of deformation) of the Reuther board; their angles of rebound were changed, resulting in conversion of more horizontal momentum to vertical momentum and increase of their takeoff velocities by approximately two and one half feet per second over their contact speeds. Kreighbaum reported the following mean values: angle of contact, 64 degrees; contact speed, 20.12 feet per second; contact time, 0.114 second; takeoff angle, 96 degrees; takeoff velocity, 22.61 feet per second; difference between contact speed and takeoff speed, 2.52 feet per second.[3]

The well-timed deceleration of the upper extremities assists in the transfer of momentum to the rest of the body segments. There is a brief flight phase as the body prepares to contact the board; consistent with any parabolic flight, the gymnast's vertical velocity is zero and potential energy (energy of position) is maximum at the peak of the hurdle. The potential energy is converted into kinetic energy (energy of motion) as his velocity constantly accelerates until the moment of contact. During early contact with the board the gymnast is in a transitional state — from primarily horizontal velocity to a decreased total velocity with a dramatically increased vertical component.[4, 5]

As in any projectile motion, the characteristics of pre-flight are determined by the velocity and angle of projection; in addition, in vaulting, the direction and magnitude of angular momentum imparted to the body is set at the time of takeoff. The farther behind the person's center of gravity the reaction force is directed at takeoff, the greater is the forward angular momentum of the body. The same magnitude of force applied to the board (same reaction force from the board against the gymnast) applied with the body inclined at different angles results in considerably different angular momentum of the body. Angle and velocity of takeoff determine the curvilinear parabolic path of the center of gravity of the gymnast, but angular momentum dictates the amount of rotational tendency that the gymnast must control during flight.

As the vaulter contacts the horse, he again has a chance to influence the flight characteristics of his body. The direction and magnitude of the angular momentum are frequently changed during contact with the horse. For example, in a **straddle vault** (Fig. 26–7), forward rotation of the body occurs during the preflight (Fig. 26–7, 1 and 2) and backward rotation occurs during the flight phase (Fig. 26–7, 3 through 6). As the gymnast approaches the horse, he rotates forward to contact the far end of the horse with his hands. A strong extension of the upper extremities downward and backward applies force through the shoulders causing an off-center force that reverses the angular momentum of the body, so that the body rotates backwards. As the body starts to come to a vertical position, the gymnast straddles the horse with his feet above the level of the horse.[6] The performer helps to stabilize

Figure 26–7. Straddle vault. Positions 1 to 2 are the preflight phase and posiions 3 to 6 are the flight phase. (Adapted from Hay,[6] p. 308.)

his flight by abducting his arms directly to his side (90° abduction) to increase his moment of inertia (resistance to angular rotation) about the forward-backward axis through his body. Even if the push-off from the horse is slightly asymmetrical, this increase in angular resistance to rotation effectively eliminates the undesirable tilting that might otherwise result.

Upon landing from the vault the gymnast must apply a force to cause his body to rotate in the direction opposite to that in which his angular momentum is taking him. The friction between the gymnast's feet and the mat applies a force to counter the backward rotation of the body during mat–foot contact. If the forces are not controlled correctly, he is pitched forward and needs to take steps that, although they serve to dissipate his linear and angular momentum, are detrimental to an otherwise good performance. As in any landing, the performer is able to dissipate some of the energy of landing with the controlled flexion of the lower extremities (lengthening contractions of hip, knee and ankle extensors).

BARS

The **parallel** and **uneven bars** are events in which a certain amount of deformation energy is used by the performer to assist in executing some maneuvers. Lascari[7] performed a comparative analysis between the late- and the early-drop styles of a "felge" (from a somersault) to a handstand (Fig. 26–8) on the parallel bars. In terms of performance, Lascari observed that, with the late-drop style, the gymnast finished the maneuver in a handstand with elbows flexed, requiring a press to a fully extended handstand. An early-drop by the same performer resulted in a fully extended handstand at the conclusion of the move. His subsequent kinetic analysis revealed that the peak vertical force toward the bottom of the early-drop was 650 pounds compared with 480 pounds for the late-drop. (The gymnast's weight was approximately 133 lbs.) Besides the tremendous grip strength needed by the gymnast at the bottom of **both** styles, one could assume that effective deformation of the bars was significantly greater in the early-drop as compared with the late-drop. The potential energy (energy of deformation) from the bars was converted into the energy of motion (upward) and, when coordinated with the movements of the skilled gymnast, resulted in a greater useful vertical impulse available for the uprise portion of the skill. The increased vertical impulse available in the early drop was directly related to the gymnast's ability to rise to a level where the fully extended handstand was possible (Compare the final positions in Fig. 26–8, A and B).

The grace of a skilled gymnast performing a routine on the uneven bars belies the complexity of the event. The performer must effectively and efficiently travel from the top to the lower bar throughout the routine. As with the parallel bars, the unevens are deformable to some extent. In giant swings from the upper to the lower bar, the gymnast frequently applies a force that deforms the bar and subsequently converts that energy of deformation to kinetic energy of the body.

The acceleration caused by gravity and the increase of angular velocity with the shortening of the radius of rotation (decreasing of moment of

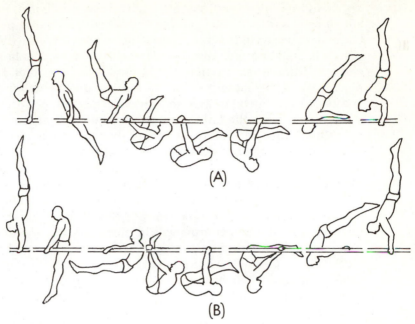

Figure 26–8. Felge handstands. The late style is shown in (A) and the early drop style is depicted in (B). There is 0.156 second between each position, for both styles shown. (Adapted from Lascari.[7])

inertia) are used to advantage in many events in which rotation around a bar is involved (particularly the horizontal bar for men and uneven parallel bars for women). Extension of the body as high as possible results in the development of maximum speed at the end of the long lever as gravity pulls the body downward. Piking at the hips shortens the radius of rotation, decreases the moment of inertia and increases angular velocity as the body moves upward against gravity.

IMPORTANCE OF BODY BUILD

At the same time mechanical principles are emphasized, it is necessary to remember that the system being analyzed, the human body, is both biological and mechanical in nature. Two examples may help to impress the importance of knowing something about both aspects of the performer.

Because the distribution of mass about a rotating body is so important to the resistance of the body to angular motion, the varying lengths of body segments would seem to be a factor to be considered. The Japanese have been consistently successful in international gymnastics competition; in 1972, five of the top eight male gymnasts in the world were Japanese. Hirata[9] reported that the gymnasts were among the smallest and shortest athletes at the Olympic games in Tokyo. LeVeau and associates[10] have also reported that Japanese male gymnasts, compared with American male gymnasts, have shorter tibias, forearms and feet. Yet the weights of the two groups are similar.

In events involving rotation, such as the side horse, parallel and horizontal bars, and still rings, an individual with a greater proportion of total body mass closer to the axis of rotation rotates more easily; the moment of inertia is less, and thus resistance to angular motion is less. The structural characteristics of the gymnast may have an important influence on the mechanics of the activity. If two gymnasts, one of whom is six feet, seven inches tall and the other five feet, seven inches tall, perform giant swings on the horizontal bar the taller one gains greater momentum as he drops because the radius of rotation is longer, but for the same reason he will be slowed more as the body rises. When a taller person attempts an iron cross on the still rings, he has to counteract a greater torque at his shoulder joints than does a shorter gymnast of equal weight; because the taller gymnast has longer arms, the distance between hands and shoulder joints is longer. Since torque is the product of force times the perpendicular distance, for equal body weights the longer arms would mean greater torques.

The skeletal structure of a person is also important when analyzing performance. Certain techniques may be the result of an effective interrelationship of biological structure and mechanical function. One example can be seen in the shoulder movements in preparation for an iron cross on the rings. The torques that must be developed at the shoulder become increasingly larger as the gymnast allows gravity to abduct his arms to 90 degrees. The torques at each shoulder are related to one-half the person's body weight and the length of the upper extremity; the heavier the gymnast and the longer his arms, the more difficult the task. Besides contracting strongly the adductors of the humerus, the gymnast may also inwardly rotate the humerus at the glenohumeral joint, to bring the greater tubercle of the proximal end of the humerus into a position of contact with the scapula much sooner than if the humerus were outwardly rotated. This can be felt by first abducting the arm while outwardly rotated and then abducting it while it is inwardly rotated. The gymnast adjusts his movements to take advantage of anatomical factors in the pursuit of mechanically efficient motion. A complete analysis of a movement should include explanation of both the internal and external mechanical effects.

NOTE

The principles of center of gravity and equilibrium (Chapter 3), motion (Chapter 4), leverage (Chapter 5), force (Chapter 6) and projection (Chapter 9) are all applicable to various gymnastic events. As indicated earlier, the preceding discussion offers only a few examples of possible applications of these mechanical principles to a few selected events.

REFERENCES

1. Bunn, J. W.: *Scientific Principles of Coaching.* Englewood Cliffs, New Jersey, Prentice-Hall, Inc., 1955, p. 201.
2. Heidloff, R. C.: A Logical Application of Physics to Selected Tumbling Stunts. Unpublished Master's Thesis, Springfield College, 1938, p. 69.
3. Keighbaum, E.: The Mechanics of the Use of the Reuther Board during Side Horse Vaulting.

In Nelson, R. C. and Morehouse, C. A. (eds): *Biomechanics IV*. (International Series on Sport Sciences, Vol. 1) Baltimore, University Park Press, 1974, pp. 137–143.
4. *Ibid.*, p. 140.
5. Gombos, E. A.: Gym Forum. *Modern Gymnast*, 4(7):23–25, 1962.
6. Hay, J. G.: *The Biomechanics of Sports Techniques*. Englewood Cliffs, New Jersey, Prentice-Hall, Inc., 1973, pp. 307–309.
7. Lascari, A. T.: The Felge Handstand — A Comparative Kinetic Analysis of a Gymnastics Skill. Unpublished Doctoral Dissertation, University of Wisconsin, Madison, 1970.
8. LeVeau, B. F., Ward, T. and Nelson, R. C.: Body Dimensions of Japanese and American Gymnasts. *Medicine and Science in Sports*, 6:146–150, 1974.
9. Hirata, K.: Physique and Age of Tokyo Olympic Champions. *The Journal of Sports Medicine and Physical Fitness*, 6:207–222, 1966.
10. LeVeau, B. F., *et. al.*: *loc. cit.*

ADDITIONAL READING

Hay, J. G.: *The Biomechanics of Sports Techniques*. Englewood Cliffs, New Jersey, Prentice-Hall, Inc., 1973, pp. 288–328 (Chapter 12)
Hay, J. G.: *A Bibliography of Biomechanics Literature*. 3rd ed. Iowa City, University of Iowa, 1976. (Gymnastics — Section T17, 167 references)

27

OTHER ACTIVITIES

Space does not permit discussion of every activity in the same degree of detail. However, some attention to other common activities may spark some thinking about the force problems involved. This chapter, therefore, treats briefly only a very few of the possible applications of mechanical principles to several activities of varying types.

ARCHERY

Archery is essentially a pulling activity as far as the force produced by the archer is concerned. The archer applies force which bends the bow; thus the bow is given potential energy, energy of deformation, which, in turn, is applied to the arrow when the force causing the bow's unnatural position is released. When the archer draws his bow, the force of his pull must exceed the sum of the two forces caused by the resistance of the two ends of the bow to being bent and, at full draw, as he holds, it must equal the sum of these two forces (Fig. 27–1).

The task of stringing the bow involves forcing it into a greater bend than is normal. This can be accomplished easily by using the two hands to produce a leverage action on the bow. The axis of the lever is the point of contact of the bow with the inside of the archer's foot. One hand grasps the bow handle to apply force to pull the center of the bow outward at the same time the other hand pushes the far end downward. These two forces acting together bend the bow and make it possible to slip the string into the nock at the end of the bow.

The position of the archer with the side toward the target makes possible the longest draw of the string in a straight line. With the head turned toward the target, the tonic neck reflex enhances the steadiness of the extended arm.[1] A stance with the feet farther apart than the width of the hips places the body in an effective position for applying sideways force since the force of the foot against the ground has an outward component. Because in drawing and releasing the bow, the forces against the body are exerted in a side-to-side direction, a square sideways stance has long been considered to be the most effective. In this position the body can be held steady during the draw and release since the right foot can exert diagonal force toward the left, and the left leg can exert force to the right.

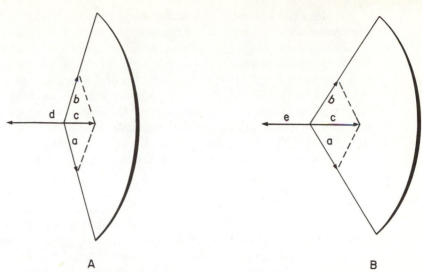

Figure 27–1. Force of draw (d) must exceed c (sum of forces from bow—a and b). To hold at full draw, force (e) must equal c.

More recently, many experts have contended that an oblique stance (open) has several advantages over the square stance. The trunk rotation required to achieve the full draw position brings the muscles of the back and trunk actively into the draw and increases the distance between bowstring and the bow arm.[2] The stance (Fig. 27–2) results in a larger base front to back (horizontal to target) and thus it is relatively easy to keep the center of gravity over the base as the body rotates during the draw. "The oblique stance does theoretically demonstrate a larger base in the direction of forward-backward postural sway."[3]

The speed with which the arrow leaves the bow depends upon the weight of the bow, its natural elasticity, its construction, the length of the draw and the sharpness of release. Woods[4] likened a **live release** to the kick of a firing gun. As the string is freed and thrusts forward, the drawing arm moves backward while the hand slides across the face and down the neck. She stated that in the release which **holds the anchor point**, "dead release", "the archer employs additional effort to counteract the natural consequence of action and reaction."[5]

Figure 27–2. Comparison of *square stance (upper figure)* and *oblique stance (lower figure)* in archery. a, Target line; b, direction of the force of the draw; c, direction of the force of bow resistance; d, direction of forward-backward postural sway. Figure adapted from Woods, Marcella D.: Archery, in *Individual Sports for Women,* Broer, Marion R. (ed.), Philadelphia, W. B. Saunders Company, 1971, Figure 2–8, p. 38.

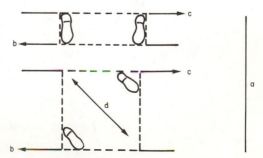

Unless the bow and arrow are angled upward considerably, the tip of the arrow is below the level of the eye. Therefore, as the eye sights over the tip a downward angle is involved. At short range the angle of projection for the arrow must be small (Chapter 9) and, therefore, the tip is well below the eye. Since the line from the eye to the tip of the arrow angles downward, the point of aim is well below the spot toward which the arrow actually points. As the flight of the arrow is lengthened the angle of projection must become greater (the arrow must be angled upward) and the tip comes up more in line with the eye. This means that, as the distance increases, the downward angle of the line from the eye to the arrow tip decreases and, therefore, the point of aim must be raised.

Any change in the position of the archer's head changes the angle at which he sights the arrow and thus affects its direction.

Wilson[6] has suggested that the aim be taken **before** the bow is drawn. He stresses that, after the archer establishes his bow hold and finger position on the string with the arms down, he raises his head and looks directly at the gold. He **then** raises the bow and, **before drawing**, shifts his eyes, keeping the head and shoulders still, to the aiming point and moves the tip of the arrow to this point. **Without moving the head or bow arm**, he shifts his eyes back to the gold and then draws. This method allows the aiming point to be closer to the gold than does aiming at the full draw position because the line of sight over the arrow tip is at a more acute angle, since the tip of the arrow is farther forward of the eyes (Fig. 27–3). The shift of the eyes back to the gold after aiming, but before drawing, is important because as the archer draws, the tip of the arrow will no longer point to his aiming point but will point progressively lower, and, if he looks at the arrow tip and shifts his position to bring the tip up to the original aiming point, the arrow will go high. Because the aiming point is on the target and the archer, after some practice, can keep his eyes on the gold and see his aiming point in his peripheral vision, this technique offers advantages that lead to more consis-

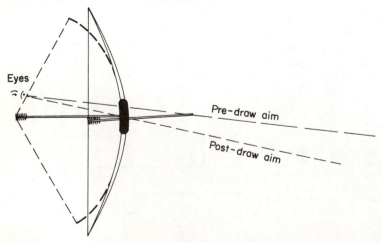

Figure 27–3. Different angles of sight resulting from pre-draw and post-draw aiming.

tent aiming. Wilson suggests using the white on the bottom of the target as the pre-draw (called by him "pre-gap") aiming point at 20 or 30 yards. He does not recommend teaching this method until the student has learned the basic fundamentals of shooting at very close range (maximum 20 feet) at a 36 inch target.

The degree to which eye dominance affects the aim of the arrow is interesting to consider. If an individual has a strongly dominant eye, an arrow drawn to the middle of the chin actually is sighted at a slight left or right angle. It may be that for the individual with a dominant right eye, the anchor point at the right side of the jaw or face is preferable as this gives a straight line from the dominant eye to the tip of the arrow. For the archer with a dominant left eye, this point of aim would cause difficulty in aiming since he would be sighting diagonally to the right over the tip of the arrow. His arrow would, therefore, go to the left. The importance of eye dominance to archery needs further study.

The application of the mechanical principles to the sport of archery is fascinating and a number of books have been written on this subject. The reader who wishes to pursue such study is referred particularly to the book, **Archery, The Technical Side**, by Hickman et al.[7] and to the chapter by Woods in the fifth edition of **Individual Sports for Women**.[8]

CANOEING

The principles of buoyancy, equilibrium, leverage and application of force are all as important in understanding canoeing as they are in understanding swimming. Application of knowledge of swimming can be helpful in learning canoeing and vice versa.

A canoe is buoyed up by a force equal to the weight of the water displaced. A sponson canoe has air chambers running from bow to stern on both sides, giving it maximum stability. These sponsons add considerably to the size of the canoe and, when in contact with the water, displace a great volume in proportion to their weight. Therefore, this type of canoe is very buoyant, particularly at the gunwales. Because of this more force is needed to push the gunwale below the surface of the water and so this type of canoe is less likely to tip over. It has certain disadvantages, however, since the paddler must reach out farther from his body to apply force against the water. As this lengthens the resistance arm, more effort is needed to overcome the resistance of the water. Canoes are made in various sizes and shapes and each is particularly effective for a specific purpose.

Both the canoe and the paddle are levers and all the principles of leverage apply. The canoe is a lever of the first class with its fulcrum at its center of gravity. The center of gravity shifts in relation to the load in the canoe. At any time a force is applied at its side, the canoe rotates around the center of gravity of the canoe plus any additional weight which it carries. The paddle, like the shovel, is a combination of levers. The resistance is offered by the water and thus is always applied against the blade of the paddle. The lower hand is the fulcrum for any force applied by the top hand (first class lever) and the top hand is, at the same time, the fulcrum for the force applied by the lower hand (third class lever). The farther down the lower hand can be placed comfortably on the paddle, the longer its force arm and the more effective the force produced by that hand.

When an individual enters a canoe or puts a pack or other object into a canoe, the center of gravity of the canoe plus the added weight must be considered. If the canoe is to remain in equilibrium, this center of gravity of the total weight must be over the base of support. Since the base of the canoe (the keel plus a few inches on either side) is narrow from port to starboard and long from bow to stern, the canoe lacks stability from side-to-side but is extremely stable from end to end. It is important for the paddler to keep his weight and that of any added load as low as possible to reduce the rotary tendency that results from a high center of gravity. To keep the center of gravity over the base it is necessary to step into a canoe directly over the keel. The canoe must be close to the dock so that the force of the step can be directed straight downward. If the weight of the individual exerts force diagonally outward and downward as he steps into a canoe, the outward force will push the canoe (and foot) farther from the dock and the paddler will be unable to get his center of gravity over this moving base. As a result, he falls into the water between the canoe and the dock.

To reduce the rotary force inherent in a high center of gravity, the paddler should immediately lower his body by kneeling on the bottom of the canoe or by squatting if he has to move toward an end. To make it possible for the individual to exert straight downward force when stepping out of a canoe, the canoe must be broadside close to the dock. The push to move the individual up out of the canoe must be straight downward. If the push is on an angle it will push the canoe away from the dock and the individual will not receive enough counter force to move his center of gravity over the foot on the dock and, again, he may find himself in the water.

To keep the center of gravity as low as possible and still leave the trunk and arms in a position to function in paddling, it is best to kneel in the bottom of the canoe. Sitting on seats raises the center of gravity and makes the canoe much less stable. To keep the center of gravity over the base from port to starboard the paddler must kneel in the center (from side-to-side) of the canoe, keeping his own center of gravity over the keel. Since the base is narrow, any slight shift of his center of gravity can put it beyond the edge of the base. When two paddlers are in a canoe, it is important that both keep their weight centered. Of course, a canoe may be balanced by both paddlers kneeling slightly off-center in opposite directions. Because one has to paddle beyond the side of the canoe there is a temptation to sit toward the paddling side to apply force more easily in the desired direction. Sitting as close to the gunwales as possible does make paddling easier because the force is applied closer to the body and the two paddlers can trim the canoe. **However**, any slight shift of either paddler toward the center of the canoe puts so much weight toward the side on which the other is paddling that the center of gravity of the total (canoe plus the two paddlers), falls beyond the side edge of the base and the canoe tips over.

To keep the center of gravity over the center of the base from bow to stern and thus keep the canoe level in the water, a single paddler must kneel in the center (bow to stern) of the canoe. The center of gravity of the canoe plus the paddler can be shifted forward or aft and still be well within the base, since the base is so large in this direction. However, when a single paddler kneels in the stern the center of gravity falls toward the stern, the weight of that area of the canoe is increased in relation to its size, and the stern moves downward in the water and the bow lifts. As a result, the broader surface of the bottom of the canoe resists forward movements through the water and more bow surface is exposed to any wind. If a cross wind is blowing the effect is magnified. With the center of gravity so far toward the stern, the force arm for the wind force against the side of the bow of the canoe lever is lengthened, increasing the cross wind's effectiveness in causing the canoe's bow to rotate in the direction the wind is blowing. When a single paddler kneels in the center of the canoe (bow to stern) so that his center of gravity is over the center of the canoe, the canoe remains level, the resistance arms are shortened, and he has equal control over both ends of the canoe. This position can be likened to one of standing astride the fulcrum of a teeter-totter so that force can be applied against both ends, either to balance the board or to rotate it around its fulcrum, and also to grasping a long blackboard on wheels as far forward and backward of its center as possible (see Fig. 16–7).

To keep the center of gravity low and over the base while changing positions in a canoe, the body should be lowered by bending the hips and knees, and a portion of the weight should be supported by the right hand on the gunwale as the remainder is taken by the left foot and vice versa. In this way the two forces on either side of the center can be balanced at all times.

Since a canoe presents relatively little surface area to resist the water when traveling forward or backward and a large surface when moving broadside, less force is required to move it forward or backward than directly to the side.

When traveling with a wind or current, both forces (wind and paddler) are acting to push the canoe ahead and the forward momentum is the resultant of the two forces. Less force is needed to maintain a given speed. When traveling into a wind or current, the force of the paddler is in direct conflict with the force of the wind (or current). The direction and speed of the canoe depend upon the relative magnitude of the two forces. If the wind (or current) is stronger than the force applied by the paddler, the canoe moves backward. If the two forces are equal, it stands still. Only if the force produced by the paddler exceeds the force of wind and current does the canoe move forward. When traveling across a current or in a cross wind, force must be exerted by the paddler in opposition (on the downwind side) if a straight course is to be maintained.

Canoeing is a pushing and pulling activity. As in swimming, the canoe moves in the direction opposite to that in which the paddle applies force. Since force must be applied at the side of the canoe (off-center), rotary motion is produced unless counteracted by another force. To produce linear motion (straight course) of the canoe, equal rotary forces must be exerted on opposite sides of the canoe, or balancing rotary forces must be exerted in opposite directions on the same side. A single paddler at the stern can control the direction of the canoe by angling his paddle outward as he draws it backward through the water. This action applies force against the water in a diagonally backward-outward direction, and the reaction force against the paddle, and through the paddler to the stern of the canoe, is forward and inward. The inward component offsets the rotating effect of the off-center force.

When paddling on the right, the force of the stroke tends to rotate the bow to the opposite side (left); the inward (left) component of the reaction to the diagonally backward-outward force exerted at the stern tends to move the **stern left**, and thus the **bow, right**, counteracting the tendency for the bow to turn left. This is called the J stroke. The older J stroke first applies force off-center straight backward which sends the canoe forward and rotates the bow to the opposite side. The final part of this stroke exerts pressure both backward and outward, sending the canoe ahead and rotating the stern to the opposite side, thus bringing the bow back toward the paddling side. In this way, the rotary force of the first part of the stroke that tends to turn the bow to the opposite side is counteracted by the rotary force of the final part of the stroke that tends to turn the bow back into the line of direction. Angling the paddle from the beginning offsets the rotary force throughout and the canoe moves straighter forward than when the bow is allowed to start to turn and then brought back into line; the necessity for overcoming rotation that has already begun is eliminated. The degree to which the paddle is angled depends upon the amount of rotation to be overcome.

When two are paddling, the bowman's off-center force may balance that of the stern or the stern may need to use the J stroke, the paddle angle will depend upon the paddling strength of the bow.

Pressure straight backward (bow stroke) on the right side of the canoe sends the canoe forward and, because the force is applied off-center, to the left. The paddle is placed in the water as far forward as possible, still allowing the blade to be almost perpendicular to the top of the water. If the reach is too far forward, the paddle must enter the water on an angle and the pull on the paddle produces force diagonally downward and backward, tending to lift the canoe as well as move it forward. The flat surface of the blade faces the direction of movement through the water so that the large area will produce as much counterpressure as possible. By pushing with the top hand and pulling with the lower hand, the blade is moved backward to the point where backward force diminishes and upward force becomes a factor. This gives the greatest distance for application of force in the direction opposite to that of desired movement. Beyond this point force pulls the canoe deeper into the water and resistance to forward progress is increased. This stroke follows the same principles of force production as the straight arm pull of the crawl (Chapter 25). By dropping the top hand in front of the body, the blade of the paddle is lifted with the side of the blade, which offers very little resistance (very small surface), cutting the water. The blade is carried forward with the edge leading to keep air resistance to a minimum.

Pressure straight in toward the canoe draws that part of the canoe toward the paddle (draw). The same principles apply as in the bow stroke; the difference lies in the fact that the reach is out to the side instead of forward and the paddle is drawn toward the canoe rather than backward. In both strokes, the canoe is pulled toward the point where the paddle entered the water. When a single paddler in the center of the canoe uses this stroke, the canoe tends to move broadside since the force is supplied in line with the center of gravity of the canoe. When two paddlers use this stroke on the same side of the canoe it again moves broadside. Since both are applying force in the same direction, both ends move in the same direction. When two paddlers use this stroke on opposite sides of the canoe, the canoe rotates sharply around its center of gravity.

Pressure straight outward from the side of the canoe pushes that end of the canoe in the opposite direction. In the pushover stroke the paddle enters the water with the blade parallel to the side of the canoe so that the flat surface is in position to push outward against the water. The paddle is pushed against the water and that part of the canoe where the paddler is kneeling moves away from the paddle.

Pressure can also be applied at an angle backward and inward, or backward and outward, and again the canoe moves in the direction opposite to that of the force against the water. The diagonal draw on the right when performed by the bow paddler moves the canoe ahead and toward the right. The sweep or C stroke combines the forces of a diagonal pushover and a diagonal draw. The complete stroke executed from the center of the canoe (bow to stern) is effective in moving the canoe in a broad turn to the opposite side. The first half of the stroke moves the canoe forward and turns the bow to the opposite side (diagonal push) while the last half of the stroke (diagonal draw) moves the canoe forward and draws the stern toward the paddle, also turning the bow toward the opposite side. Because the force against the water exerted by the first half of the C stroke has an outward component and that by the last half has an inward component, the **total** stroke is effective for turning the canoe **only** when used in the **center**. If used in the bow (or stern), the inward and outward components of the total stroke tend to rotate the bow (or stern) first one way and then the other and so will offset each other; thus force is wasted and no turn results.

The cross bow rudder is a stroke in which the paddle is held against the resistance of the water and the momentum of the canoe actually creates the force that turns the canoe.

There has been much discussion of "bent arm" and "straight arm" paddling. Bent arm paddling has the advantage of using a leverage action of the arms since the top arm can push while the lower arm pulls. Its disadvantage is that much of this action is accomplished by the muscles of the arms and shoulder girdle which are weaker than the larger back and trunk muscles. Straight arm paddling involves more of a pull with both arms, accomplished to a great degree by the larger back and trunk muscles. When paddling in a situation that does not require a great deal of force, and much of the paddling that is done is of this type, the bent arm stroke probably conserves energy. However, when maximum power is needed, the straight arm stroke, which does away with dependence on the weaker arm muscles and uses the stronger back and trunk muscles to advantage, is more effective. Paddlers should be familiar with both methods and understand the advantages of each so that they can choose intelligently according to the demands of a particular situation. In paddling for a long period of time, a change from one method to the other could give considerable relief to tired muscles.

FIELD HOCKEY

Field hockey is essentially a game of running, changing direction and striking with an implement. The underhand throw pattern is involved in rolling the ball onto the field from out of bounds. The principles discussed in Chapter 12, Running, and Chapter 19, Striking, are applicable to this sport. Only a few of the applications of mechanics that are unique to hockey are discussed here.

In many sports, for example, tennis and badminton, the object's direction is reversed and the momentum of the oncoming object adds to the effectiveness of the return hit. In hockey, however, frequently the purpose is to apply force to keep the ball moving, or to accelerate it in the direction in which it is already moving; when the direction must be reversed it is wise, for safety, to absorb the force of the oncoming ball before applying force to reverse its direction. Since the ball approaches the vertical hitting surface of the stick with forward spin, it tends to rise as it rebounds. As players are close and the ball is hard, injury is likely when a ball rebounds into the air. In hockey, loss of control is likely if the momentum of an oncoming ball is not absorbed when the purpose is to reverse the ball's direction. Because the ball tends to rebound upward, the handle of the hockey stick should be held forward of the blade when a ball is to be stopped. Then, as the blade gives to absorb the force of impact, the angle of the stick causes the ball to rebound toward the ground rather than upward.

Certain restrictions are placed upon movement by the rules of various games. In hockey, for the sake of safety, one such rule restricts the motion of the stick to the height of the player's shoulder ("sticks").

Two methods for preventing the foul of "sticks" are most frequently suggested. One involves a tight wrist on backswing which keeps the blade of the stick low and a rotation of the blade downward on follow-through. This method makes the use of wrist action to produce force impossible, but is successful in avoiding "sticks." In the second method, the well bent right elbow is swung away from the body and up on the backswing and, on follow-through, the left elbow is well bent and swung out from the body. This method allows for the use of wrist action and, at the same time, makes it impossible for the stick to rise above the shoulder. Some individuals are more successful with the first method and others with the second; both techniques effectively prevent "sticks."

In performing the scoop the stick is used as a combination of first and third class levers. This can be likened to the use of a shovel (Chapter 5). While the scoop movement, being a light task, is rapid and the heavy task for which the shovel is employed demands a slower movement, the leverage employed is the same.

There is some disagreement as to the "best" method for carrying the hockey stick while running any distance on the field. Some have insisted that the stick be carried low with both hands well up toward the end of the handle. The advantage of this position is that the stick is close to the ground at all times and thus is always in position to play the ball. Its disadvantage is that, because it is a long implement, considerable effort is required to control the head of the stick in this position and it is in the way of the forward moving legs as the player runs.

Others have insisted that the stick be carried in a horizontal position close to the front of the body, the left hand at the top of the stick and the right well down on the handle. The advantages of this position are that the stick is easier to hold and control and is out of the way of the legs as the player moves forward. Its disadvantage is that the hand position must be adjusted and the blade of the stick dropped before control of the ball is possible. However, the right hand can slide up the handle very rapidly. It would seem that, instead of insisting on the use of one method or the other, the wise teacher discusses the advantages and disadvantages of each and allows the player to select that method which can be used most effectively by that individual.

A study of the effect of position in the striking circle from which the ball is hit, on the degree of error possible if the ball is to pass through the goal, is interesting.[9] Except when the ball is hit from directly in front of the goal, the "opening of the goal," that is, the area through which the ball must pass to go into the goal, is actually smaller than the 12 foot width of the goal (Fig. 27–4). As in basketball, the opening of the goal available to the ball varies with the angle of the ball's approach. The size of the angle is important to the forward since this indicates the error possible for the shot if the ball is to pass through the goal. The opening of the goal is important to both the defense and the forward since it is easier to defend a small area. When a ball is approaching from a point 11 feet toward the sideline from the center of the goal and 6 feet out from the goal line, it must pass through a 4 foot space in order to pass between the goal posts (Fig. 27–4). Thus, if the goalie stands diagonally out from the near goal post facing the oncoming ball only the four foot area must be guarded.

If shooting from (approximately) opposite the center of the goal, the angle through which the path of the ball may vary and still go into the goal is greater as the player approaches the goal line, and the entire width of the goal is always available.

Feet in Front	Feet to the Side	Angle	Opening of Goal
41	0	17°	12 ft.
21	0	32°	12 ft.
6	0	90°	12 ft.

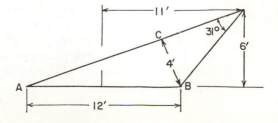

Figure 27–4. Ball must pass through area BC in order to enter goal AB.

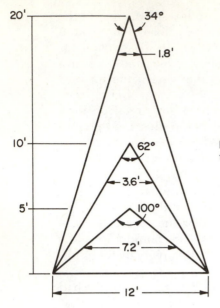

Figure 27–5. Increase in width of area that must be guarded to prevent a goal as the forward approaches the goal line.

Therefore, it is advantageous for the center forward to come in close to the goal line before shooting (assuming that the opposing defense, with the exception of the goalie, has been passed). The center halfback should tackle the opposing center forward to force a shot for goal as far out in the striking circle as possible. The farther out, the less area the defense must cover to prevent the ball from passing between the goal posts (Fig. 27–5).

When the ball is hit from a point farther toward the sideline, away from the center of the goal, the opening of the goal diminishes as the player approaches the goal line. The angle increases slightly and then, after the player reaches a point approximately midway to the goal line, it also diminishes.

Feet in Front	Feet to the Side	Angle	Opening of Goal
41	21	13°	10 ft.
21	21	17°	8 ft.
6	21	9°	3 ft.

It is advisable, therefore, for the inner to shoot for the goal from a point approximately halfway from the edge of the circle to the goal line, since the angle of possible error is slightly larger at this point. This is true **if** the player is not too far out toward the sideline. After the player reaches a point approximately 30 feet out toward the sideline, both the angle and the opening of the goal diminish as the goal line is approached. The fullbacks should attempt to force inners to shoot from far to the side and close to the goal line to decrease the margin of error possible for the shot and the area that must be guarded.

Feet in Front	Feet to the Side	Angle	Opening of Goal
31	31	11°	8 ft.
21	31	10°	6 ft.
6	31	4°	2 ft.

Since wings are normally far from the center of the field, any shot taken from their positions must be extremely accurate. These shots are easy to guard since the opening of the goal is small. It is advisable, therefore, for wings to pass to inners or the center forward since these players are in more advantageous positions for shooting. Obviously, the halfbacks should attempt to force the wings to stay out and should be alert for passes toward the center of the field.

It is important that the goalie come out to meet a forward **who has passed all other defense and is well ahead of the rest of the forward line** so that the forward is forced to shoot at a point where less area needs to be guarded. The goalie must know where to stand to cover the opening of the goal through which a ball must pass when shot from various angles. If two forwards are approaching together, the goalie must stay back since the shot for goal could come from either.

Strings stretched out on the field to indicate angles and the width of the opening of the goal at various points clearly demonstrate the reason for the coaching suggestions given.

SKIING

In many skiing techniques, gravity is the primary force that causes the movement. The position of the skier on an incline gives him potential energy.

As the skier stands on a slope, gravity pulling him straight downward acts at an angle to the slope; one component of the force is effective in holding the skier to the slope and the other in moving him downhill (Fig. 27–6). The friction between his base (the skis) and the surface offers little resistance to gravity's force as it moves the skier downhill. The skier's main problems involve balancing his center of gravity above a moving base and producing forces to cause rotation of his skis when he wishes to change

Figure 27–6. Forces effective against skier standing on slope: a, gravity; b, component perpendicular to slope, holding skier to slope; c, parallel to slope, moving skier downhill.

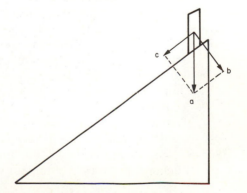

direction, or to overcome gravitational force and momentum when he wishes to stop. Because of the leverage of the long skis, many legs have been broken when skiers have fallen. Bindings that are made to release the boot so injury is less likely must be so engineered that they will release under two types of forces: when the force of the heel lift exceeds a certain limit and when the twist on the leg exceeds an allowable torque. However, they must not release when the skier is traversing rough and icy terrain.[10]

Bindings are adjusted according to the skill level of the skier, his weight and height and the size of the bones of his lower extremities. These factors are directly or indirectly related to the skier's potential to develop and absorb the forces involved in skiing. A beginner's bindings are set looser than those of a highly skilled alpine skier of the same size. A novice usually travels at slower velocities than the expert, and it is the slow twisting falls that are particularly dangerous. It is important that the beginner's bindings release appropriately in the slower twisting of the lower leg because it has been shown that a long bone such as the tibia withstands less twisting prior to fracture with **slow** twisting than with **fast** twisting. Much more energy can be absorbed by the bone before it is damaged if a rapid torque is applied.[11]

Because the expert skier travels at high velocities, the bindings may be set tighter because the bones are able to withstand higher stresses before damage occurs. The expert skier also needs to have tighter bindings because of the high frequency "chattering" of the skis that may result as he is racing downhill. Inadvertent release of bindings while the skier is traveling at high speeds can also result in injury, although in this instance, the upper extremity is more likely to be injured. The ideal for any set of skis and bindings depends on the skier as well as the skiing conditions, but the setting should always be such that the bindings will release if there is danger of serious injury to the skier, but will not release if the skier is not in jeopardy.

A collection of significant research related to skiing biomechanics and injury mechanisms resulted from an international symposium on skiing safety and trauma.[12] The papers contained in this collection provide numerous facts and additional sources related to skiing.

Walking on the Level. The reduction of friction presents a problem when walking on skis on the level. Since there is little friction between the ski and the snow, the backward push of the foot, through the ski, against the snow cannot be as great as in walking, or slipping will result. To compensate, the poles are used for a point of contact to apply force by use of the arms and shoulders. Since the tips of the poles actually sink into the snow, the backward force against the poles is more directly backward and causes counterpressure from the snow which sends the skier forward. To increase the horizontal component of the force, the pole is planted in the snow slightly behind the foot. In order to apply as much force as possible in line with the center of gravity to decrease the rotary force, the hands are kept close to the sides of the body. The body is inclined forward from the ankles (as in walking) to move the center of gravity ahead of the pushing foot and pole so that there will be a horizontal component to the force applied.

The amount of lean and the push of the foot need to be adjusted according to the friction between the ski and the snow. This depends upon both snow conditions and the wax on the skis. In general, the stickier the wax and the wetter (heavier) the snow, the greater the friction between the two surfaces. As friction decreases, there is less resistance to the pushing force from the foot and thus less reaction force to push the ski ahead; the ski may slide backward rather than move ahead. Thus less pushing force can be exerted by the feet and the body lean must be decreased. Use of alternate leg and arm gives more effective application of force and better balance since any force applied away from the center of gravity has a rotary effect. If the push of the arm coincides with the push of the opposite foot, the rotary tendencies tend to balance.

Downhill Running.   The potential energy of the skis is imparted to the body of the skier since he is attached to the skis by the bindings. Because the force is applied to the skier at considerable distance from the center of gravity of his body, there is a tendency for this force to produce rotary movements of the body that tend to move the legs forward and out from under the body. To compensate the skier must move his center of gravity forward. This forward lean should take place from the ankles with the heels kept down so that the surface area between boot and ski is as large as possible, thus making use of the entire ski as a base of support.

The forward lean of the body is in proportion to the degree of steepness of the slope. In general, the body is usually very slightly ahead of the line that is perpendicular to the skis so that air resistance to the body of the skier is counteracted. The faster the skier is moving, the greater the air resistance and the greater the forward lean necessary to counteract it.

If the center of gravity of the body gets behind the line perpendicular to the skis (perpendicular to the slope), the body weight tends to push the skis forward and then two forces are acting on the skis in a forward-downward direction, the body weight and the force of gravity. As a result, the skis move out from under the body.

The degree to which the motion of the skis caused by the force of gravity is imparted to the skier is dependent upon the angle between the body of the skier and the skis. The speed of the skis depends upon both the angle of the slope and friction. The steeper the slope, the greater the downhill component of force in relation to the force pulling the skier against the slope and, therefore, the skier moves down the hill faster (Fig. 27–7). The less the friction between the surfaces of the slope and the skis, the less resistance offered to the motion of the skier. The less solid the surface (in general, the deeper and less packed the snow), the more the skis drop down into the snow and the greater the resistance to the forward momentum.

In applying this principle, the wetness of the snow must be considered. Very dry, powdery snow, even though fairly deep, may offer little resistance. If the crust is so thick that the skier does not break through, it offers little resistance. In fact, so little resistance is offered that control is difficult. If the skier does break through the crust, the crust becomes a wall that the tip of the ski must break, and great resistance to forward motion results.

Skiing with one ski ahead of the other reduces the surface offering resistance, and puts the skier in a position to apply pressure effective in moving the center of gravity of the body backward or forward more easily. The base is enlarged in the direction of the force and, therefore, the body is

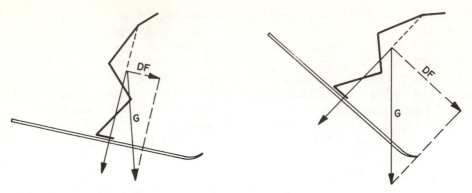

Figure 27–7.   Greater downhill component of force with steeper grade.

more stable. When one ski is forward the base is enlarged in the forward-backward direction, the direction of any probable impacts from bumps or change in snow conditions. If a slowing of the skis is anticipated, the skier must be ready to shift his center of gravity back to be in position to resist the tendency for the upper body to continue moving ahead at the faster speed. Because of the inertia of the trunk the body tends to keep moving forward at the same speed. Also, the force causing the slowing of the skis is applied against the body at the feet which are a long way from the body's center of gravity and therefore, the lever arm is long.

Since the speed of the skier is affected considerably by the conditions of the snow, it is dangerous for a beginner to ski when the snow conditions vary on the same slope. A great deal of control is needed to adjust the center of gravity as the speed of the skis changes. It takes a skillful skier to control skis on ice since the lack of friction causes any slight change in weight to send the skis off in the opposite direction.

Short skis (3 feet) have been introduced to simplify the beginning skier's problems in controlling the skis. The shorter levers offer less resistance to turning, and thus the beginner experiences earlier success. The same reasoning applies to the use of short skis as to a short racket by the beginning tennis player (see p. 314).

The skier skis with flexed knees to lower his center of gravity and thus increase his stability, and to make it possible to absorb the shock caused by bumps. The knees should not be bent so far that further flexing is impossible when it is necessary to absorb shock.

The principle that the more nearly the center of gravity is over the center of the base the more stable the body, is important in skiing. When the center of gravity is over the center of the width of the base the skis are weighted evenly and so they move together. If the center of gravity is off-center one ski is weighted more than the other, causing the skier to turn.

Because it is more disastrous to catch an outside edge than an inside edge, some instructors teach students to edge slightly toward the inside to avoid catching an outside edge. Catching an inside edge of a ski places the foot in such a position (ankle rotated in and sole of the foot facing out) that the body weight exerts force away from the center of the stance and the ski moves away from the center. The base is widened and, up to a point, balance is not reduced. The foot is in position to push out against the wall of snow and to push the body in over the other ski, so that the ski that had a caught edge can be lifted and brought back into position. When an outside edge is caught, the foot is placed in such a position (sole of foot facing in) that the body weight exerts pressure toward the center of the stance and the ski moves in, tending to cross the other ski. The base is narrowed and stability is reduced. If the ski does cross, momentum is sharply reduced and, because of inertia, the skier is likely to fall forward. It is difficult to exert pressure in the direction that will move the center of gravity over the flat ski. When an edge is caught, the weight must be moved onto the flat ski so that the weight can be removed from the edged ski and it can be flattened.

Snowplow. In a snowplow the skis are more or less on their inside edges. Hutter[13] stated that since the ski is longer in front of its binding than behind it, the resistance of the snow is greater in front of the foot and the ski turns around this pivot point. The resistance in front of the binding can be increased by dropping forward into the knees more and the greater the difference in resistance between the front and rear of the ski, the tighter the turn.

Sideslip. To slide sideways, the weight must be kept evenly distributed over the length of the skis. In discussing this technique, Hutter[13] stated that leaning too far forward puts too much pressure on the tips of the skis, the resistance is increased and the skis turn to point uphill. The skier then slides backward. If the pressure is placed too much on the back part of the skis they tend to turn downhill.

Parallel Skiing. In recent years there has been a swing from stem skiing to parallel skiing.[14, 15, 16] In general, the parallel turns are made by first unweighting the skis and then thrusting the heels in the direction opposite to the direction of the turn. (The tails move to the right when making a left turn.) A forward-upward motion of the body effected by extending the knees and ankles, in combination with a push against the pole placed in the snow about three feet ahead of the foot on the inside of the turn, unweights the tails of the skis and shifts the weight onto the tips. The pole must be placed well ahead of the foot since the body is moving forward and will be even with the pole by the time of the push. It is the inside pole that is used since it is the pivot for the turn. The momentum of the skier causes him to turn around the pole. Reaching with the inside pole rotates the shoulders away from the turn and puts them in position to counterbalance the heel thrust. The heel thrust which moves the tails of the skis farther around, occurs as the weight drops back and the legs again go into flexion.

The forward-upward movement of the body, which unweights the tails of the skis and shifts the weight forward, can be demonstrated by standing on a bathroom scale and flexing and then extending the knees. As the knees bend there is a split second drop of the needle to zero and then the needle returns to the original reading. If the legs are extended, the needle jumps higher as the body pushes down against the scale to initiate the movement, drops to zero as the feet follow the body's upward movement, and then settles back to the beginning weight as the upward momentum of the body is overcome by gravity. It is at the moment during extension (when the scale needle would drop), that the tails of the skis are unweighted and the skier's momentum is effective in causing him to turn about the fixed point, his pole. As the turn is completed, the skis are edged on the uphill edge to prevent side slipping down the slope.

DANCE

The application of the principles of mechanics to the various types of dance is as important as to any other activity. All principles that deal with equilibrium, motion, leverage and force application and absorption must be applied in any dance activity. On the whole the rhythm of body movement is set by an outside stimulus. This fact causes problems for some individuals who find it difficult to move in a superimposed rhythm (see p. 33).

The walk of ballroom dancing is a modification of the natural walk necessitated by a difference in purpose. While the purpose of normal walking is to conserve energy over a period of time, the purpose of the dance walk is to produce a smooth gliding movement which allows for easy and immediate change of direction. Sliding the toes forward rather than walking heel first and rolling forward onto the toes, keeps the ball of the foot along the floor, resulting in a gliding movement, and places the ball of the foot and the toes in a position that makes possible immediate application of force whenever change of direction is desired. The reduced friction between the surface of the dance floor and the shoe makes it possible to slide the foot along the floor with ease and necessitates a smaller step to reduce the forward or backward component of the force exerted against the floor in order to prevent slipping.

A major purpose of some forms of dance may be to convey certain emotions and ideas or to demonstrate body control and patterns. These purposes are accomplished through position or movement and various degrees of energy expenditure. While other activities may seek to produce force with the least expenditure of energy, in dance energy may be sacrificed in order to create a given impression or to express a certain mood or emotion. This is not unlike the strategic use of a forceful movement pattern which is checked at the last moment to deceive the opponent in a game such as badminton.

In dance the sole tool is the body. While props may be used to create atmosphere, they are not generally used as instruments for the production of force as are the various pieces of sport equipment.

In all dance activities, an understanding of the importance of the eyes and the semicircular canals of the ears to balance is extremely important. When turning rapidly, the dancer fixes his eyes on a spot and quickly turns the head to that spot so that the eyes have a point of focus and the head is stationary for a part of the time that the body is executing each turn.

Contemporary dance and folk dance use walking, running, sliding, galloping, leaping, jumping, hopping and many combinations of these activities (Chapters 11, 12, 13). Although they may be modified slightly because of purpose, the basic mechanics are the same as when these techniques are used in the performance of any other activity.

The buzz step turn, used frequently in folk dance, is unique with the dance activities, although the pivot in basketball is certainly related to it. In executing this turn, an off-center application of force by one foot causes the body to move in a circle about the other foot, the center of rotation. In this it is the same as the pivot. When this turn is performed by two individuals, double rotary force is produced. Since the dancers are moving in a circle, centrifugal force acts to pull them apart; this force becomes much greater as the speed of rotation is increased and as the dancers lean their shoulders farther away from each other (hips remain close together). If they are able to produce the greater force required to maintain their angular velocity as they lean further outward, the linear velocity of their upper bodies increases (p. 73). The dancers need to realize that they will need to exert greater force with their arms to keep from flying apart.

Although the feet are used somewhat differently, the pivot turn in peasant position has many of the same problems. In this turn the placement of the man's hands **behind** his partner's hips and of her hands **over** his shoulders, results in hand positions that are effective for applying forces directly inward at hip and shoulder to resist the outward pull of centrifugal force. With the arms straight the elbow joint tends to support this position relieving the elbow flexors from the strain of keeping the dancers from being pulled apart and thus making a fast turn easier.

Ballet dancers and skaters frequently spin at high speeds. The arms are outstretched and the non-supporting leg swings wide as rotary momentum is developed; suddenly the arms and leg are brought close to the body's vertical axis, shortening the radius of rotation and greatly increasing the rotary velocity. Slowing down is accomplished by again lengthening the radius of rotation through extension of the arms and the leg.[17]

The transference of momentum from a part to adjoining segments is seen when the dancer, having first rotated the arms, shoulders and head with the feet firmly on the surface, jumps into the air; the rotation transfers and the whole body twists.[18]

The techniques involved in leading are important in both ballroom and folk dance. The best position for a man's right hand for leading differs somewhat according to the dance involved. The accepted position for most ballroom dancing involves placement of the man's right hand just below the woman's left shoulder blade. The flat hand increases the surface contact and makes possible the application of force over a broad surface area. Pressure of the whole hand applies force which moves the woman forward. Pressure with the heel of the hand applies off-center force which rotates her to her own right. In order for pressure of the fingers to rotate the woman to her own left, the fingers of the man's hand would need to extend beyond the woman's spine so that the force is applied on the right side of her back. Use of both hands, the right to push on one side or the other of the woman's back and the left to pull or push her hand, makes possible excellent control of rotary movement. Two forces, both off-center, can be applied at the same time to produce rotary motion in either direction. **The pressure exerted in leading is slight, giving a suggestion of desired direction of movement more than force.** For difficult leads requiring considerable hip movement, such as those found in the Latin American dances, the man is in a better position to assist rotation of the hips of the woman when his hand is placed nearer her hip than her shoulder.[19]

Tap dance requires that the individual become adept at maintaining his equilibrium on one foot (or a part of one foot), a small base, while moving the other foot in various ways. It involves rapid transference of weight from one foot to another. The use of the arms to counterbalance the movements of the legs is extremely important. As in several other activities, the tap dancer must learn to use the loss of equilibrium to initiate movement while maintaining an erect position.

In contemporary dance the body must frequently supply the resisting force as well as the force being applied. For example, when the dancer wishes to convey the idea of forceful pushing, he assumes the "push position" which is dictated by mechanical principles; with the feet in a forward-backward stride (stable base in direction of force), knees flexed (force applied by strongest muscles), body angled forward from ankles (force applied in desired direction — forward), the trunk is stabilized **but**, in the absence of an object or outside force to resist the pushing force, the antagonists to the prime movers must be contracted at the same time. Thus the mechanical principles are followed to convey an idea rather than to apply force to an object.

Inexperienced dancers need to start their practice of many of the fundamental contemporary dance techniques while sitting or lying on the floor. A wide base of support and low center of gravity make it possible to concentrate on the movements being practiced without concern for the maintenance of balance. Practice at a bar is useful in minimizing balance problems while learning certain techniques that cannot be executed in a sitting or lying position. In general, the individual progresses from a wide base to a narrow one, from a low to a high center of gravity, and from performing a technique over a stationary base to performing it over a moving one.

Because of the importance of the length of the lever, small light movements of the extremities can be performed away from the center of gravity but strong heavy movements need to be executed close to the body.

In performing the various dance falls, the center of gravity is lowered as far as possible before it is allowed to move beyond the edge of the base. The weight is then rapidly spread over as large an area as possible so that the force per unit of area will be small. All of the principles of force absorption are extremely important since the dancer must continually absorb the kinetic energy produced by a leap, jump, or even a run.

In general, the dancer, just as the gymnast performing free exercise, must become skilled in the control necessary to maintain positions and to move under conditions that make equilibrium difficult. He must know the principles of mechanics in order to be able to produce the amount of force desired for the particular technique or to convey the desired impression to others. He must be able to apply the principles of force absorption if he is to avoid injury.

BODY CONDITIONING EXERCISES

As in dance, the lying and sitting positions, because of the broad base and low center of gravity, make it possible to concentrate on an exercise without concern with the maintenance of balance. The difficulty of some exercises is increased by changing the starting position from the sitting or lying position to a standing position and finally to performing the exercise above a moving base.

The force of gravity is used to increase the stretch and thus to aid in the development of flexibility. It is also used as a resistive force in the development of strength. In the forward-downward bending of the trunk, gravity assists in pulling the upper body downward and increasing the stretch of the muscles of the leg, hip, and lower back. In exercises in which the weight of the body itself, or of a body part is lifted or lowered slowly, gravity supplies the resistance against which the muscles must work. When lying on the side and lifting the leg upward, the weight of the long lever must be lifted against gravity's pull. In lowering the leg, effort is increased by controlling the speed of the drop so that, again, gravity's force must be resisted.

An understanding of the importance of the length of the lever is extremely important in the choice of body conditioning exercises. Since more velocity can be developed at the end of a long lever, the lengthening of the lever is important in producing additional force to stretch tight areas. For example, a certain amount of stretch results from trunk twisting performed with the hands on the hips. However, when the arm on the side toward which one is twisting is flung diagonally upward and backward, the stretch is increased considerably because of the momentum transferred from the long arm lever to the trunk to which the arm is attached.

Lengthening the lever being lifted or slowly lowered against the pull of gravity greatly increases the effort required. Therefore, those exercises using long levers are more effective for the development of strength. In the well known sit-up exercise, the long trunk must be lifted against the force of gravity. Adjustment of the position of the arms and hands varies the degree of difficulty of this exercise because of the change in the distance of the center of gravity of the segments to be lifted from the fulcrum for the movement (the hips). When the arms are held forward, the center of gravity of the upper body is as close to the fulcrum as possible. Reaching forward with the arms increases the ease of the sit-up, since the momentum of the arms is transferred to the trunk and aids the abdominal muscles in overcoming inertia. When the hands are placed on the hips, the center of gravity moves slightly upward from the hips (the fulcrum) and the arms are no longer useful in supplying initial momentum. Therefore, this method is somewhat more difficult. Crossing the arms over the chest and placing each hand on the opposite shoulder further lengthens the distance from the hips to the center of gravity of the upper body and increases the difficulty of the lift. The position with the hands placed at the back of the neck is even more difficult as the weight is still further from the fulcrum. However, in this position there is a tendency for the performer to swing the elbows forward and thus gain momentum which reduces the difficulty of the exercise. If the strongest exercise is desired it is important that the elbows remain out to the side throughout the exercise. Placing the arms straight above the head lengthens the lever to its maximum. Because this makes the exercise so difficult (**if** the arms are really kept in this position), it is impossible to resist the tendency to swing the arms forward; since the lever is so long, if this is done the momentum that can be developed is considerable, and when this is transferred to the trunk the exercise becomes easier instead of more difficult.

Since the psoas muscles, which are strong hip flexors, are put on the stretch when one lies on the back with the legs straight, they are in an excellent position to assist the abdominal muscles in the sit-up movement. Bending the legs and placing the feet flat on the floor releases the stretch of this muscle and it can no longer assist the movement **to the same degree.** When the feet are held down on the floor by placing them under a bar or a piece of furniture or by having them held by a partner, the psoas is more effective than when the feet are free. Therefore, for maximum exercise of the **abdominal muscles**, the knees should be well bent and the feet should not be held.

The psoas and iliacus muscles have some attachments on the lumbar vertebrae and therefore, any strong pull by these muscles with the legs stabilized will pull on the lower back and can cause strain if the upper body is allowed to lag behind so that the lower back is arched. Therefore, this exercise should always be executed with the knees bent and by **curling** the back rather than allowing the back to arch.

In developing the abdominal muscles through the use of this exercise, the position should vary with the present strength of the individuals in a group. All should have the knees bent and the feet flat on the floor. Some may need to reach forward with their arms in the beginning. Others may be able to place the hands on the back of the neck and still keep the elbow out to the side. Still others may find the other positions necessary. Many may be unable to perform a sit-up when the feet are not held. Since holding the feet brings the psoas muscle to the assistance of the abdominals, it would be advisable for these individuals to use a curl-up exercise that can be performed without this assistance in place of the sit-up exercise. Effort to lift by curling and to hold the upper body a few inches off the floor may be more effective in abdominal muscle development than the complete sit-up exercise for these individuals.

The part of the sit-up exercise calling for maximum expenditure of effort is the first part of the movement. As the trunk is lifted off the floor inertia must be overcome, the center of gravity of the upper body is the farthest from the fulcrum and the angle of pull of the muscle is most disadvantageous. As the upper body nears the position above the base, the exercise becomes progressively easier. Once the movement has started inertia helps the movement. The resistance arm progressively shortens and the angle of pull becomes increasingly larger and therefore becomes more advantageous. It might be wise to change the concept of this exercise; instead of starting from a lying position, the individual might start from a sitting position with the legs bent and feet flat on the floor, lower the curled trunk backward and downward as far as can be controlled with the feet on the floor, and hold the upper body suspended above the floor for a period of ten seconds[20]; or he might lower as far as possible to control and then lift the trunk slightly, lower again and lift, repeating this several times before returning to the sitting position. The second method results in isotonic exercise rather than isometric. As abdominal strength increases the individual will be able to hold, or exercise in, a position closer and closer to the floor.

If the sit-up exercise needs to be modified, an alternate approach to starting the exercise from a sitting rather than a lying position and slowly leaning backward is to start from a supported position in which the trunk, neck and head are angled upward from the hips; the degree of the angle depends on the strength of the abdominal muscles: the less the strength, the greater the angle. This eliminates the most difficult portion of the exercise. A hinged board can be adjusted to various angles of trunk support from which the exercise can be started and, as abdominal strength develops, the trunk can be supported lower and lower (closer to the floor) gradually increasing the length of the upper body lever and the distance it must be lifted and thus the difficulty of the exercise. If such a board is not available another approach is for a partner to hold the two hands of the individual who is unable to perform a sit-up and, by standing in a forward-backward stride and transferring the weight to the back foot, to assist by pulling on the individual's hands during the beginning of the sit-up exercise. Starting a sit-up while lying **head down** on an inclined board greatly **increases** the difficulty of the exercise since the upper body must then be lifted against gravity to get to a position even with the hips, the starting position for the normal sit-up.

Analysis of the frequently suggested straight leg lifting, and slowly lowering exercises makes it clear that this exercise should be used **with caution**. Since the strong hip flexors are attached to the pelvic girdle, vertebral column and the thighs, effort to hold the long leg lever against gravity results in a pull against the pelvis and the lower back. As in the sit-up exercise, the greatest strain comes when the legs are closer to the floor or when the angle of pull (angle between muscle and thigh bone) is smaller. It is easy to hold the legs straight up above the hips. The force of gravity pulls them down onto their base and the angle at which the muscles are functioning is advantageous (large). As the legs are lowered this angle of muscle function becomes smaller and, at the same time, the distance from the center of gravity of the legs to the fulcrum (the hip joint) is increased. Both factors increase the effort required to control the legs against the force of gravity. **If the abdominal muscles are not strong enough to stabilize the lower back, pelvis and lumbar vertebrae, strain is likely.** The leverage and angle of muscular pull involved in this exercise must be recognized so that injury to the lower back is avoided. If the individual **flattens his back** against the floor, draws the knees into the chest, straightens the legs and then, as he slowly lowers, at the instant he **begins** to feel the lower back leave the floor (when he is no longer able to stabilize), allows the knees to flex and the feet to drop to the floor, no strain of the lower back will result. If he continues the exercise with an arched lower back, strain is likely. Placing one hand on the floor beside (touching) the lower back will make it possible for the individual to know immediately when the back begins to lift.

In suggesting body conditioning exercises, the condition of each individual must be considered and exercises must be adjusted to the present level of strength, flexibility, coordination, and endurance. **Application of the mechanical principles** indicates adjustments in movements that increase difficulty and effectiveness, and reduce the possibility of injury due to strain.

REFERENCES

1. Houtz, Sara Jane: Personal communication, July, 1963.
2. Woods, Marcella D.: Archery. In *Individual Sports for Women*. 5th ed. Broer, Marion R. (ed.) Philadelphia, W. B. Saunders Company, 1971, p. 37.
3. *Ibid.*
4. *Ibid., p. 41.*
5. *Ibid., p. 42.*
6. Wilson, R. I. (Dick), Manager, Archery Division, Shakespeare Company, Kalamazoo, Michigan, personal correspondence, June, 1965.
7. Hickman, C. N., Nagler, Forrest and Klopteg, Paul E.: *Archery, the Technical Side*. Milwaukee, The North American Press, 1947.
8. Woods, *op. cit.*, pp. 17–75.
9. MacLean, Dorothy, and Broer, Marion R.: Angles in Hockey Goal Shooting. Unpublished study, University of Washington, 1949.
10. Outwater, John O., and Ettlinger, Carl F.: The Engineering of Ski Bindings, *Medicine and Science in Sports*, 1:4:200, Dec. 1969.
11. Asang, E.: Experimental Mechanics of the Human Leg — A Basis for Interpreting Typical Skiing Injury Mechanisms. *The Orthopedic Clinics of North America*. 7:63–73, 1976.
12. Eriksson, E. (ed.): Symposium on Ski Trauma and Skiing Safety. *The Orthopedic Clinics of North America*, 7:1:3–250, 1976.
13. Hutter, Clemens Maria: How You Can Learn Wedeln, Part I: Boil Your Skiing Down to the Absolute Essentials. *Ski*, 21:22, November, 1956.
14. Schaeffler, Willy, Bowen, Ezra and Riger, Robert: The New Way to Ski. *Sports Illustrated*, 7:22:34–42, Nov. 25, 1957; 7:25:60–69, Dec. 16, 1957; 7:26:94–106, Dec. 23, 1957.
15. Throw Away that Stem. *Sports Illustrated*, 21:21:46–51, Nov. 23, 1964.
16. Hutter, Miki: Technique Today: An Evaluation: *Skiing*, 17:3:92, 154–157, Dec., 1964; 17:5:58–60, Feb., 1965.
17. Dyson, Geoffrey H. G.: *The Mechanics of Athletics*. London, University of London Press Ltd., 1964; p. 75.
18. *Ibid., p. 82.*
19. Wilson, Ruth M.: University of Washington, Seattle, Personal Conference.
20. Waite, Elizabeth M.: Conditioning Exercises. Unpublished paper, University of Washington, 1958.

ADDITIONAL READING

Hay, James G.: A *Bibliography of Biomechanics Literature*. 3rd ed. Iowa City, University of Iowa Press, 1976.
  Archery — Section T1 (26 references)
  Calisthenics — Section D (17 references)
  Canoeing — Section T8 (4 references)
  Dance — Section F (4 references)
  Field Hockey — Section T14 (5 references)
  Skiing — T30 (53 references)

APPENDICES

Appendix A

SYMBOL IDENTIFICATION

a   Linear acceleration

$\bar{a}$ Average linear acceleration

D   Distance

F   Force

FA   Force arm — *perpendicular* distance from line of force to fulcrum

F_c Centrifugal force

g   Acceleration of gravity (32.2 ft/sec/sec at earth's surface)

I   Moment of inertia (angular motion)

k   Radius of gyration

KE   Kinetic energy

m   Mass

M   Momentum (linear motion)

N   Newton(s) (force)

PE   Potential energy

r   Radius

R   Resultant (addition of forces)
Resistance (leverage)
Range (projection)

RA   Resistance arm — *perpendicular* distance from line of resistance to fulcrum

S   Displacement (distance) along an arc

t   Time

T   Total time (projection)

V   Linear velocity

$\bar{V}$ Average linear velocity

V_v Vertical velocity

V_h Horizontal velocity

V_i Initial velocity

V_f Final velocity

W   Work

Wt   Weight

Greek Letters

β (beta)   angle of attack (motion thru fluid)

ϵ (epsilon)   coefficient of restitution

α (alpha)   angular acceleration

ω (omega)   angular velocity

θ (theta)   angle

Appendix B

FORMULAS

CENTER OF GRAVITY

$$DLG = \frac{D(W - SW)}{W} \quad \text{(p. 47)}$$

ACCELERATION OF GRAVITY $= 32.2$ ft/sec/sec

$$D = \frac{1}{2}gt^2 \quad \text{(p. 49)}$$

LEVERAGE

Moment $= F \times FA$ (p. 81)

$\Sigma M = 0$ **or** $F_1 \times FA_1 = F_2 \times FA_2$ **or** $F \times FA = R \times RA$ (for equilibrium)

FORCE

$R^2 = F_1^2 + F_2^2$ (square of hypotenuse $=$ sum of squares of other two sides) (p. 96)

$$\sin \theta = \frac{F_v}{F} \quad \text{(p.97)}$$

$$\cos \theta = \frac{F_h}{F} \quad \text{(p. 97)}$$

$$W = F \times D \text{ (p. 104)}$$

$$\text{Power} = \frac{F \times D}{t} \quad \text{(p. 104)}$$

$$PE = Wt \times Ht \text{ (p. 105)}$$

$$KE = \frac{1}{2}mV^2 \text{ (p. 106)}$$

$$Wt = m \times g \text{ (p. 66)}$$

LINEAR MOTION

$$\bar{V} = \frac{D_f - D_i}{t} \quad \text{(p. 61)}$$

$$\bar{a} = \frac{V_f - V_i}{t} \quad \text{(p. 63)}$$

$$a = \frac{F}{m} \text{ or } F = m \times a \text{ (p. 66)}$$

$$F \times t = mV_f - mV_i \text{ or } F = \frac{m(V_f - V_i)}{t} \quad \text{(p. 67)}$$

ANGULAR MOTION

$$\omega = \frac{\theta_f - \theta_i}{t} \quad \text{(p. 70)}$$

$$S = r\theta \quad \text{(p. 69)}$$

$$V = r\omega \quad \text{(p. 69)}$$

$$\alpha = \frac{\omega_f - \omega_i}{t} \quad \text{(p. 70)}$$

$$F_c = \frac{m \times \omega^2}{r} \quad \text{(p. 73)}$$

$$\text{Torque} = I\alpha \quad \text{(p. 74)}$$

$$\text{Angular momentum} = I\omega \quad \text{(p. 71)}$$

PROJECTION

Vertical

$D_v = V_i t + \frac{1}{2}gt^2$ simplified to $D_v = \frac{1}{2}gt^2$ when $V_i = 0$ (p. 137)

   or

$$D_v = \frac{V^2}{2g} \quad \text{(p. 136)}$$

$$t = \frac{V_f - V_i}{g} \quad \textbf{or} \quad t = \frac{V_v}{g} \quad \text{(p. 141)}$$

$$T = 2t \quad \text{(p. 141)}$$

$$\epsilon = \frac{\text{ht. bounce}}{\text{ht. dropped}} \quad \text{(p. 126)}$$

NON-VERTICAL

$$V_v = V \sin \theta \quad \text{(p. 140)}$$

$$V_h = V \cos \theta \quad \text{(p. 140)}$$

$$D_v = V_v t + \frac{1}{2}at^2 \quad \textbf{or}$$

$$D_v \text{ (to high point)} = \frac{1}{2}gt^2 \quad \text{(p. 137)}$$

$$D_h = V_h \times T + \frac{1}{2}at^2 \quad \textbf{or}$$

$$D_h \text{ (air resistance negligible)} = V_h \times T \quad \text{(p. 142)}$$

$$R = \frac{V^2}{g} \sin 2\theta \quad \text{(p. 142)}$$

$$t = \frac{V_v}{g} \quad \textbf{or} \quad \frac{V \sin \theta}{g} \quad \text{(p. 141)}$$

$$T = 2t \quad \textbf{or} \quad T = \frac{2V \sin \theta}{g} \quad \text{(projection height = landing height) (p. 141)}$$

$$T = \text{time to high pt.} + \text{time high pt. to ground} \quad \text{(p. 145)}$$

Appendix C

SUMMARY OF TRIGONOMETRY

Because the solutions to many motion analysis problems involve the use of a right triangle, a basic understanding of the fundamentals of trigonometry is needed. The literal meaning of the word "trigonometry" is the measurement of triangles. The various parts of a right triangle are defined in Figure C–1. Regardless of the lengths of the three sides of a right triangle, their **relationships** to each other are constant. This principle is expressed by the formula:

$$X^2 = Y^2 + Z^2 \text{ (square of hypotenuse} = \text{sum of squares of other two sides)}$$

Three facts are known about any right triangle: (1) like any other triangle it contains a total of 180 degrees; (2) one angle is 90 degrees; (3) the relationships among sides are constant. Because of these three facts, if the lengths of any two sides, or the magnitude of one acute angle and the length of one side are known, it is possible to calculate the length of any side or the

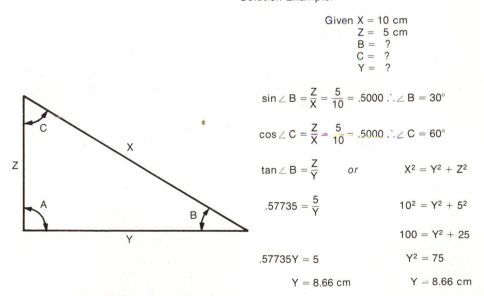

Solution Example:

$$\text{Given } X = 10 \text{ cm}$$
$$Z = 5 \text{ cm}$$
$$B = ?$$
$$C = ?$$
$$Y = ?$$

$$\sin \angle B = \frac{Z}{X} = \frac{5}{10} = .5000 \therefore \angle B = 30°$$

$$\cos \angle C = \frac{Z}{X} = \frac{5}{10} = .5000 \therefore \angle C = 60°$$

$$\tan \angle B = \frac{Z}{Y} \quad \text{or} \quad X^2 = Y^2 + Z^2$$

$$.57735 = \frac{5}{Y} \qquad\qquad 10^2 = Y^2 + 5^2$$

$$\qquad\qquad\qquad 100 = Y^2 + 25$$

$$.57735Y = 5 \qquad\qquad Y^2 = 75$$

$$Y = 8.66 \text{ cm} \qquad Y = 8.66 \text{ cm}$$

Figure C–1. Right Triangle.
one angle (A) = 90°
two acute angles (B and C), the sum of which = 90°
hypotenuse (X) is the longest side (opposite the right angle)
side opposite (Z, opposite angle B; Y, opposite angle C)
side adjacent (Y, adjacent to angle B; Z, adjacent to angle C)

magnitude of the other acute angle (or of both if only lengths of sides are known) by applying one of the following trigonometric functions:

$$\sin \theta = \frac{\text{side opposite}}{\text{hypotenuse}} \qquad \sin B = \frac{Z}{X} \qquad \sin C = \frac{Y}{X}$$

$$\cos \theta = \frac{\text{side adjacent}}{\text{hypotenuse}} \qquad \cos B = \frac{Y}{X} \qquad \cos C = \frac{Z}{X}$$

$$\tan \theta = \frac{\text{side opposite}}{\text{side adjacent}} \qquad \tan B = \frac{Z}{Y} \qquad \tan C = \frac{Y}{Z}$$

In problems of motion the sides can represent magnitudes of forces, distances or velocities.

While there are six trigonometric functions, the three stated here (sine, cosine and tangent) are sufficient for most practical problems. A summary table including trigonometric values for various angles follows (Appendix D).

Appendix D

TABLE OF TRIGONOMETRIC FUNCTIONS *

Angle θ Degree	Angle θ Radian	sin θ	cos θ	tan θ	Angle θ Degree	Angle θ Radian	sin θ	cos θ	tan θ
0	0.0000	0.0000	1.0000	0.0000					
1	0.0175	0.0175	0.9998	0.0175	31	0.5411	0.5150	0.8572	0.6009
2	0.0349	0.0349	0.9994	0.0349	32	0.5585	0.5299	0.8480	0.6249
3	0.0524	0.0523	0.9986	0.0524	33	0.5760	0.5446	0.8387	0.6494
4	0.0698	0.0698	0.9976	0.0699	34	0.5934	0.5592	0.8290	0.6745
5	0.0873	0.0872	0.9962	0.0875	35	0.6109	0.5736	0.8191	0.7002
6	0.1047	0.1045	0.9945	0.1051	36	0.6283	0.5878	0.8090	0.7265
7	0.1222	0.1219	0.9925	0.1228	37	0.6458	0.6018	0.7986	0.7535
8	0.1396	0.1392	0.9903	0.1405	38	0.6632	0.6157	0.7880	0.7813
9	0.1571	0.1564	0.9877	0.1584	39	0.6807	0.6293	0.7771	0.8098
10	0.1745	0.1736	0.9848	0.1763	40	0.6981	0.6428	0.7660	0.8391
11	0.1920	0.1908	0.9816	0.1944	41	0.7156	0.6561	0.7547	0.8693
12	0.2094	0.2079	0.9781	0.2126	42	0.7330	0.6691	0.7431	0.9004
13	0.2269	0.2250	0.9744	0.2309	43	0.7505	0.6820	0.7314	0.9325
14	0.2443	0.2419	0.9703	0.2493	44	0.7679	0.6947	0.7193	0.9657
15	0.2618	0.2588	0.9659	0.2679	45	0.7854	0.7071	0.7071	1.0000
16	0.2793	0.2756	0.9613	0.2867	46	0.8029	0.7193	0.6947	1.0355
17	0.2967	0.2924	0.9563	0.3057	47	0.8203	0.7313	0.6820	1.0724
18	0.3142	0.3090	0.9511	0.3249	48	0.8378	0.7431	0.6691	1.1106
19	0.3316	0.3256	0.9455	0.3443	49	0.8552	0.7547	0.6561	1.1504
20	0.3491	0.3420	0.9397	0.3640	50	0.8727	0.7660	0.6428	1.1918
21	0.3665	0.3584	0.9336	0.3839	51	0.8901	0.7771	0.6293	1.2349
22	0.3840	0.3746	0.9272	0.4040	52	0.9076	0.7880	0.6157	1.2799
23	0.4014	0.3907	0.9205	0.4245	53	0.9250	0.7986	0.6018	1.3270
24	0.4189	0.4067	0.9135	0.4452	54	0.9425	0.8090	0.5878	1.3764
25	0.4363	0.4226	0.9063	0.4663	55	0.9599	0.8192	0.5736	1.4281
26	0.4538	0.4384	0.8988	0.4877	56	0.9774	0.8290	0.5592	1.4826
27	0.4712	0.4540	0.8910	0.5095	57	0.9948	0.8387	0.5446	1.5399
28	0.4887	0.4695	0.8829	0.5317	58	1.0123	0.8480	0.5299	1.6003
29	0.5061	0.4848	0.8746	0.5543	59	1.0297	0.8572	0.5150	1.6643
30	0.5236	0.5000	0.8660	0.5774	60	1.0472	0.8660	0.5000	1.7321

*For values of angles falling between those listed (Example: 26°34′) consult a book of logarithmic and trigonometric tables.

TABLE OF TRIGONOMETRIC FUNCTIONS *Continued*

Angle θ Degree	Angle θ Radian	sin θ	cos θ	tan θ	Angle θ Degree	Angle θ Radian	sin θ	cos θ	tan θ
61	1.0647	0.8746	0.4848	1.8040	76	1.3265	0.9703	0.2419	4.0108
62	1.0821	0.8829	0.4695	1.8807	77	1.3439	0.9744	0.2249	4.3315
63	1.0996	0.8910	0.4540	1.9626	78	1.3614	0.9781	0.2079	4.7046
64	1.1170	0.8988	0.4384	2.0503	79	1.3788	0.9816	0.1908	5.1446
65	1.1345	0.9063	0.4226	2.1445	80	1.3963	0.9848	0.1736	5.6713
66	1.1519	0.9135	0.4067	2.2460	81	1.4137	0.9877	0.1564	6.3138
67	1.1694	0.9205	0.3907	2.3559	82	1.4312	0.9903	0.1392	7.1154
68	1.1868	0.9272	0.3746	2.4751	83	1.4486	0.9925	0.1219	8.1443
69	1.2043	0.9336	0.3584	2.6051	84	1.4661	0.9945	0.1045	9.5144
70	1.2217	0.9397	0.3420	2.7475	85	1.4835	0.9962	0.0872	11.430
71	1.2392	0.9455	0.3256	2.9042	86	1.5010	0.9976	0.0698	14.301
72	1.2566	0.9511	0.3090	3.0777	87	1.5184	0.9986	0.0523	19.081
73	1.2741	0.9563	0.2924	3.2709	88	1.5359	0.9994	0.0349	28.636
74	1.2915	0.9613	0.2756	3.4874	89	1.5533	0.9998	0.0174	57.290
75	1.3090	0.9659	0.2588	3.7321	90	1.5708	1.0000	0.0000	∞

Appendix E

CONVERSION TABLE

ABBREVIATIONS

in	= inch	mm	= millimeter
ft	= foot	cm	= centimeter
yd	= yard	m	= meter
mi	= mile	km	= kilometer
oz	= ounce	g	= gram
lb	= pound	kg	= kilogram
sec	= second	slg	= slug
hr	= hour	N	= Newton

LINEAR MEASURES

1 ft = 12 in
1 yd = 3 ft
1 yd = 36 in
1 mi = 5280 ft
1 mi = 1760 yd
1 cm = 10 mm
1 m = 100 cm
1 km = 1000 m
1 in = 2.54 cm
1 cm = 0.3937 in
1 ft = 30.48 cm
1 cm = 0.0328 ft
1 in = 0.0254 m
1 m = 39.37 in
1 ft = 0.3048 m
1 m = 3.2808 ft
1 yd = 0.9144 m
1 m = 1.0936 yd
1 mi = 1609.34 m
1 mi = 1.6093 km
1 km = 0.6214 mi

AREA MEASURES

1 sq in = 6.4516 sq cm
1 sq cm = 0.155 sq in
1 sq ft = 929.03 sq cm
1 sq ft = 0.0929 sq m
1 sq m = 10.7636 sq ft

VOLUME MEASURES

1 cu in = 16.387 cu cm
1 cu cm= 0.061 cu in
1 cu ft = 0.0283 cu m
1 cu m = 35.3147 cu ft
1 cu yd = 0.7645 cu m
1 cu m = 1.3080 cu yd

MASS MEASURES

1 lb = 16 oz
1 kg = 1000 g
1 oz = 28.35 g
1 g   = 0.0353 oz
1 kg = 2.2046 lb

1 lb = 0.4536 kg
1 lb = 0.0311 slg
1 slg = 32.2 lb
1 kg = 0.0685 slg
1 slg = 14.6 kg

VELOCITY

1 ft/sec = 0.6818 mi/hr
1 mi/hr = 1.467 ft/sec
1 m/sec = 3.60 km/hr
1 km/hr = 0.2778 m/sec
1 ft/sec = 30.48 cm/sec
1 cm/sec = 0.0328 ft/sec
1 ft/sec = 0.3048 m/sec
1 m/sec = 3.281 ft/sec
1 mi/hr = 44.7041 cm/sec
1 mi/hr = 0.4470 m/sec
1 m/sec = 2.2369 mi/hr
1 ft/sec = 1.097 km/hr
1 km/hr = 1.467 ft/sec
1 mi/hr = 1.609 km/hr
1 km/hr = 0.6214 mi/hr

FORCE

1 lb = 4.45 N
1 N = 0.2248 lb
1 kg = 9.8 N
1 N = 0.1020 kg

WORK

1 ft-lb = 0.1383 kg-m
1 kg-m = 7.2307 ft-lb

ENERGY

1 ft-lb = 1.3558 joules
1 joule = 0.7376 ft-lb
1 kg-m = 9.8068 joules
1 joule = 0.1020 kg-m

INDEX

419